KV-638-370

Contents

Part 3: Banking and Finance

Part 4: Legal Issues

Doing Business with
Spain

in association with

PRICEWATERHOUSECOOPERS 🅚

Spanish Chamber of Commerce
in Great Britain

Second Edition

Consultant Editor:
Nadine Kettaneh

KOGAN
PAGE

Publishers' note

Every possible effort has been made to ensure that the information contained in this book is accurate at the time of going to press and neither the publishers nor any of the authors can accept responsibility for any errors or omissions, however caused. No responsibility for loss or damage occasioned to any person acting, or refraining from action, as a result of the material in this publication can be accepted by the editor, the publisher or any of the authors.

This book is intended as a general guide only. Its application to specific situations will depend upon the particular circumstances involved. The environment for foreign direct investment in Spain continues to be subject to rapid change. It is therefore important to be aware that the information given in this book is time sensitive and should not be relied upon as a substitute for obtaining professional advice.

First published in 2001

Kogan Page Limited
120 Pentonville Road
London N1 9JN

Web site: www.kogan-page.co.uk

Kogan Page Limited and contributors, 2001

British Library Cataloguing in Publication Data

ISBN 0 7494 3139 3

Typeset by Saxon Graphics Ltd, Derby
Printed and bound in Great Britain by Bell & Bain Ltd., Glasgow

Part 5: Accounting Issues

Part 6: Taxation

Appendices

ewoo, Daimler-Chrysler, Bridgestone, IBM, General Electric, Michelin, Rolls yce, Embraer, Sikorsky, Mead Packaging, Chase Manhattan, ITT Hartford, csson, Reckitt & Colman, ACB, Pepsico, Elf Atochem, Guggenheim Museum...

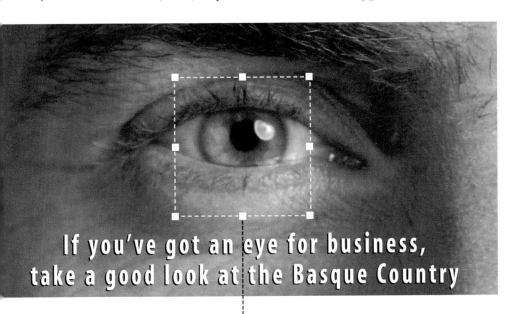

If you've got an eye for business, take a good look at the Basque Country

k at the Basque Country, and you'll see profit aplenty.

e a close look at a region that is a magnet for or firms and businessmen from all over the 'ld who demand excellent king conditions and a place ere life can be lived to the full.

e a close look at a highly ustrialised region that put its full king behind quality and ovation as a way of improving its npetitiveness on international rkets.

e a close look at an area that is eptive and open to Europe and world, a region ready for new lenges.

e a look at the Basque Country. a great place to do business.

Take a good look and you'll see:

- Superb communications.
- Infrastructures that constantly adapt to changing market needs.
- Leading-eddge technology.
- A first-class financial network.
- Mayor industrial developments in significant sectors like the iron and steel industry, capital goods, machine-tools, automotive components.
- A highly-skilled workforce.
- Environmental awareness.
- An administration in close contact with the local population and the region's entrepreneurs.
- A mild climate and magnificent countryside providing unbeatable surroundings.

BASQUE COUNTRY

For more Information: ■ BASQUE GOVERNMENT
Vitoria-Gasteiz (Spain)
Tel.: +34 945 188 092 - FAX: +34 945 188 081
On Internet: http://www.euskadi.net

■ SPRI. BASQUE DEVELOPMENT AGENCY
Bilbao (Spain) - Tel.: +34 944 797 012 - Fax: +34 944 797 023

List of Contributors

BBVA emerged as the result of the merger between Banco Bilbao Vizcaya and Argentaria agreed in October 1999. BBVA is the largest financial group in Spain by profits and shareholders' equity. It has a market share of 20 per cent in credit investment and of 17 per cent in deposits plus mutual funds. BBVA is an internationally diversified financial group with a strong presence in Latin America, a region in which leads in pension fund management with a market share of 30 per cent.

Bové Montero & Cía is a firm of auditors, fiscal advisors and management consultants founded 20 years ago, with offices in Barcelona, Madrid, Pamplona and Palma de Mallorca.

The firm services are available in English, French, German and Italian as well as Spanish and Catalan. In order to provide services in such a wide range of languages the firm's qualified professional staff in addition to their professional specialities speak one or more languages and are supported by an excellent team of secretaries/translators.

Natalie Corcoll has a Degree in Economics (Universidad Autónoma de Barcelona) and a Diploma in International Tax Advising and has worked at Bové Montero & Cía. since August 1999. She speaks several foreign languages, German (mother tongue), English and French.

Cranfield School of Management is a leading European university management school. It is part of Cranfield University, renowned for its high quality postgraduate teaching and research and its strong links to industry and business. Management education has been offered at Cranfield since the late 1940s and during that time we have continued to develop our range of educational services for the international business community.

Cranfield School of Management aims to contribute to the improvement of management practice and leadership in both the national and international arena, through education and research. Pursuit of this mission is based on a virtuous circle in which research feeds into teaching programmes, and teaching and consultancy experience contribute to research intitiatives. This ensures that high academic standards are complemented by strong practical relevance for today's businessmen and women.

Elena Liquete-Collis MA DipM MCIM is Client Liaison Manager at Cranfield School of Management. In that capacity, she works with clients to develop programmes that meet their needs. As a Spanish national, she maintains close links with Spain and has led joint research projects with Spanish universities, financed by the British Council and the Spanish Ministry of Education. She is also a contributor to the "Business Culture in Spain", one of the electives in Cranfield's MBA programme.

Professor Chris Brewster BA(Econ) PhD MIPD is Professor of International Human Resource Management at Cranfield. He is Director of the Centre for European Human Resource Management (a leading research unit, examining human resource issues in Europe) and of the Centre for Strategic Trade Union Management (working with senior union officials to improve the effectiveness and efficiency of their organisations. Professor Brewster has consulted with multinational companies, taught on management programmes throughout the world and is a frequent conference speaker. He has a particular interest in the subject of international and comparative human resource management. He is the author of several books and many journal articles.

Fairbanks Consultancy specialises in the development of international business, particularly in mainland Europe, for companies and organisations operating in the consumer goods sector fairbank@surfaid.org.

Hay Consulting S.A. is a dynamic Human Resources consultancy firm located in the cultural heart of Modernism in Barcelona. This privileged environment is the meeting-point for companies and professionals willing to offer the highest quality services in town.

Hay Consulting's quality approach includes the establishment of a relationship with clients based on trust and understanding, as well as on personalised assessment activites.

For more details about our services, please see page 402 for contact details.

Investment Promotion Bureau (SEPI) is a national government's development agency devoted to assisting and advising foreign companies with location planning needs for their direct investment projects. The Bureau acts as a one-stop-shop and implements location consulting strategies for foreign investors in Spain.

Juan José Berbel is deputy general manager of the Investment Promotion Bureau Studies Department. Graduated in International Relations in Barcelona, he is also an academic member of the Pompeu Fabra University in Barcelona as an expert in international political economy.

Margarita Lainez is a senior project manager at the Studies Department of the Investment Promotion Bureau. Graduated in business administration in Bilbao, she has developed her professional career as a senior controller evaluating firms' economic operating planning.

Josefa Mateos is a senior project manager at the Studies Department of the Investment Promotion Bureau. She is an expert in regional analysis and research as well as in labour legislation subjects related to industry.

Jones Lang LaSalle is the world's leading real estate services and investment management firm, operating across 96 key markets in 34 countries on five continents. The company provides comprehensive and wide-ranging integrated expertise on a local, regional and gloval level to owners, occupiers and investors.

Dr Mikel Navarro Arancegui has been Professor of Economics at the University of Deusto since 1994. In addition to a manual on Spanish economics, he has contributed to plenty of plenty of publications on competitiveness and the manufacturing industry.

PricewaterhouseCoopers (www.pwcglobal.com) is the world's largest professional services organisation. Drawing on the knowledge and skills of more than 160,000 people in 150 countries, they help clients solve complex business problems and measurably enhance their ability to build value, manage risk and improve performance in an Internet-enabled world.

PricewaterhouseCoopers provides a full range of business advisory services to leading global, national and local companies and to public institutions. These services include audit, accounting and tax advice; management, information technology and human resource consulting; financial advisory services including mergers & acquisitions, business recovery, project finance and litigation support; and legal services through a global network of affiliated law firms.

PricewaterhouseCoopers currently employs more than 3,200 people, in Spain. It operates through 20 offices in Barcelona, Bilbao, La Coruña, Las Palmas de Gran Canaria, Logroño, Madrid, Málaga, Murcia, Oviedo, Palma de Mallorca, Pamplona, San Sebastián, Santander, Sevilla, Santa Cruz de Tenerife, Valencia, Valladolid, Vigo, Vitoria and Zaragoza.

Joaquim Verges is a Professor of Business Economics & Management, at the Department of Business Economics, Autonomous University of Barcelona, (UAB), since 1980. He has been Vice-chancellor for Economics Affairs of the UAB (1980–1986), and Director of the Department of Business Economics of the same University (1986–1994). He also acts as a consultant and adviser for firms and organisations both in the private and public sectors.

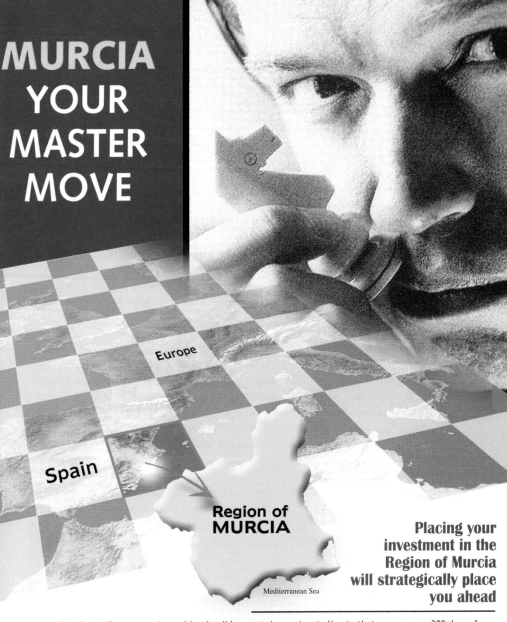

MURCIA YOUR MASTER MOVE

Europe

Spain

Region of MURCIA

Mediterranean Sea

Placing your investment in the Region of Murcia will strategically place you ahead

- Located in the Mediterranean Arc, with splendid economic development.

- Classified as primary objetive by the European Union, benefiting from the highest grants and subsidies available within the EU.

- Well developed industrial parks at prices lower than the national average.

- Shipping facilities for world wide transportation through the port of Cartagena.

- Well qualified technical labor force.

- Most economic rates for utilities.

- A prominent climate that assures over 300 days of sunshine per year.

- Excellent quality of life with a variety of leisure activities.

Invest in Murcia.
The right place. The right time.

INFO
INSTITUTO DE FOMENTO
REGION DE MURCIA

Foreword

There could hardly be a better environment in which to invest one's capital than that provided by Spain's expanding and successful economy. Over the last few years, Spain has developed all the right macroeconomic conditions to promote solid and sustainable growth. The country now ranks amongst the world's top ten in terms of GDP and has one of the highest growth rates within the European Union.

The Spanish economy is, of course, now fully integrated into world financial, commercial and business structures and guarantees of stability and profitability have contributed to Spain's huge success in attracting direct international investment.

A climate of vigorous competition has been established as a result of a privatisation process that has seen the liberalisation of many traditionally public sectors such as telecommunications, transport and power. Spain's open, dynamic and flexible economy is not only booming, but doing so in the context of stable labour relations, high internal demand and very low inflation.

The advantages offered to the investor by Spain's complete integration into the European Union and by its being a member of the European Monetary and Economic Union (EMU) are not negligible and act as further incentives to potential investors.

Above and beyond the purely economic rationale for doing business in Spain, we should also remind you that Spain is an enjoyable country to work and spend time in. We trust that this edition of *Doing Business in Spain* will serve as a useful and practical guide to further your interest in Spain.

The Spanish Chamber of Commerce in Great Britain

Can you imagine what could fit in a hat?

Can you imagine what could fit in a small
territory like Alava?

Fortunately surprising places still exist

Discover Alava

FOR ITS POTENTIAL LOGISTICS • FOR ITS AUXILIARY INDUSTRY • FOR ITS QUALIFIED LABOR FORCE • FOR ITS INCENTIVES

ALAVA DEVELOPMENT AGENCY

Landázuri, 15. 01008 Vitoria-Gasteiz (Alava) SPAIN
Tel. +34 945 15 80 70 Fax. +34 945 15 80 71
E-mail: alavadesarrollo@jet.es

Arabako
Foru Aldundia

Diputación
Foral de Alava

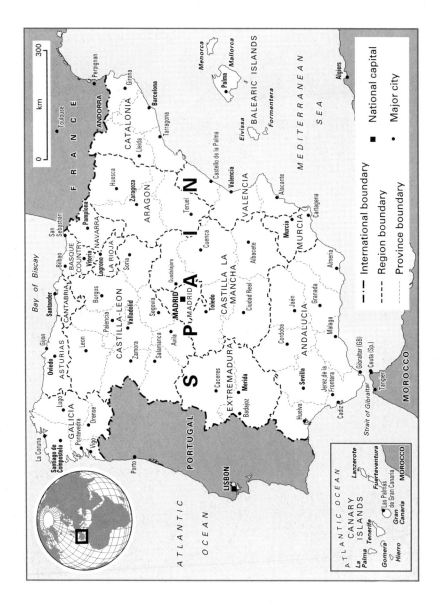

Map 1: Spain and its neighbours

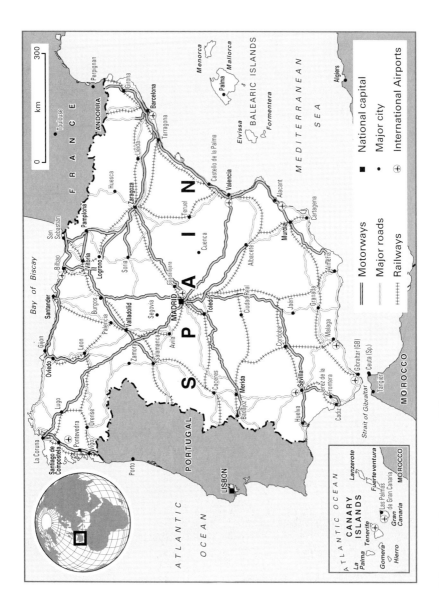

Map 2: Infrastructure of Spain

A Strategic Location

The region of Valencia on the eastern coast of Spain is situated right at the core of the Mediterranean Arc. Valencia is the perfect location from which to serve European, north African and Mediterranean markets. The European Union is one of the world's largest markets, made up of more than 370 million consumers with a high standard of living.

This region offers a well developed infrastructure for transportation, telecommunications, banking and accounting. Operating costs are low by European standards thereby reducing start-up costs and increasing the return on investment.

Spain enjoys a stable economy and provides excellent conditions for financing investment projects. 1998 economic indicators show that Spain had a 2% inflation rate, a growth rate of 3.8% (above the U.S., Japanese and EU averages), as well as an 11% Savings rate.

A STABLE AND COMPETITIVE ECONOMY

The region of Valencia accounts for 10% of Spain's economy, both in terms of GDP and of the relative size of the industrial, services and agricultural sectors.

Valencia offers a market made up of well managed and diversified manufacturers, a growing service sector, and unlimited subcontracting opportunities. Many operate under ISO 9000.

Here 13,500 exporters, nearly a third of the national total, account for 14% of Spain's exports. The Valencian region consistently shows the country's largest trade surpluses, which have remained in the range of 140% in recent years.

LOW OPERATING COSTS

— The corporate tax rate in Spain is 35%. This figure is lower than the European average of 38% and the OCDE 36.86%.
— Spain offers one of the most competitive labor costs in Europe and Valencia's labor cost remains lower than Spain's average.
— Industrial land is affordable in Valencia, at costs ranging from $4/sq.ft. to $8/sq.ft.

INVESTMENT INCENTIVES FOR THE FOREIGN INVESTOR

Valencia's low operating costs and the financial incentives provided by the government assure a high investment return for companies achieving their expected corporate targets.

Regional incentives, the major mechanisms whereby financial aid is provided, include the entire Autonomous Region of Valencia. This region is eligible for investment incentives to a maximum of 30% of total investment.

This important incentive provides non-refundable subsidies calculated as a percentage of total funds spent on a project approved for investment.

Financing is also available in the form of long term credit (5 to 10 years) to a maximum of 75% of total investment. A rebate on the interest rate is provided by local financial institutions.

The regional and central governments offer a range of employment incentives and tax credits to promote the hiring

STANDARD RATE OF CORPORATE TAX

Source: The Economist Intelligence Unit, 1997

TOTAL LABOUR COSTS (WAGE AND NON-WAGE) IN MANUFACTURING INDUSTRY
US$ per hour, male and female workers

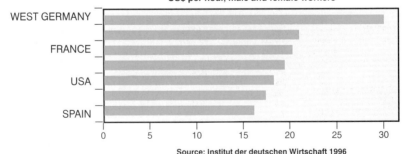

Source: Institut der deutschen Wirtschaft 1996

contract qualifies for a subsidy of the employer social security tax. Also available, are training incentives and financing for Research and Development activities at 0% interest rate.

READY AVAILABILITY OF HIGH QUALITY STAFF

Valencia offers a large labor force of 3.2 million educated and motivated young people.

The region is home to 5 prestigious universities with 132,000 students.

There is also a network of Technological Institutes, which companies can refer to for any valuable technical resources they may need to improve management policies and production processes. Currently the network consists of 15 centers (footwear, ceramics, furniture, textiles, toys, biomechanics, metalmechanics, agricultural industry, optics, building materials, plastics, information technology, electronic technology, ceramics, industrial design and containers and packaging)

Additionally, there are several international schools, including an American, British, Irish, a Scandinavian and a French school.

DIRECT CONNECTIONS WITH THE REST OF EUROPE

Valencia lies only a short distance from the rest of Europe. Its excellent transportation infrastructure makes it an open door to worldwide markets. Two international airports, an efficient railway system, an extensive road network and five commercial ports link the region of Valencia to the rest of the world.

It is worth mentioning that the Port of Valencia, which has been recently expanded, is the largest commercial port of Spain, and one of the three most important ports in the Mediterranean. It is also the gateway to foreign markets for the 20% of Spanish exports.

The Port of Valencia is served by 143 regular shipping lines linking destinations all over the world such as:

USA and Canada (27 weekly services)
Far East (13 weekly services)
Atlantic South America (10 weekly services)
Pacific South America (8 weekly services)

THE MOST PRESTIGIOUS MULTINATIONALS ARE LOCATED IN THE REGION OF VALENCIA

More than 260 multi national corporations have chosen Valencia as a manufacturing or distribution center for Europe and the Mediterranean, including Japanese, American, German and French companies.

LARGE AVAILABILITY OF COMPETITIVE INDUSTRIAL LAND

The Region of Valencia has, at present, an extensive and competitive supply of over 120 million square feet of industrial land.

lighting, collection of industrial waste, purifying plants, optic fiber, natural and propane gas, etc. and are well connected to the main highway networks in the Region of Valencia.

Among them, is the industrial Park of Sagunto, where we find two of the most relevant foreign investment projects of 1998 for the region of Valencia. Namely the opening of the Sidmed-Galmed Iron & Steel Plant and the Pilkington-Glaverbel plant which is currently under construction.

- The Sidmed-Galmed Iron & Steel complex is an investment project of more than 30,000 million pesetas (approx. US$206 million) and is expected to convert Sagunto into one of the most important centers in the world, for metal and iron production, using a new cold treatment method. It is estimated that by the year 2001 SIDMED-GALMED will have the capability to manufacture 800,000 tons of galvanized sheets and 2 million sheets produced by cold treatment.
- The British company, Pilkington, and the Belgian company, Glaverbel, decided on a 50-50 joint venture for installation of a float glass manufacturing plant in Sagunto. This joint investment project, worth an approximate 20,000 million pesetas (approx US$138 million), will be an important supplier to the automobile and construction industries, in which 150,000 tons of glass are estimated to be produced. It is also important to note that this project gives an important boost to employment. This new plant which is expected to open in the year 2000, will create some 150 direct jobs and roughly 500 indirectly.

INSTITUTO VALENCIANO DE LA EXPORTACIÓN (IVEX)

IVEX, was created by the autonomous government of Valencia, to attract investment to the region and to provide advice and support to companies in the Valencia area interested in exporting their products and services to foreign markets. In order to achieve its objectives IVEX has developed a network of 20 branch offices throughout the world, with the most recent ones opening in Asia, America and Europe.

IVEX takes an active and dynamic role in defining projects and getting them underway. Thanks to the institution's proximity to different levels of administration, IVEX is in the ideal position to help companies take the correct steps and expedite the necessary procedures. The support provided encompasses anything from providing general information on the region of Valencia, to advising on available regional incentives, to research of available industrial land, funding sources, and much more. From start to completion of a project, IVEX is committed to lending its full support.

INDUSTRIAL FOREIGN COMPANIES LOCATED IN VALENCIA

BAYER	Germany	Pharmaceuticals	BP OIL España	UK	Oil
PLEXI	Germany	Plastics	LAWSON MARDON SUÑER	UK	Packaging
THYSSEN ROS CASARES	Germany	Steel	TEXTAR	UK	Brakes
VB AUTOBATTERIES	Germany	Batteries	TETRA PAK	Sweden	Packing materials
ZENDER	Germany	Plastics	BRITAX	UK	Automotive
ESSILOR	France	Optics	DANONE	France	Food
ALSTOM	France	Trains	BAXTER	USA	Pharmaceuticals
RHÔNE POULENC	France	Chemicals	FORD España	USA	Cars
SCHNEIDER ELECTRIC	France	Electric devices	FREEPORT MCMORAN	USA	Chemicals
SIDMED GALMED	Luxembourg	Steel	JACOBS SUCHARD	USA	Food
TOTAL España	France	Oil	JOHNSON CONTROLS	USA	Car seats
PLASTIC OMNIUM	Belgium	Plastics	MASCOTECH	USA	Car Parts
BOSAL	Belgium	Exhaust Pipes	MB	USA	Toys
ISSA	France/Japan	Coil springs	MSL	USA	Electronics
MITSUBISHI MATERIALS	Japan	Cutting tools	PITTSBURG PAINT GLASS	USA	Car paints
UBE Industries	Japan	Chemicals	TENNECO AUTOMOTIVE	USA	Exhaust pipes

Part 1

Economic and Business Conditions

1.1

A Brief History

Juan José Berbel, Investment Promotion Bureau, SEPI

Whatever your perception of Spain, reality would surely change it. This would hold true not only in the context of the past seven years' outstanding economic results, but also with respect to the country's democratisation and to its participation as a 'founder member' of the European Economic and Monetary Union (EMU). Spain has also successfully established a degree of social welfare that has been praised by the United Nations Human Development Programme, among other institutions. These are all developments that reveal a deep structural change and evolution from the basic economic, political and social patterns that characterised Spain in the 1960s and 70s.

In essence, three main factors have guided Spain through this transformation process: European integration, the re-democratisation of political and social structures, and economic liberalisation. Let us review the influence of each factor.

European integration

Complete European integration has been a fact since Spain's accession to the European Economic Community in 1986, after it followed a convergence schedule for income levels as well as for working and living conditions for the Spanish population. From a starting point of near complete isolation following the end of the Spanish Civil War (1936–39), the European reference reveals itself as an important key for understanding Spain's current situation. In 1999, Spain became a founding member of the so-called 'euro-zone', shaped by 11 EMU member countries.

Spain has turned towards Europe at all levels: Spanish citizenry is one of the most trusting of European institutions and holds much 'optimism' with respect to the common currency (the euro). Internationalisation of the economy is largely due to growing trade and investment with European Union (EU) partners, while the Spanish political representatives' involvement in European policy has been increasingly powerful, as Spain is now able to exercise more influence in EU legislative activity.

New institutions for a democratic system

Spain has had a healthy democratic political system since all its outdated institutions and structures were removed through the approval of the 1978 Constitution, drawn up by the first democratically elected government since the end of the Civil War. The current constitution is not the first Spanish Constitution in force: since the 1812 Constitution – which set up one of the first European Democratic Parliaments – there have been more than eight other Constitutional regimes. But the importance of the 1978 Constitution is its spirit of overseeing a peaceful and integrative transition to democracy and its flexibility in achieving institutional and social changes, all of which have placed Spain in a strong position to face the new challenges of the 21st century.

Spanish international presence and participation in world-wide and regional intergovernmental organisations has greatly increased in the past two decades. Spanish representatives show a significant influence not only in EU institutions, but also in Nato structures, UNESCO, the European Central Bank, and in initiatives for the resolution of conflicts in the Balkans and the Middle East.

The following provides a general profile of Spain through some relevant and up-to-date facts about the country:

Capital	Madrid
Other main cities	Barcelona, Valencia, Seville, Zaragoza, Bilbao, Málaga, Las Palmas, Murcia, Valladolid, Palma de Mallorca
Surface	504,782 sq km
Population	39,628,000 inhabitants
Currency	Peseta (euro)
Languages	Spanish, Catalan, Euskera and Galician
State regime	Constitutional monarchy
Government system	Parliamentary democracy
Head of state	King Juan Carlos I (Borbón). Since 22/11/1975
President	Sr José Mª Aznar López. Since 4/5/1996
Main political parties	Central state level: • *Partido Popular* (centre right party: in government) • *Partido Socialista Obrero Español* (centre left party; social democratic) • *Izquierda Unida* (left-wing party)

Autonomous communities level:

- *Partido Nacionalista Vasco* (PNV) (right-wing nationalist party)
- *Convergència i Unió* (CiU) (centre-right nationalist party)
- *Bloque Nacionalista Galego* (left-wing nationalist party)

Towards international economic competitiveness

Spain's pattern of economic development does not differ much from patterns of industrialisation or services development in other European countries. The only difference of note is in the divergence in timing needed to complete the economic development process. In this sense, Spain, as is the case of other southern European economies, has been traditionally considered a 'latecomer' to that process, although this assessment is currently being reviewed in light of the country's present economic situation. It is therefore useful to have a brief overview of the stages of development completed by the Spanish economy to this day – the academic mainstream agrees on the following main stages as determining moments of modern Spanish economic history:

The Industrial Revolution happened, as in the majority of European continental countries, in the middle of the 19th century. Since then, the Spanish population has more than doubled and real income per inhabitant has increased more than ten-fold.

The period between 1900 and 1936 was characterised by the loss of Spain's last colonies in America. Apart from a certain social disappointment, the real effect on the economy was to bring on a period of new progress and growth in many fields such as industry, finance and agriculture. The return of capital and human resources from the colonies, and the fostering of public works, brought about economic modernisation and diversification, both in sectoral and geographical terms, providing a significant increase in industrial density throughout the Spanish map. The sound growth was also backed by a renewal of industries such as chemicals, automotive, electrical, machinery, metal components and construction, among others. A 'spill-over' effect was evident in relation to services, contributing to the soundness of the private banking system, the strong development of telecommunications, transportation and the finance sector.

The outbreak of the Civil War in 1936 stunted this modernisation process, while the post-war economy, directed by an isolationist regime, slumped into an economic autarchy based on an attempt at national self-sufficiency. Public intervention and minimum levels of external exchanges in the economic sphere were typical characteristics of this period.

From 1950 to the 1970s, a process of structural transformation of the economy was begun, leading to increasing external openness, a slight improvement of wealth ratios and a more than slight liberalisation policy. In the 1970s, the world-wide energy and other basic raw materials crisis brought on a necessary economic adjustment in Spain which was to last until 1983, approximately. Effects of this adjustment explain some current traits of the Spanish economic model, the most evident of these being the high unemployment rates, and the business and industrial investment crises during those years.

But these years did not constitute a 'lost decade' for Spain, at all. Though the economic sphere may have been dampened by the general recession, a simultaneous transition to real democracy was taking place. A 1977 agreement called *Pactos de la Moncloa* laid the foundations of the new democratic period that began in 1978. Negotiations between all social actors and the fulfilment of institutional reforms in taxation or finance sector systems led to the restructuring of the country's political and economic bases.

Economic consolidation began in 1985, leading to a more flexible and liberalised economy that is able to be more competitive internationally, and to a higher level of internationalisation and openness. In the political arena, democratic institutions set up by the 1978 Constitution made big strides in instituting a culture of stability, which has since then become strongly established in Spain.

The latter half of the 1990s showed the positive effects of European synergies on internal economic development in Spain. Some of the principal effects include: high economic growth rates, sharp increases of Foreign Direct Investment inflows into Spain (2nd in European ranking), great improvements in the relative position of Spain (10th in world-wide ranking) in terms of Gross Domestic Product (GDP), and economic openness. Other benefits have derived from integration into the EU structure, such as direct income in terms of net funds received from EU partners.

Lastly, it is worth mentioning that Spain has already reached a high standard of population welfare, even when compared to other European countries. Indicators such as equitable income distribution, and the increase in the working population's qualifications (Spain has one of the highest university enrolment rates amongst industrialised countries), show the commitment of the whole society in turning its economic growth into human development. That is the real image of Spain.

1.2

The System of National Government and the Political Party Structure

Juan José Berbel, Investment Promotion Bureau, SEPI

Introduction

Two phrases define, in less than ten words, the current political scene in Spain: a democratic state organisation and healthy political stability. As in most cases, reality is far more complex than it first appears, though it is true that the present parliamentary system in Spain is widely accepted, both internally and internationally, as being reasonably effective in its performance.

The representative democracy established by the 1978 Constitution, and currently in force, overcame traditional Spanish social cleavages, mainly between different nationalist sensibilities, and it did so in an extremely short time period. At present, at least three democratic parties have taken turns in the state government, maintaining similar structural policies and a political direction based on a moderate ideology. Until the 1980s this pattern of continuity reinforced the transition to democracy, and its current benefits are the consolidation of this transition and full involvement of Spain in the international arena.

The system of national government

The 1978 Constitution: the essentials of the political system

The political power structure established by the 1978 Constitution has become an unavoidable reference point for democratic transition processes in the international arena, such as those happening in Poland or the Baltic republics. These countries have been studying the Spanish political model and ways of applying its flexibility and administrative decentralisation.

The organisation of Spain's political system can be defined through two different lines of analysis. The first is related to the geographical distribution of political power, and will be discussed in the following chapter. The second is related to the division of political power between different public organisms, and is covered briefly below.

It is important, firstly, to differentiate between the head of state and the President. The monarch, currently Juan Carlos I de Borbón, is the head of state; the President, currently Sr José Mª Aznar, is elected by parliament after a democratic poll by universal suffrage.

The royal role is merely formal, and includes representation of the state at both domestic and international levels. Since his designation in 1975, the current monarch has greatly contributed to the achievement of social and political stability, as well as to the expansion and importance of Spanish foreign policy around the world, especially in Latin America, North Africa and countries of the Middle East.

The Spanish parliament consists of a lower house, the *Congreso de los Diputados* (Congress of Deputies), whose members are called *diputados* (deputies), and of an upper house, the *Senado* (Senate), whose members are called *senadores* (senators). The President is elected by members of parliament, and is responsible for the country's political leadership and for the appointment of the government cabinet of ministers.

Both parliament and government have the power to approve laws and regulations, although in practice this function is mainly undertaken by the government. In the context of this arrangement, the parliament acts as a deliberative forum and as a controller of the government by means of questions, appeals or motions. Other controlling and balancing organs are the Accounts Court, which supervises the management of the public budget, and the Ombudsman, which defends the individual rights guaranteed by the Constitution.

An independent judicial system also verifies that the government's legislation is in keeping with the Constitution. Following the German judicial system, a Constitutional Court was established to fulfil that purpose.

The lower house of parliament has 350 seats, and its members are elected for a maximum term of four years by proportional representation. Formally, it is the central institution of the state, although the close relationship existing between this house's majority and the government puts the political initiative quite clearly into the hands of the government.

The upper house is formed along traditional senate lines, revising legislation passed by the lower house and, theoretically, providing a representative forum for the Spanish Autonomous Communities. Twenty per cent of its members are nominated by each of the 17 Spanish Autonomous Regions, while the remaining 80 per cent of its 257 members obtain their seats in general elections. Nevertheless, the Senate frequently reproduces the same majorities as in the lower house.

The following table shows the distribution of seats in the two houses of the Spanish parliament as a result of the last general election, in March 2000.

Table 1.2.1   Distribution of seats in parliament

Party	Congreso de Diputados Seats	% of votes	Senado Seats
Partido Popular (PP)	183	44.54	127
Partido Socialista Obrero Español (PSOE)	125	34.08	61
Convergència i Unió (CiU)	15	4.2	8
Izquierda Unida (IU)	8	5.46	–
Partido Nacionalista Vasco (PNV)	7	1.53	6
Coalición Canaria (CC)	4	1.06	5
Others	8	9.13	1
TOTAL	**350**	**100**	**208 (+49)**

The electoral system is one of proportional representation, with voters choosing from closed lists previously approved by the different political parties, except in the case of the Senate, whose members are selected from open lists. Elections for the parliament's two houses are held on the same day. Traditionally, Spanish voting has mainly been driven by economic conditions at the time of polling and by the personality of political leaders, although foreign policy issues have also had a certain influence (mainly those issues related to specific EU negotiations).

The structure of government

As previously mentioned, the President is elected by the parliament, and the different ministries are appointed by the President. Together, the President and ministers exercise the government's functions and take executable decisions in weekly meetings of the Council of Ministers (cabinet meetings). The Spanish system makes no distinction between the government and the cabinet. At present, there are two vice-presidencies (political and economic) that give their holders a higher profile than other cabinet ministerial positions. Minister of the Economy is also considered a high profile position, mainly because of the budget perspective.

The ministries that make up the Spanish national government are currently:

- Presidency
- Foreign Affairs
- Domestic Affairs (Home Office)
- Justice
- Labour
- Science and Technology
- Education and Sports
- Defence
- Economy
- Treasury
- *Fomento* (Public Works)
- Agriculture, Fishing and Food
- Public Administration
- Health and Consumption
- Environment

Recent political developments

Since the first democratically elected government in 1978, three different political parties have been in government. In 1979, a centrist party (the *Unión de Centro Democrático*, now no longer existing in its original form) was elected by simple majority to rule over the initial transition to democracy. Its mandate was altered, mainly as a result of the economic crisis and of an increase in terrorist violence in the Basque Country, in the north of Spain. From 1982 to 1996, four general elections were won by the PSOE (socialist party), the last one in 1993 by simple majority. The development of the system of autonomous regions, the accession to the European Economic Community and the need to restructure outdated industrial structures were some of the main topics included in the socialist agenda.

In 1996, the general election was won by the Popular Party (centre-right) by a simple majority. That government registered outstanding economic results following a successful macroeconomic policy that saw Spain become a founding member of European Monetary Union (EMU) and register the strongest economic performance among the EU countries. Other relevant issues in the government's agenda were the reform of the taxation system, a pro-business-oriented industrial policy and a market liberalisation trend both through *ad hoc* regulations and through the gradual restructuring and the privatisation of former state-owned companies. In March 2000 the Popular Party was returned to power for a second consecutive term.

As a general pattern, moderation has been a constant guide of different governments' policies. To a certain extent, this is due to the pluralist party system, and to the fact that there are no extremist right-wing or anti-democratic parties in either state institutions or in the party system itself. Thus, the governing parties' general attitude is one of both reformism and continuity, without sharp ideological polarisation along a right-left axis.

In the general election in March 2000, the current politically centre Popular Party regained the majority of seats in parliament. Hence, these results confirm a clear tendency towards a two-party system (PP and PSOE), which should be added to the Spanish party system profile.

The continuity pattern will be underlined by maintenance of the government agenda for the next four years. That agenda will be based on five main topics: Spanish economy liberalisation (policies towards no-deficit national accounts, Euro currency introduction, sector deregulation, and privatisation of previously state-owned companies); social dialogue with labour agents (trade unions, employers' confederations among others); huge investment in public works; policy commitment towards public and private technology and R&D expenses, as well as a reinforcement of the Spanish position in the European Union.

1.3

The System of Autonomous Regions

Juan José Berbel, Investment Promotion Bureau, SEPI

Introduction

Spain has three different levels of administrative territorial distribution: national, regional and local. This chapter outlines the system of government for the country's 17 Autonomous Regions (*Comunidades Autónomas*), and also explains the principal differences between a classic federal system and the one existing in Spain at present. The chapter will also focus on the general political structure and rules guiding the internal organisation of the regions as a whole. A map of the regions can be found at the beginning of the book and a comprehensive profile of each in Appendix 1.

The third territorial level is that constituted by local councils and provinces – inner divisions within the Autonomous Regions.

A new form of administrative and political autonomy

An unprecedented (and original, in international terms) geopolitical structure was provided for by the 1978 Spanish Constitution. One of the main purposes guiding the complete change in administrative and political power in Spain was the attempt to give due consideration to nationalist demands – mainly Catalan and Basque – in the democratic and constitutional spheres. Another objective was the improvement of administrative effectiveness by means of a decentralisation process, and increased closeness between government and citizens. This redistribution of political power has been considered a decisive factor in creating legitimacy for the nation-wide democratic process.

The Constitution has, therefore, provided for a system of administrative and political self-government for the 17 regions of Spain that involves a transmission of sovereignty to the regions from the national level, but not in the other direction.

To those unfamiliar with the decentralised Spanish regional model, experts explain the system by likening it to a federal one, although from a constitutional point of view, Spain is not a federal state. Nevertheless, it is the facts and not the terminology that matter, and the current distribution of political powers and budgetary resources does make the dynamic very close to the relationships that exist between central and federal states, as developed in classic federal models.

However, some differences between the models of Spanish Autonomous Regions and classic federal states should be underlined:

- The Spanish Constitution, as mentioned above, does not establish a federal system as such, although it borrows many features of political power distribution from federal models, such as Germany.

- Sovereignty does not lie in each individual Autonomous Region. It is derived from the Constitution, which transfers its material powers to the three territorial levels (national, regional and local).

Even among federal states, models of government that recognise intermediate territorial governments constitute a rare exception, but this arrangement does work in the Spanish case. Decentralisation of political power as it is currently organised has enabled the different regions to approve their own 'Home Rules', which include basic features of self-government. For example, all Spanish regions have budgetary autonomy and freedom for resource allocation, and it is worth noting that over 20 per cent of the public sector budget is managed by these territorial entities.

Home Rules also cover areas of action for which the regions can introduce their own laws, though always in compliance with the Constitutional legislative framework. The Constitution defines the powers that can be exercised by the Autonomous Regions and those exclusive to the state. In this way, powers of self-government are devolved according to the political experience and traditions of each region. Differences in the degree of self-government derive from this 'asymmetric speed' allowance. Thus, Catalonia, the Basque Country, Galicia, Navarre, Valence and the Canary Islands have assumed a higher degree of political powers than the other regions, which maintain lower legislative activity levels.

The state exercises exclusive power over the following areas of government:

- regulations relating to the constitutional framework;

- nationality, immigration, status of foreigners and political asylum;

- international relations;
- defence and security;
- justice administration;
- external trade;
- the monetary system;
- general planning for economic activity;
- social security, taxation, general labour and commercial legislation;
- other general legislation (without prejudice to its execution by the authorities of the Autonomous regions).

The devolution of political and management powers in certain areas of government from the central state to the autonomous regions is not yet complete. Although there has been a slowing down in the pace of transfer of political power, administrative and budgetary management powers are still being devolved, and this continues to contribute to the strengthening of links and confidence between the central and regional levels of power.

Political structures

Each Autonomous Region has a legislative assembly (for example, the *Junta de Gobierno* in Castilla–León; the *Parlament* in Catalonia; and the *Cortes* in Aragón), as well as an executive government elected for a maximum term of four years by a majority of the legislative assembly. Legislative representatives are elected by universal suffrage for a maximum term of four years.

This democratic parliamentary system has a practical bias towards the governing executive, and its president. In fact, the political and legislative initiative for each Autonomous Region lies mainly with the executive government and, more specifically, the region's president, who, in terms of public opinion, is the most recognisable institution and whose performance is easiest to evaluate.

On the national level, there is much discussion about redefining the Senate's role to make it an institution that would bring real value by deepening the relationship between the regions and the state.

Regional political party structure

The regional political party structure is not particularly complex. Three Autonomous Regions, those with the most complex multinational and multilingual societies, the Basque Country, Catalonia and, to a lesser extent, Galicia, have political parties that are specific to them at the regional level. For example, there are at least three parties with representation in the Basque parliament that are specific to that region. In Catalonia, there are four region-specific political parties with a regional parliamentary presence. These are the best examples of a sub-national multi-party system in Spain and it is also worth noting that Catalonia and the Basque Country regions, between them, provide nearly three-quarters of the total number of the country's regional parties of consequence.

As well as running the regional government, some of the regional parties are also represented in the national parliament. This is the case of *Convergència i Unió* (Catalonia) and the *Partido Nacionalista Vasco* (Basque Country), two nationalist centre-right parties that hold their respective regional governments while maintaining a presence in the national parliament. Moreover, these two political parties, the Catalan party in particular, have provided constant and faithful support to the simple majorities of the two main Spanish political parties during the last two governmental periods (1993–1996 with the PSOE government, and 1996–2000 with the government of the Popular Party).

Most other regions have at least one regional political party, following a similar pattern to that found in other European countries' administrative regions, such as the Scottish National Party in Scotland or the *Véneto* in Italy. The regional government in these other Autonomous Regions is usually held by a national party, such as the Popular or the Socialist party.

As a general rule, it is the Minister for Domestic Affairs who calls elections for regional legislatures, and elections for town council representatives are usually held on the same day. Andalusia, Galicia, Catalonia and the Basque Country are the exception to that rule. In the case of those regions, election day is decided and announced by their own governments, whether or not that date coincides with other elections, be they for the European parliament, Spanish parliament, other regions' parliaments or town councils. For example, the recent March 2000 election returned representatives to both the Spanish national parliament and to the Andalusian regional legislature.

1.4

Economic Performance

Margarita Lainez, Investment Promotion Bureau, SEPI; statistics compiled in collaboration with Maite Yusta, Investment Promotion Bureau, SEPI

Introduction

At the dawn of the 21st century, it would, at the very least, be risky to analyse the macroeconomic performance of a European country such as Spain without taking into account the world-wide globalisation of the economy. This is even more relevant when one considers that Spain is a founding member of the European Economic and Monetary Union (EMU), a regional economic group and basic component of the triad structure of the world economy. In this sense, the increase in the number of 'competitors' on the international level that this globalisation process has produced has resulted in the need to make some strict structural adjustments in the economies of industrialised countries and to maintain budgetary discipline in public finances.

In this context Spain has, over the past few years, developed the right macroeconomic conditions to foster solid and sustained economic growth. In fact, Spain is registering the strongest economic indicators of all European countries, in addition to ranking tenth in the world in terms of Gross Domestic Product (GDP) (outstripping economies such as those of The Netherlands, Australia and Russia). Spain has also had one of the highest economic growth rates in the European Union (EU) in recent years, and the outlook for the next few years is equally encouraging.

Spain's economic achievements have been made possible, to a large extent, by the rational use of capital and highly skilled human resources. The country's current success is a great encouragement to investment, both for companies that operate in Spain – which have seen their profits increase – and for potential foreign investors. Improvements have been registered in all areas of economic activity, and these have been accom-

Table 1.4.1 Spanish GDP

1998 Population	Inhabitants	39,371,147
GDP (1998)	Ptas (millions)	84,634,836
	US$ (billions)	566,498
	Yen (million)	74,241,084
Annual growth in real GDP	1999/1998	3.7
	Forecast 2000	3.7*
Per capita GDP (1998)	Ptas	2,120,744
	US$	14,195.07
	Yen	1,860,301
	Index: EU = 100	81.45

US$ = Ptas 149.40 (1998) / ¥1 = Ptas 1.14 (1998) / 1 DM = Ptas 84.90 (1998) / €1 = Ptas 167.49 (1998)

* *Forecast Source:* Spanish Ministry of Economy

Sources: Spanish National Statistics Institute; FIES Savings Banks Foundation; Bilbao-Vizcaya Bank Foundation 1999

panied by some significant investments, such as those made to create an optimal infrastructure network. All this has led to an increase in wealth for companies and households, which is accompanied by an increase in employment levels and a healthy climate for relations between labour and employers. Spain's economic structure comprises very diversified companies, belonging to a broad variety of industrial and service sectors, in line with its more industrialised European partners.

Economic performance

Recent evolution

The current economic situation shows solid and sustained growth, the incorporation of the Spanish economy into world financial, commercial and business structures, and the success of Spain in attracting direct international investment through guarantees of stability and profitability. This all takes place against a backdrop of lower production costs and an outlook for growth in the foreign market. The economy has been liberalised and opened up through the passing of business-oriented legislation; the process of privatisation of public companies, begun in 1996 with a strict timetable for completion, has enabled competition to become a major factor of Spain's economic system. Furthermore, deregulation and liberalisation have taken place in sectors that were traditionally dominated by monopolies, such as telecommunications, hydrocarbons, transportation and power.

Spain is one of the countries that has most intensely felt the consequences of globalisation, mainly because of the efforts made to qualify as
a founding member of EMU, an objective it easily achieved. As a result, an
open, dynamic and flexible economy has been established, with stable
growth: in 1999, GDP increased by 3.7 per cent, a rate much above the
euro zone average. The following table compares Spain's performance to
that of the other 15 countries of the EU, the USA and Japan.

Internal demand

One fundamental reason for Spain's stable growth rate is the significant
increase in internal demand, driven by the constant generation of employment, the stability of interest rates, and the fact that in 1999 an ambitious
reform of personal income tax was begun. The growth in consumer spending has generated an increase in investment and in gross fixed capital
growth, translating into better business competitiveness and excellent
expectations for the future. The impact of government spending on final
consumption was moderate, as the government is exercising budgetary
restraint in its objective of containing the deficit.

Investment

Gross capital growth in recent years has maintained high growth rates of
around 9 per cent, with accelerated investment in construction. This
growth has meant an increase in the number of companies created, which
has given rise to an increase in employment and general wealth.

Profitable investment, especially in capital goods, is the essential element that explains Spanish economic growth, along with the strong performance of exports of goods and services and the aforementioned
growth in consumer spending. A large part of this investment dynamic has
resulted in an increase in direct foreign investment flows (US$ 22 billion
in 1998) and in investment for new technological assets, with businesses
taking advantage of the current low interest rates. The increase in the
level of new technology will soon show results with respect to the cost
effectiveness of profitable investments.

Indications from the industrial production index, levels of installed
capacity utilisation, and electricity consumption show that demand is
healthy and that there exists a certain level of confidence in the Spanish
economy.

Inflation

The significant decrease in the inflation rate is a fundamental indicator that
Spain is in a new economic cycle. In 1998, the Consumer Price Index (CPI)
registered a new record low of 1.8 per cent, thus proving the economy's

Table 1.4.2 GDP, inflation and unemployment in Spain, the EU, USA and Japan, 1997–2000

Country	% increase in GDP*				Inflation (%)†				Unemployment (%)†			
	1997	1998	1999	2000	1997	1998	1999	2000	1997	1998	1999	2000
Germany	2.2	3.0	2.0	2.5	1.8	0.9	0.6	1.0	9.9	9.4	9.1	8.6
Austria	2.5	3.3	2.8	2.6	1.3	0.9	1.0	1.3	4.4	4.7	4.3	4.2
Belgium	3.0	2.9	2.4	2.3	1.6	1.0	1.1	1.4	9.4	9.5	9.2	9.2
Denmark	3.3	2.6	1.7	2.0	2.2	1.7	1.9	2.1	7.7	6.3	6	6.2
Spain	**3.5**	**4.0**	**3.7**	**3.7**	**2.0**	**1.8**	**2.9**	**2.1**	**20.8**	**18.8**	**15.7**	**14.0**
Finland	6.0	5.5	4.0	2.7	1.2	1.5	1.5	2.0	12.6	11.4	10.3	9.2
France	2.3	3.1	2.6	2.8	1.2	0.7	0.5	1.1	12.5	11.6	11.3	10.7
Greece	3.5	3.5	3.7	3.9	5.5	4.8	2.5	2.9	10.3	10.1	10.3	10.2
Ireland	9.8	9.5	6.7	6.4	1.5	2.4	2.0	2.0	9.8	7.7	6.5	6.2
Italy	1.5	1.8	2.5	2.8	1.7	1.8	1.3	1.5	11.7	11.8	11.7	11.4
Luxembourg	4.8	4.1	3.9	4.4	1.4	1.6	1.7	1.7	3.4	3.1	2.9	2.8
Netherlands	3.6	4.0	2.2	2.2	2.2	2.0	1.6	2.2	5.5	4.1	3.6	3.7
Portugal	3.8	4.2	3.5	3.2	2.2	2.8	2.3	2.0	6.7	5.0	4.6	4.6
United Kingdom	2.2	1.0	2.5	2.7	2.8	2.7	2.7	2.4	5.7	4.7	4.8	5.3
Sweden	1.8	2.8	2.2	2.6	0.5	-0.1	0.2	1.0	8.0	6.5	5.4	5.1
EU (15)	2.7	2.8	1.8	2.7	1.9	1.5	1.3	1.6	10.4	9.6	9.1	9.8
USA	3.9	3.9	3.3	2.2	2.3	1.6	2.1	2.4	4.9	4.5	4.3	4.5
Japan	1.4	-2.8	-1.4	0.3	1.7	0.6	-0.2	-0.2	3.4	4.1	5.0	5.0

* Spanish GDP from the National Statistics Institute for 1998 and 1999, forecast from the Spanish Ministry of Economy for 2000. Rest of GDP from *1999 Annual Economic Report*, European Commission. (1999 and 2000 are forecasts, except EU, USA, Japan and Luxembourg from International Monetary Fund *World Economic Outlook 1999*.)

† International Monetary Fund *World Economic Outlook 1999*. (1999 and 2000 are forecasts, except inflation figures for Spain in 1999.)

ability to make growth compatible with price stability. In 1999, the CPI increased slightly because of a series of exogenous factors, such as the strong rise in international oil prices and the depreciation of the euro. Nevertheless, the elements that make up trend inflation (non-power industrial goods and services) demonstrated deceleration with respect to the previous year.

Interest rates have decreased steadily from 13 per cent in 1993 to 3.25 per cent in February 2000, one of the lowest rates in the past three decades, and one that makes investment appealing.

Figure 1.4.1   Inflation and interest rates

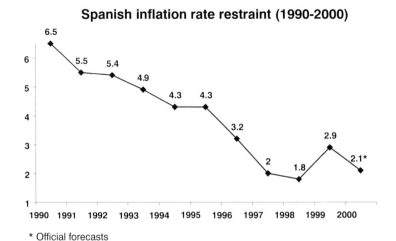

Spanish inflation rate restraint (1990-2000)

* Official forecasts

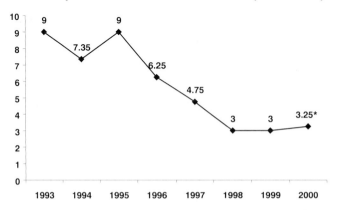

Spanish interest rate decrease (1993-2000)

* February 2000

Source: Bank of Spain; Spanish Economy and Treasury Ministry, 1999

Foreign sector

As in many other industrialised countries, Spain's balance of trade is traditionally in deficit. Nevertheless, a rapid improvement in the level of exports is expected to result from the upswing in the international economic situation. As far as imports are concerned, it should be noted that a significant increase has been registered as a consequence of the boom in internal demand. In 1999 exports increased by 1.5 per cent and imports by a high 5.6 per cent.

As far as the current account balance is concerned, one need only mention the increase in capital inflows, mainly originating in the EU, as well as the now traditional surplus in the balance of invisible items.

Labour climate

The structural, long-term change in the Spanish economy has led to an increase in employment, and this has been characterised by good relations between employers and trade unions. The sustainable expansion of income and employment has not affected the policy of moderation in salary increases, which has been reflected both in collective bargaining agreements and in individual salary raises.

The unemployment rate was greatly reduced by close to five percentage points, placing it at around 15 per cent at the end of 1999. Despite this being one of the highest unemployment rates within the EU, one should not underestimate the ability of the Spanish economy to create new jobs in the short term.

Public deficit

The intensification of the fiscal consolidation process led to a reduction in the public deficit of nearly two points in terms of the country's GDP, placing it at 1.3 per cent in 1999, a figure which is lower than the goal of 1.6 per cent set in the government's Stability Programme of 1998. Likewise, a decreasing trend has been established in the ratio of public debt to GDP, which in 1999 approached the threshold of 60 per cent. The impact of the low interest rates applied to the interest on public debt has also contributed to the drop in this ratio.

Economic forecast

The recovery of the emerging economies, the continuing and noteworthy growth of the US economy and the general improvement in outlook for the EU is likely to stimulate growth rates of around 2.6 per cent in industrialised countries (that belong to the Organisation for Economic Co-operation and

Development – OECD), for the period 2000–2003. The expected progressive growth in both the foreign markets and internal demand of the euro zone will foster a level of growth in the coming fiscal years that is superior to that registered in 1999. A flexible monetary and fiscal policy, along with previously initiated structural reforms, will allow stable growth to be guaranteed.

The Spanish economy will continue to benefit from high growth rates, which are expected to be 3.7 per cent in the year 2000 and 3.3 per cent in the triennium 2001–2003. The increases in internal demand and exports are expected to be maintained, due to stable wage costs and an improved international situation. This, in turn, should lead to a higher inflow of international investments.

The Spanish economy is expected to continue to make gains in productivity levels while the unemployment rate should continue to fall and reach less than 10 per cent by 2003. Inflation, on the other hand, is expected to remain stable at 2 per cent between 2000 and 2003.

In conclusion, it should be pointed out that the Spanish economy has successfully faced the challenge of opening up and liberalising its markets, and of doing so in a highly competitive context. This achievement, along with a significant reduction in the deficit and ample compliance with euro convergence criteria, indicates that the conditions are right for solid, stable and lasting growth. The favourable evolution of the labour market and inflation rates, and the stability of interest rates, provide the right conditions for the successful development of business activities. Similarly, foreign companies requiring a stable environment to develop their potential for growth and expansion should find that establishing their business in Spain will bring the success and growth they seek.

1.5

The Internationalisation of the Spanish Economy

Margarita Lainez, Investment Promotion Bureau, SEPI

Introduction

In keeping with the internal growth that the Spanish economy is experiencing, a very important process of internationalisation is taking place. The internationalisation of an economy is measured through two basic indicators: the flow of direct investment and the rate of opening-up (trade flow in relation to gross domestic product).

Direct Spanish investments overseas in 1999 were double the previous year, reaching US$30,665 million and surpassing 3 per cent of Gross Domestic Product (GDP), primarily in companies in the telecommunications, banking and tourism sectors. In some countries, such as Brazil, Spain is the leading foreign investor and in the Latin-American area, it ranks second, only outstripped by the United States. In the coming years, one of the main challenges of the Spanish economy will be to increase exports to Eastern Europe and, primarily, to Asia.

With regard to foreign investments in Spain, these have risen to US$8,398 million, growing by 44 per cent in the first six months of 1999; this increase is due in great part to the boom in Spanish internal demand.

Foreign trade

A new pattern is emerging in the nature and make-up of exports from Spain, and one that is an improvement for the external sector. In the past decade, four sectors in particular have seen strong growth in demand and exports: the automotive, equipment, financial and audiovisual industries; there has been a fall in exports in the sectors faced with weak demand.

The increase in commercial transactions with developed countries is a further indication of the strength of Spain's external sector.

Exports and imports (both goods and services) as a whole have risen in the last decade from 37.4 per cent of GDP in 1991 to 60.5 per cent in 1999. This opening-up rate is one of the highest in the OECD, with countries such as Germany and France having a lower opening-up rate, of 53.8 per cent and 51.2 per cent, respectively.

Figure 1.5.1   Economic opening-up rate: exports and imports in relation to GDP

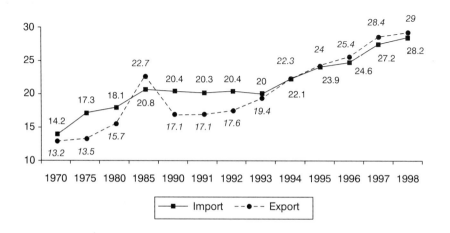

Source: Bilbao Vizcaya Bank

Liberalisation steps

The process of opening up trade in Spain to foreign countries began in 1959, at the end of the period of autarchy that followed the Civil War, and culminated in 1986 with entry into the European Economic Community (EEC). The year 1959 marks the beginning of the liberalisation of trade, as Spain joined organisations of international co-operation such as the OECD (the previous year it had entered into the International Monetary Fund and the World Bank), and began a search for stable monetary ties. The most significant sign of liberalisation took place between 1964–67, when Spain participated, as a member with full rights, in the Kennedy Round of the General Agreement on Tariffs and Trade (GATT). At this meeting, the reductions in tariffs that were agreed upon represented for Spain a linear average of 18 per cent, and the reductions began to be applied between 1968 and 1972.

Later, in 1970, the signing of the Preferential Agreement with the EEC took place. The result was a reduction in the Spanish tariff for products coming from member countries of between 25 and 60 per cent of the rate according to the product, as well as expansion of the quotas that were gradually introduced until the end of 1976. In 1977, Spain participated in the Tokyo Round of the GATT, and as a result there was a further reduction in tariffs.

The integration of Spain into the EEC took place in 1986. This fact meant the complete opening up of foreign trade as a consequence of the elimination of tariffs for the rest of the member countries and the adoption of a common customs tariff, as well as a whole set of community trade policies.

In 1987, the Single European Act was signed, whose purpose was to build a single market and to form the European Economic and Monetary Union (EMU). There followed the 'Delors Plan,' whose objective was the European Union Treaty through which the EEC became the European Union (EU).

Spain's trade relations with foreign countries are now completely liberalised, most markedly by free trade with the other members of the EU. Spain's relations with countries outside the EU are governed by a series of general principles (common customs tariff and quotas in certain cases) and preferential agreements, regulated by the EU and within the framework of the World Trade Organisation (WTO).

Trends in the foreign sector

As in many other European countries, the balance of trade in Spain has traditionally been in deficit, with no change to positive figures expected in the coming fiscal years. Nevertheless, an improvement is expected in the deficit as a result of the increase in exports and of the maintenance of the growth rate in imports. This improvement is based on the recovery of international economies, the depreciation of the euro with respect to the dollar, and the rise in internal demand of European partners. All these factors are stimulating the recovery of exports, both those directed towards Europe and to the rest of the world.

According to the latest foreign trade data provided by the Customs Department, the recovery of exports is evident. In monetary terms, there has been a steady increase throughout 1999, from first quarter negative growth of 2.8 per cent, to a positive 3.2 per cent in the second quarter and closing the fourth quarter at 5.9 per cent growth. Simultaneously, imports that had shown growth in the first and second quarters of 10.8 per cent and 15.4 per cent, respectively, saw a visible deceleration in the third quarter, in which the increase in imports had fallen to 11.5 per cent.

The latest projections made by the OECD indicate that the estimated increase for Spanish exports in volume of goods for the years 2000 and 2001 will be 7.1 per cent and 7 per cent respectively, while for imports increases of 11 per cent are expected.

Figure 1.5.2   Current account balance

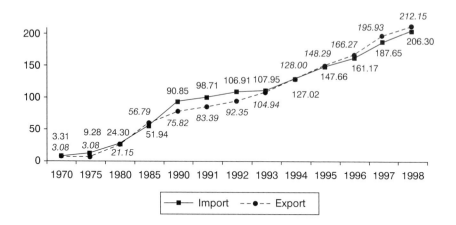

Exchange rate: Average 1975-1998, 1 US$ = 112.82 Pts
Source: Bilbao Vizcaya Bank

The increase in export activity is anticipated to be generalised in all branches of activity, with greater impact in metal products, tobacco, wood and furniture, manufactured goods, rubber and plastic products, automobiles and parts, minerals, electrical products and some foodstuffs. With regard to imports, inflows increased in the automotive and manufactured consumer goods sectors.

The positive outlook for exports is supported by a survey made by the National Council of Chambers, which shows that 95 per cent of Spanish exporters surveyed expect to increase or maintain their foreign sales.

As far as the concentration of activity is concerned, it should be noted that 72.8 per cent of exports and 67.2 per cent of imports take place as trade with other countries of the EU, thus confirming the high quality of Spanish products.

Finally, it should be noted that, given the positive outlook for the Spanish economy, it is foreseeable that a significant increase will take place in trade relations with other countries both in terms of exports and investments. This should give rise to great increases in activity for companies established in Spain. These will see their turnover grow by capturing market share, and this will be accompanied by improvements in efficiency, and by the offering of highly competitive products in line with those offered in the international markets.

Table 1.5.3   Sectoral ranking of exports and imports in 1998

Sector	Exports	Sector	Imports
Automotive	21,445,139.41	Chemical	15,810,965.59
Automotive components	9,804,276.94	Automotive components	13,683,808.52
Chemical	8,855,368.77	Automotive	12,732,729.11
Fresh and frozen fruit and vegetables	6,070,897.76	Electronic and computer	9,234,404.06
Iron and steel	3,961,802.92	Combustibles and petrol derivatives	8,492,905.73
Electronic and computer	3,718,736.19	Iron and steel	5,605,431.76
Textile	3,012,727.99	Electric material	4,087,041.27
Electric material	2,724,759.63	Raw materials	3,641,590.36
Electrical appliances	2,416,263.53	Textile	3,292,539.75
Combustibles and petrol derivatives	2,249,066.13	Seeds and fruits	3,231,063.42

(Thousand current US$)
Source: ICEX (Spanish External Trade Institute, 2000)

Table 1.5.4 Country ranking: Spanish exports and imports, 1998

Countries	Export	Countries	Import
France	21,332,867.74	France	24,170,895.16
Germany	14,844,335.95	Germany	20,423,237.07
Portugal	10,167,763.19	Italy	12,915,887.49
Italy	10,147,943.07	United Kingdom	10,278,582.35
United Kingdom	10,006,241.61	United States	7,746,022.55
United States	4,591,885.40	Netherlands	5,702,532.89
Netherlands	3,760,895.56	Belgium and Luxembourg	4,520,235.63
Belgium and Luxemb0urg	3,039,676.93	Japan	4,048,608.42
Brazil	1,300,493.32	Portugal	3,720,461.87
Argentina	1,250,620.76	China	3,252,297.35

(Thousand current US$)
Source: ICEX (Spanish External Trade Institute 2000)

1.6

Competitiveness: The Corporate Perspective

Juan José Berbel, Investment Promotion Bureau, SEPI

Introduction

With increasing economic globalisation over the last two decades, our perception of what it is to be competitive has changed, both in respect to companies and their operations, and to countries and their performance in the global economy.

There are many challenges that countries and firms must now face in order to maintain a 'competitive' position within the global economic network. These include:

- Sharp increases in foreign investment and trade.

- Free movement of capital.

- New location patterns of international production.

- Changes in the relationships between partners in technology transfers.

- New production and distribution processes.

- The changing nature of the relationships between states and other non-state actors, such as multinational firms, among many others.

Spain has evolved in light of the above and whatever your image of Spanish competitiveness has been, its reality will probably have changed in these last two decades.

To begin with, the external image of the country is rather different. These days, Spain has even become fashionable. The global magazines *Newsweek* and *Businessweek* have international editions that cover Spanish culture, companies, the economy and the political situation. For Worldinvestor.com technology consultants, Spain comes second among the most advanced countries in Europe with regards to telecommunications networks. In the last survey of world leaders by United Parcel

Service (UPS), Spain is shown as the country with the best expectations over the next three years, with regards to the prospects of both economic and business operations. Managers of the international location departments at KPMG and PricewaterhouseCoopers (PWC) consultants agree that Spain is a privileged destination for direct foreign investment in Europe, as a result of the Economic and Monetary Union (EMU).

The aim of this chapter is to throw some light on the relative competitive position of Spain, both in the European and global frameworks. First of all, it is worth analysing corporate competitiveness by reviewing the results of companies operating in Spain. These results will show important patterns with regard to the second issue to be discussed here: country competitiveness. The Spanish economy's output will be presented and followed by a review of the main factors of competitiveness that impact on Spain's position.

Business competitiveness in Spain

Three main indicators will be addressed in order to emphasise the importance of company output in the context of Spanish competitiveness.

As can be seen in Figures 1.6.1, 1.6.2a and 1.6.2b, the Organisation for Economic Co-operation and Development (OECD) forecasts for the year 2000, regarding the return on the investment ratio (ROI) for companies operating in Spain, show an outstanding 18.3 per cent; the third highest rating in the OECD. In addition, non-public companies operating in Spain are among those with the best corporate profitability in Europe, with a steady upward trend since 1994 and reaching net profit figures of around 19.8 per cent in 1999, and a return on their own capital of 10.6 per cent.

Business operations profits OECD Countries. Return on capital ratio (ROI), 2000

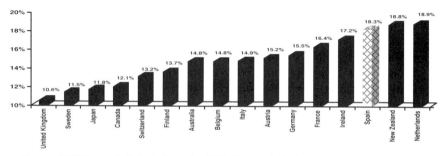

Source: OECD Economic Outlook, December 1998, (Last available data)

Figure 1.6.1   Return on capital ratio stands for dividends that return to the company from its investment calculated on a yearly basis (Forecasts for 2000)

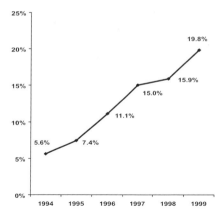

Figure 1.6.2a   Profits over production value (net results)

1999 figures are estimations calculated by the Bank of Spain Quarterly Survey

Source: Bank of Spain, Company Balances Office, 1999

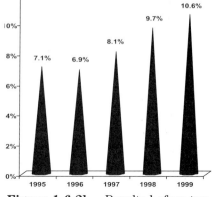

Figure 1.6.2b   Results before-tax over own-capital (own-capital profitability)

Figure 1.6.3a shows that out of Western European countries, Spain has the best expectation of sustaining these results in the future (in the opinion of its own entrepreneurs). These results are both with regards to the growth of its economy in the next three years and to the optimism surrounding the success of its companies.

Corporate investment and more specifically, direct foreign investment inflows, received by a country are reliable indicators of competitiveness. Almost 7,500 companies affiliated to multinational companies are currently operating in Spain in a wide range of productive and service sectors; a tally only surpassed by Germany within the European Union (EU). According to the United Nations Conference for Trade and Development (UNCTAD), Spain also ranks tenth in the world in terms of direct foreign investment inflows, a good indicator of Spain's relative competitiveness in a global context.

In addition, the reinvestment ratio in Spain accounts for nearly 30 per cent of total direct foreign investment inflows, proving the steady commitment of foreign capital towards Spain.

Analysis of country competitiveness

A quick look at the macroeconomic indicators that influence a country's competitiveness is useful here as it is essential to the success of a country's businesses that they operate in an environment that encourages sustained growth.

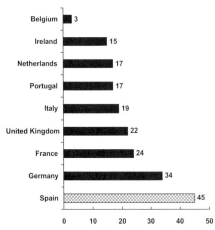

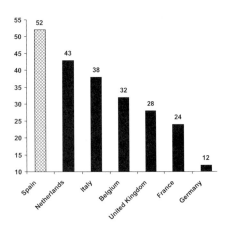

Figure 1.6.3a In the next three years, which Western European countries will show the strongest economic growth?

% of countries mentioned by business leaders

Figure 1.6.3b Will the economic position of your company be better or worse in 12 months time?

Net optimism (greater number denotes more net optimism)

Source: UPS Europe Business Monitor 1998 edition
Survey over European business leaders

Today, Spain presents an optimal macroeconomic environment with Gross Domestic Product (GDP) growth forecasts of more than 3.7 per cent over the next three years. With rates of growth of private consumption of around 4.4 per cent and growth of gross fixed capital formation of more than 8 per cent (twice the European average).

Spain, as a founder member of the EMU, has also achieved reliable control over classic economic imbalances. After six years of constant lowering and stabilisation of inflation index, annual inflation is now under 3 per cent. However, the Spanish government has launched a new package of economic liberalisation measures for the last term of the year 2000, in order to lower consumer prices.

Other macroeconomic indicators, such as the Budget Deficit, are no longer a problem in the Spanish economic framework, as it is expected to become positive by the end of 2000.

An optimal economic framework is also relevant to both public infrastructure investment and public capital flow towards the corporate world. To this end, Spain will receive funds for structural and cohesion purposes from the EU that amount to over €43,000 million for the period 2000–05 (Figure 1.6.4). This should guarantee public investment in the economy and once again, show the steady commitment of the EU towards Spanish competitiveness.

European Union funds: country breakdown

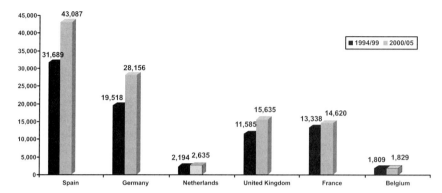

Figure 1.6.4   1994–99 & 2000–05 periods comparison

Figures expressed in Million Euros (€ 1 = 166.386 Ptas / US$ 1.11). Data is referred to EU monetary transfers to EU member States mainly for the strengthening of infrastructures, business financing and environment

Source: European Commission, 1999

Drive towards competitiveness

The combination of several optimal economic and social conditions will lead to the success of a corporate investment project and a country holding a strong global competitive position. This is known as the 'agglomeration effect': a number of factors of competitiveness which taken together, identify the leading locations in Europe, in terms of corporate investment and best operation practices.

Some of the factors whose 'agglomeration' makes it possible to assess Spain's competitiveness are as follows:

● **Full availability of skilled and qualified human resources.** With enrolment rates in Secondary and University Education above the EU average and a good knowledge of foreign languages.

● **Labour productivity**. Amongst the highest in Europe with a 2.7 per cent average increase in the last twenty years (Figure 1.6.5), but with rather moderate labour costs at an annual growth of around 2.8% in the last six years; several times below the inflation rate (Figure 1.6.6).

● **Integrated communication networks and telecommunications infrastructures.** A system of highways, centres of logistics, international airports and industrial seaports, combined with one of the most state-of-the-art telecommunications infrastructures in Europe, meet the wide ranging need of hard infrastructure-related services required by companies.

Constant labour productivity standards increase

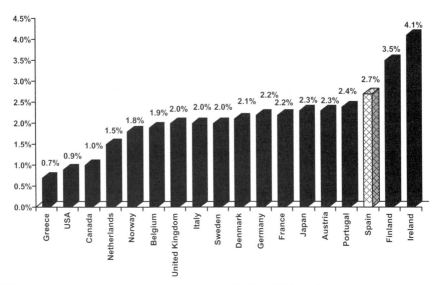

Figure 1.6.5   Percentages of increase 1979–1997 period average

Source: OECD, Economic Outlook, December, 1998 edition. Last available figures for each country

The highway and railway network will have top priority in the agenda of the Ministry of Public Works for the period 2000–06, in which almost €20 million will be invested in the expansion and improvement of the current facilities.

- **Production costs.** Between 10 per cent and 30 per cent lower than the European Union average (construction, land, buildings, electricity, gas, water, transport and logistics, etc.).

- **Tax pressure.** Amongst the lowest in Western Europe. The corporate tax rate actually paid by companies in Spain is at 24.11 per cent; the theoretical rate is set at 35 per cent.

- **Diversified economic structure.** The growing importance of the service sector, but a relatively larger industrial sector than the European average.

- **Quality of life.** One of the highest standards in the world. United Nations (UN) statistics point to a long life expectancy (78 years), together with optimal health and education infrastructure. According to its Development Programme, the UN has stated that Spain is the most

Labour costs

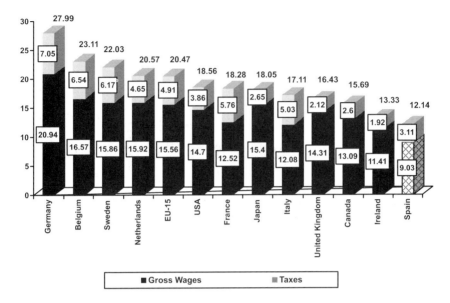

Figure 1.6.6   Labour costs worked per hour in manufacturing (all sectors)

Figures in current US$
Source: US Department of Labour, Bureau of Labour Statistics, 2000. (Last available data for 1998)

Tax charges

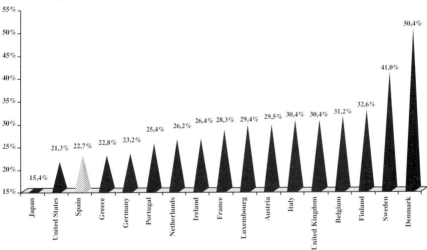

Figure 1.6.7   Compared tax charges among European union members (selected countries)

Figures in percentages over GDP. Japan and USA figures are shown for comparative purposes
Source: European Commission, 1999 figures

Spanish economic structure

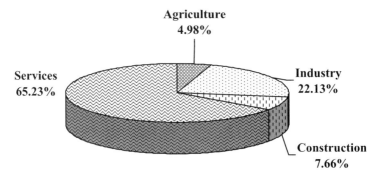

Agriculture
4.98%

Services
65.23%

Industry
22.13%

Construction
7.66%

Total Spanish Gross Added Value
in 1999: US$ 586.79 Billion

Figure 1.6.8   Percentages over total Spanish Gross Added Value for 1999

Source: FIES Savings Banks Foundation, 2000

successful country in the world in converting its income into human development.

- **Emerging markets.** At present, Spanish companies are major investors in almost all Latin American countries. Spain has privileged business relationships with, and direct accessibility to, emerging markets such as the Latin American or Mediterranean markets.

Supportive policies for investment

The last factor that impacts on competitiveness in Spain consists of the policies that are being developed by the Spanish government to support productive investments in the country. In fact, investment oriented policies are considered to be the core of a general policy towards business. The main goal of these public initiatives is the improvement of the Spanish corporate, economic and social environment by establishing and consolidating industrial and service networks, as well as through the creation of stable employment. The underlying basic theory is to consider that private initiative is an essential factor in guaranteeing job creation. In this sense, public actions oriented to support corporate investment can be summarised in five points:

- Improvement of the legal framework that is related to company activities; mainly, the tax system, labour and company law, as well as the financing system.

- In keeping with the above, plans are underway to free industries that are less transparent to the participation of private companies (such as, telecommunications, energy, airports and seaports, etc).

- Launching of investment programmes with regards to infrastructure, both for highways and for communications (such as motorways, improvement of seaports and airports, optic fibre wiring and broadband networks among others), as well as for services oriented to private companies (such as test laboratories, technology transfer centres, quality certification laboratories, etc).

- Active financial support, mainly orientated to technology and Research & Development (R&D) activities, as well as to on-going employment training. More than €3,000 million will be allocated to the National Plan of Research & Development (PROFIT Plan). This plan aims to help scientific and technological research in Spain as a means of increasing in-house industrial competitiveness in specific technology-related sectors.

- Through the Sociedad Estatal de Participaciones Industriales (SEPI), setting up an Investment Promotion Bureau (IPB); a public office that offers location advisory services to foreign investors at no cost and preserves confidentiality. The IPB is devoted to giving specialist advice to all needs of a direct investment project, both in case of greenfields or expansions of activities already developed in Spain. The advisory services cover different stages of the investment project: from decision-making to effective implementation, facilitating analysis and search of locations, identification of industrial partners and suppliers, feasibility studies for the project and tailor-made incentive packages, among other services.

Incentives to foreign investment in Spain

The last big area of governmental activity is devoted to providing attractive packages of grants and incentives for companies operating in Spain. A brief review of the main programmes available is offered here as useful complementary information.

As the great majority of affiliated companies of multinational groups cannot benefit from the status of being a Small and Medium-sized Enterprise (SME), the following review only takes into account the main incentives for which large companies could be eligible.

Within the territory of the EU, these grants are subject to the competition rules published by the European Commission, as they appear in the 'map of regional aid' approved for each country. The map shows maximum aid figures that governments are allowed to grant in different regions to corporate investment.

The aim of granting different levels of aid to different regions within a country is to attempt reducing regional differences in favour of a new territorial economic balance. This aim, however, must not lead investors to think that areas in which higher aid can be granted are inappropriate for the location of a productive operation. At present, the criteria used by the European Commission for classifying the different areas are very heterogeneous; it is possible to see regions with solid industrial structures enjoy a higher aid ceiling than others, oriented maybe towards agriculture, that do not have a consolidated corporate structure. This paradox could, for instance, be a result of unemployment figures that may be above the national average in some industrial areas.

In this sense, the diversity of the Spanish regions makes it easy to find appropriate locations for many different kinds of corporate activities. For example: the location of a shared services centre that makes high use of human resources, does not require the same conditions as an investment in capital intensive industry. In this sense, Spanish economic geography has proved to be suitable for the performance of diversified activities, even when companies choose to take advantage of the benefits resulting from the regional convergence policy.

In fact, there are successful examples, such as those of Dupont and Suzuki in Asturias; Ford and Fujitsu in Andalusia; Rhone-Poulenc, Renault and other call-centre activities in Castile-León; Solvay and Alcatel in Cantabria; Valeo in Aragón; Thomson in Castile-La Mancha; the PSA Automotive Group in Galicia, amongst many others.

Grants should not be too strong an argument in taking a decision about a new productive location. As has already been mentioned above, that decision must take into account the overall 'factors of the agglomeration of competitiveness', although the specific weight of the grant must not be underestimated.

The basic scheme of incentives that constitutes the current offer of aids to companies in Spain is concentrated on four basic pillars:

- Grants for investments on fixed assets.

- Employment grants (job creation and training).

- Technology and research orientated investments.

- Tax credits on the corporate tax rate.

A review of these programmes appears in Table 1.6.9.

However, all Regional Governments, as well as many of the Spanish town councils, have their own aid programmes, which in many cases can be availed of at the same time as those mentioned above.

Table 1.6.9 Programme of Government aid to companies

Type of Grants	Grant Level
Fixed Assets	
• Regional incentives	Up to 50% of the net aid equivalent to the investment expenses on fixed assets
• Development of mining areas	Up to 60% of the expenses
• Reindustrialisation	Long-term loans without interest of up to 70% of the investment expenses in fixed assets
Employment	
• Job creation	Up to €4,500 for each job created (depending on the regions)
	A reduction of the employer's contribution to the Social Security between 20% and 60% during the first two years of the work contract (depending on the employment group)
• Training	Up to 100% of aid for employment training programs
	Between €1,000 and €1,800 of aid for each participant in continuous training
Technology and Research	
• National Plan of Research & Development (PROFIT Plan)	Non-refundable aid or loans at zero interest of up to 85% of the eligible expenses (depending on the regions and type of projects)
Corporate and other Tax Relief	
	Rate deductions of the corporate tax for expenses of: R&D: deduction of up to 40% Innovation: up to 15% Environment: up to 10% Export Promotion: up to 25% Training: up to 5%
	Local tax allowances in certain town councils

Conclusion

The accession of Central and Eastern European countries to the EU at the end of this decade will certainly produce new challenges for the current member countries. Although a competition within a zero-sum game is not taken into consideration, the better the relative position in terms of competitiveness a country has, the better it will face economic changes in the near future.

With a sound economic background and strong prospects regarding corporate performance output, Spain must not be underestimated – it is a front runner in the race for competitiveness.

The Impact of the Euro

Margarita Lainez, Investment Promotion Bureau, SEPI; statistics compiled with the collaboration of Maite Yusta, Investment Promotion Bureau, SEPI

Introduction

The fact that Spain has belonged to the European Community since 1986, and was a founding member of the European Economic and Monetary Union (EMU) in 1998, has placed the country in a position of strength in the world markets. This is as a result of being part of an integrated group that carries a certain weight and that increasingly gains in effectiveness and in decision-making capability within the world economic framework. In addition, the upcoming use of a common currency will provide significant benefits both for Spain and for the companies that operate in its territory. These benefits can be summarised, among others, as: the full integration of European financial markets, the elimination of risk from exchange rate fluctuations, and the reduction in commercial transaction costs.

Thus, the single currency will cause an increase in competitiveness and effectiveness in companies, which will see their transaction costs decrease. There will also be fewer uncertainties regarding the stability of the growth rate and of traditionally volatile indicators such as inflation and interest rates, as far as trade with other companies forming part of the euro zone is concerned.

In addition, an increase in productivity levels is expected as well as an improvement in competitiveness, which should result in higher economic growth and employment. Spain has already initiated this process by implementing plans to increase gross fixed capital growth through programmes promoting Research & Development (R&D), professional training of workers and by improving the country's infrastructure. This process of modernising Spanish business is enabling it to successfully face the challenges of competition in the euro zone.

The competitiveness of a nation in the euro zone will thus be measured through factors such as relative labour cost, productivity, the training of human capital or the technological level of business. The achievement of an optimal level in these areas requires the deregulation of markets as well as the simplification of public finance and administration.

Main stages for the EMU

The EMU was first proposed as a formal objective of the European Community at a summit meeting at The Hague, in December 1969. As a result of that meeting, the Weber Report of June 1970 was prepared and it suggested the establishment of the EMU over a ten-year period, with three stages for its development.

Table 1.7.1   Developmental stages towards the EMU

Rome Treaty	Weber Report	Single European Act	Delors Report	Start of 1st stage	European Union Treaty	Start of 2nd stage	Start of 3rd stage
1957	1970	1987	1989	1990	1992	1994	1999
Creation of EEC Monetary Committee	Proposed 10-year year plan for EMU	Co-operation in economic and monetary policies	Three stages of EMU	Freedom of capital movement	Convergence criteria	European Monetary Institute	Single currency

The sequence for the introduction of the single currency, which was agreed upon at the European Council of Madrid (December 1995), encompasses three stages:

● The first stage or preparation period began in early 1998 and ran until 1 January 1999. During this period, the countries that complied with the criteria for convergence, and thus qualified for the single currency, were chosen. Those criteria were:

  – Inflation to be no higher than 1.5 points above the average of the three countries with the lowest inflation rate;
  – Long-term interest rates to be no higher than 2 points above the average of the three countries with the lowest inflation rate;
  – Public deficit to be no higher than 3 per cent of Gross Domestic Product (GDP);
  – Public debt to be no higher than 60 per cent of GDP;
  – A stable rate of exchange in the two previous years, with neither devaluation nor major stress on the national currency.

● The second stage or transition period began on 1 January 1999, with the introduction of the EMU, and will run to 1 January 2002. In this stage, the euro operates as the official currency and may be used as 'written money' but not in cash.

● The third stage, or definitive changeover, will run from 1 January 2002 until June of the same year. During this period, central banks will proceed to replace national bank notes and coins with euro-denominated currency.

As of 1 January 1999, the euro is the official currency of the 11 countries that have joined EMU (the 'euro zone'). The euro zone includes Spain, Portugal, France, Italy, Germany, Belgium, Luxembourg, The Netherlands, Ireland, Austria and Finland, which all complied with the convergence criteria. Greece, which had been left out because it did not meet the criteria, has now qualified for inclusion in the euro zone; the United Kingdom, Sweden and Denmark have chosen to remain outside it.

Converging to euro standards

The following table shows Spain's economic performance relative to other countries with respect to indicators that are relevant to the convergence criteria for EMU.

Table 1.7.2   Indicators relevant to convergence criteria, Spain and other countries, 1999

Countries	1998 Inflation (%)	Interest rate (%)	Public Deficit (%/GDP)	Public Debt (%/GDP)
Belgium	1	3.29	(1.0)	118.2
Germany	0.9	3.32	(1.7)	61.1
Spain	1.8	3.32	(2.3)	65.1
France	0.8	3.29	(2.7)	58.8
Ireland	2.4	3.29	2.0	49.5
Italy	2.0	3.29	(2.7)	118.7
Luxembourg	1	n/a	2.5	6.9
Netherlands	2	3.29	(0.8)	67.5
Austria	0.9	3.29	(2.4)	63.0
Portugal	2.8	3.36	(1.5)	57.8
Finland	1.4	2.43	1.4	49.7
Denmark	1.8	3.49	0.9	58.0
Greece	4.8	9.80	(2.5)	106.3
Sweden	0.4	3.58	2.3	74.2
United Kingdom	3.4	5.90	0.2	48.7
Japan	0.6	0.21	(5.9)	37.2*
United States	1.6	6.08	1.4	43.9*

* OECD Economic Outlook, Forecast for 1999
Source: Inflation figures taken from OECD Economic Outlook, December 1999. All other figures taken from European Commission Autumn Report

The period leading up to the beginning of 2002 is one of transition, during which public administrations, economic agents and citizens in general will be able to influence the development of the euro through their daily approaches and actions. Spain has plotted a course of direction for the transition period by, in the first instance, preparing the Economic Stability Programme. In the second instance, a set of legislative measures, such as the Plan for Transition to the Euro and the Law for the Introduction of the Euro, has been developed. Finally, the government has sought to reinforce and support social dialogue so that society itself adapts easily to the new reality of Spain adopting a new, common currency.

EMU is intended to be an area of macroeconomic stability, an important condition for the development of business activity, for the maintenance and improvement of consumer purchasing power, and for the creation of employment. Macroeconomic stability is to be achieved through adherence to three principles:

- Monetary stability, through the creation of the European Central Bank, which will be responsible for the design and execution of a single monetary policy.

- Budgetary stability, a consequence of meeting the convergence criteria.

- Stability in the rate of exchange, resulting from the existence of a single currency.

The most important consequences of this macroeconomic setting for Spanish business are the following:

- Currency devaluation is no longer an option for improving the competitive position of exports.

- Stable and moderate inflation.

- Lower interest rates.

- Reduction of uncertainties, both in exchange rates as well as inflation.

- Lower transaction costs.

- Greater transparency in markets and improvement in the price system for decision-making.

- Simplification of procedures and documents in international relations.

What impact for companies? Balancing the pros and cons

The introduction of the euro will be felt differently by each business depending, among other things, on factors such as its openness to foreign markets, its volume of cash transactions, its dependence on foreign supply, and finally, its size, type of activity and the sphere in which it performs its activity.

Chambers of commerce, industry and shipping in Spain, co-ordinated by the National Council of Chambers, are developing the Single Currency Programme, whose objective is to facilitate the adaptation of Spanish companies to the euro. Among the activities performed by this programme is an annual survey that tracks the degree of preparedness among businesses for the euro.

According to the latest survey, taken in 1999, 63 per cent of companies surveyed feel that the introduction of the euro will present more advantages than drawbacks. 57 per cent anticipate that new business opportunities will appear and 65 per cent have already begun to study the implications of the single currency. As far as dates are concerned, 62 per cent will begin to use the euro during the transition period (1 January 1999 to 31 December 2001). Likewise, 77 per cent feel that prices will not be affected.

By sectors, it should be mentioned that the industrial sector is the most optimistic, and shows a greater degree of awareness and preparedness for the euro. Trade and restaurant/hotel activities, along with construction, have experienced noteworthy advances with respect to 1998.

Finally, the impact of the introduction of the single European currency in Spain cannot be considered of great importance, as it will not substantially affect the internal functioning of already-established companies, and will therefore also not mean any problem for the establishment of new investment projects. However, the introduction of the euro will have an important positive effect in relation to the level of competitiveness that companies established in Spain enjoy. The elimination of exchange rates and their associated costs and uncertainties, along with a lower comparative labour cost and greater productivity of the work force, place Spain in an excellent starting position as far as the impact of the euro on the economy is concerned.

1.8

Business Culture

Elena Liquete-Collis and Chris Brewster,
Cranfield School of Management

Introduction

Spain has a distinct culture that is different from British culture. Yet, when it comes to business practices, the general assumption seems to be that there is a 'right way' and a 'wrong way' of conducting business. Needless to say, each national culture believes its approach to be the correct one. In this section we would like to suggest that while business practices in Spain are different from those of the UK, they are neither better nor worse. The British traveller doing business in Spain has a clear choice:

- To try to conduct business as he or she would in the UK. This is often stressful and may lead to failure; or

- To acknowledge that business practices in Spain are different, learn about them and enjoy the experience.

What follows is a brief outline that will help you when conducting business in Spain. In order to deal with such a vast subject in such a short space we have had to make a fair number of generalisations. Please bear in mind that while our comments will be broadly accurate, they will not apply to every situation you may encounter. In particular, Spain is a large and varied country with marked regional variations. There is not space here to consider these differences, but in some cases they can be quite significant. Any time that one can invest in learning about Spain and the Spanish will help in the achievement of business objectives and make the experience more enjoyable.

Work practices

Business hours

The structure of the working day in Spain is different to that of a working day in the UK. Offices generally open at 9am and senior managers are unlikely to be in before that time. In some instances, the more senior the person, the more likely he or she is to arrive late. Traditionally, business activity would stop from 1pm to 3 or 4pm for lunch. In the smaller towns and cities this long lunch break allows the family to get together for the main meal of the day. In larger cities, such as Madrid or Barcelona, this is no longer practical, as the distances are now too great and the traffic too congested to allow people to travel back home for lunch. Hence, some businesses now follow more anglicised practices and have shorter lunch breaks.

Either way, lunch remains the main meal of the day and if it is not practical for people to return home, there are plenty of restaurants offering reasonably priced meals. The Spanish view the British practice of eating sandwiches at one's desk as an unsociable and unsophisticated one, and to be discouraged. Equally, coffee breaks are often taken outside the office. It is perfectly acceptable to leave the office for 15 minutes to pop over to the nearest coffee shop with a colleague, but it would be seen as highly unusual to have coffee at one's desk.

Offices close around 7pm although senior staff generally stay on. This is often the time when the 'real work' is done, as it is easier to gain access to key people who have very busy diaries. Business discussions will often continue over a drink at a bar nearby.

If you are being entertained, dinner is not likely to start before 9 or 10pm and will often go on past midnight. If you had an early start, or have just flown in having already put in a full day's work in the UK, you may not be at your best by 10pm, let alone midnight. If, however, you have planned for a long day and allowed yourself a late start you may even enjoy your night out!

During the summer, working hours may change, and this is particularly true of the hottest areas of Spain, where offices tend to work from 8am to 3pm.

Public holidays

The Spanish enjoy 14 public holidays per year. While the majority are national public holidays and apply to the whole of Spain, each region can also nominate a number of public holidays. Public holidays can fall on any day of the week. If they happen to fall on a Thursday, for instance, people will often take the Friday off in order to have a long weekend. It is always worth checking a Spanish calendar when planning a business trip.

The typical holiday entitlement in Spain is 30 days, often taken as a whole calendar month. Many businesses actually close down for a month in the summer, generally in August.

Human resources practices

Human resources practices in Spain are generally less formalised than in the UK. Recruitment is still largely conducted through informal networks, with many key posts never reaching the job pages. Performance appraisals are not yet popular with the Spanish, although are widely used by multinationals and larger Spanish companies.

Cultural issues

Use of English

English is well established in Spain as the international business language. There is, however, something of a generation gap and one may find that older executives in smaller companies are less likely to speak English. Conducting business in a second language seems to add to the potential for costly or embarrassing misunderstandings. While a Spanish business-man may speak very good English, his understanding of the meaning behind the words is likely to be shaped by his own culture. Care should be taken to spell out any assumptions and clarify what is understood in the particular context of the negotiation in hand.

Conducting negotiations

British businessmen and women conducting negotiations in Spain often voice a common complaint: things *take too long!* While in the UK they may be able to fit in three or four important meetings within a day and move negotiations on fairly quickly, in Spain they may only manage one meeting in a day and still walk away empty-handed.

The difference revolves around different attitudes to what is important in a business relationship. In the UK, business and personal lives rarely cross. The British see little value in getting to know business partners personally. The assumption is that the contract is there to resolve any differences that occur between the parties as the relationship develops. This is not the assumption in Spain. The Spanish are highly sociable people who need to know and like their business counterparts. They prefer to do business with people they trust, so that the paperwork becomes redundant or the contract becomes merely a formalisation of an on-going relationship. It is therefore well worth investing the time to develop business relationships.

If you insist on conducting your negotiations in the same way as you would in the UK, you are not only likely to fail, but your stress levels will go through the roof. If, on the other hand, you do your best to adopt the Spanish way, you will achieve your objectives in the end and you may even enjoy it.

In a similar vein, what British businessmen and women also find very irritating is the Spanish unwillingness to commit anything to paper, preferring a more direct means of communication such as the telephone or face to face discussion. If you feel you need to write, it is probably a good idea to follow it up with a telephone call or you may never get a response.

The Autonomous Regions

Spain has 17 Autonomous Regions with varying degrees of freedom to legislate and raise taxes. Some regions also have their own language in addition to Spanish. Regional languages have the same standing as the national language. When conducting business in any of the Autonomous Regions it is well worth investing a little time to do some basic research. Legislation on local matters may vary, as indeed do the incentives to set up businesses in certain areas.

The Spanish executive

Spanish executives are generally educated to degree level, with law and economics being the most popular degrees. They are likely to have a masters degree, sometimes from a north American university, and tend to speak good English. They will generally develop their careers in one organisation and are characterised by a 'hands-on' approach. Management is not yet seen as a discipline and therefore Spanish managers are generally expected to be technical experts in their subject area.

The Spanish organisation

The Spanish business scene is largely populated by Small and Medium-sized Enterprises (SMEs), with 90 per cent of Spanish companies employing less than 50 people. This figure would help to explain the small number of Spanish multinationals operating internationally. In many industries, financial services in particular, recent years have seen an increase in mergers and acquisitions in an attempt to make Spanish organisations more competitive within the European Union (EU).

Spanish organisations tend to be more hierarchical than British companies. Care should be taken to pursue any issues through the correct channels, as ignoring the hierarchy is likely to cause offence.

Mode of address

The fact that the Spanish have two surnames seems to puzzle the British. The explanation is quite simple; when a child is born he receives his father's surname as well as his mother's, in that order. For instance:

Father	José **Rodríguez** Pérez
Mother	María **Suárez** Martínez
Child	Francisco **Rodríguez Suárez**

Some writers insist on the use of both surnames when addressing a Spaniard. In practice, the use of both surnames is only required when filling in official paperwork. In business correspondence it is quite acceptable to use just the first surname.

In a formal business context, the correct way of addressing a Spanish colleague is as follows:

Señor Rodríguez or Don José Rodríguez
Señora Suárez or Doña María Suárez (for a married lady)
Señoríta Suárez or Doña María Suárez (for a single lady)

Christian names can be used when invited to do so.

Please bear in mind that women in Spain do not change their names when they get married. They simply become Señora instead of Señorita (Mrs instead of Miss).

Part 2

Business Practice and Development

2.1

The Structure of Industry

Professor Mikel Navarro, ESTE-Universidad de Deusto

Introduction

Manufacturing industry accounts for 18 per cent of Spain's value added and of its workforce. This figure is slightly higher than that of the USA but clearly lower than the rest of the European Union (EU) or Japan. This weakness in Spain's manufacturing industry is even more evident when industrial value added per capita is taken into account: €2200 in 1997 compared to the EU-15 average of €3700, €3900 in the USA and €6900 in Japan.

The weakness in Spain's manufacturing industry is due to its late industrial growth. In the 1960s and the first half of the 1970s, the so-called development phase of Spain's economy, the country's industry became unstuck. The aforementioned development process was cut short by the petrol crisis: between 1975–1985 Spain suffered a 40 per cent drop in industrial employment. This loss is vastly greater than the EU average and contrasts with the maintained and even increased level of industrial employment in US and Japanese industries during the same period. However, and despite the strong influence of the recession between 1990–94, employment in industry has increased in Spain relative to other leading countries since 1985: employment in industry has risen by 14 per cent while it has remained more or less the same in other leading countries.

Industrial structure

The location of industry has traditionally been based in Catalonia, the Basque Country and Madrid. It has recently expanded to other communities, in particular towards the Mediterranean coast and the Ebro region (Navarra and Zaragoza). Today both Catalonia and the community of Valencia account for 30 per cent of Spain's industrial activity while the Basque Country and Madrid claim 11 per cent each. With regard to sectorial specialisation, the chemical industry is flourishing in Catalonia; textiles, non-metallic mineral and other manufacturing industries are doing well in the community of Valencia; metallurgy, machinery and transport equipment in the Basque Country; electrical, electronic and optical equipment and materials in Madrid.

Key sectors of Spanish industry
Looking at how each sector contributes to overall manufacturing production, it is clear that the sectors that stand out are food, cars, pharmaceuticals and chemicals and non-metallic mineral products. Spain also has other highly specialised areas (in particular the drinks, leather and footwear industries), however these hold less weight in the manufacturing sector. The sectors that stand out by their low specialisation level are instruments of optical precision, non-electrical machinery and electrical and electronic materials and equipment, all with a high level of technicality. However, growth analysis shows that Spanish industry is undergoing significant structural change, as a result of which the more traditional sectors (iron and steel, textiles, leather and footwear) have lost ground to the more attractive sectors such as cars, non-electrical machinery, electrical materials and the chemical industry. This has brought Spain sectorial specialisation closer to the standard of the leading countries.

Foreign trade
To complete the analysis of Spain's production structure, an examination of its foreign trade is necessary. Spain's current account is clearly in deficit, but has traditionally been compensated for by the surplus in tourism, transfers and the movement of capital. The sectors that contribute negatively to the trade balance are the chemical industry, non-electrical machinery, electrical goods and professional materials, whereas the sectors that contribute positively are cars and, at the other end of the spectrum, non-metallic mineral products, leather and footwear.

Generally speaking, the contribution to the balance of the Spanish trade is positive in the sectors of production of consumer goods, in the industries that require low- to medium-level technology where growth in demand is low to medium and where economies of scale and use of natural resources are intensive. Conversely, the contribution of the balance of the foreign trade is negative in the sectors producing capital goods and intermediary goods, sectors with a high technological level and high growth in demand, and sectors that make intensive use of science and technology and are very differentiated. However as a proviso to what has previously been indicated, the specialisation profile of Spain's trade is rapidly improving and catching up with EU standards.

Competitiveness

Size of enterprises

It is now necessary to examine a series of factors specific to each sector which influence Spain's competitiveness and give a clearer picture of its manufacturing industry. To be considered in the first instance, is the size of the existing enterprises and business groups. Reports from Eurostat and the European Commission clearly state that Spanish businesses are, on average, small and the importance of the small- to medium-sized business sector is very high. Of the top 500 firms worldwide (based on their stock market value) only ten are Spanish, and none of these are manufacturers. One of the main reasons for Spain's weak economy is precisely its lack of powerful industrial corporations. This is clearly reflected in the international dimension of Spain's economy. Since 1997, direct investment by Spanish businesses abroad has been significantly greater than direct foreign investment in Spain, the latter going largely into industry while Spanish investment abroad goes to the service sectors (finance, transport, communications), energy, and only a small proportion to industry.

Ownership

Following recent privatisation, the presence of influential state owned companies in Spanish industry is rather small. From the end of the 1970s to the mid-1990s the banking sector began to reduce its industrial holdings, which today are relatively low, although still higher than the European average. It is foreign capital that has increased its investments in Spanish businesses, so much so that, up until the mid-1990s at least, companies controlled by foreign capital claimed over 40 per cent of industrial gross value added. Holdings by some companies in the capital of other companies, although higher than the average in the Anglo-Saxon model, is still low compared to the continental average. And families who had been losing ground in industrial businesses as shareholders, after 1995 began to see their position improve and are now, along with foreign capital, the principal shareholders in industry. Generally speaking the ownership structure of Spanish companies is very similar to that of its continental peers, where investments are concentrated mainly in a small number of companies that have a major shareholder, and with little investment from institutional investors, in contrast to the Anglo-Saxon model.

Labour costs

Secondly, we must take into account labour costs, productivity and the stock of fixed capital of Spain's manufacturing businesses. The cost of labour per employee, calculated in dollars, is a third lower than the EU average and half the German average, yet double that of Portugal. These differences are compensated for in part by existing differences in productivity. The final result shows that labour cost per unit of product (which varies according to both labour cost per employee and productivity) is 16 per cent lower in Spain than the European average, over 25 per cent lower than in Germany but almost 25 per cent higher than in Portugal.

Investment

Productivity and efficiency of production is largely determined by the stock of fixed capital available and it is, in turn, influenced by investment. Analysis shows that investments per employee made by Spanish companies are clearly lower than the average US investments and, needless to say, lower than those made in Japan. In addition, one needs to look not only at the size of the investment but also how effectively it is used. This could be determined by looking at the rate of asset turnover.

Although comparisons based on statistics for different countries should be taken with great caution, figures indicate that Spain's manufacturing companies have radically changed their approach in that regard. Thus, unlike in the past, Spain's manufacturing companies presently have asset turnover rates similar, if not superior, to other countries included in the database of the BACH project.

Technology

Another key factor regarding competitiveness lies in technical superiority, an area in which Spain's economy is known to be generally weak. Research and Development (R&D) spending represents only 1 per cent of GDP, while in the EU that figure is 2 per cent and in the USA and Japan, nearly 3 per cent. Moreover, the proportion of spending by businesses is clearly less in Spain than in other leading countries. And if we look at the manufacturing industry the percentage of Spain's value added spent on R&D is only 1.4 per cent, a figure three times lower than leading EU countries and five times lower than that of the USA and Japan. This low figure is partly explained by the little weight of the low- to medium-level technology sector within the Spanish manufacturing industry, referred to previously. It is also explained by the fact that a large number of high-level technical businesses are owned by foreign investors (for example, in cars and the chemical industry), in which a fundamental part of their research is carried out by their parent company.

The technological weakness in Spain's manufacturing businesses, which has been highlighted by its low level of spending on R&D, is further confirmed by more general data relating to numbers of patent requests (per 1000 inhabitants), the rate of coverage in the technological balance, the percentage of companies that have brought a new or improved technological product or process to market.

Financial Structure

Finally, a comparison between the factors that have a bearing on competitiveness and the financial structure of Spain's manufacturing companies must be made. Again, caution is needed when comparisons are made based on data from different businesses and countries. The figures show that the percentage of own funds used is higher overall in Spanish businesses than the average in European, Japanese or US companies. In other words, the debt level of Spain's manufacturing businesses is lower than other countries. This is also reflected in the low percentage of financial expenses in relation to financial incomes.

This is the result of the reinvestment policies and debt recovery carried out by Spain's manufacturing businesses during the best part of the 1980s and 1990s, in a context of high interest rates and poor financial profitability. The stock market and venture capital firms have hardly contributed to the capitalisation of Spain's manufacturing industry. Today, in a new context, with very low interest rates and high financial profitability, Spain's manufacturing enterprises are using credit again and are increasing their level of indebtedness.

What is noticeable, on the one hand, is the great importance of short-term debt in relation to total debt (higher than in other countries) and on the other hand, the importance of commercial debt in Spain's manufacturing industry.

Profitability
Finally, we should look not at other factors influencing competitiveness in the manufacturing industry, but at the very indicator of this competitiveness: the profitability of manufacturing companies. It would appear that the profitability of Spanish manufacturing companies has traditionally been inferior to the European Community and US averages. However, the strong progressive recovery of companies since 1994 has altered this. In the last year for which comparable figures are available, 1997, profit margins after tax were clearly lower in Spain than they were in the rest of Europe and in the USA. However, thanks to the improved asset turnover today, when after tax results are seen in relation to assets, the profit ratio of Spain's manufacturing industry is close to the EU average, although a long way short of the USA. And taking into account the relatively favourable growth shown by the activity and profitability of Spanish enterprises in 1998–99 (years when Spanish businesses witnessed record profits), indicators suggest that the current profitability levels of Spain's manufacturing enterprises will have reached if not surpassed the EU average.

2.2

State-owned Enterprises and Privatisation

Joaquim Vergés, Department of Business Economics, Universitat Autònoma de Barcelona

Introduction

The number of State-Owned Enterprises (SOEs), and their economic weight in the national economy, have decreased impressively in Spain since 1985, when the government of the socialist party (PSOE) began a process of restructuring and modernisation as well as of selective privatisation of these public enterprises. Some SOEs were privatised by direct sale to a private firm or business group, generally belonging to the same production sector. Several of the larger SOEs were partially privatised by the state's sale of share packages by means of public offerings in the stock market. This meant that they became 'mixed capital companies', though continuing to operate under state control, as the state's remaining stake in the firms' capital allowed it to retain control. The first block (those firms privatised by direct sale) consisted mainly of manufacturing firms, and most of these were loss-making before being privatised. The second block, on the contrary, was referred to by the economic press as 'the crown jewels', as the firms were and remain large and highly profitable enterprises, with a strong market position and a remarkable international projection.

This privatisation process was, of course, strongly accelerated when the conservative party (*Partido Popular*) won the elections in 1996. The most remarkable change in privatisation policy was that the above mentioned large and profitable firms (Repsol, Endesa, Argentaria, Tabacalera and Telefónica) were totally privatised over the first two years of the conservative government's term of office.

It is worth pointing out that, by 1985, the size of the public enterprise sector in Spain was relevant, although smaller than in most European countries. The value added of all the Spanish public firms represented some 8.5 per cent of Gross Domestic Product (GDP), and employed a similar percentage of the labour force. Their share of national investment was somewhat greater, at 20 per cent. Most public enterprises were industrial firms and public services. They ranged from the coal mines to the national airline company, from single Spanish companies in industries such as aeronautics and the automotive industry*, to almost all the aluminium sector, and the greater part of the iron and steel industry. They also included a great part of the national producers of electricity, the national telephone company, a major part of the oil sector and a significant part of the chemical industry and the banking sector.

To all these must be added two traditional Public Enterprises (PEs), which were the holders of two public monopolies that existed at that time (among others): the distribution of tobacco and the distribution of fuel. Overall, there were some 130 'direct' PEs, plus approximately 850 'indirect' ones (that is: subsidiary or sub-subsidiary firms of the aforementioned). And we must also add to the list the PEs belonging to the regional governments and municipalities.

By 2000 the picture had changed dramatically. Almost all the large SOEs have now been privatised either totally or partially, and the economic weight of the public enterprise sector in the national economy has fallen to just over 2 per cent. Nevertheless, there remain some large SOEs (airlines, aeronautical industry, railways, shipbuilders, defence industry and others; as well as the more traditional ones such as the postal service, airports, ports etc), and many others of lesser importance. Some of these remaining SOEs already have specific privatisation plans drawn up for them.

Management and legal features

The great majority of Spanish public enterprises (either at the state, regional, or municipal level) were and are legally formed joint-stock companies (*sociedades anónimas*, SA). This makes them subject to private law in their commercial and labour relations, and in the way managers and staff are recruited, and thus subject to the same conditions as a private company. Therefore, their proprietors – usually public agencies or control holdings – do not need any legal authorisation to completely or partially sell their shares. This explains why, unlike in countries such as the United Kingdom, France or Italy, the process of privatisation was not preceded by

---

* There were other companies in the automotive industry (as there are now). They were the Spanish subsidiaries of the large European and American car manufacturers such as Renault, Peugeot, Citroen, Ford, General Motors.

the adoption of an *ad hoc* law, but rather, each privatisation is undertaken through a specific governmental decision.* There are exceptions, since some SOEs have a legal status of public entity†, which makes them dependent upon public law procedures. For example, the national railway company (Renfe), the airports or the postal service fall into this category. But in general, the SOEs have always depended upon public agencies or holdings that acted as their major shareholders and, therefore, also as their privatising agents. The most important public agency at present is the *Sociedad Estatal de Participaciones Industriales* (SEPI).

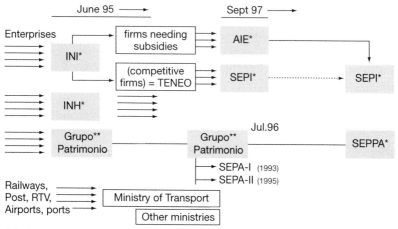

INI = Instituto Nacional de Industria   SEPI = Sociedad Estatal de Participaciones Industriales
INH = Instituto Nacional de Hidrocarburos SEPA = Sociedad Estatal de Participaciones Accionariales
AIE = Agencia Industrial del Estado   SEPPA = Sociedad Estatal de Participaciones Patrimoniales

*Subordinated to the Ministry of Industry
**Subordinated to the Ministry of Economy and the Exchequer

Figure 2.2.1   Public agencies that control state owned enterprises

---

* Somewhat late in the day, in March 1995, the socialist government of Felipe Gonzalez presented and saw passed through parliament a law 'On Privatisations', which is actually, as is clear from its official title, simply a 'law of juridical rules for the transfer of public shares of certain enterprises', that is to say a law more of administrative proceedings than of political content. Later on, in June 1996, the cabinet of the new conservative government passed and made public a resolution (not even a decree, just a governmental declaration) on the 'basis for a programme of modernisation of the public enterprise sector'. This resolution's most notable contents were, in the first place, an explicit political commitment by the new government to expand the process of privatisation to the maximum, and, secondly, the setting up of a Consultative Council for Privatisations, whose members were appointed by the government itself.

† *Empresa/Sociedad Estatal* or *Organismo Autónomo Comercial y Industrial*

State-owned enterprises in 2000

The selling of shares in profitable large SOEs can be considered as having been completed by the end of 1999, with some notable exceptions, such as the remaining 60 per cent of Iberia, the remaining 25 per cent of Red Electrica Española, and the remaining 40 per cent of Retevisión.

Nevertheless, the declared policy of the ruling conservative party (returned to power in the March 2000 elections) is considering the privatisation of all the remaining state-owned firms, the more traditional ones – such as railways and airports – included. Therefore, new sales can be expected from 2000 onward. By the end of 1999, the government had already decided to privatise some of these firms. However, the implementation of the privatisation process has been subordinated either to an improvement of the economic and strategic position of the given firm, or to more favourable conditions in the stock market for the launch of new public offerings. The following are the SOEs for which the government, the public agencies (which act as privatising bodies) or the public enterprises' management have explicitly indicated that definite plans for privatisation exist:

Table 2.2.1   SOEs for which specific plans for privatisation exist (from 2000 onward)

Firm	Sector	Economic performance	Method of privatisation (as announced)
Belonging to Ministerio de Fomento:			
	Telecommunications	High profits record	By public offering (PO) in the stock market
Retevisión (40%)*			
Belonging to SEPI:			
Iberia	Airlines	Among the most profitable international airlines in 1997	40% by direct sale[+] 60% by PO
Babcock Wilcox Española	Machinery construction	Losses (approaching to balance in 1998)	Direct sale
Santa Barbara	Armament	Losses (but with some profit-making divisions)	By direct sale
Ence (51.3 %)*	Paper	Steady profits	25% by direct sale 26.3% by PO
REE (25 %)*	Bulk electricity carrier	High profits record	By PO
Casa	Aeronautical industry	Balanced	Not yet known
Musini	Insurance	Steady profits	By direct sale
Inisias			
Crédito y Caución			

Table 2.2.1 *continued*

Firm	Sector	Economic performance	Method of privatisation (as announced)
Belonging to SEPPA:			
Transmediterránea	Sea transport (passengers' lines)	Steady profits	By PO
Coosur	Olive oil	Balanced	N/A

* The whole (remaining) public ownership

†10% to 'industrial partners' (British Airways 9%, and American Airlines 1% – in this way Iberia will be part of a strategic alliance, and in a stronger position to face international competition.); 30% to 'institutional partners': Caja Madrid, BBVA, Logística, Ahorro Corporación, and El Corte Inglés. (These agreements were already signed by the beginning of 2000).

Source: author's own compilation from several primary sources (government officers' statements and economic press information)

Other than those mentioned above, by the end of 1999 there were 44 other directly state-owned PEs for which no privatisation plans had been announced by government, as well as all the commercial ports, airports and other similar public entities. To all these enterprises remaining in state hands, we must add the existing municipal public enterprises (about 800) and those controlled by the regional governments (about 490); two blocks of public enterprises in which privatisation operations have been rather scarce.

Table 2.2.2 Most notable SOEs for which no specific privatisation plans had been announced by the end of 1999

Firm	Sector	Public holding controlling the firm
Aviaco	Airlines	SEPI
Aluminio Español	Aluminium	
Ensa	Nuclear equipment	
Enusa	Uranium processing	
Infoinvest	Financial services	
(and 14 others of less importance)		
Hunosa	Coal mining	SEPI ('inherited' from AIE)
Minas de Figaredo	Mining	
Potasas de Subiza	Mining	
Presur	Mining	
Bazan	Shipbuilders	
Astano	Shipbuilders	
Astilleros Españoles	Shipbuilders	
Minas de Almadén	Mining	SEPPA (*G. Patrimonio*)
Tragsa	Agriculture services	
Alimentos y Aceites	Agriculture products	
Agencia Efe	News agency	

Table 2.2.2 *continued*

Firm	Sector	Public holding controlling the firm
Cesce	Financial & Insurance Services	
Cetarsa	Financial & Insurance Services	
Enausa	Toll highways	
Paradores Nacionales	Hotels	
Mercasa (and 9 others of less importance)	Dairy foods central markets	
Renfe	National railways	*Ministerio de Fomento**
RTVE	Radio & television	
Feve	Regional railways	
Aena	Airports	
Puertos autónomos	Main ports	
Autoridad portuaria	Other ports	
Hispasat	Communications satellites	
Conf. Hidrográficas (and some others of less importance)	Canals	

* Ministry of Public Works
Source: author's own research

Public enterprises controlled by regional governments and local (municipal) authorities

While the process of privatisation of SOEs by successive central governments continues, the Spanish regional governments have become engaged in a process of creating public firms geared towards development and other socio-economic policy goals. These enterprises are usually given the legal status of private law (joint-stock) companies, as is the case for most SOEs.

As a consequence of these concurrent processes, the number of public firms depending on regional governments has steadily increased over the past 15 years. Furthermore, this is a general trend and is not influenced by the political leaning of the regional governments in office. Thus, the number of 'regional public enterprises' grew from 247 in 1990 to 493 in 1998. Some of these firms provide the services that have been devolved from the regional administration's responsibilities, but most carry out business related to the development of regional economic activity and employment (from innovative fisheries to new energy development and high-tech communications services). Most regional PEs are therefore created as an element of industrial development policy, in its more traditional sense.

As far as enterprises depending on local councils or other local authorities are concerned, the most important ones are the public transport companies (bus and metro) of Madrid and Barcelona, both giving service to metropolitan areas of more than three million people. These two public firms are followed in the ranking by similar companies in Valencia and Bilbao and other cities, and hundreds of others local public companies of less importance (local radio and television stations, housing, water supply, waste disposal and a wide range of other municipal services). It is worth pointing out that no significant privatisation initiatives have taken place in this sector of Spanish public enterprises.

2.3

The Role of Small and Medium-sized Enterprises

Bové Montero & Cia

Introduction

A well-known characteristic of Spanish enterprises is that they are, on average, small in size. Size is a factor that conditions the behaviour of a business and that can affect, in part, the structural character of the country's economy.

This chapter looks at the quantitative and qualitative importance of Small and Medium-sized Enterprises *(SMEs)*[1] in Spain, paying special attention to their role in creating employment and in acting as a dynamic and creative force for economic success. The chapter will conclude with a look at the future role of SMEs.

Some statistics

According to figures from the National Institute for Statistics (INE), on 1 January 1999 there were more than 2.5 million businesses in Spain, of which 99 per cent were SMEs. It is predicted that this trend in Spanish business will continue to develop.

As illustrated in Figure 2.3.1, the majority of Spain's businesses are either very small or micro-businesses; Figure 2.3.2 shows that over half these businesses (55.5 per cent) are very small and, in addition, do not employ salaried workers. It must be remembered that the proportion of freelancers in Spain is 5 per cent higher than the European average.

---

[1] This article uses the most common definition for SMEs, also used by the OECD, which considers small businesses to be those with no more than 100 employees, medium-sized businesses to have between 101 and 499 employees and large businesses to have over 500 employees.

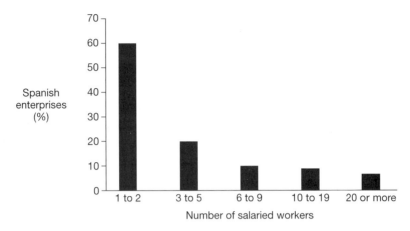

Figure 2.3.1   Number of salaried workers employed by Spanish enterprises

Source: National Institute for Statistics (INE), 1999

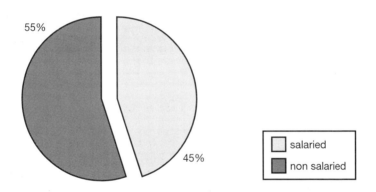

Figure 2.3.2   Percentage of enterprises with salaried or non-salaried workers

Source: National Institute for Statistics (INE), 1999

There are 1,130,685 businesses that have salaried employees – they represent 44 per cent of all Spanish businesses. Of these, 57.4 per cent employ one or two salaried persons. Only 5.8 per cent employ 20 or more salaried workers.

Table 2.3.1 shows an analysis of the different economic sectors and illustrates the fact that most large enterprises are found in the industrial sector, where 9.2 per cent of businesses have over 20 salaried employees.

The 'other services' sector boasts the highest proportion of small businesses, with 85.6 per cent of enterprises employing two or fewer salaried persons, followed by the 'commerce' sector where 83.5 per cent of enterprises employ at least two salaried persons.

On the basis of the location of the head office, the Autonomous Communities that are home to the most registered companies are, in order of importance: Catalonia, Andalucia, Madrid, the Valencian Community, the Basque Country and Galicia. Catalonia also boasts being home to more financial sector companies than any other area, and is consequently one of the principal engines of the Spanish economy.

Table 2.3.1   Enterprise assets by economic sector 1 January 1999 (Ptas million)

Number of salaried workers	Economic sector				
	Industry	Construction	Commerce	Other services	Total
Non-salaried workers	78,587	124,332	433,336	751,871	1,388,126
1–2	61,297	68,586	223,519	298,369	651,771
3–5	34,888	35,218	72,852	92,173	235,131
6–9	20,507	18,251	26,984	35,975	101,717
10–19	20,718	14,913	18,266	25,526	79,423
20 or more	21,785	10,326	11,427	22,105	65,6433
Total	**237,782**	**271,626**	**786,384**	**1,226,019**	**2,521,811**

Source: National Institute for Statistics (INE)

The importance of the SME sector

SMEs and their potential for job creation

Due to their dynamism and ability to adapt, the greatest potential for job creation lies with the SMEs. Indeed, according to data compiled by the government, the SMEs provide some 80 per cent of jobs in Spain.

The fact that there are so many small businesses in Spain (normally micro-businesses with fewer than 10 workers) and that they are often run by families, is due, among other things, to the relative ease in establishing such businesses.

In Spain, the minimum amount of share capital needed to set up a limited company is Ptas500,000. Also, the government offers subsidies and assistance for the creation of businesses, which are particularly targeted towards certain groups such as young people and women. It is therefore quite easy to become an entrepreneur in Spain, since the most important factor for success is not necessarily capital, but rather having an enterprising nature and business acumen.

There are several factors that motivate Spanish people to set up their own business, but on the basis of a study carried out in Andalucia,[2] it appears that the main motivation is the desire to prosper. The second motivating factor is self-employment (particularly people who have not felt fulfilled as employees in previous jobs). The third factor is bringing an idea to fruition and the fourth, to secure independence and own earnings. Generally, SMEs in Spain are great creators of wealth and self-employment.

SMEs in a competitive environment

It is obvious that in an economy such as the Spanish one, with over 2.5 million businesses, there should be enormous competition. Also, in an environment of increasing globalisation, competition is no longer only local, provincial or national but increasingly global in nature, particularly due to the free movement of goods and services, people and capital and the increasing use of new technologies such as the internet.

It is therefore clear that, in the framework of this new global environment, SMEs should have certain disadvantages in comparison with larger companies with regard to their capacity to invest in Research and Development (R&D) and in new technologies, access to information, export, etc. It should also be taken into account that the large companies are becoming even larger as a result of the many mergers that have been taking place over the past few years.

The next few paragraphs discuss the problems now faced by Spanish SMEs and how they are being resolved.

The challenges facing SMEs

SMEs and R&D

Carrying out technological and R&D activities is very important for businesses, so much so in fact that the degree of innovation shown by some companies can actually determine their survival and positioning in the market. However, SMEs are at a disadvantage in this regard in comparison with the larger companies. In Spain, the probability that a large company will spend resources on R&D is almost 70 per cent, while for smaller companies, the probability is only 20 per cent. This is in keeping with R&D spending patterns in other European countries.

There are several initiatives designed to counter this imbalance. National programmes, attractive tax rebates for R&D expenditure, European co-operation networks such as the 'Technological Research and

---

[2] Díez de Castro (1995) *Business in Andalucia*

Development Plan' (TRDP) or the 'Leonardo Plan' are all designed to facilitate the acquisition of technological competencies by SMEs.

SMEs and access to information

One of the principal concerns for decision-makers is to have access to relevant information affecting their business directly or indirectly, in order to reduce the uncertainty of the whole decision-making process. Increasing competition pushes businesses to look for sustainable competitive advantages by taking adequate strategic decisions.

Access to communication/information has therefore become a *sine qua non* condition for companies to remain competitive in the current market. As previously mentioned, of all the mediums available, the internet has become an important means of communication and access to information.

Here again, the larger companies have an advantage in that they have more resources available to them and can, and indeed do, dedicate more spending towards gathering information, while SMEs are generally still in the process of modernising. In the last few years however, businesses (mainly SMEs), aware of the problem that SMEs face in gaining access to information, have sprung up to offer their services in accessing the internet, adapting computer programmes and tailoring other solutions exclusively for small and medium sized businesses.

SMEs and exports

The size of an enterprise directly influences its ability to export, as its means of production is directly related to its size. Thus the average exportation rate of large enterprises is double that of small enterprises: only 20 per cent of enterprises with a workforce of 20 or less export goods compared to 80 per cent of enterprises with a 500 plus workforce.

There are three reasons why it is advantageous to be a large enterprise in the export market:

1. Large enterprises are better able to redeem export-related fixed costs and can therefore more easily meet the minimum standard/level for effective exportation.
2. Large enterprises are better able to spread the high-risk element of exportation over a larger number of export transactions.
3. The larger the company, the higher the possibility of differentiation in production.

Being conscious of the disadvantages faced by SMEs and recognising the importance of exports for the economic growth of a country, local and central governments have created a number of support organisations that offer a multitude of services and financial subsidies designed to strengthen SMEs' international activities. Amongst these, the Spanish External Trade Institute (ICEX) stands out as being one of the most effective. In addition, banks are becoming more involved in strengthening the international side of SMEs' business by providing financing and advice for export.

It is expected that Spanish enterprises will continue to become increasingly international. Indeed, Spanish businesses have achieved a lot in a short space of time, especially considering the disadvantages that they started off with in comparison with other European businesses. It is worth noting that, in the last four years, Spain has doubled its exports and now ranks among the world's top ten investors and exporters. SMEs have not been left out of this development.

The internet has taken on an important role for Spanish exporters as it has drastically reduced costs (including the fixed costs referred to earlier as being advantageous to the larger companies). The market is global and the internet is able to connect buyers and sellers anywhere in the world. In addition, companies no longer need to have a physical presence abroad, thus noticeably reducing one of the disadvantage that SMEs had in relation to the larger enterprises. With this new outlook, the talk will soon be of 'virtual internationalisation' rather than of the traditional approach of actually having a business in a foreign country.

Future outlook

Small and medium sized enterprises are a vital part of any country's economy. Not only do they create jobs but they also contribute to economic growth through their flexibility and their constant challenge to larger businesses and monopolies. However, Spain's SMEs (like others in Europe) still remain at some disadvantage compared to larger enterprises.

On the one hand, co-operation between SMEs must increase in future to enable them to share common experiences, knowledge and information, but on the other hand, they must begin to collaborate more closely with large enterprises. If SMEs were able to provide more goods and equipment to the larger firms without neglecting their traditional areas of business, they would have access to a very large market. Small and large businesses both complement and need each other, and the philosophy of SMEs should evolve from that of 'fight them' to that of 'join them'.

However, government must further lower the administrative, bureaucratic and financial barriers that SMEs face in order to facilitate their creation and survival so that they are able to continue creating more jobs and contributing further to Spain's economic growth. Despite their difficulties therefore, Spain's SMEs have a very optimistic future.

2.4

The Labour Market

Bové Montero & Cía

Introduction

In recent years, the labour market and its functioning have taken an important position in industrialised economies, especially in Europe. Spain still has one of the highest unemployment rates among European countries, although it has recently fallen greatly from 24.2 per cent in 1994 to 15.4 per cent in 1999. The objective for Spain is to create some 1000 jobs net each day, in order to achieve full employment within a reasonable period of time.

This chapter begins with a presentation of recent figures on unemployment, continues with a description of how the Spanish labour market is structured, and concludes with a short reflection on the future of the Spanish labour market.

A few relevant figures

From 1996 to 1999, unemployment decreased by more than one million people, reflecting the radical change in the outlook of labour in recent years; this is illustrated in Figure 2.4.1. The figures for the last quarter of 1999 illustrate two remarkable facts. First, that the Spanish economy already employs over 14 million people, and second that its capacity to create jobs has by far exceeded the real increase in Gross Domestic Product (GDP). GDP rose by approximately 3.8 per cent in 1999, but employment increased by 5.24 per cent in the same year.

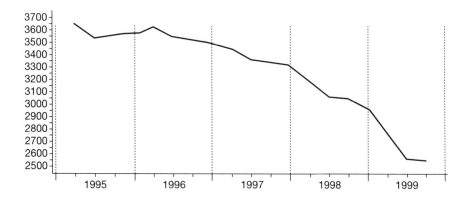

Figure 2.4.1   Spanish unemployment rate

Source: EPA *(Encuesta de la Población Activa – Inquiry of the Active Population), 1999*

The distribution of employment in different economic sectors is quite similar to that in other developed countries. In 1999, approximately 7 per cent of the working population worked in the agricultural sector, 20 per cent in the industrial sector, 11 per cent in the construction sector, and most, namely 62 per cent, in the service sector. This trend is illustrated in Figure 2.4.2.

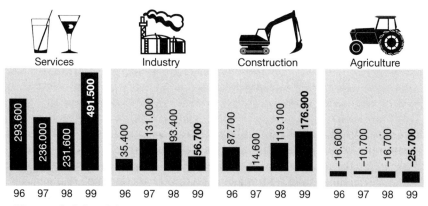

Figure 2.4.2   Job creation by sector with yearly figures, 1999

Although there remains a difference between the registered unemployment rates for men and women, with the unemployment rate for men being lower, this discrepancy will be slowly eroded. This development is anticipated given that 60 per cent of the jobs created in 1999 were for women and that this trend is likely to continue in the next few years. Figure 2.4.3 illustrates the discrepancy in male and female employment rates.

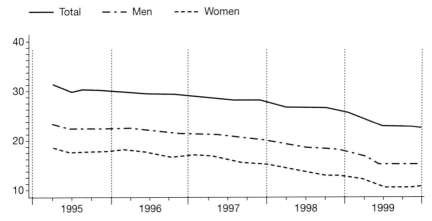

Figure 2.4.3   Unemployment rate among men and women

Source: EPA (1999)

Structure of the labour market

Below is a discussion of the structure of the labour market and of its institutional mechanisms through the working cycle:

- starting off;
- permanence;
- leaving the labour market.

Searching process and availability of information

In order to find a job, it is essential to get information about the availability of jobs. The broader and more extensive the information, the better the adjustment between vacancies and unemployed persons. In Spain, the INEM (Spanish Office of Employment) is the institution that has traditionally been the link between firms and employees, and it was only in 1994, as a result of labour reform, that public and private employment agencies were allowed. As of that time, temp agencies (ETTs) were introduced, and although they usually only provide work for a short period of time they play a strong role in keeping the labour market flexible and in creating new jobs that may turn into permanent positions.

At present, besides the traditional methods of searching for a job (newspapers, labour magazines, etc), the internet is becoming an increasingly important tool in the process.

Process of starting a job – different kinds of contracts

The Spanish entrepreneur, just like any other, is more or less willing to hire new employees according to the choice of contracts available and that may be adapted to the firm's needs.

It is possible to hire employees on one of the following types of employment contracts:

- Unlimited contract: in this case, the entrepreneur receives a bonus from the government (less social security contribution);
- Part-time contract;
- Temporary contract or contract of a determined duration;
- Practice contract;
- Training contract.

Relationship with the firm

Collective bargaining
Wage negotiations normally take place between the trade unions (the most important ones are UGT and CCOO) and the employers' association (CEOE) at the beginning of each new year, and are conducted separately in the different economic sectors.

This model shows a few problems. On the one hand, since negotiations are held independently within all sectors, the result is an excessive fragmentation. On the other hand, the system of wage setting does not always take into consideration macroeconomic conditions (for example, the level of unemployment in an economy), neither does it adjust perfectly to the different levels of productivity of independent firms. This method of wage negotiation should be improved in the future.

Wages[*]
Employees are entitled to receive the equivalent of at least two extra monthly payments per year and therefore gross annual wages are divided into 14 payments. There are collective wage agreements that provide for a *pro rata* of said extra payments throughout the whole year. There is also a minimum wage per year set by the government, which for the year 2000 amounts to Ptas70,680 per month.

Working time
The maximum duration of ordinary working time is of 40 hours per average week of the year. Working hours cannot exceed 9 hours per day, unless

[*] *Source: Doing Business in Spain*, by Bové Montero & Cía, Gestión 2000 (2000)

otherwise agreed in the collective wage agreement or between the entrepreneur and the employees' representatives. In any case, a rest of at least 12 hours between working days has to be respected. Overtime cannot exceed 80 hours per year.

Holidays amount to 30 calendar days per complete year of service, ie both working days and holidays are included. There are also national, regional and local holidays throughout the year, hence the maximum number of holidays is limited according to Spanish law.

Social security
Contributions to social security are paid both by the firm and by the employee. In general, the firm pays 30.6 per cent and the employee 6.4 per cent. Employees are classified in various professional categories in order to determine their contribution to social security. Each category has a minimum and a maximum contribution, which is normally revised every year.

Social situation of the citizens of EC countries
Since 1 January 1992 and the application of the EC-normative, citizens of EC countries may work in Spain under the same conditions as Spanish citizens. They do not need work or residence permits. EC-members who wish to reside in Spain for more than three months must, however, obtain a residence permit.

Termination of a work contract
Traditionally, the dismissal of an employee with an open-ended work contract was a very expensive decision for the entrepreneur, as the firm would have to pay a high indemnity to that employee. In times of economic growth, this restrained the firm from hiring too many employees for fear of the consequences of recession-induced redundancies. The reform of the Labour Law in 1984 was intended to give the labour market more flexibility by introducing temporary contracts. The objective was to encourage entrepreneurs to hire employees in times of economic growth, without the fear of dire financial consequences if those employees were later made redundant. However, the abuse of those temporary contracts made employees lose confidence in their future, and the fear of job loss led to spending restraint and to a decrease in consumption.

The latest labour reforms of 1994 and 1997 sought, with very good results, to avoid the overuse of temporary contracts, which not only led to halting growth in private consumption, but also caused firms to be understaffed and suffer losses in productivity and competitiveness. The reforms were designed to reduce the effective cost of a dismissal and to promote the use of unlimited contracts by decreasing legal indemnity payments in case of dismissal.

Unemployment benefits

The idea behind a protection system in case of unemployment was to guarantee a minimum level of income to those who lost their jobs. In 1999, unemployment benefits ranged between Ptas60,611 and Ptas177,793 per month, according to the applicant's individual situation and the last job worked. The effects of unemployment benefits are always far-reaching and difficult to balance in a labour market. Potentially, the higher the economic cover provided to an unemployed person, the less their interest in finding a new job.

In 1992, when the highest unemployment rate was registered in Spain, this system had to be reformed due to its high cost for the state. The reform did not have a profound impact, but did extend the period during which an employee made contributions in order to qualify for unemployment benefit, thus automatically reducing the amount of benefit paid out and the period of time in which benefit could be paid out. With the reforms adopted in recent years, the country is close to finding a fair system that satisfies the needs of both entrepreneurs and employees.

Re-training, training and public employment programmes

The growth and persistence of unemployment as a problem has proved that passive politics (unemployment protection) must be complemented by active methods of putting people back to work. These methods relate to the qualification, retraining and training of unemployed people and to public employment programmes in the labour market.

In Spain there are different support programmes, such as those that are specific for young people, those that provide resources for professional training, those that make grants for direct job creation or for personnel hiring, and those that encourage the employment of disabled people. There are also training courses for jobs for which firms have been unable to fill their vacancies.

Future prospects

It should now be clear that more profound structural reforms of the Spanish labour market are necessary in order to gain more flexibility. It is evident that within a frame of increasing globalisation, international competitiveness and continuous technological breakthroughs, an adjustment of the labour market to this new environment is essential. Therefore, all market actors and foreign investors need to co-operate, as Spain offers some excellent prospects in every field of investment. Soon, one will not discuss the unemployment crisis but rather contemplate the reality of full employment in a continuously strengthening Spanish economy.

2.5

Personnel Recruitment

Hay Consulting, S.A.

Current labour market

Now, and over the past two decades, a clear trend has emerged in Spanish society showing a preference for university education over technical training courses of shorter duration. This preference is most likely born of the influence of Spain's recent history, including factors such as the Civil War and 40 years of Francoism, and to the notion that a university degree is a symbol of wealth and power and brings with it access to top positions in the labour market. Furthermore, the long period of isolation from the international community imposed by Franco's policy of self-sufficiency had the effect of limiting opportunities for Spaniards to be in contact with other cultures and languages.

Starting in the 1960s, Spain gradually opened its doors to foreign investment and influence. This coincided with a rise in economic growth that provided the country with more flexibility and opportunities, helped by a favourable political environment and the globalisation of markets. The main consequences of all these factors have been:

- A major improvement in employment rates;

- An increase in the number of women working;

- Greater ease of access to higher education for all social groups and the devaluation of professional training qualifications, considered socially inferior and quite removed from the European dual model of education/training;

- The opening of new markets;

- A need for knowledge of foreign languages.

As a result of this new environment, Spain now has an excess of professionals with university degrees and a clear and worrying deficit of technical and specialised professionals, thus creating recruitment difficulties in this area.

The solutions put in place to overcome this last problem are twofold. One is to enhance the social image and prestige of technical education. The other looks abroad to the importation of professionals from other countries and the search for professionals among immigrant workers.

Human resources services

Among services provided by companies specialising in the human resources (HR) sector, recruitment is the service whose aim it is to find the right employee to fill a client firm's position. It can be seen as supplying clients with a solution to their search for candidates by finding the employee whose profile corresponds to the requirements of the firm, its needs and corporate culture.

The added value offered by this vocation is to bring a high level of objectivity to the selection process, helping clients define the competencies they require for a certain position in a particular environment. Furthermore, companies can reduce the expenses related to time and organisational structure and resources by externalising the human resources function.

The evaluation systems adopted by different HR consultants may vary, but the most reliable is one that compares interview results with the results of personality and competency tests in order to identify those professionals that could offer the company the most effectiveness. HR consultants usually present a personalised report of the three final candidates whose profile and experience best correspond to the vacancy.

Sources of external HR services

Companies have access to several sources of recruitment to organise their manpower, mainly through public institutions and private companies.

Public institutions
This category of recruitment source includes non-profit making institutions that possess databases gathering *curricula vitae* (CVs) or lists of people looking for a job or a change in career. The service offered by public institutions is limited to verifying applicants' details and drawing up a broad profile of applicants based on their studies, years of experience, languages, computer skills, etc. They can neither provide an evaluation service nor an idea of the availability of potential candidates. Furthermore, their information is seldom updated. The following are examples of such institutions:

- **INEM:** National institute of employment, whose main task is to review the list of unemployed persons and compare it with lists of job opportunities.

- **Training centres for unemployed:** Databases include the names of people who have attended, or are willing to attend, courses subsidised by the state.

- ***Bolsa de Trabajo* (careers offices):** In universities and public centres of education, usually have a specialised database of former students organised by area of study. These lists are not always updated and list young people with little or no professional experience.

Private companies

- **ETT (temporary employment companies):** Their activity is to select personnel for positions that offer a fixed period contract. Their databases are generally extensive but have a high turnover rate, and are therefore not always up to date. They usually have difficulty in filling positions in certain professional categories. They tend not to resort to conventional recruitment and evaluation processes and if they do, these are very basic. Finally, they offer a guarantee of replacement in cases of non-satisfaction of the client or of voluntary dismissal of the worker before the contract ends.

- **Service companies/outsourcing:** They are responsible for the whole structure of personnel in a department/service of a company that wishes to outsource some of its personnel issues, thereby optimising its resources and reducing its costs. The department in question is usually not considered a key department, and could, for example, be cleaning, maintenance or telemarketing. Service companies are organised by areas of activity.

- **Human resources consultants:** Among the broad range of services these offer is that of personnel selection, a highly specialised service, as the recruitment of professionals is for permanent, and not temporary, vacancies. They resort to several forms of recruitment such as their own database, advertisements published in the press, and networking contacts for direct searches. They focus the process of selection on the study and understanding of corporate cultures and environments, in order to define quite accurately the personal and professional features making up the best profile for the position to be filled. HR consultants usually offer a guarantee of replacement during the first three months. During this trial period they will follow up on the evolution of the chosen candidate within the company. Their fees are usually fixed in relation to the salary of the position to be filled, the resources required to complete the recruitment process, and the level of difficulty in finding candidates, taking into consideration the situation of the labour market.

- **Business schools, private universities and private professional schools:** They have a list of their former and current students. They do not follow a standard approach and some charge fees for consulting their database and for having access to the CVs of students. Generally, the databases are of young professionals with up-to-date knowledge and strong potential but, generally speaking, with little experience. These institutions may also offer a personnel selection service, in which case the service is similar to that provided by HR consultants, and generally comes with similar fees and conditions.

- **Chambers of commerce:** Some have a *bolsa de trabajo* at companies' and members' disposal for a fee. They do not follow any standard way of operating and it is therefore advisable to check this information beforehand.

- **Internet:** The internet has specialised web sites offering CV databases at a relatively low cost. Their main advantage is the rapidity of the search and the principal disadvantage is that the contact is impersonal and not always up to date.

Finding an HR consultant
There are several sources of information, the most important being:

- AEDIPE (*Asociación de Directivos de Recursos Humanos y Personal*): HR managers association;

- Chambers of commerce;

- City halls (information services for companies);

- City services guides;

- Telephone directories;

- Specialised web sites.

You can also consult HR publications such as:

- *Capital Humano* (Human Capital)

- *Factor Humano* (Human Factor)

- *Staff*

- *Empleo y Desarrollo* (Employment and Development)

Finally, in the employment section of national and local newspapers, job advertisements are published either by companies themselves or by HR consultants. The latter usually indicate their address, fax number, telephone number, e-mail and, sometimes, a person to contact.

2.6

Investing in Spain

Colin P Blessley, Partner in charge of Financial Advisory Services, PricewaterhouseCoopers, Spain

Introduction

Since 1996, the strength of the economy in the USA and the recovery in Europe has spawned a succession of multibillion-pound Mergers and Acquisitions (M&A). The venture capital industry continues to be extraordinarily active on all fronts, across borders and in many industries, involving both financial and strategic buyers. The mood of optimism is stronger in the USA than in Europe or Asia in terms of the amount of activity.

For many years Spain has been a recipient of significant amounts of foreign investment, with this activity intensifying in the 1980s. In the early 1990s, Spain had been seriously affected by the recession that hit other markets, and was slow to emerge from it. M&A activity resented the slowdown and the number of transactions dropped off considerably in the first half of the decade.

In 1995, the economy started to recover and, with it, so did M&A activity. However, the nature of the transactions has changed. With Spain's accession to the European Union (EU), the early and middle 1980s were characterised by the scramble of international businesses seeking to secure a foothold in a market of 40 million consumers, hitherto protected but now suddenly opened wide. Thus, the 1980s was more speculative, whereas the deals that are taking place nowadays have a more solid underlying rationale, companies are better valued, and the targets have stronger links with the real economy. Generally, today we see a concentration based operations with business criteria – such as industrial synergies, new markets, privatisations and strategic divestments. Now that economic activity has picked up, driven largely by strong domestic demand and exports favoured by a weak currency, there has been an increase in M&A activity. The Spanish economy is currently among the best-performing in Europe, with good GDP growth predicted to continue for the next few years; unemployment is down and, in general, the outlook is comparatively healthy.

The venture capital industry appeared in the Spanish economic scenario in the late 1980s. As in the rest of Europe, private equity in Spain has experienced a sharp development over the past decade, although following a discontinuous pattern. After the period of recession early in the decade, in 1995 the amount of new equity invested bounced back to 1990 levels reaching Ptas 26.5 billion. The improved focus of the venture capitalists is evidenced by a substantial increase in average deal sizes. A significant aspect to be noted is that, during 1997 and 1998, management buy-outs (MBOs) and management buy-ins (MBIs) gained market share among total venture capital investments, thus demonstrating that the Spanish market has become more mature in terms of private equity.

One of the most important factors driving M&A activity in Spain at present is the positive economic cycle, which has stimulated an increasing interest from foreign companies in building their presence in this market. With the suppression of barriers to EU trade and the entry into the Economic Monetary Union (EMU), Spanish companies are also gaining in efficiency.

Other factors that have been decisive for M&A transactions include the Spanish government's privatisation programme, which, after languishing for many years, was revitalised by the current centre-right government. The stock market is now very efficient, and the attractive opportunity for initial public offerings (IPOs) has affected company valuations and made Spanish private companies more attractive.

Cultural issues

In a world where national trends are converging into a common behaviour, there are still some cultural differences to be identified between Spain and other European and international communities. Local practices can differ and in this section we seek to provide some insight into these practices.

Family-owned businesses are still the backbone of Spanish industry. But more open-minded generations with foreign education are joining companies, information is flowing more easily and M&A activity in Spain is growing. There is still a considerable number of deals that are completed in Spain without involving an M&A consultant or adviser, but which are closed with the help of the local tax adviser, family lawyer or accountant. However, this is changing, and Spanish companies fully understand the importance of seeking adequate advice, especially in the case of a cross-border transaction.

Gathering information

A common issue that purchasers come up against is the availability of information in Spain. All companies are required to file their annual financial statements with the local Mercantile Register, plus a copy of the management report and of the auditors' report if the company is audited. Listed companies are further required to file copies of their financial statements and related auditors' report with the National Securities Exchange Commission. All this information can be obtained by the general public. However, the majority of medium- and small-sized Spanish companies do not disclose much information in their annual accounts and, therefore, there is no substitute for good commercially orientated due diligence.

Even though Spain has improved significantly in the implementation of modern management techniques, there is still a general lack of sophisticated management information systems, budgeting and forecasting procedures, strategic planning and the preparation of business plans, as compared to Anglo-American companies. Treasury management and cost-accounting can sometimes be somewhat rudimentary.

Deal sources

In Spain there is a considerable number of small- and medium-sized family owned companies that can have succession problems and that can, therefore, be the target for foreign investment. Additionally, in recent years there has been a structural reform of the economy, with sectors such as the telecommunications and electricity industries being liberalised, the pensions and health systems profoundly reformed, and a number of state-owned companies privatised. The stock market reached an all-time high, reflecting the confidence of investors. In addition, the pressures towards the globalisation of the economy means that, in order to compete in the regional or global marketplace, unless they have a particular, specialised niche position, Spanish companies will be forced to seek strategic solutions to remain in business. All these factors will generate more transactions.

Analysing accounts

Spanish accounting policies aim to ensure that a company's annual financial statements are clear, and reflect a true and fair view of its net worth, financial position and operating results. The preparation of accounts subscribes to the principal accounting concepts such as prudence, going concern, recording, cost basis, accrual basis, consistency, etc, stated in the National Chart of Accounts (PGC). The PGC has also been adapted for various industries (for example, construction, electric utilities, real estate), and contains a description of the rules of valuation based on the foregoing accounting principles.

However, Spanish principles are not entirely in accordance with International Accounting Standards and caution should be taken when analysing financial information. Therefore, restatement may be necessary for compliance. It is always advisable to seek guidance from a local accounting firm familiar with cross-border and international accounting conventions.

Due diligence

A detailed business investigation into the target is crucial when considering a merger or acquisition, in order to identify the key commercial issues, the strengths and weaknesses, and areas of potential concern.

The results of the due diligence can often help to highlight difficulties or problems and to confirm the bidder interest in the target. It is essential to protect the acquirer from surprises at a later stage. Based on information obtained as part of the due diligence, the purchaser should also be able to prepare a detailed post-acquisition integration plan.

A merger or acquisition represents a major challenge to the parties involved. The decision-makers on both sides of the transaction must, therefore, obtain and absorb a significant amount of technical data from internal and external experts, decide on an optimal course of action, and successfully negotiate this result, usually within severe time constraints. Accordingly, it is important to involve experienced professional advisers in the due diligence process, with a proven background in the local market and multidisciplinary capabilities, who will also be able to assist in overcoming the target company's unfamiliarity with these procedures.

Valuation

A key objective in any acquisition is not to overpay for the target company. It is essential to ascertain the market value of the company and to have all the information necessary to estimate the possible price, also considering the possible synergies that might be expected from the transaction.

The larger Spanish corporations have very quickly understood the importance of financial theory in relation to the creation of value. Theories and methodologies such as discounted cash flows, weighted average cost of capital, and adjusted present value are widely accepted, understood and applied in these large corporations. However, the same cannot be said about medium and small-sized Spanish companies.

There is still an important part of the Spanish economy made up of small- and medium-sized family-owned companies, who often do not have the financial sophistication to follow theories of value and value creation. Some typical characteristics that help identify such businesses are:

- balance sheets with important levels of owned real estate;
- large amounts of excess cash and no interest-bearing debt;

• limited information on future prospects, ie budgets and forecast.

In these situations, the basic concept of value is the equivalent P/E obtained on disposal by an acquaintance operating in a completely different sector. Negotiations in these circumstances can become relatively frustrating. In many cases, the purchaser and his advisers will endeavour to educate the target company. However, the seller's scepticism is understandable when the educator is trying to acquire the business. In such cases, it is always worthwhile recommending the target to find a professional adviser to assist him in such a process. Often, one can suggest a small list of names of suitable advisers.

Venture capital

Recently, a new venture capital bill was passed that significantly benefited venture capital activity and encouraged new investments. One of the main changes brought by the bill is the fact that supervision, inspection and penalties for private equity houses depend exclusively upon the National Securities Exchange Commission. However, venture capitalists are now allowed to invest through institutional preference shares in any company, and not only in non-quoted shares as was the case previously.

In terms of fiscal aspects for private equity, two significant changes have arisen from the bill:

• VAT exemption for management fees;

• 99 per cent allowance of the Corporation Tax for the capital gain resulting from disposals of portfolio investments until the 12th year (the previous regulation was until 10th year).

In other words, the changes to the legal and fiscal framework sought to stimulate a new investor cycle for venture capitalists in Spain, and they did so with success. Some statistics for private equity in the aftermath of the bill are set out below.

Table 2.6.1   Private equity in Spanish markets

	1995	*1996*	*1997*
Accumulated funds	184.9	188.9	229.1
New funds raised	23.1	8.6	67.7
New equity invested	26.5	31.0	43.2
Total portfolio	**98.0**	**111.6**	**121.2**

Source: Martí Pellón, J (1998) El capital inversión en España, 1997. Civitas, Madrid

Table 2.6.2   Breakdown of the annual investment

	Investments (Ptas million)						Number of transactions					
	1995	(%)	1996	(%)	1997	(%)	1995	(%)	1996	(%)	1997	(%)
By destination												
New participated companies	20.0	75.5	23.7	76.3	36.9	84.6	132	60.6	100	63.3	180	73.8
Companies in portfolio	6.5	24.5	7.3	23.7	6.7	15.4	86	39.4	58	36.7	64	28.2
Investment of the year	**26.5**	**100**	**31.0**	**100**	**43.5**	**100**	**218**	**100**	**158**	**100**	**244**	**100**
By level of expansion												
Seed capital	0	0.0	0.3	1.1	0.4	0.9	1	0.5	7	4.4	14	5.7
Start-up	2.9	10.8	1.6	5.1	3.1	7.2	52	23.9	35	22.2	51	20.9
Expansion	18.8	71.2	26.7	86.0	28.1	64.6	144	66.1	106	67.1	152	62.3
Substitution	0.8	3.0	0	0.0	1.0	2.3	2	0.9	0	0.0	1	0.4
LBO/MBO/MBI	3.9	14.6	1.9	6.1	10.9	25.0	17	7.8	6	3.8	26	10.7
Restructuring	0.1	0.4	0.5	1.8	0	0.0	2	0.9	4	2.5	0	0.0
Investment of the year	**26.5**	**100**	**31.0**	**100**	**43.5**	**100**	**218**	**100**	**158**	**100**	**244**	**100**
By size of transaction												
0 to Ptas 9 million	0.1	0.5	0.1	0.4	0.1	0.4	31	14.2	27	17.1	41	16.8
10 to 49 Ptas million	2.0	7.5	1.4	4.4	1.7	3.9	76	34.9	53	33.5	67	27.5
50 to 99 Ptas million	2.6	9.9	1.6	5.2	2.7	6.1	36	16.5	23	14.6	41	16.8
100 to 199 Ptas million	3.9	14.5	2.7	8.6	3.9	9.0	30	13.8	19	12.0	33	13.5
200 to 499 Ptas million	10.5	39.5	6.8	22.0	10.8	24.8	34	15.6	21	13.3	37	15.2
Above Ptas 500 million	7.4	28.0	18.4	59.4	24.3	55.9	11	5.0	15	9.5	25	10.2
Investment of the year	**26.5**	**100**	**31.0**	**100**	**43.5**	**100**	**218**	**100**	**158**	**100**	**244**	**100**
By number of employees												
0 to 9 employees	4.1	15.6	2.7	8.9	6.0	13.7	69	31.7	50	31.6	85	34.8
10 to 19 employees	1.9	7.3	0.8	2.5	1.1	2.6	25	11.5	17	10.8	25	10.2
20 to 99 employees	6.1	23.1	8.9	28.7	7.9	18.1	68	31.2	58	36.7	82	33.6
100 to 199 employees	4.2	15.9	2.5	7.9	9.0	20.7	19	8.7	9	5.7	22	9.0
200 to 499 employees	6.6	24.6	4.8	15.6	13.4	30.8	30	13.8	11	7.0	20	8.2
Above 500 employees	3.6	13.5	11.3	36.5	6.1	14.1	7	3.2	13	8.2	10	4.1
Investment of the year	**26.5**	**100**	**31.0**	**100**	**43.5**	**100**	**218**	**100**	**158**	**100**	**244**	**100**

Source: Martí Pellón, J (1998) El Capital inversión en España, 1997. Civitas, Madrid

Legal acquisition issues

The acquisition of more than 5 per cent of the share capital of a listed company must be notified to the National Securities Exchange Commission. Public offers must be made to acquire significant shareholdings. Contingent liabilities cannot normally be avoided by an acquirer purchasing assets rather than shares, since liabilities can be deemed to follow assets on the transfer of a business.

Employees in Spain have strong rights; for example, permanent employees made redundant without cause are entitled to 45 days' redundancy pay for every year of service, up to a maximum of 42 months' pay. These rights are almost always upheld by tribunals.

Environmental legislation in Spain is relatively recent and has not yet been totally developed in terms of enactment from a practical standpoint.

In accordance with EU directives for environmental regulation, several bills have been passed that affect administrative and penal issues. Even if Spain has incorporated environmental legislation later than most of its European neighbours, there is a tendency to harmonise with the rest of EU countries and more and more companies are obtaining ISO 14.001 certifications on environmental management. However, caution should be taken when investing in a Spanish company in order to take into account possible contingencies arising from environmental issues.

Taxation issues

The transfer of shares is not normally subject to indirect tax. However, transfer tax of 6 per cent is due on the acquisition of shares in any company where at least 50 per cent of the assets comprise Spanish real estate, as far as the acquirer gets the ownership of that net worth or at least a position of control in the company. Transfer tax of 1 per cent is payable on share capital increases or on reductions where there is a distribution to shareholders.

In sales of shares by individual shareholders, a progressive reduction due to monetary depreciation is applied to the acquisition value in order to determine the taxable capital gain for acquisitions of shares in which the vendor was the owner of the shares prior to December 1994. A 20 per cent flat tax rate is applied to capital gains derived from transfers of shares acquired at least two years before the transfer takes place.

Under the new Corporation Tax Act, applicable since 1 January 1996, goodwill may be amortised for tax purposes over a period of 10 years, when it arises due to a purchase between non-related entities. The same treatment applies to certain other intangible assets.

Interest expense is tax deductible for a Spanish company borrowing to acquire Spanish or foreign companies. However, a thin capitalisation rule (debt/equity 3: 1) may be applied if the Spanish company borrows directly or indirectly from any related foreign company. There is no withholding tax on interest payments to EU resident parent companies.

According to the new Corporation Tax Act, following a merger or a takeover, tax losses from the non-survivor company may be transferable to the surviving entity. The capital gain obtained, after adjusting for inflation, from the transfer of tangible or fixed assets (basically buildings) may be deferred, provided that the proceeds from such transfers are reinvested in assets connected with the company's activity. The adjusted capital gain is apportioned on a straight-line basis over the tax periods that conclude in the seven years following the three-year period for reinvestment, or the tax period over which the assets are depreciated, at the taxpayer's choice.

There are no limits on the repatriation of dividends. Withholding tax is not payable on the payment of dividends to an EU parent company, provided that it has owned 25 per cent of the share capital for at least one year. Otherwise, the tax credits available depend upon the applicable treaty.

Conclusion

As mentioned earlier, the definitive incorporation of Spain into the EU in 1986 added a fully open market of some 40 million consumers to the greater Europe. This was one of the most decisive events in Spain's history in the 20th century, both from economic and political viewpoints. In the 1990s, Spain implemented a series of economic adjustments and policies in compliance with the criteria required for its entry into the EMU, which have led to economic growth and low inflation. This has provided companies with a stable environment in which to plan expansion.

In this context, there are still many opportunities for interesting deals in Spain, as the marketplace develops and becomes increasingly sophisticated. In the fields of private trade deals, development capital and flotations, there are still many parts of the economy where successful transactions can be carried out.

Venture capitalists will contribute to the process of concentration of medium/small companies. Therefore, the higher demand of non-quoted companies would offset the excessive demand of quoted companies and the resulting increase of their share price. Finally, there are several sectors where the number of transactions is likely to increase in the future and these include construction, pharmaceuticals and healthcare, hospitals, food distribution chains, such as supermarkets, IT, food and paper. Also, a wider use of the internet as a distribution channel will bring more business for IT and logistics companies.

The continuing privatisation programme at national, regional and local levels will also continue to provide sources of investment opportunities. The form in which these opportunities will arise will be varied, depending on the sector, public service and political context, but it is clear that in Spain the private sector involvement in public activities, either investments or services, will increase. A number of factors will drive this trend:

- the need for more and better infrastructure and services demanded by a developed and growing economy;

- pressures for reduction or contention of the tax burden;

- greater budgetary discipline imposed by the EMU;

- a more favourable political attitude towards private sector management of public infrastructure and services.

Nowadays in Spain the use of project finance and private sector related schemes for investments in infrastructure is becoming more frequent, with shadow toll schemes starting to be implemented in roads. There are areas where the presence of the private sector will be increased or introduced in some form in the near future: airports, railways, postal services, public television, water treatment, local transport and public health services.

Additionally, Spain has a strategic key role as a springboard for accessing Latin American markets. A number of European companies have already followed this route with considerable success and no doubt more will follow.

2.7

The Property Market

Jones Lang LaSalle

Madrid office market

In 1999, the Madrid office market was characterised by a lack of supply, a low level of available office space and strong demand (see Figure 2.7.1). Most companies had to rent office space in buildings still under construction through pre-letting agreements.

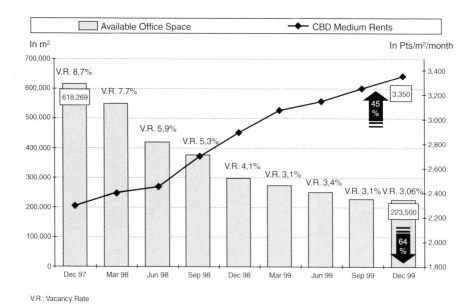

V.R.: Vacancy Rate

Figure 2.7.1 Madrid office supply 1997–2000

Source: Jones Lang LaSalle Research, January 2000

Rents

- The highest rent in the Central Business District (CBD) increased to Ptas4,100/m^2/month, which represents an increase of 6.5 per cent during the last quarter of 1999 and of 17 per cent for 1999 as a whole.

- In the secondary area and the periphery, the highest rents increased by 11.5 and 11 per cent respectively during the last quarter of 1999, and by 26 and 30 per cent during the year.

- In satellite locations, the highest rents increased by 6 per cent during the last quarter and by 20 per cent in 1999.

- The highest rents were achieved in high quality and well-located buildings but generally transactions were not signed at the maximum prices.

Supply

- Available supply dropped from 3.1 per cent during the third quarter to 3.06 per cent during the last quarter of 1999. This rate is more stable in 2000, as a consequence of the gradual delivery of new buildings on the market.

Take-up

- During the last quarter of 1999, 204,000m^2 were rented in Madrid, of which 114,000m^2 represented letting transactions in office buildings, 74,000m^2 represented pre-let transactions in new buildings which were put on the market before their tenants left, and 16,000m^2 were purchases.

- Total take-up in Madrid increased every quarter, and the total take-up for 1999, including letting, pre-letting and purchase transactions was 663,800m^2.

- Pre-letting and letting transactions in 1999 reached 595,400m^2, which is a high figure compared to the previous years when pre-letting transactions were rare. This reflects a high take-up level.

Future supply

Most of the new buildings will be constructed in the periphery, with a majority of the projects located in the north and east of the periphery (see Figure 2.7.2). The projects at Olivar de la Hinojosa and Arroyo de la Vega near Campo de las Naciones are the most important, since they are located in the area with the highest absorption capacity, and level of demand in the case of Arroyo de la Vega. A large reserve of land will come on the market in 2002 or 2003.

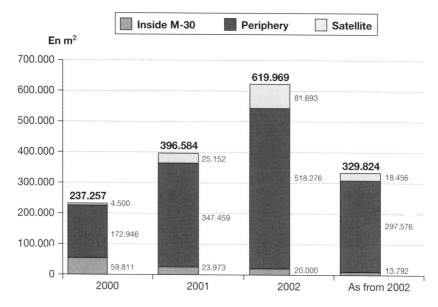

Figure 2.7.2   Madrid future supply 1999–2002

Source: Jones Lang LaSalle Research, January 2000

In 2001 and 2002, approximately 106,000m² will come on the market in the satellite locations. This area includes the business centres of San Fernando de Henares, Tres Cantos, San Sebastián de los Reyes and Las Rozas. More than half of these 106,000m² will be concentrated in San Sebastián de los Reyes, in the La Marina business park.

Given the high number of transactions, the trend will be for developers to try to deliver their buildings as quickly as possible in order to take advantage of the poor supply. The increase in the number of projects will lead to a competitive situation between the builders, particularly at the beginning of construction. Potential tenants will probably prefer the buildings that offer characteristics to suit their needs.

Tenants are beginning to consider the turnkey or pre-letting possibilities as the only way to rent modern and high technology buildings with floor space large enough for their headquarters. During the next few months, other potential tenants will begin to look for smaller office space (ranging from 3000 to 5000m²) and will consider the pre-letting possibility to be the best option.

Barcelona office market

In 1999, the Barcelona office market was characterised by a decrease in available office space, an increase in rents and an office stock with only 30,000m² of new buildings (see Figure 2.7.3).

Rents

- In 1999, the trend in the Barcelona office market was clearly an increase in rents. The highest rental increase took place in the CBD at 36 per cent. Rents remained stable in the periphery, while they increased by 25 per cent in the secondary area and by 22 per cent in the prime area.

- The highest increase was registered in the new buildings located in the prime area and the CBD.

Supply

- The available office space dropped significantly (by approximately 44 per cent).

- In the city of Barcelona, there is currently only 95,000m^2 of available office space, of which 13,200m^2 have been constructed recently.

- The vacancy rate fell from 2.74 per cent during the first quarter of 1999 to 2.19 per cent during the last quarter of 1999. The vacancy rate in the prime area and the CBD is approximately 1.93 per cent.

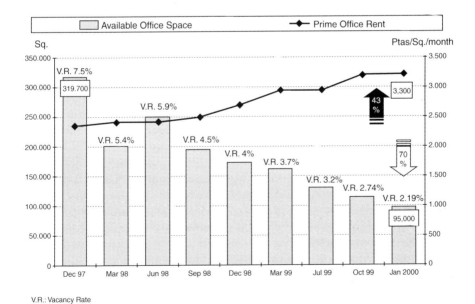

V.R.: Vacancy Rate

Figure 2.7.3   Barcelona office supply 1997–2000

Source: Jones Lang LaSalle Research, January 2000

Transactions

- Total take-up in 1999 (including letting and pre-letting transactions) reached 305,000m^2, of which 18 per cent was to pre-letting operations.

- Due to the lack of supply, a high percentage of the offices available in 1999 were immediately rented.

- In 1999, take-up increased by 21 per cent compared to 1998. Purchase transactions remained at the same level as in 1998 and reached 38,000m^2.

- Due to the poor supply, companies are beginning to choose the pre-let option, especially if they need large office space. In 2000, this trend will continue for office space larger than 2000m^2.

- The largest number of transactions was in the CBD. However, the average office space per operation was only 313m^2, compared to 575m^2 in the periphery.

Future supply

- By the end of 2000, as shown in Figure 2.7.4, approximately 76,000m^2 of office space will have been delivered in new buildings, and 16,000m^2 of office space in buildings being refurbished. From the total area of this supply, 19,000m^2 have already been pre-let, reflecting a market with a lack of high quality supply.

- The secondary area also plays an important role in the market, with a future supply of 33,000m^2. One of the most important buildings under construction is the Sertram 2 in Zona Franca with 11,000m^2.

- In 2001 most of the ongoing projects will be delivered in the secondary area. However, starting in 2002, land available for construction will be located in San Cugat, the airport area, or Sabadell.

Investment

Total investment in Spain for offices, shopping centres and industrial product reached Ptas 245,000 million in 1999, excluding the land purchases and development cost. The most important investors and developers wish to continue having a strong position in the Spanish market, because of the strong economic outlook and property market indicators. The products offering the highest yields continue to be offices and shopping centres, although investment is expanding to other sectors.

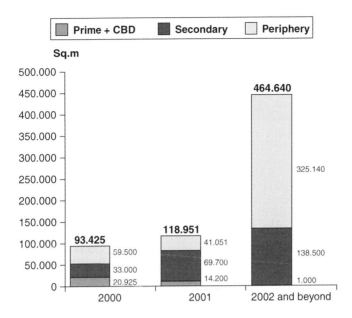

Figure 2.7.4   Barcelona future supply 1999–2002

Source: Jones Lang LaSalle Research, January 2000

Offices

Offices represent the most interesting product for investors, and the total investment volume (excluding land purchases and development cost) reached Ptas175,600 million in 1999, of which 170,000 million were for office-only buildings and the rest for purchases of office/industrial or office/residential buildings.

The investment market increased by 8.3 per cent compared to 1998 (with a total investment of Ptas157,000 million). However, supply was much lower, yields remained stable and the supply changed to 'turnkey with no tenant' promotions, which represent a higher risk for investors. The investment activity was principally focused on Madrid and Barcelona, where office investments reached Ptas131,000 and Ptas23,000 million, respectively. The investment activity in Barcelona is lower than in Madrid, due to the lack of product.

Yields remained at the same level during the year, at approximately 5 per cent for well-located and high quality buildings in Madrid and at 5.75 per cent in Barcelona (see Figure 2.7.5). In the development areas of business parks and office areas located far from the city centre, yields were approximately at 6 per cent in Madrid and 6.75–7 per cent in Barcelona.

There is a strong demand for office buildings in Madrid and Barcelona, and investors are looking for high quality buildings with a good location.

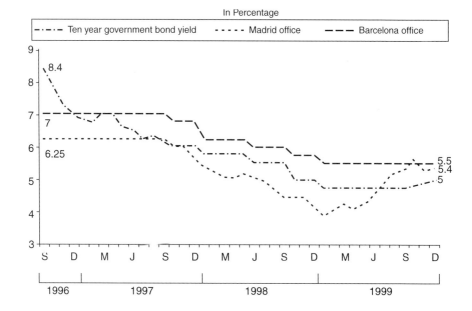

Figure 2.7.5   Yield comparatives

Source: Banco de España y Jones Lang LaSalle Research, January 2000

Many investors are anticipating a rise in rents for the next few months. However, high rental increases have already taken place in Madrid and it is expected that the increases will be lower during the next few years. On the other hand, high rental increases are expected in Barcelona (see Figure 2.7.6) due to the lack of available space for rent and the small number of office buildings due to be constructed during the next years.

In Madrid and Barcelona, the demand is concentrated in the prime area and the CBD, although high quality projects being delivered in the Madrid periphery, at Campo de las Naciones, Arroyo de la Vega and Avda. de América, created great interest among investors.

Shopping centres

In 1999 the investment in shopping centres reached Ptas42,000 million, excluding projects investment or the cost of the project. The investment market continues to expand, and important Spanish (Riofisa, Metrovacesa, Vallehermoso, GE Capital, Neinver, etc), and foreign (TrizecHahn, Rodamco, THI, Trema, Heron, Lend Lease, ING, Chelverton, MDC, etc) developers and investors are looking for good investment opportunities in Spain. Although yields fell due to the increasing demand and the lack of high quality products, they remain higher than the European average.

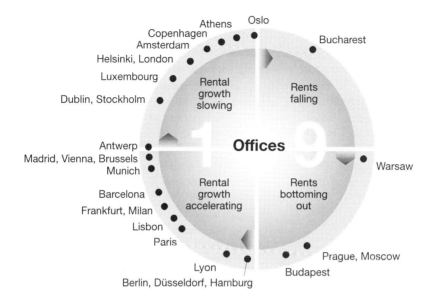

Figure 2.7.6   Short term rental cycle, 4th quarter 1999

There is a high level of demand to let premises in high quality shopping centres, and the available space is limited. Initial yields for this kind of shopping centre are approximately 7 per cent. The best option for an investor who wishes to invest in shopping centres is to become associated with a developer and to assume the risk involved by the development of the project.

Industrial

In the Spanish industrial market, companies traditionally bought to consequently occupy the premises. This trend changed during the last few years as a consequence of the diversification of the investments and the low initial yields achieved by office buildings.

The demand is concentrated on new, large and high quality warehouses located in new areas with a high industrial capacity and with good communications to the main roads and highways. However, investors were frustrated by the lack of high quality warehouses in the important cities, where the industrial park is generally obsolete.

In the prime area, yields range from 7.75 to 8.25 per cent, while the investment volume, essentially located in Madrid and Barcelona, reaches approximately Ptas13,300 million.

Industrial property

The industrial market is in the same situation as the office market, as it benefits from a strong economy, and demand is higher than supply for all kinds of industrial space. In 1999, developers were not able to react quickly to the industrial needs of the important cities, and the town halls did not help to resolve this problem, as they only freed pieces of land very slowly. Therefore, some initiatives were frustrated.

In the Barcelona metropolitan area, future supply is limited by the geographical location of the city between the sea and the mountains. The available space in Madrid and Barcelona is of medium and low quality, sometimes obsolete, and therefore does not meet the industrial needs of the companies. The few new promotions are generally small ones with high sales prices. In some cases, prices are too high for small companies, thereby slowing down the industrial growth of some Spanish cities (Madrid and Barcelona). As there were few speculative promotions, turnkey transactions represent the only option to buy or rent high quality warehouses and large areas.

Madrid

- Highest rents reach €7.81/m^2/month (Ptas1,300) in the best areas of Madrid (Alcobendas-San Sebastian de los Reyes and the industrial estate las Mercedes).

- In the other areas of Madrid, rents range from €3.6/m^2/month (Ptas600) to €6.01/m^2/month (Ptas1,000) depending on the area and the quality of the warehouse.

Barcelona

- Highest rents reach €7.21/m^2/month (Ptas1,200) in the best areas of Barcelona (Gran Via Sur and Pedrosa).

- In the other areas of Barcelona, rents range from €3/m^2/month (Ptas500) to €6/m^2/month (Ptas1,000), depending on the area and the quality of the warehouse.

- Prices in Barcelona increased by between 15 and 20 per cent during the last few years.

The trend followed by investors is to invest in large areas that will be occupied by logistic operators or distribution platforms. The Barcelona market is mostly composed of user owner buildings. Some areas are being improved, such as Pueblo Nuevo (PN 22@), and logistic parks are being created, such as the Parc Logistic 'La Granada' in Gerona, the logistic park of the Zona Franca with 400,000m^2, and Prologis Parc St Boi in el Baix Llobregat with warehouses of 140,000m^2. The autonomous government (*generalitat*) of Catalonia has as a project to create two new Goods International Centres (CIMs) in Lérida and Gerona based on the model of the 200,000m^2 centre in Mollet.

2.8

The Retail Market

Elsie Fairbanks, Consultant working for Trade Partners UK, Business in Europe Section

The Spanish market is an exciting and diverse one, offering a wide range of opportunities for companies involved in the consumer goods sector. The purpose of this chapter is to provide a broad overview of the sector and give a brief indication of the trends, highlighting some of the opportunities available.

Background

Much has been written about social change in Spain in the last quarter of the 20th century, and this is particularly reflected in the radical restructuring that has taken place in the retail market. In a society that has seen major changes in virtually all aspects of life since the end of the Franco era in the mid Seventies, and with a general increase in affluence since Spain joined the European Union (EU) in 1986, evolving lifestyles have resulted in many changes to the way in which Spaniards shop.

Until the 1970s, Spanish retailing was dominated by small family businesses, typically operating from old buildings with a local focus from one or at most two or three outlets, and little communication with other companies in terms of marketing, purchasing or logistics. By the end of the 1990s around 21 per cent of retail establishments had become part of some kind of chain, franchise, purchasing syndicate or co-operative, and these represent a major share of retail turnover in Spain.

The removal of restrictions on foreign ownership, investment and capital in the 1970s has had a profound effect on the structure of Spanish retailing. Spain has followed similar trends to other European countries in terms of concentration and the growing presence of foreign-owned establishments in the high streets, as well as in the growth of hypermarkets and shopping centres.

The urban population is moving out of the cities into new residential areas often some distance from the traditional city shopping areas. More women are entering the job market and therefore looking for ways to save time in making their household purchases.

In July 1996, the government passed a new law, *the Ley de Ordenacion del Comercio Minorista*, the corporate law to regulate retail development. This law has had a major impact on retail expansion. It seeks to regulate:

● the development of large new commercial establishments;

● opening hours;

● different types of selling, for example banning below-cost sales; and

● payment to suppliers.

Spain's regional authorities, as opposed to central or local government, have the most influence on planning policies. Planning approval for retail development requires three licences:

● the building licence relating to location and design area of the development;

● the retail licence itself; and

● the operating licence which confirms that the finished building satisfies the specified regulations.

Requirements of the licences vary depending on the size of the proposed development and the size of the town, and licences are only granted subject to the results of an impact study. The net effect of this is to make the whole planning process considerably longer and more expensive, with permission taking between two and eight years depending on the size of the project.

The new law also imposes restrictions on trading hours and Sunday opening, which vary by region.

Economic situation

All the main indicators now testify to the buoyancy of consumer confidence in Spain. Steady growth of the Spanish economy is reflected in a continued increase in household consumption helped by low interest rates and an improved employment situation. The retailing sector is particularly buoyant, with services an expanding sector in Spain.

Structure of the retail sector

As part of the inevitable modernisation of the Spanish retail market, the sector is currently faced with a series of developments that are having a direct and serious impact, namely:

- the move towards business integration, enabling major retail groups to increase their market share;

- increased involvement of major European distribution groups, particularly French, German and Dutch;

- the constantly evolving behaviour of Spanish consumers as a result of social change; and

- the implementation of the single currency, which is requiring considerable adaptation.

According to a recent report prepared by the Spanish Ministry of Internal Trade (*Dirección General de Comercio Interior*): 'Distribution has reached a stage of maturity in which neither is expansion awesome nor recession a concern; rather, it tends to maintain its current dimensions, adapting its infrastructure to developing social needs.'

Outside the major chains, the application of modern management techniques and systems and a relatively low level of computerisation of retail stores are an added difficulty for smaller retail businesses. The existence of barcode optical readers in retail shops is still low – in 1998 only 38.3 per cent had this facility, although this is now growing, together with facilities for credit card transactions.

Staff training, although actively encouraged by the state, is still very low.

Mass distribution

Compared to the UK and to other northern European markets, the Spanish grocery retail market is still relatively fragmented, with the top ten chains only covering just over 50 per cent of the market. Small traditional grocery shops are disappearing rapidly in Spain although, according to figures supplied by AC Nielsen for 1998, Spain, together with Italy and Greece, still has one of the highest percentage of independent retailers in Europe. However, this figure is expected to continue to fall until it reaches levels similar to the rest of Europe. To compare the situation in Spain with that of the UK, the share of grocery sales in 1998 was as follows:

Table 2.8.1   Retailers' market shares, Spain and UK

	Spain (%)	UK (%)
Traditional shops	20	5
Supermarkets	48	50
Hypermarkets	32	45

The last couple of years have seen a significant consolidation of ownership, with small regional supermarkets constantly being acquired both by the major pan-European chains such as Promodès and Auchan, as well as acquisitive Spanish groups such as Eroski, Mercadona, Caprabo and Superdiplo.

The full impact of the recent merger between the French retail groups Carrefour and Promodès has yet to be seen in Spain. At the beginning of 2000, the two groups had between a 27 and 46 per cent share of the market, depending on the region. As this is up to three times larger than the nearest competitor in Spain, the European Commission has ruled that competition authorities must now rule on whether the merger is against public interest. Experts in Spain expect that the final outcome will be that the group is ordered to sell off a certain number of stores, particularly in regions where the market share is unusually high. As the management function merges, fundamental changes will also take place in the branding, buying and logistics structures of the new organisation both at a national and global level.

Following the rapid expansion of the hypermarket model in the 1990s, major groups are now steering their strategy towards the smaller supermarket format that appears to be more successful in Spain.

The discounting sector continues to grow and currently accounts for around 15 per cent of sales of packaged groceries with further growth forecast. This sector is dominated by foreign-owned companies, with the most important chain being Día, a subsidiary of the French Promodès Group, which has around 2000 stores, followed by the German chain, Lidl, which is expanding rapidly with over 270 outlets.

The non-food sector is continuing to grow, with an 11.5 per cent rise in sales in 1998, mainly attributed to improved consumer spending. Particularly interesting sectors are toys (+16.7 per cent), textiles (+14.5 per cent), cosmetics and personal hygiene (+12 per cent). Large-scale stores specialising in areas such as DIY, toys, household appliances, gardening, culture and sport are becoming increasingly important in Spanish mass distribution.

The following chart lists the top ten chains in 1998, and also indicates the extent of foreign ownership:

Table 2.8.2   Top ten retail chains, 1998

Group	No. of retail outlets	Market Share (%)	Main shareholders
G Promodes: Continente, Dia, Simago/Champion, Punto Cash, Ilturgiana, Costasol	2033	13.52	Promodès Group (France)
CC Pryca	56	8.90	Carrefour B.V. (France)
G Auchan	203	7.47	Samu-Auchan (France)
G Eroski: S.Coop. Eroski, Consum, Erosmer, Udama,Supera, Cenco, Coop.C. Ntra Sra.Merced	1012	6.48	Mondragon Corporation Cooperative (Spain)
Hipercor/El Corte Ingles	64	6.09	El Corte Inglés Group (Spain)
Mercadona/A. G Serrano	403	4.73	Privately owned by Roig family (Spain)
Makro	19	1.86	Metro Beteiligungs AG (Germany)
G Unide	1371	1.32	G. Eroski
Lidl Descuento	150	0.91	Lidl & Schwarz Group (Germany)
Inter-Marche	40	0.30	Intermarché (France)

Source: Distribution Yearbook 1998/Alimarket

When the figures of some of the groups are broken down further, the following chart gives the top twenty companies on the Spanish market (food and non-food):

Table 2.8.3   Sales of top 20 retailers in 1997

Company	Sales 1997 (Ptas bn)	Increment 97/96 (%)
El Corte Inglés	920,000	10.27
Pryca	528,000	−1.84
CC Continente	496,000	2.28
Alcampo	415,000	37.47

Table 2.8.3 *continued*

Company	Sales 1997 (Ptas bn)	Increment 97/96 (%)
Eroski	378,850	13.14
Mercadona	287,500	12.75
DIASA	273,313	7.26
Hipercor	268,000	11.67
Caprabo	129,000	49.75
Makro	127,517	10.18
G Superdiplo	120,000	33.33
S Sabeco	103,162	28.93
Unigro	95,200	3.48
Grupo Syp	90,000	53.85
Unide	87,000	–5.43
GOASAM (Zara)	83,810	10.97
Cortefiel	72,040	4.67
Simago	69,862	0
Lidl Auts.	65,000	30.00
Gadisa	58,157	10.62

Source: La Distribución Comercial en España 1999, from various reports

House brands

While representing a smaller market share than in most EU markets, particularly the UK, house-branded or private label products account for around 12 per cent of the market and are particularly important in the discount sector. As these brands are an important tool for developing customer loyalty, all the major chains are developing and promoting ever increasing ranges of products from basic items to innovative specialities.

This area is a particularly interesting one for UK companies experienced in meeting the stringent demands of the UK multiples in their sourcing of private label products

El Corte Ingles

One of Spain's largest privately owned companies, the El Corte Inglés group owns a diverse range of businesses including department stores, travel agents, computer distribution, clothing manufacturing, and the Hipercor chain of hypermarkets. The Group employs over 57,000 people.

El Corte Inglés department stores dominate the Spanish retail scene, with over 40 stores, and it is by far the most important store group in Spain, accounting for around 56 per cent of the specialised distribution business. In 1995, El Corte Inglés took over the store group Galerias Preciados, and has now absorbed these stores into the El Corte Inglés format. The head office is in Madrid and the company also has buying offices in several centres across the world including London.

Contact details for this important chain including its London office, together with other important groups and chains are given in Appendix 6.

Clothing market

Traditionally, Spain had a very fragmented retail distribution system for clothing, with small independent retail shops playing an important role. However, this situation is changing and the development of shopping centres has helped to bring about this change. There has been a significant development of retail chains such as Zara, Mango, Adolfo Dominguez, Cortefiel and Springfield both nationally and internationally. Spanish clothing retailers are now playing a significant role in the international fashion scene with their vertically integrated systems of design, manufacture, distribution and retailing. Hypermarkets have made steady gains in market share and department stores, primarily El Corte Inglés, continue to maintain an important share. Spanish consumers tend to place considerable importance on brand names with strong loyalty to the well-known Spanish design houses.

Three Spanish companies in particular dominate the market:

Table 2.8.4   Major Spanish retail groups and their subsidiaries

Group	Trading names
G Inditex	Zara, Pull & Bear, Bershka, Stradivarius Lefties, Massimo Dutti
Cortefiel	Cortefiel, Milano, Springfield, Women's Secret, Don Algodón
Induyco	Part of the El Corte Inglés group

Shopping centres

In spite of economic recession in the mid 1990s and the adverse legislation of July 1996 governing the opening of new shopping centres, this is proving to be one of the most interesting retail developments in Spain. According to the *Asociación Española de Centros Comerciales* (AECC), the Spanish Association of Shopping Centres, from only 22 shopping malls in 1977, there are now around 400 shopping centres in Spain. Furthermore, there is still considerable growth potential and shopping centres are continuing to be developed.

The shopping centre sector is undergoing growth and consolidation both in terms of new projects and of the entry of international investors, and shopping centres continue to be star performers on the real estate market.

At present most of the shopping centres are located in three regions, Andalucia, Madrid and Catalonia, and there is considerable scope for expansion in the other 14 regions of Spain. International investors generally consider Spain to be an attractive proposition and, having initially concentrated on Madrid and Barcelona, are now investing in developments of a more regional nature and also in cities and towns with populations as small as 50,000.

Hypermarkets are the dominant anchor stores but recently this has been changing, as leisure activities play an increasing role. It has been noted that while the 'built area' has grown in recent years, the area devoted to sales constitutes a smaller proportion of the total surface area – devoting more space to leisure time, personal services and catering. This trend is expected to continue. Formats such as factory outlets are also starting to develop well.

Faced with problems in obtaining planning permission, developers are considering different strategies for expansion, including mergers and acquisitions. This activity is usually a catalyst for refurbishment, and many Spanish shopping centres are either currently refurbishing or forced to consider refurbishment in the near future.

As the shopping centres face increased competition there is a growing opportunity for companies offering management services, creative marketing concepts and specialist design features such as lighting and glazing.

Franchising

Although it is difficult to obtain accurate figures, it is estimated that in 1999 there were around 750 franchise networks operating in Spain, having increased from 640 in 1998. Although growth of new networks is slowing down, expansion of existing networks and brand names continues and this is considered to be a dynamic sector. One limiting factor is the difficulty in finding suitable premises. Of the trade names currently operating in Spain, around 75 per cent are Spanish, with the balance made up mainly of US, French, Italian and UK brand names. US franchises, not surprisingly, tend to be mainly in the restaurant and fast food trade.

This is considered to be a commercial formula with ample development potential in the current retail climate, particularly in the shopping centre sector.

Service stations

Convenience stores at service stations are relatively new in Spain, and are either managed by the petrol companies themselves, or by a joint venture with another retail group; for example, Repsol, Spain's number one petrol company and El Corte Inglés have joined forces to recreate Supercor stores. The number of service stations is growing at around 300 per year and approaching saturation point.

Direct marketing

This is becoming one of the most favoured marketing and distribution tools in Spain, with sales forecast to top US$ 2 billion in the year 2000. Several factors are contributing to this, including technological advances in printing and distribution, a steady growth in credit card use and changing lifestyles – as more people move out of the major cities into residential areas, which are often away from the main commercial centres. Also, an improved Spanish national postal service responsive to the demands of direct marketing is helping to develop the sector.

Mail-order companies lead the direct marketing sector although television marketing is becoming increasingly popular, and telemarketing is becoming the fastest growing sub-sector. Spaniards expect speedy dispatch of orders and there tends to be a high percentage of returned orders for goods received late. Trust in the direct marketing company is an important factor and generally consumers prefer companies that are members of The Spanish Association of Direct Marketing (AEMD). There are no restrictions against establishing a direct marketing operation in Spain although strict laws do exist for data protection. The AEMD has strict ethical codes to regulate mail order and telemarketing. Contact details for this organisation are given in Appendix 6.

Of the mail order volume sold in Spain, 58 per cent comes from four regions: Andalusia, Catalonia, Madrid and Valencia. Catalonia is considered to be the best area for mail order and many companies in this sector operate from Barcelona.

Spain still has a long way to go to reach the sales figures achieved in other European countries or in the USA. Whereas Spaniards spend an average of €14.4 per capita on mail-order goods, the French spend €180 and Americans spend €510. However, the largest sales volumes are provided by books and CDs, followed by household appliances and textiles. The social and economic profile of home sales consumers tends to consist of people in the middle/high income bracket.

E-commerce

Spain still falls behind other European countries in the progress being made with the internet market, but it is generally accepted that prospects are promising. The Spanish Association of E-Commerce (AECE), established in May 1998 in association with AEMD calculated that e-commerce accounted for approximately US\$ 5.3 million in 1997, growing to US\$ 23 million in 1998, and had forecast a figure of US\$ 66 million for 1999.

It has been suggested that the main reasons for the difference in growth in Spain to other markets is the basic infrastructure, insufficient investment in research and development, and the cost of the service. Furthermore, there is only a limited amount of Spanish language on the internet (estimated to be less than 2 per cent of available content), a small number of PCs in Spanish homes and a low level of penetration in small and medium-sized companies. The following charts may help to put this into context.

Table 2.8.5   Number of internet hosts

Country	Number of internet hosts – Feb 2000	Number of internet hosts – July 1998	Growth (%)
Spain	487,851	258,015	89
United Kingdom	1,677,946	1,321,905	27
Germany	1,640,343	1,308,706	25.4
Italy	644,399	357,919	80

Source: RIPE NCC www.ripe.net/

Table 2.8.6   Internet sales by percentage of population

Country	Percentage of the population that buys on the internet			
	1999	2000	2001	2002
Spain	0.6	1.0	1.6	2.4
United Kingdom	2.7	4.5	6.9	10.5
Germany	3.2	5.1	7.7	11.3
Italy	0.9	1.5	2.5	3.9

Source: 1999 Jupiter Communications

The most important categories of products sold on the internet in Spain are books and magazines, computer equipment, food and drink, travel and tourism.

Although familiarity with the internet and e-commerce and an appreciation of the benefits that these offer is increasing, Spain is considered to be in the early stages of e-commerce – there is still some concern about on-line payments and the reliability of the delivery service for orders. This must present a substantial commercial opportunity for e-services such as consulting, marketing, entertainment, education and travel as well as hardware and software.

Also, the potential from Spanish language web sites in South America must be considerable.

The euro

The Spanish government has undertaken major reviews of the distribution sector and introduced a programme of training and modernisation, and in particular taking into account the problems associated with the implementation of the euro. The priority is to ensure that personnel working in the sector are sufficiently well trained to ensure reliable conversion.

Dual pricing in both pesetas and euros has gradually been appearing since 1 January 1999 on counter signs, price lists, cash register receipts and advertising material. All outlets must be able to return change in euros from 1 January 2002.

The irrevocable conversion rate is €1 = Ptas166.386.

Doing business in retailing

Broadly speaking, the opportunities in the sector can be divided into two main areas:

- the supply of goods and services to Spanish consumers;

- the supply of equipment and services to the retail sector.

There are various tried and tested ways of selling goods and services to the Spanish market, and it is not the purpose of this chapter to go into this in detail. However, the following observations may be helpful.

In the days when the Spanish retail market was made up of a large number of small independent retailers the only realistic way to approach the market was to appoint either an agent or a distributor to sell on your behalf. However, with the growth of large distribution groups, there is an increasing trend towards direct selling to these companies. Competition is fierce and the cost of supporting a local distributor in the price structure may well make prices non-competitive, forcing suppliers to consider the direct approach.

Provided that the chains have central distribution facilities and can accept cost-effective minimum orders, and that the supplier has the appropriate resources to service the business from a UK base, supported by regular visits to the market, then this option is viable and preferred by

Spanish buyers. However, UK suppliers do have a reputation for sometimes giving poor service, with a tendency to make late deliveries. Many Spanish buyers still consider it important to have local representation, even if this is merely a point of contact in the event that a problem arises. It is therefore worth considering the possibility of appointing a local representative to fulfil this role or establishing a local sales office.

Opportunities

There is every indication that there are many opportunities available for UK companies, particularly in the retail services sector. Trade Partners UK, through its offices in London and the British Embassy in Madrid, will be running a series of activities to help companies to take advantage of these, including Meet the Buyer events and workshops. If you would like to be included on the mailing list for these events, please contact the Southern Europe Desk on +44 20 7215 4772.

Summary

While not wishing to be unrealistic about the competitive nature of the market, Spain is currently experiencing strong economic growth and this, together with an environment of rapid social change, means that the Spanish market is open to new retail concepts and products, with opportunities existing throughout the supply chain. Spain is the UK's 8th largest export market and is easily accessible to UK companies.

Sources
Dirección General de Comercio Interior (Spanish Ministry of Internal Trade)
British Embassy, Madrid
Trade Partners UK
Food from Britain Spain S.L.
Alimarket
RIPE NCC
Asociación Española de Centros Comerciales
Spanish financial press

Part 3

Banking and Finance

The Banking Sector

Carmen Hernansanz, BBVA, Research Department, Madrid

Credit institutions

The Spanish financial system is comprised of the credit institutions that, together with the Bank of Spain, constitute the core of the system known as the credit system (see Figure 3.1.1). Spain's credit institutions can be divided into three categories.

The first category consists of deposit institutions, and comprises commercial banks, savings banks and credit co-operatives. This group corresponds to the banking system in its strictest sense, as these are the only institutions that can receive deposits. It accounts for an overwhelming proportion of the total balance sheet of credit institutions. In November 1999, banks held around 55 per cent of total credit system assets, followed by the savings banks with a 35 per cent share. Co-operatives, meanwhile, come in a long way behind banks and savings banks, with a 3.5 per cent share of the total assets of credit institutions.

The second category is made up of Specialised Credit Institutions (*Establecimientos Financieros de Crédito*), the assets of which account for just under 3 per cent of the total assets of credit institutions. These institutions are authorised to engage in specialised lending activities such as leasing, mortgage lending, financing of equipment and other capital goods, and factoring.

Finally, there is the Official Credit Institute (ICO), which in terms of assets is comparable to the specialised credit institutions. When acting as a specialised credit institution, the ICO provides medium- and long-term financing to Spanish firms, while in its capacity as the state financing agency, it allocates finance as directed by the government to those affected by severe economic crises, natural catastrophes or other similar circumstances.

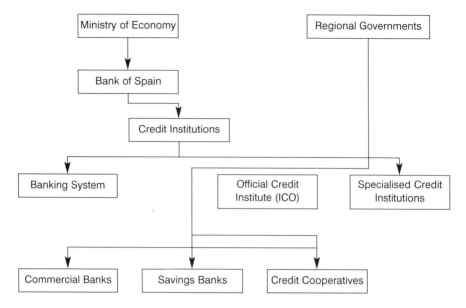

Figure 3.1.1   The Spanish financial system

The Bank of Spain

The Bank of Spain is the Spanish central bank. Its origins go back over two centuries, although its functions as a central bank only began to be defined in the 1921 Bank Ordinance Law. In the second half of the 1970s, the Bank of Spain completed its transformation into a central bank with full responsibility for the regulation and supervision of the financial system.

The Treaty on European Union requires that all central banks of member countries of the Economic and Monetary Union (EMU) be independent of their respective governments. In compliance with this requirement, the Spanish government approved the Law of Autonomy of the Bank of Spain in June 1994. This legislation makes the Bank of Spain a special institution within the public administration, which, though subordinate to the government in general terms, does not allow the Treasury to run overdrafts on its account with the central bank. Also, the Bank of Spain may not acquire directly from the Treasury any securities issued by it. The Law of Autonomy extended the term of office of the Governor and Deputy Governor, and lists specific reasons for their possible dismissal, thus reinforcing the autonomy of the decision-making bodies of the central bank.

Spain's entry into EMU in January 1999 meant that the functions hitherto entrusted to the Bank of Spain had to be redefined. The Spanish central bank was already fully integrated into the European System of Central

Banks (ESCB), meaning that it is subject to the provisions of the Treaty on European Union and to the statutes of the ESCB. As a result, the Bank of Spain participates in several of the functions attributed to the ESCB:

- Defining and executing EMU monetary policy, with the principal aim of maintaining price stability across the Euro area.

- Implementing exchange rate policy and conducting currency exchange operations consistent with the Treaty on European Union, and managing official currency reserves.

- Promoting the sound working of payment systems in the euro area.

- Issuing legal tender bank-notes.

In addition to the functions that the Bank of Spain performs as a member of the ESCB, the Spanish central bank has the following responsibilities:

- The holding and management of currency reserves not transferred to the ECB.

- The supervision of the solvency and behaviour of credit institutions.

- The promotion of the sound working and financial stability of the Spanish financial system and of national payment systems.

- The placement in circulation of coins.

- The provision of treasury and financial agent services for government debt.

- The role of adviser to the Spanish government, preparing of appropriate reports and studies.

- The preparation and publication of statistics relating to its functions, and assisting the ECB in the compilation of the necessary statistical information.

The governing bodies of the Bank of Spain are the Governor, the Deputy Governor, the Governing Council (formed by the Governor, the Deputy Governor, six council members, the Managing Director of the Treasury and the Vice President of the National Securities Exchange Commission) and the Executive Commission (formed by the Governor, Deputy Governor and two council members).

Privately owned banks

Following the privatisation of the last public stake in Argentaria in February 1998, all of the banks operating in Spain are now privately owned. Spanish banks are public limited companies and are required to have a minimum capital base of Ptas3,000 million (around €18 million). The establishment of a bank must be approved by the Ministry of the Economy on the basis of a report submitted by the Bank of Spain. The Second Directive on Banking Co-ordination makes it possible for a credit institution authorised in one EU country to open branches and offer banking services in all countries of the EU. To do so in Spain, the foreign bank must first request its central bank to write to the Bank of Spain outlining the activities in which it intends to engage. The foreign bank may then establish itself as soon as the Bank of Spain certifies that it has received this notification. This procedure is valid only for the opening of branches; the establishment of a subsidiary requires the authorisation of the Ministry of the Economy.

In 1999, there were 146 banks in Spain, with a network of 16,905 branches and 131,460 employees. In November 1999, Spanish banks managed 49 per cent of loans to the domestic private sector and 42 per cent of deposits. Table 3.1.1 shows the structure of banks' balance sheets. Lending activity accounts for around 46 per cent of the banks' total balance sheets. Financing through customers' deposits has a 45 per cent share of the balance sheet, though financing from the Bank of Spain and the inter-bank market is also significant, representing 37 per cent of the total liabilities.

The establishment of EMU has acted as a catalyst for the gradual process of banking consolidation that was already under way in Spain. The two largest mergers in Spanish banking history were announced in 1999. In January, Banco Santander merged with BCH to create BSCH, and, in October, BBV and Argentaria announced that they were merging to form BBVA.

As a result of the above, the 31 Spanish financial groups at a consolidated level can be sorted into three broad groupings. The first of these comprises the large banks arising out of the recent mergers (BSCH and BBVA), which together account for 79 per cent of private-banking assets and manage 77 per cent of loans and 80 per cent of deposits. The second consists of medium-sized banks, defined as those that have total assets of over €5,000 billion, and including Banco Popular, Banco de Sabadell, Bankinter, Deutsche Bank España, Banco Pastor, Banco Atlántico, Barclays Bank and Banco Zaragozano. This group has a 15 per cent share of total private-banking assets, and manages 19 per cent of loans and 16 per cent of deposits. The third group is made up of the other private banks, with a share of assets, loans and deposits in the private-banking sector of approximately 5 per cent.

Table 3.1.1   Balance sheet structure (Jan–Sept 1999)

Average of total assets (%)	Total (1)	Banks	Savings banks
Assets			
Cash and central banks	2	1	2
Interbank Market	20	24	14
Credits	50	46	57
Securities Portfolio	20	20	20
– Fixed Income	15	15	16
– Equity	5	5	5
Other assets	8	8	7
Liabilities			
Bank of Spain & interbank market	27	37	12
Client liabilities	56	45	74
Capital	6	5	6
Special Funds	3	2	3
Subordinated Debt	2	2	1
Other liabilities	6	8	4
Avge. Assets (EUR bn)	937	580	325

(1) Banks, savings banks and credit cooperatives
Source: Bank of Spain

Savings banks

Spanish savings banks have a private legal nature, but they are not public limited companies. There are several areas in which regional governments have a say in their regulation and management. Their status as credit institutions predominates, though they also have a social role – in this way, saving banks' profits have two different end-uses. At least 50 per cent of profits are required by law to be assigned to reserves, while the remainder must be devoted to social projects in the territory where they operate. Savings banks do not pay out dividends. In the period 1996 to 1999, Spanish savings banks devoted an average of 26 per cent of their profits to social projects and an average of 74 per cent to increase their reserves.

Savings banks are managed by a general assembly, a board of directors and a supervisory committee. The assembly is the supreme governing body. It comprises between 60 and 160 members representing depositors, local governments, founding institutions and employees. The board of directors is the body to which the general assembly delegates the management of the institution under the supervision of the supervisory committee.

The regional governments have a variety of powers relating to the management of savings banks, chief among which are the authorisation of their establishment, merger or liquidation, the supervision of management and lending activity, and the development of functions pertaining to inspections and sanctions. Any change to a savings bank's statutes must be approved by its corresponding regional government, and, indeed, recent years have seen an increase in political representation in these institutions.

Savings banks are permitted to engage in all types of activity, and have been able to perform the same operations as banks since 1997, so that the regulations are the same for both. Although previously confined to operating in their Autonomous Region of origin, savings banks have been able to open branches throughout the country since 1989, making them strong competitors for banks. In a number of cases, the expansion of savings banks came about through the acquisition of the networks of smaller banks. However, the statutes of savings banks shield them from being taken over by banks.

In 1999, there were 50 savings banks, with a network of 18,337 branches and 92,276 employees. In November 1999, the Spanish savings banks managed 40 per cent of credits to the domestic private sector and 51 per cent of its deposits. Lending activity accounted for around 57 per cent of their total balance sheet, 15 percentage points more than in the case of banks. Financing through customers' deposits is of great importance, holding a 74 per cent share of the balance sheet, 29 percentage points above that of banks. These figures reflect the fact that savings banks focus on traditional retail banking business much more than private banks.

The pace of consolidation in the savings bank sector is very slow in comparison with that of banks. Their lesser vulnerability to take-overs, their non-dependence on market valuations, their greater emphasis on traditional business, and the political considerations that have to be overcome before a merger, are all factors that stand in the way of the sector's consolidation. As a result, there has only been some movement towards mergers of savings banks within the same Autonomous Region. As a consequence of weaker merger activity, the level of concentration in the sector is much lower than is the case with banks.

At the end of 1999, the 35 savings bank groups existing in Spain could be classified into three groups. The first comprises the two major savings banks: La Caixa and Caja Madrid. This group has a 37 per cent share of the sector's total assets, and manages 36 per cent of credits and 33 per cent of deposits. It should be noted that the size of the largest savings banks is much smaller than that of the group of largest banks. The assets of the two largest savings banks represent one quarter of those of the two largest banks. In the case of deposits, the two large savings banks have just over one third of the deposits managed by the biggest two banks.

The second group is composed of savings banks with total assets of over €10,000 billion. This threshold is higher than the one established for banks, reflecting the lower segmentation by size that exists in this sector. The following seven savings banks can be included in this segment: Caixa Catalunya, Bancaja, Caixa Galicia, Caja del Mediterráneo, Ibercaja, Bilbao Bizkaia Kutxa and UNICAJA. These institutions account for around 30 per cent of savings banks' total banking business. Finally, the other smaller savings banks have a share of around 33 per cent of the total.

Banking system activity

As the balance sheet structure of banks and savings banks reflects, the activity of the Spanish banking system conforms to the universal banking model, with a sharp bias towards retail banking.

The environment for banking activity in Spain is highly competitive in spite of the increase in banking concentration. This is the result of stiff competition from savings banks (their share of the banking system is very similar to that of banks) and of the establishment of EMU – which eliminated the exchange rate as a barrier to the entry of foreign banks. A further threat is the entry of foreign banks via the internet. The evolution of MIBOR-current account differentials, which narrowed by some 300 basis points between 1995 and 1999, and mortgage rates that are among the lowest in the euro area, reflect this highly competitive environment.

The process of financial liberalisation, the decline in interest rates in Spain as a consequence of convergence with the more macro-economic stable euro area countries, the financial disintermediation process, and stiff competition, have translated into a gradual reduction in Spanish banking margins. Spanish institutions have reacted to this decline in a variety of ways. First, Spanish banks, to a much greater extent than savings banks, were the pioneers of the commercialisation of mutual funds in Spain. This has given them a leading position in this segment of the financial industry. Second, Spanish institutions have striven to reduce costs as a means of enhancing their efficiency.

Finally, one of the responses to the difficulty of dealing with a more adverse banking environment has been the expansion of Spanish banks into Latin America. This process, which began in 1995 and intensified in subsequent years, has been dominated by the two leading commercial banks. The acquisition of stakes in Latin American financial institutions has allowed the large Spanish banks to build up a significant presence in twelve countries in the region, and to occupy the leading positions in foreign bank rankings in Latin America.

Banking regulation

Spanish banking legislation has undergone significant changes over the past twenty years. Following the banking crisis in the 1980s, the Bank of Spain adopted a variety of measures to liberalise and deregulate the banking system. When Spain joined the EU in 1986, the EU Directives had to be gradually incorporated into Spanish legislation. Spanish banks may now engage in any type of financial activity envisaged in the Second Directive on Banking Co-ordination.

Like all other financial institutions in the euro area, Spanish banks are subject to a minimum reserve requirement of 2 per cent of the liabilities included in their reserve base, remunerated at the average rate of the main refinancing operations of ECB monetary policy.

Each type of credit institution (bank, savings bank or co-operative) must have its own deposit guarantee system, with its own legal personality and full capacity to act. This provision has a twofold objective. On the one hand, it protects the interests of depositors by providing surety of up to €20,000. Second, it guarantees the stability of the financial system by safeguarding against bank runs prompted by the difficulties of any one specific institution. The deposit guarantee funds are composed of contributions from its members up to a maximum level of 0.2 per thousand of the deposits guaranteed.

Banking supervision

The Bank of Spain supervises solvency, conduct and compliance with specific rules for lending activities. It does so without prejudice to the prudential supervisory function performed by the Autonomous Regions in the exercise of their responsibilities, and in co-operation with the Bank of Spain. The legal framework for banking supervision was developed by the Law on Governing Bodies of the Bank of Spain of June 1980, which reflected the need to subject credit institutions to a special system of stricter administrative supervision than the one in force for the other sectors of the economy. This law specified the obligation of these credit institutions to provide the supervisory authority with full information on their situation and performance, limiting or prohibiting practices liable to increase the risks of insolvency or lack of liquidity.

The Law of July 29 1988, the Second Directive on Banking Co-ordination, and the Law of Autonomy of the Bank of Spain, constitute the key pieces of legislation upon which supervision is based. Among the Bank of Spain's supervisory functions, two in particular are worth mentioning:

- The monitoring and supervision of credit institutions, an area of competence that applies to all their branches or centres in Spain or abroad.

- The Bank of Spain co-operates with the authorities entrusted with similar functions in foreign countries, providing them with information on the management and ownership of Spanish financial institutions and any other information necessary to facilitate the monitoring of their solvency.

3.2

The Role of the Banking Sector in Economic and Industrial Development

Carmen Hernansanz, BBVA, Research Department, Madrid

The role of the banking sector in the Spanish economy

The Spanish financial system, like that of other countries in continental Europe, is characterised by the major role that is played by banks in their position as financial intermediaries. The assets of credit institutions accounted for 178 per cent of Gross Domestic Product (GDP) at the end of 1999, while the share of financial markets in the Spanish economy amounted to 140 per cent of GDP (equities: 81 per cent of GDP, fixed-income: 59 per cent). Nonetheless, the distance between banks and markets has been narrowing in recent years as a result of the financial disintermediation process and the greater development of financial markets driven by Spain's entry into the Economic and Monetary Union (EMU).

In addition, the favourable economic climate of the past few years has made it possible for firms to generate sufficient funds to reduce their need for external financing and to increasingly fund expansion with their own resources. According to the Bank of Spain, the share of own resources in total financing (internal and external) has risen from 37 per cent in 1993 to 45 per cent in 1998.

Nonetheless, Spanish firms are still heavily reliant on bank financing. In 1998, lending by credit institutions accounted for 28 per cent of Spanish non-financial firms' total liabilities. One source of short-term financing often used by Spanish firms is inter-firm lending, which makes up 16 per cent of their total liabilities. Particularly significant within these internal financial flows in the sector is commercial credit stemming from deferrals of payment for goods, transactions or services rendered as part of a firm's traditional business. Conversely, short-term securities and bonds account for a meagre 4 per cent of Spanish firms' total liabilities. It is reasonable to assume, however, that, as a result of the recent growth observed in private fixed-income markets, this form of financing is increasing and will continue to do so in the future.

In spite of the above, the degree of reliance on bank financing and the possibility of tapping alternative funding channels depends to a large extent on a firm's size. Among small and medium-sized firms, dependence on bank credit is much higher, and their capacity to diversify funding channels is very limited. Given that, in general, Spanish firms are smaller than their European counterparts, it may be concluded that dependence on bank lending is higher in Spain than in other European Union countries.

Consequently, in spite of the growth of financial markets, banks will continue to be one of the main funding channels for small and medium-sized firms. In September 1999, bank lending for productive activities accounted for 52 per cent of total credit extended by banks, savings banks and credit co-operatives. These funds were largely allocated to the services sector (54 per cent of total credit provided for productive activities), followed by industry (28 per cent), construction (13 per cent) and agriculture (4 per cent). Bank lending as a proportion of gross value added in each of these sectors amounted to 48 per cent in the services sector, 75 per cent in construction, 56 per cent in industry and 40 per cent in agriculture. The construction sector is therefore particularly dependent on bank lending. Indeed, it is traditional in Spain for housing and mortgages to be sold in tandem, the conditions generally being negotiated by the property developer.

Similarly, households will also continue to be highly reliant on bank lending. 41 per cent of credit extended by banks, savings banks and co-operatives is allocated to individuals. A very large portion of this segment is accounted for by house purchases and renovations (72 per cent), though credit for consumer durables consumption has grown rapidly in recent years, accounting for 10 per cent of bank lending to individuals in September 1999.

The changes observed in households' saving habits have brought about a major shift in the composition of the funds used by banks to finance their lending business. In 1990, 61 per cent of Spanish households' financial assets were invested in cash and deposits. This percentage had fallen by 20 percentage points by the end of 1998. Conversely, the proportion of households' financial wealth invested in mutual funds rose from 2 per cent to 22 per cent over the same period, which would seem to suggest that there has been a significant decline in the importance of banks in the Spanish financial system.

Nonetheless, the role of banks is more important than a first glance at these figures would suggest. The ten leading Spanish fund-management companies belong to the major Spanish banks and savings banks, and control almost three quarters of the total assets in mutual funds in Spain.

Industrial shareholdings

Relations between the banking system and non-financial firms have a long historical tradition in Spain dating back to the early stages of Spanish industrialisation in the 19th century, when most of the leading Spanish banks were born. As a result, the Spanish banking model corresponds to the universal banking concept in its broadest sense.

The relationship between the banking system and industry in the past consisted, to a great extent, in direct support from credit institutions to firms in which they had acquired a stake, in the form of credits to finance their productive activity. There is widespread agreement that this was one of the factors that triggered the severe banking crisis in the 1970s. This also explains the misgivings sometimes generated by the presence of Spanish banks in the body of shareholders of leading Spanish firms. Indeed, it is sometimes perceived as a reflection of a high concentration of power, and as a mechanism for the allocation of finance that does not benefit from the constraints of market discipline. However, the management of industrial shareholdings has changed significantly over the past twenty years, a significant contributing factor in this change being the tightening of the regulations governing such shareholdings.

Banking regulations set out clear limits for the concentration of risk taken as a result of relationships between banks and non-financial firms. Firstly, the total risk (through shareholdings and lending activity) incurred by a credit institution, not only with an individual firm but also with its industrial group, must not exceed 25 per cent of its capital base. Furthermore, the Bank of Spain defines a 'large risk' as one incurred by a credit institution with an individual firm or group, the value of which exceeds 10 per cent of the institution's capital base. The legislation sets out that the sum of such large risks must not be more than eight times greater than the financial institution's capital base.

The strategies guiding industrial shareholding policy have also changed in the past few years. First, the practice of providing direct support to firms simply because a credit institution is a shareholder has disappeared and the control exercised over these firms has also diminished. Banks now have separate departments to handle the management of their industrial portfolio, and their activities are completely distinct from those relating to corporate banking.

Second, industrial shareholdings are now seen as a way to offset the reduction in margins obtained from traditional intermediary activity. Accordingly, the decision to invest in a particular firm is now taken on the basis of strictly financial criteria, an essential condition being that such firms or sectors offer high growth potential. As a result, the industrial port-folios of large Spanish credit institutions yielded returns on investments of over 20 per cent in the 1990s. The reason for such a strong recent perfor-mance is that large banks have opted to acquire stakes in leading Spanish firms in relatively non-cyclical sectors and, besides, have actively managed these positions, liquidating them when their growth potential is considered to have fallen relative to other alternative investments.

At the end of 1999, the three main financial groups, BSCH, BBVA and La Caixa, had industrial shareholding portfolios with a market value of €11.6 billion, €14.4 billion and €14.6 billion, respectively. This repre-sented cumulative unrealised capital gains for these financial groups of €6.6 billion, €6.4 billion and €7.5 billion, respectively, giving an indication of just how profitable investing in industry has been for Spanish banks.

Raising Finance for Corporate Investment

Introduction

As a result of growing demand for equities in the past few years, Spanish firms have opted to increase their presence in the stock exchanges. In addition, the development of alternative sources of financing to bank loans or to the traditional equity and fixed-income markets is very recent in Spain. The latest funding channels are aimed at firms whose characteristics hamper their access to the usual sources of external finance. This chapter describes the requirements with which Spanish firms must comply in order to obtain a market listing, the recent developments of venture capital in Spain and the creation of the New Stock Exchange (*Nuevo Mercado*) which began operations in April 2000.

Listing on the Spanish stock exchange

The Securities Market Law (Law 24/1988) established the freedom to issue shares without prior authorisation, except in certain exceptional cases. In addition, it acknowledges the right of the issuer to choose the placement method, with no requirement other than a public announcement prior to its launch. The Securities Market Law brought the regime for public share offerings into line with that for issues of other types of financial products, such as fixed-income securities. Nonetheless, firms wishing to go public must comply with a number of requirements. These include:

- the filing of a registration statement with the Spanish Securities Exchange Commission (*Comisión Nacional del Mercado de Valores, CNMV*);

- the submission of documents certifying the issuance agreement;

- the registration of an audited financial statement;

- the elaboration of a prospectus. The prospectus is the key piece of information provided by the firm about the financial operation's details and about itself.

The CNMV acts as a depository for the information provided by firms, and facilitates its dissemination. It is expected to verify that the contents, format and frequency of submission of the information comply with the principle of transparency.

Firms listed on the stock exchange must audit their annual accounts and make them available to the public through the CNMV, together with a management report and other documents making up the annual report. In addition, they must provide a variety of information on a quarterly and half-yearly basis. Two months before the end of each half-year, firms must present a detailed analysis of their financial and economic situation for the January–June and January–December periods. This involves the submission of consolidated and individual balance sheets and profit and loss accounts, together with a summary of relevant facts. The half-yearly accounts do not have to be audited.

No later than 45 days after the end of each calendar quarter, firms must supply information on subscribed capital, number of employees, business trends and results, and paid-out dividends. When developments in a firm may affect its share price, Spanish legislation requires that these relevant facts (*hechos relevantes*) be made public as quickly as possible.

The past few years have seen a considerable number of firms entering the Spanish stock exchanges. In 1998, the value of new firms coming to the market totalled €1.3 billion. These firms represented sectors that were new to the Spanish stock exchange, such as textile design, the hotel industry, distribution, the environment and the wine-making industry. In most cases they were family-owned or medium-sized businesses that saw the stock exchange as the ideal place in which to raise funds and acquire liquidity. In 1999, the value of new firms entering the market rose to €25.2 billion. Some of the most recent, and most successful, listings have been large firms and start-ups from technology sectors that were previously not represented on the stock exchange.

Public offerings are the normal procedure chosen for stock exchange listings. This type of operation allows firms to attain the wide distribution required by share issues, both in order to comply with legal requirements and to ensure an adequate level of liquidity. In the absence of any benchmark, it is difficult to set an initial price for this type of firm. The analysis and preparation of 'order books' by the underwriters prior to listing are normally important clues as to a share's coming-out price. In general, most initial public offerings by private firms have been over-subscribed several times and have been subject to considerable scaling back.

Venture capital

The scarcity of permanent resources means that new firms, especially technology start-ups and small and medium-sized firms, tend to begin operations with capital raised through venture capital companies. In Spain, the acquisition of temporary and minority stakes in firms by financial institutions dates back to 1972, though most of the initiatives were promoted by the public sector as a means of encouraging regional development. Private investors, for the most part foreigners, only began to show an interest in this type of investment in Spain in 1986, the year of Spain's entry into the European Union. The Spanish Association of Venture Capital Companies (ASCRI) was founded in the same year, incorporating both public and private Spanish investors.

These new investments largely took the form of management companies for venture capital (*Sociedades Gestoras de Entidades de capital riesgo*). These companies do not invest their financial resources, but rather promote the setting-up of funds to be placed under their management. In the 1987–1991 period, venture capital activity grew at an average annual rate of 31 per cent and the private sector's share of the total funds under management rose to almost 61 per cent.

The rationale behind investment by public and private institutions differed considerably. The public sector concentrated on modest investments in small firms or start-ups in limited geographical areas. Conversely, private venture capital focused on larger, growth or later-stage firms. Investment in the form of venture capital slowed during the 1992–1996 period as a result of the high prices paid by investors in previous years, the abundance of funds available for investment and the scarcity of investment opportunities. To these factors were added the difficulties encountered in disposing of investments, the absence of a liquid stock exchange for small or early-stage firms and the lack of specific and neutral regulations for long-term capital gains.

Nonetheless, several factors have markedly improved the outlook for venture capital in Spain. The Royal Decree 7/1996 improved the tax treatment of long-term capital gains, thus enhancing the appeal of this type of investment, which needs a long time horizon to be profitable. Spain's entry into the European and Monetary Union (EMU) represents a first step towards the creation of a venture capital market in the euro area, with the resulting interest of EMU investors in the Spanish market. Law 1/1999 regulating venture capital companies and their management companies drew up the regulatory framework for venture capital operations in Spain. This law sets out the legal system governing authorisation, supervision, inspection and sanctions for venture capital companies. The new legislation is a reflection of the increased importance placed by the economic and regulatory authorities in small and medium-sized firms. Another example of the interest in promoting these firms is the recently created New Market

(Nuevo Mercado) in Spain (see below), which should encourage the emergence of new firms and hence an increase in the liquidity of venture capital investments in Spain.

As a result of these recent developments, the volume of venture capital under management grew by 71 per cent in 1998, registering an all-time high of Ptas344 billion (around €2 billion). An analysis by type of investor shows that non-residents, chiefly financial institutions and pension funds, accounted for 40 per cent of total funds. Public investors came next with a share of around 18 per cent of the total. The withdrawal from the market of a number of operators, and the modest amount of new contributions from the Autonomous Regions, have combined to bring about a gradual decline in the weight of the public sector in venture capital over the years. Domestic financial institutions are the third biggest investors, with a 15 per cent share of the total funds under management, followed by domestic private non-financial firms, with an 8 per cent share. It is worth highlighting the absence of venture capital investment by Spanish pension funds and other institutional investors in contrast to the situation in other developed markets, for instance in the United States.

Investment patterns in venture capital have gradually been converging with international standards, though the level of concentration remains relatively high. In 1998, 42 per cent of total investment took the form of LBOs, management buy-outs (MBOs) and management buy-ins (MBIs). This was followed by funds invested in growth firms, with 39 per cent of the total. Nonetheless, the bulk of investment was concentrated in relatively large firms (firms with over 200 employees accounted for 50 per cent of investment, as against the 8 per cent received by firms with less than 20 employees).

By sector, investment shows a high concentration in consumer goods industries, which absorbed 41 per cent of total investment in 1998, followed by information technology and communications, each with an 11 per cent share.

Preliminary data for 1999 allow cause for optimism in relation to venture capital developments in Spain. It is estimated that the volume of investment in 1999 grew by between €90 and €140 billion, to reach an all-time high. Between 25 per cent and 27 per cent of total new investment was in internet and telecommunications companies, in contrast to past investment patterns, which focused more on early-stage or growth firms. Although the proportion of investment in new technologies is much lower than in countries such as the United States, the trend shows that the financing of seed and start-up firms has increased and that this rise will probably continue.

The CNMV is the main regulator of venture capital in Spain.

The New Market *(Nuevo Mercado)*

In December 1999, the CNMV published the rules and regulations for the creation of a special trading segment in the stock exchange called the *Nuevo Mercado* (New Market). This market is aimed at firms engaged mainly in activities in one of the cutting-edge technology sectors or in potentially high-growth sectors, given their potential market. That is, it is a market aimed at those firms with a higher level of perceived risk and hence greater share price volatility than that of traditional shares.

Firms wishing to be listed on this market face no additional requirements to those applicable in the main market, meaning that firms must have a minimum capital of Ptas200 million (around €1.2 million), there being no minimum initial placement. Nonetheless, before trading can begin, a firm must obtain a non-binding report from the stock exchanges on its suitability for a market listing, prior to final approval on certification of its prospectus.

This prospectus, while similar to that of all other public offerings, must contain the following additional information:

• It must provide a description of the operational environment of the firm, including details of its potential market, technological aspects and elements of uncertainty or risk, etc;

• It must present full information on concrete future operations and plans for investment and funding;

• It must contain details of the commitments given by shareholders with significant stakes as to the length of time they will remain in the firm's capital. It must also show these shareholders' participation in financing operations and their membership of the board of directors, though it does not set a time limit on their commitments with the firm; and

• It must include details of the scope of any agreements the firm may have established with stock exchange members (market makers) under which the latter would foster the liquidity of the firm's shares. The regulation of market makers is covered by a different specific set of rules.

In addition, firms that obtain approval for a listing on this segment of the market will face stricter disclosure and transparency requirements than those of traditional firms; this is in order to ensure adequate protection for investors. Firms must make reports at least once a year on their business performance and outlook and on their anticipated funding and investment plans for future expansion and development.

As far as trading rules are concerned, the new stock exchange is characterised by its flexibility. The price at which new issues will come on to the market will be set according to real supply and demand. In contrast to traditional shares that have a maximum limit of 50 per cent relative to the issue price, there will be no limit on coming-out prices for shares on this market. Under normal conditions, prices will be able to move by 25 per cent, compared with the 15 per cent limit for traditional shares. Nonetheless, if exceptional circumstances are affecting supply or demand, special adjustment periods will be set up to allow supervisors to examine the circumstances surrounding trading. Following the adjustment period, an increase in the maximum price variation may be authorised for such shares, meaning that very large fluctuations will be possible in a single session. Finally, in the event of increases higher than the maximum variation, it will be possible to change the normal duration of the session (from 9am to 5.30pm), extending trading beyond the market close.

3.4

Capital Markets

Carmen Hernansanz, BBVA, Research Department, Madrid

Government debt market

The Book-Entry Public Debt System is the securities clearing and settlement system introduced in 1987 to encourage trading in book-entry public debt. This system is managed by the Bank of Spain's Book-Entry Office, which, on the one hand, performs a recording function and, on the other, the function of market administrator, responsible for the daily settlement of the transactions executed. This system is based on the instrumentation of public debt securities through accounting records, implying the elimination of the physical movement of paper certificates or documents. Only accounting records are kept, with the holder being registered at the Book-Entry Office. The Spanish Treasury has the power to approve the inscription of securities issued by the Autonomous Regions and other public organisations in the Book-Entry Office. Several of them do so, though, with the exception of Madrid, the Autonomous Regions which have a stock market (Catalonia, Valencia and the Basque Country) trade a portion of their public debt securities on this market, together with issues from other public and private organisations.

The Spanish Treasury regularly issues two types of instrument: Treasury bills (*Letras del Tesoro*) and government bonds (*bonos* and *obligaciones*). As of January 1999, as a result of Spain's entry into the Economic and Monetary Union (EMU), all outstanding balances of government debt securities were re-denominated in euros.

Treasury bills were created in 1987 with the launch of the Book-Entry Public Debt Market. These are discount securities with original maturities of six months, one year and eighteen months. At the end of 1999, the outstanding balance of Treasury bills registered for trading in the Bank of Spain's Book-Entry Office amounted to €53 billion.

Government bonds are securities paying regular coupons with maturities of two years or longer. The original maturities of short-term bonds (*bonos*) range between two and five years, while long-term bonds (*obligaciones*) always have original maturities of over five years. Currently, the Treasury issues 3-year and 5-year *bonos* and 10-year, 15-year and 30-year *obligaciones*. Bonds issued after July 1997 are strippable – that is, each bond can be separated into as many discount securities as there are cash flows paid by the bond. At the end of 1999, the outstanding balance of bonds registered for trading in the Bank of Spain's Book-Entry Office amounted to €206 billion.

Spanish Treasury securities are issued on a competitive bid auction basis. The annual auction calendar for the different instruments is published in the Official State Gazette at the beginning of each year. Any individual or institution can participate in tenders through registered dealers (*entidades gestoras*), which are the financial institutions authorised by the Treasury to hold government debt records on behalf of their clients. The Bank of Spain is one of these registered dealers, and, as such, receives applications from investors to access tenders through direct accounts (*cuentas directas*) which, in general, allows investors to benefit from lower commissions.

All Treasury securities are traded on a highly active secondary market in which most of the Spanish financial intermediaries are present. The bulk of trading on this market takes place through the Book-Entry system. The secondary market for government securities is a decentralised market in the sense that there is no trading system through which all transactions are executed. There are two types of transaction: simple transactions and double transactions. Simple transactions consist of a single purchase/sale and double transactions are made up of two purchases/sales in reverse directions. There are, in turn, two types of simple transaction: spot transactions and forward transactions:

- Spot transactions are those in which transfer of the security takes place on a date no more than five business days after the trade is struck, with the settlement date generally being: transfer date plus three business days.

- For forward transactions the transfer date is more than five business days after the contract date.

There are three types of market member:

- **Account holders (*titulares de cuenta*)**: are financial institutions authorised to purchase and hold book-entry public debt in individualised accounts in the Book-Entry Office;

- **Registered dealers (*entidades gestoras*)**: as described earlier, which can be subdivided into two types. These are:

  - fully-fledged registered dealers or *entidades gestoras de capacidad plena* (account holders that can conduct all kinds of transactions with their clients);

– restricted registered dealers or *entidades gestoras de capacidad restringida* (these can only act as dealers on behalf of third parties).

Other market participants, though not members of it, are the inter-dealer brokers, which perform the function of conveying information and bringing together the different parties without taking any position in the market.

Trading is generally divided into two segments: the market between account holders, and the market with third parties (involving participants that are not account holders and which must resort to the services of registered dealers). In trading between account holders, it is worth distinguishing between the anonymous market (or first tier), in which the institutions operating do not know the identity of their counter-party, and the second-tier market, in which the counter-party is known.

In 1999, turnover in Treasury bills was €2416 billion. Of this amount, €79 billion corresponded to simple spot transactions, €2154 billion to fixed-date repurchase transactions, and €183 million to sight repurchase transactions. Trading volume in bonds amounted to €8751 billion, distributed as follows: €2409 billion in simple spot transactions, €5912 billion in fixed-date repurchase transactions, €411 million in sight repurchase transactions, and €19 billion in simple forward transactions. This shows that in both the Treasury bill and bond markets, trading is heavily dominated by repurchase transactions.

The Bank of Spain is responsible for the supervision and monitoring of this market.

Corporate debt market

Private fixed-income trading is spread over two markets: AIAF (the Spanish association of brokers and securities dealers) and the four Spanish stock exchanges. However, the importance of the former dwarfs that of the stock exchanges. Thus, in 1999, the trading volume for short-term and long-term bonds alone (*bonos* and *obligaciones*) on the AIAF market was €56.8 billion, compared with a turnover for corporate debt on the four stock exchanges of only €1.7 billion. The agreement between AIAF, the stock exchanges and the Securities Clearing and Settlement System (see below), to harmonise settlement procedures for fixed-income securities traded on these markets, should help to reduce operating costs in the corporate debt secondary markets.

The AIAF Fixed-Income Market was authorised to operate as an organised securities market in August 1991. The assets traded on this market comprise commercial paper, mortgage bonds, corporate bonds, some regional government bonds, matador bonds, mortgage-backed securities, asset-backed securities and preferred shares. Trading on this market is limited to institutions that are market members. It is decentralised and only securities that comply with certain requirements, and which the issuer has registered on the exchange, can be traded. The organisation governing the market is the Securities Exchange Council (*Sociedad Rectora*), comprising 68 shareholders made up of 34 banks, 17 savings banks and 17 Spanish securities broker-dealers (*sociedades de valores*) and securities brokers (*agencias de valores*). As with the public debt market, new issues have been represented in book-entry form since 1998.

The market has two trading segments: the wholesale segment, in which trading takes place between members, and the retail segment, which covers trading between members and final clients. Prices are communicated through a system of normalised screens showing the best prices for the whole of the market. Transactions between members are carried out by phone, though there is an anonymous segment channelled through specialised intermediaries. Membership of this market is open to credit institutions and securities broker-dealers and brokers, provided that they are stock exchange members. A distinction is made between two types of market member: members in general and specialised members, either in trading with specialist inter-dealer broker systems or in trading of matador bonds. In any case, members must act as counter-parties to their clients.

Firms or entities wishing to include their issues on this market must submit a prospectus verified by the National Securities Exchange Commission (CNMV) giving details of the nature, denomination and characteristics of the securities to be issued. In cases where the issuers are Autonomous Regions or international organisations of which Spain is a member, securities will be approved for listing by virtue of the issuer's application.

At the end of February 2000, the balance of securities listed on this market amounted to €71 billion, which represents a 79 per cent increase relative to the end of 1998. A number of developments underpinned rapid growth. The appeal of commercial paper increased after its tax treatment was changed to make it exempt of withholding tax. Meanwhile, the decline in the public-sector deficit has reduced the central government borrowing requirement, making room for issues from the private sector. In addition, several regulatory changes – such as the regulation of non-mortgage-backed securities – freed up issuance of private fixed-income securities by making issuance simpler, cheaper and more flexible and widening the range of available instruments. Finally, some private fixed-income securities are eligible for use as collateral in ECB monetary policy operations, increasing the demand for these financial instruments.

Banks and savings banks constitute the most active sector in fixed-income issuance in this market, with a 42 per cent share of the total outstanding balance. The second most active issuers are other lending institutions with a 17 per cent share. With respect to type of instrument, commercial paper and long-term corporate bonds, each with 20 per cent of the total, feature prominently, followed by mortgage-backed securities and short-term corporate bonds, each with 15 per cent of the total. Finally, matador bonds and preferred shares each have a 10 per cent share of the total.

Turnover on the AIAF market in 1999, at €86 billion, was double that of the previous year, showing the solid expansion of activity in this market. The largest part of this turnover corresponded to mortgage-backed securities, with 44 per cent of the total, followed by commercial paper, with 21 per cent, and long-term corporate bonds, with 17 per cent.

The CNMV is responsible for supervising and monitoring this market.

Stock exchanges

The 1988 Securities Market Law brought sweeping changes to the organisation of the stock exchanges. The concept of market member was created, and securities broker-dealers (*sociedades de valores*) and securities dealers (*agencias de valores*) became considered as such. All purchases and sales of listed securities require the intervention of a market member. The organisation and functioning of each market became the responsibility of Securities Exchange Councils (*Sociedades Rectoras*), limited companies whose capital was distributed among their members, and which are organised according to professional and profitability criteria. The Securities Exchange Councils are the sole shareholders of the Stock Exchange Association, which manages the Stock Market Interconnection System (SIBE), another of the key changes introduced by the Securities Market Law.

The SIBE is an order-driven electronic market, thus allowing it to operate for longer trading hours (the continuous market). This system was developed as a common trading platform for the members of the four Spanish stock exchanges (Madrid, Barcelona, Valencia and Bilbao), so that, after authorisation by the CNMV, it is open to any share listed on one of these markets. The traditional open outcry trading system exists alongside the SIBE, but liquidity has been declining steadily. The bulk of trading takes place on the SIBE. In 1999, share dealing on the SIBE amounted to €292 billion, compared with €5.9 billion on the traditional trading system.

Clearing and settlement in the stock exchanges is entrusted to the Securities Clearing and Settlement System, a limited company whose capital is distributed among the securities exchange councils of the stock exchanges and other institutions (mainly market members).

Trading on the Spanish stock exchanges is not confined to shares. Government debt, the debt of a number of Autonomous Regions and some segments of private fixed-income securities are also traded. The so-called second market was founded in 1986 with the aim of furnishing an organised market for small and medium-sized firms that are not able to fulfil the necessary requirements for a full listing on the main market. This market has been very slow to develop, however.

The creation of a New Market (see Chapter 3.3) was aimed at providing a fresh stimulus to listings of small firms and start-ups. Finally, the Latin American stock exchange in euros (Latibex) was created at the end of 1999. Six Latin American Companies were listed on this market by the end of September 2000, and the listing of another five companies is expected soon.

The main indicator of the Spanish stock exchange is the Ibex-35 comprising the 35 most liquid shares listed on the continuous market.

The market capitalisation of shares included on the SIBE stood at €454 billion at the end of 1999. Several factors have contributed to the spectacular expansion of the market in recent years, notably the rise in share prices (the average annual Ibex-35 rose by 209 per cent between 1995 and 1999) and capital increases (€39 billion in the past two years). Also helping were new listings (public offerings by private firms in the period 1998–1999 amounted to €26 billion, while capital flows deriving from the privatisation of state-owned enterprises totalled €12.4 billion over the same period).

Trading volume on the SIBE has been rising steadily since its inception. In 1999, share dealing through this system amounted to €286 billion, up 11 per cent from the previous year. Market expansion, the growing appeal of equity in the low interest rate environment ushered in by Spain's entry into EMU, and the large weight of non-resident investors (48 per cent of total turnover) lie behind this increase.

This market is regulated and subject to oversight by the CNMV.

Futures and options

MEFF Holding, created at the end of 1991, incorporates the organisation and functioning of the two electronic futures and options markets existing in Spain: MEFF Fixed Income and MEFF Equity.

MEFF acts as both market and clearing-house for the trading of futures and options contracts in Spain. Access to the market is only possible through a market member. There are three types of market member: custodian clearing members, clearing members and trading members:

- **Custodian clearing members:** These members can trade directly on the market for their own account and on behalf of clients, and must assume the responsibility for transactions executed both for their own account and for clients and other members for which such an agreement exists (and has been submitted to MEFF). They also act as custodians for all margins posted by clearing members. They are required to be Government Debt Book-Entry registered dealers with full powers to hold accounts for third parties.

- **Clearing members:** These members can trade directly on the market for their own account and on behalf of clients. Like custodian clearing members, they must post margins for open positions and settle daily profits and losses for all transactions executed for their own account and on behalf of clients and other members for which such an agreement exists (and has been submitted to MEFF). Clearing members must also have a contract with one or more custodian clearing members with which margins will be posted and adjusted; that is to say, clearing members post margins with the clearing house through the 'agency' services of custodian clearing members.

- **Trading members:** These can trade directly on the market for their own account and on behalf of clients. They must establish an agreement with one or more clearing members through whom trades will be settled and appropriate margins posted for house account and clients' accounts.

There is a fourth complementary category in addition to the above three, the market maker category, whose function is to supply liquidity to trading by quoting bid and offer prices.

One important feature of MEFF's activity as a clearing-house is that it interposes itself between parties, assuming counter-party risk.

MEFF Fixed-Income

MEFF Fixed-Income is the market on which interest rate derivatives are traded. A broad range of futures and options contracts on government debt and the MIBOR at different time horizons was traded in past years. Nonetheless, Spain's entry into EMU has meant that other products traded on bigger and more liquid European futures exchanges have become substitutes for MEFF products, leading to the suspension of trading in several contracts. In February 2000, open positions in this market amounted to €15.5 billion, of which €15.4 billion corresponded to the future on the 10-year notional bond, for which the underlying asset is the 10-year government bond. In 1999 MEFF Fixed-Income signed an agreement with MATIF, the French futures exchange, whereby MEFF members gained access to the trading of futures contracts on the 3-month EURIBOR. Open positions on this contract at the end of February 2000 totalled €181 million.

MEFF Equity

MEFF Equity includes the futures and options market on the Ibex-35 and options on several listed stocks: Acerinox, Acesa, Banco Popular, Bankinter, BBVA, BSCH, Endesa, Fecsa, Gas Natural, Iberdrola, Repsol, Sevillana, Altadis, and Telefónica. This market provides access to futures on the DJ Eurostoxx and DJ Stoxx indices, which are traded on the French

MONEP exchange. The open position in terms of number of contracts at the end of 1999 amounted to 55,949 in Ibex-35 futures, 70,958 in Ibex-35 options and 2,053 in share options.

This market is regulated and subject to oversight by the CNMV.

3.5

Insurance

Carmen Hernansanz, BBVA, Research Department, Madrid

Structure of the insurance industry

In 1997, the Spanish insurance sector was the seventh biggest in Europe, with a market share of 4 per cent. The weight of premiums in Gross Domestic Product (GDP) for the entire European Union amounted to 7.3 per cent, while in Spain it was only 5.4 per cent. Although more recent data permitting a fuller comparison with the rest of Europe are unavailable, the insurance sector in Spain has experienced a marked acceleration in growth over the past two years. Insurance premiums rose by 7.1 per cent in 1998, and, on preliminary data, were up by a record 27 per cent in 1999, to Ptas5.6 trillion. This increase was largely attributable to the sale of unit-linked products (policies linked to baskets of assets or mutual funds), which increased by 230 per cent, pulling in around Ptas800 billion. Mass commercialisation of this type of product began in September 1999, as soon as the uncertainty about its tax treatment had disappeared. The rapid expansion of the insurance sector in 1999 was therefore largely prompted by savers' reactions to the fiscal changes stemming from the implementation of the 1999 personal income tax reform.

Nonetheless, the growth rate of premiums (excluding unit-linked products) accelerated to 12 per cent, with growth in car insurance after several years of slackness particularly significant, at 14 per cent, partly because of higher charges. According to preliminary data for 1999, the volume of life insurance premiums amounted to Ptas3.0 trillion, while that of non-life insurance totalled Ptas2.6 trillion. A breakdown of the share of each type of insurance is reported in Table 3.5.1 below.

In spite of increased business volume, insurance companies' earnings performance has been poor in recent years. In 1998, gross profit in the insurance sector fell by 16 per cent, to stand at Ptas139 billion. The price wars that hit a number of sectors (car and homeowner insurance), and a rise in claims of almost 20 per cent, lay behind this result. Reflecting these

Table 3.5.1   The insurance sector (1999)

Premiums	Growth (%)	Ptas (trillion)
Life	**42**	**3.0**
Unit-linked	232	
Other	13	
Non-life	**11**	**2.6**
Cars	14	
Health	9	
Homeowner	8	
Other	6	
Total	**27**	**5.6**
Total ex-unit linked	**12**	**4.8**

Source: ICEA

developments, profits in the traditional insurance business recorded a decrease of almost 9 per cent. A smaller decline in interest rates than in previous years, and the resulting impact on financial income, also had a dampening effect on earnings, as 60 per cent of insurance companies' portfolios are invested in fixed-income securities, of which half is government debt. In 1998, the technical financial result, which includes financial income, decreased by 30 per cent. The outlook for 1999, however, suggests that earnings may have picked up relative to the previous year.

Companies in the Spanish insurance sector are grouped together in UNESPA, the Spanish Union of Insurance and Reinsurance Companies. This organisation brings together more than 300 companies, representing over 90 per cent of the Spanish insurance market.

The five main life insurance companies in terms of premium volumes in 1998 were: Vidacaixa (Ptas137 billion), Argentaria Vida y Pensiones (Ptas116 billion), Mapfre Vida (Ptas92 billion), Barclays Vida y Pensiones (Ptas89 billion) and Euroseguros (Ptas82 billion). The leading positions in the non-life ranking were occupied by Mapfre Mutualidad (Ptas151 billion), Axa Aurora Ibérica (Ptas109 billion), Winterthur (Ptas104 billion), Zurich España (Ptas89 billion) and Asisa (Ptas76 billion).

As is evident from the names of the insurance companies listed above, a large number of the leading companies in Spain are owned by banks and savings banks. In Spain, the distribution of insurance products through bank branches is standard practice. In 1998, 42 per cent of business volume was distributed via this channel, followed by 32 per cent through insurance agents and 14 per cent through the offices of insurance companies. The latest trends show that the role of banks is increasing. Thus, for the new production traded in 1998, 64 per cent was channelled via bank branches, while only 19 per cent was sold through insurance agents.

This trend has led independent insurance companies to strengthen ties with banks with a view to using their extensive branch networks to sell insurance products. Thus, Mapfre recently signed an alliance with Caja Madrid for the creation of an insurance holding, a strategy that has been copied by other smaller insurance companies.

The insurance sector in Spain has undergone a process of considerable restructuring in the past few years, following a host of mergers. As a result, there has been an increase in the concentration of insurance business in a number of segments. In the case of the non-life branches, the percentage of premiums managed by the five leading companies increased from 22 per cent to 24 per cent between 1996 and 1998. Given that the Spanish insurance sector has been characterised by a lower efficiency ratio than its European counterpart, it seems reasonable to assume that this restructuring will continue in the period ahead.

Regulation

State intervention in the insurance sector is high as this business involves the exchange of a current payment by the policyholder for another future and random one by the insurance company. The basic legislation for the sector is contained in the Insurance Contracts Law (Law 50/1980), the Law on the Regulation of Pension Plans and Funds (Law 8/1987), and the Law on Private Insurance Provision (Law 9/1992). These three laws were modified by the Law on the Ordinance and Supervision of Private Insurance (Law 30/1995).

Access to insurance activity in Spain is contingent upon administrative authorisation from the Ministry of Economy and Finance. Institutions must always have an adequate solvency margin composed of the total assets of the insurance company free of all anticipated obligations after deduction of intangibles. One third of the minimum amount required for solvency margins constitutes the guarantee fund, which cannot be less than the equivalent in pesetas of €800,000 for life insurance and reinsurance companies, €400,000 for companies in the surety, credit and public liability branches and €300,000 for the others.

Spanish insurance companies that have been authorised may conduct their business under the right of establishment or the freedom to provide services in the whole of the European Economic Area (EEA). Conversely, insurance companies registered in EEA countries other than Spain, and that have been authorised to operate in their member state of origin, may do business in Spain.

The powers of the Spanish government in the regulation and supervision of private insurance are discharged through the Ministry of Economy and Finance, which delegates these functions to the General Insurance Office.

The General Insurance Office is entrusted with the following functions:

- monitoring compliance with precise requirements for access to and extension of private insurance and reinsurance activity, the general overseeing of conduct and the supervision of requirements demanded of the administrators and partners of insurance companies;

- supervising mergers, associations, portfolio transfers, transformations, spin-offs, and, in general, all proposals for operations that involve changes to the sector's structure;

- supervising access to insurance brokerage activity, and monitoring and performing the other supervisory functions of this segment of the sector;

- monitoring compliance with the precise requirements for access to the activity of pension fund-managing companies, and their supervision;

- inspecting the conduct of activity and analysing the documents that insurance companies are required to submit;

- preparing regulatory proposals;

- resolving claims filed against insurance companies;

- undertaking studies on the sector.

Future outlook

The outlook for the Spanish insurance sector cannot be viewed in isolation from developments in the industry at a European level. Changes in the sector will be driven by greater competition and the corporate movements that unfold in Europe. In this sense, given the large number of companies operating in Spain, a further round of mergers can be expected, while the large Spanish companies should continue to strengthen ties with other European companies.

The tax treatment of insurance products is a key aspect in the development of the insurance sector. Given the close link between saving and taxation, it is important for tax systems to be maintained over time in order to prevent 'fiscal uncertainty' from paralysing the sector. In addition, it is important that taxation be conducive to long-term private and corporate saving in order to ensure adequate safety thresholds for long-term savings.

The income tax (IRPF) reform introduced in 1999 represents a step in the right direction, as it establishes a favourable tax treatment for insurance products. Following the reform, insurance contracts are classed as investment returns. Capital gains and returns generated by life insurance products up to two years are taxed at the marginal rate. For longer-dated products the tax base is gradually reduced, to 70 per cent for time horizons over eight years. In regular-premium insurance policies, 70 per cent of the returns are tax exempt if more than 12 years have passed since payment of the first premium, though the reduction in the tax liability of 10 per cent of the amount paid in premiums in the year has been withdrawn.

Life insurance has a promising future in Spain given its use as a complement to public pension systems. Indeed, Spanish firms, except for banks, savings banks, insurance companies and securities broker-dealers, are required to transfer management of their employees' pension funds to specialised institutions before the end of 2000, a process known as pension exteriorisation. Insurance companies will pick up part of this business, estimated at some Ptas 4 trillion, though fears have emerged in the sector over the risk of a potentially damaging price war as occurred with car insurance. The creation of dependant insurance policies (cover for individuals that need the support of another person) is at the development stage, which, given the lack of State cover for this type of service, will provide insurance companies with a new source of income.

The maturity reached in other segments suggests that future development of the insurance industry will be directed towards civil liability or health or unemployment risks. In the case of the troubled car insurance sector, recent data hint at a recovery, though a decisive turnaround will only be achieved with the introduction of new management models.

Part 4

Legal Issues

4.1

The Legal System

Eduardo V Tejero and Miriam Ruiz de la Prada, Landwell Abogados y Asesores Fiscales – A Correspondent Law Firm of PricewaterhouseCoopers

Within Western legal systems, the Spanish system pertains to the Continental European family, which is different from the Anglo-American system. The Spanish system is based mainly on Roman law and the Napoleonic Codes, and it is deeply influenced by Germanic law. The basic premises of private law were established at the end of the 19th century, whereas those governing public law were developed during the 20th century. During the last third of the 20th century the Spanish legal system adopted many legal structures from Anglo-American law, particularly in financial and technological areas.

Sources of Spanish law

The sources of the Spanish legal system are the law, custom and general legal principles:

- General principles, which are developed by jurisprudence and academic doctrine, only act to inform and integrate the legal system and are only applicable in cases where there is no applicable law or custom.

- Custom is only applicable in the absence of a law, provided that it is not contrary to moral standards or public order and when it can be proved that it has been established by tradition.

- The fundamental cornerstone of the Spanish legal system, which all other provisions must respect, is the Spanish Constitution of 6 December 1978.

The rules of law contained in international treaties are directly applicable in Spain as soon as they are introduced into internal legislation, after being published in the Official State Gazette (*Boletín Oficial del Estado*). As a result, Spain is fully subject to the legislative provisions issued by the

European Union (EU) in the terms contained therein. Therefore, it must be taken into account that not only must Spanish legal provisions respect the principles established by EU legislation, but also, in some cases, European legislation may be directly applicable in Spain.

Although jurisprudence is not, strictly speaking, a source of law, it complements the legal system with doctrine that is repeatedly established by Supreme Court rulings when interpreting and applying the Law, custom and general legal principles.

Judges and tribunals have the inexcusable obligation to resolve all cases submitted to them, and to respect the established order of sources of Spanish law.

Spanish laws

Characteristics of a law

In order for a provision to be called a law it must emanate from parliament (*Cortes Generales del Estado*) or from the Legislative Assemblies of the Autonomous Regions (*Asambleas Legislativas de las Comunidades Autónomas*).

National laws must be published in the Official State Gazette (*Boletín Oficial del Estado*). Laws emanating from the Autonomous Regions must follow the provisions of the respective Statute of Autonomy (*Estatuto de Autonomía*), which normally follow the criteria of publication in their respective Region Official Gazettes (*Boletín Oficial de la Comunidad*).

Classes of laws

Territorial
- **General laws:** Applicable throughout Spain.

- **Local laws:** Applicable in certain territories of Spain. They consist either of special regional laws (*normas forales*), which are historical laws of a civil character in force in certain territories (Vizcaya, Alava, Catalonia, Balearic Islands, Galicia, Aragon, Navarre); or of laws emanating from the Autonomous Regions (since 1978).

Rank
- **Organic laws:** These require the approval of an absolute majority of parliament. They govern certain areas reserved for this rank of law, relating to the development of basic rights and public liberties, the approval of Statutes of Autonomy, election systems and others defined by the Constitution.

- **Ordinary laws:** A simple majority of the parliament is sufficient for approval.

- **Framework laws:** These define the principles, guidelines and limits within which other rules of law must be developed. Their content normally coincides with matters with respect to which the central government has authority, but which are delegated to Autonomous Regions, and even matters reserved for the authority of the Autonomous Regions, such that the framework law is intended to avoid conflicts between national and regional laws.

- **Laws of the Autonomous Regions:** The legislative authority of the Autonomous Regions only requires that it be recognised in the relevant Statute of Autonomy. Among these laws, the following are notable:

  - Those which regulate matters which are the exclusive responsibility of the Autonomous Regions.
  - Those governing matters which are the responsibility of the central government, when covered by a framework law.
  - Those governing matters which are legally shared with the central government.

Legal provisions with the rank of Law
- **Royal Decree-Laws:** These are provisional legislative provisions issued by government in the event of extraordinary and urgent need to regulate matters which are normally within the domain of parliament. Subsequent to entering into force, parliament must either approve or eliminate the provision.

- **Legislative Royal Decrees:** Legal provisions with the rank of law which are issued by government decree by virtue of express delegation by parliament for each specific case.

Government legislative powers

Apart from the Royal Legislative Decrees and Royal Decree-Laws, the government may create other legal provisions, although they are of lower rank than a law. These provisions may take the form of Royal Decrees issued by the prime minister, Royal Decrees issued by the Council of Ministers or Ministerial Orders.

These provisions:

- may not regulate matters reserved for laws or infringe upon laws or provisions with the rank of law;

- cannot create crimes, or administrative offences, establish penalties or sanctions, taxes, levies or other charges. They are used to develop or enable a law;

- must be published in full in the Official State Gazette in order to enter into force;

- may be appealed against under the contentious-administrative court jurisdiction.

Principles governing the legislative powers

The Spanish Constitution expressly defends: the principle of legality, legislative hierarchy, publishing of legal provisions, the non-retroactive nature of penalty clauses which are unfavourable or restrictive to individual rights, legal security, responsibilities; and prohibits arbitrary public powers.

The Civil Code establishes that laws shall not have retroactive effect unless otherwise stipulated. In addition, it states that the ignorance of the law shall not excuse the failure to comply.

A summary of the basic aspects of Spanish legislation

The Spanish legal system is widely codified: Civil Code, Code of Commerce, Civil and Criminal Trial Laws, Penal Code, Workers' Statute, General Tax Act, Contentious-Administrative Jurisdiction Act. There are also other codes which regulate other legal disciplines.

In essence, Spanish legislation distinguishes between private and public law. In both areas, and since the 1978 Constitution, the Autonomous Regions of Spain have been recognised as having certain legislative powers. Even prior to the Constitution of 1978, certain Regions were already recognised to have their own private law different to that established in the Civil Code, which is applicable to most of Spain.

The Civil Code

The basic legislation body in Spanish private law is the Civil Code of 1889, which is applicable on a supplementary basis to public law jurisdictions. The Civil Code is inspired by the dominant ideologies present at the end of the 19th century, and based on the liberalism that began to be filtered by public interest.

The Code consists of a preliminary Title which regulates the application and interpretation of legal provisions. It is divided into four sections, devoted, in general, to:

- Family law.

- Assets and property.

- Property acquisition including inheritance law.

- Contracts and obligations.

Private law also includes the Code of Commerce of 1885, which specifically regulates commercial matters and mercantile contracts, as well as matters relating to maritime commerce.

Property

One of the basic classifications that Spanish law makes regarding assets is a distinction between personal and real property. The latter includes machinery and instruments used in industry or operations carried out on real property, moving or stagnant waters, and real rights to property. Personal property is deemed to be all assets not classified as real property. Another relevant classification is that which is based on whether the property is public or private.

In Spain the right to private property and inheritance is constitutionally recognised although the content is limited by the social purpose, in accordance with the relevant laws passed in this respect. This means that property rights are limited by public needs relating to urban development, agriculture and livestock, environment, resource access, consumer defence, etc. Ownership and other rights concerning assets are acquired and transferred by law, donation, inheritance, succession, forfeiture and as the result of the delivery subsequently to certain contracts (*traditio*).

Under the Spanish legal system ownership cannot be transferred merely by mutual agreement. The object of the contract must be formally delivered to the acquirer by the transferor and the former must take possession of the item (*traditio*). Contracts are a legal instrument in which the parties only convey the item for which ownership will be transferred. This principle is qualified by the fact that 'fictitious' possession is allowed: for example, for sales executed in a public deed, in which case the execution of the deed is equivalent to the delivery or receiving of the possession of the object of the contract.

Real property may be entered into the Property Register, which is a public office devoted to keeping records of the real rights affecting real property. This is a voluntary step, although the failure to enter records into the register means that the property owner or real property rightholder does not enjoy the full protection that registration provides with respect to the presumption of integrity and accuracy of the registry entry. Making an entry into the Property Registry is therefore not a prior requirement, except in certain cases such as mortgages. The Property Registry is open to the public.

Contract law

The principles governing contract law are those regarding contractual freedom, autonomy of the will of the parties and freedom of form, with no other imperative limits than public morality and order. However, as in the case with property law, these basic principles are being progressively limited, due to motives of public interest, and many provisions have been passed in defence of this interest which limit, to a certain extent, private autonomy and freedom of form.

Debt

Under Spanish law debtors are liable for their obligations against all present and future assets. A debtor may cede assets to the creditor to repay debts. Creditors, after pursuing the debtor's assets to realise the amounts owed, may exercise the debtor's rights for the same purpose. In addition, a creditor may challenge any action a debtor may have taken to defraud the creditor's rights. Although the ceding of debts must be approved by the creditor, with the creditor's approval the law does allow the debtor to be substituted without the knowledge of the debtor.

When a debtor's net worth is insufficient to fully meet incurred debts, a special procedure, called a creditors' meeting (*concurso de acreedores*) is invoked, which aims to avoid discrimination between creditors and prevent only some of them from obtaining full satisfaction from the debtor's net worth, to the detriment of the remaining creditors. The final goal is to classify credits by nature and distribute the debtor's net worth proportionally over all the outstanding debts. Under this procedure some credits have privilege over others, such as wages and salaries or those covered by a real right (pledges, mortgages, etc).

Under mercantile law the creditors' meeting, although based on the same idea, presents certain particulars with respect to regulations and procedures. A distinction is made between suspension of payments, when a debtor has sufficient assets to cover all debts but lacks liquidity to satisfy them within the stipulated period, and bankruptcy, when liabilities exceed assets. Depending on the manner in which bankruptcy is reached, there may be criminal law repercussions.

Liability

With respect to strict liability (*responsabilidad civil extracontractual*) the Civil Code is based on subjective liability (*responsabilidad sujetiva*), ie: a person is liable for his/her own negligent actions, but it also recognises liabilities arising from the actions of others (parents for children, employer for employees, etc). However, jurisprudence has made strict liability more objective, not only by inverting the burden of proof to lie with the causer of the harm, but also by declaring that with respect to certain risky activities, the causer of harm is liable even if no negligence took place. This line of jurisprudence has been included in legislation governing certain activities (nuclear energy, hunting, air navigation, etc).

Mercantile law

As in other areas of private law, mercantile legislation has been strongly influenced by public law, which establishes behaviours relating to the contractual relationships between individuals. The most notable regulatory steps in this respect include: advertising laws, consumer protection, competition defence, product liability, retail business regulations, company regulations, stock market regulation, agency contracts, personal data protection.

The official public registry for mercantile matters is the Mercantile Registry. Whereas the registration of individual businessmen, except for shipping enterprises, is optional, the registration of any legal entity (*persona jurídica*) engaged in trade is obligatory and even constituent. As is the case with the Property Registry, the Mercantile Registry is open to the public.

Administrative law

Under the Spanish legal system, public law includes, among others, criminal, labour, procedural and, especially, administrative law, which is the body of law common to the Administration.

Although Spanish administrative law grants a series of privileges to the government, at the same time it provides for a series of guarantees for citizens. One of the fundamental principles which governs this body of law is that of legality, under which the Administration cannot operate without legal coverage.

In principle, public assets are unalienable, unattachable, cannot be forfeited, and are governed by special legislation. The Constitution permits the expropriation of assets and rights for public use, under payment of the relevant indemnity and in accordance with the provisions of the relevant legislation.

The contracts concluded by the Administration must meet legal requirements set in this respect. They must be made public and subject to a bid process, with some exceptions, and are subject to the principle of equality and no-discrimination. Requirements for the concluding of administrative contracts are as follows:

- the contracting body must be competent;

- the successful bidder must have the capacity to fulfil the contract;

- the object of the contract must be defined;

- the price must be set;

- there must be adequate and sufficient credit;

- the processing of the file, which must include the tender in which the

Administration establishes the clauses governing the contract to be concluded and the budgeted amount of the relevant expense;

- all administrative action which entails economic outlays must be previously accounted for;

- the expense must be approved by the competent authority;

- the contract must be duly concluded.

Nationals of EU member countries shall have the same capacity to enter into contracts as Spanish nationals.

Contracts may be ceded by the successful bidder with the authorisation of the contracting Administration. Partial subcontracting of the contract is also permitted. Once the contract is concluded the Administration may only make modifications due to public interest arising from new or unforeseen circumstances. The price of the contract may be modified during execution, and the price review formula must be contained in the administrative contract clauses.

Any claims regarding the liability of the Administration and authorities and staff are subject to a special legal system and specific procedures.

Organisation of the Spanish government

Spain is organised on a territorial basis by municipalities, provinces and Autonomous Regions. Each of these bodies is autonomous in the management of its respective interests. The central government must defend economic balance adequately and fairly for the many territories of Spain. The differences between the Autonomous Regions' Statutes may not give rise to economic or social advantages. The authorities may not adopt measures that impede the freedom of movement and settlement of persons and assets in any part of Spain.

Apart from the heads of areas and directors, who are political appointees, the staff of the Administration is made up of civil servants or employees. Civil Service appointments are granted after a selective test process, in accordance with merit and capacity principles. Civil servants are governed by a special statute that differs from the normal employment system.

The State

The Head of State is the King of Spain. The government directs interior and exterior policies as well as civil and military administrations. The government is formed by the President, Vice Presidents (if more than one) and Ministers.

The organisation of the central government relies on the division of ministerial departments and territorial management through government delegates in the Autonomous Regions.

The duties with which ministers are charged include the exercising of authority over matters governed by their ministries. The Council of Ministers approves Bills and Royal Decree-Laws and Legislative Royal Decrees and the enabling regulations under which laws are developed and executed.

Government delegates in Autonomous Regions represent the central government in those territories. In turn, a sub-delegate of the government exists in each province. Their main duties consist of co-ordinating central government activities and public bodies with those of the Autonomous Region and municipalities.

Dependent on or linked to the central government are public bodies that are charged with the execution or management of activities and which, although dependent on a ministry, operate with a certain level of autonomy. Examples of this are the Stock Market Commission, the Telecommunications Market Commission, the Personal Data Protection Agency, the State Tax Agency, the Economic and Social Council and the National Energy Commissions.

Public bodies may also be public companies, which are charged with providing services, managing services or producing goods that are in the public interest and that may be sold. Such companies are governed by private law, except for certain internal matters.

The Autonomous Regions

The basic institutional regulation governing each Autonomous Region is the relevant Statute of Autonomy. The Statutes define the territory, its name, organisation and the seat of the regional government, as well as their jurisdiction within the framework of the Constitution.

Among the authority that Autonomous Regions may assume are the following:

- organisation of its self-government institutions;

- ordering of its territory, urban development and housing;

- public works;

- railroads, roadways, road and rail transport which takes place entirely within the Autonomous Region concerned;

- ports of refuge, and recreational ports and airports;

- agriculture, livestock, mountains and forest, and hydraulic resources;

- environmental protection management;

- internal fisheries, hunting and aquaculture;

- historical, artistic and tourism heritage management;

- promotion of sports, social welfare, health and hygiene.

The institutional organisation of the Autonomous governments is based on a Legislative Assembly elected by universal suffrage and a Government Council with executive and administrative powers. These are accompanied by a President, who leads the Government Council, and a Superior Court of Justice that is the leading judicial body within the Autonomous Region.

The activities carried out by the public entities within each Autonomous Region are supervised by the Constitutional Court, and by the Central Government when activities delegated by this authority are involved. The Contentious-Administrative court jurisdiction supervises activities involving the Administration of the Autonomous Region, and the Court of Auditors supervises those activities involving economic and budget matters.

Local administration

Local territorial entities are as follows:

- municipalities;

- provinces;

- individual Islands in the Balearic and Canary Islands;

- provincial regions;

- metropolitan areas;

- associations of municipalities.

Municipal governments, which are autonomous entities, are headed by the respective city or town council (*Ayuntamiento*), made up of a mayor (*Alcalde*) and council members (*Concejales*) all of whom are elected under universal suffrage. State legislation and the Statutes of Autonomy must guarantee the attribution of authority to municipalities.

Provinces are local entities, defined by groups of municipalities, and are territorial divisions into which state activities may be carried out. The activities of the Autonomous provincial government and administration are carried out by representative bodies. The content and scope of these entities are developed in more detail in the Statutes of Autonomy than by State legislation.

Local governing bodies have, among others, the following authority:

- regulation and self-organisation;

- taxes and finance;

- urban planning;

- expropriation;

- application of sanctions.

4.2

Company Formation

Carlos Ulecia and Eduardo V Tejero,
Landwell Abogados y Asesores Fiscales –
A Correspondent Law Firm of
PricewaterhouseCoopers

The Code of Commerce (*Código de Comercio*) is the reference law in Spanish company law. The Spanish Companies Act (*Ley de Sociedades Anónimas*), the Spanish Private Limited Companies Act (*Ley de Sociedades de Responsabilidad Limitada*) and the Mercantile Registry Regulations (*Reglamento del Registro Mercantil*) complete the main framework of Spanish company law. All these regulations are in line with the principles contained in European Union (EU) directives.

Legal structure for foreign investors: branch, company or representative office

Companies that wish to carry out their business activity in Spain may do so through a branch or by setting up a separate legal entity, which will normally take the form of a company. Also, under the Spanish legal system, foreign companies may carry out their business activity in Spain through a representative office.

The main difference between a company and a branch is their legal status. Branches have no independent legal identity separate from that of their head office. They are simply extensions of the head office. Although they may take part in legal operations and assume the corresponding rights and obligations, they are regarded as doing so on behalf of their head office. The head office and the branch have the same legal personality. It is therefore impossible to make a distinction between the responsibilities assumed by the head office and those assumed by the branch.

A company has its own separate legal identity, independent of that of the parent company. It may therefore enter into agreements and participate in all operations of a legal nature acting in its own name and right.

Both subsidiaries and branches are required to register with the Mercantile Registry. However, in the case of a subsidiary, the first entry in the Mercantile Register is that of its formation as an entity with its own separate legal identity independent of that of any other entity. The first entry in the page opened in the name of a branch is that of the formation of the head office in the relevant country and the subsequent opening of a branch in Spain will be the second entry.

Representative offices

Representative offices are a legal device with a strong fiscal component. The Double Taxation Treaties concluded between Spain and several countries* provide for a particular rule whereby, in connection with direct taxation, the performance of a certain number of operations and activities is not deemed to constitute a permanent establishment in Spain. These activities include:

• the storage or delivery of merchandise belonging to the head office;

• promoting and providing information;

• any other activity of a preparatory or auxiliary nature with respect to the head office.

From a formal viewpoint, the representative office means that the head office must execute a public document in its country of residence, resolving upon the opening of a representative office in Spain and authorising an individual to exercise certain powers.

For the representative office not to be regarded as a permanent establishment it must be used for one of the aforementioned purposes (activities of a preparatory or auxiliary nature) and it must comply with the requirement that the person in charge of the representative office must not be authorised to conclude contracts on behalf of the head office.

Setting up a company

The types of business organisation normally used in Spain to carry out business activities, are as follows:

• General Partnerships (*Sociedades Colectivas*).

• Limited Partnerships (*Sociedades Comanditarias*).

• Private Limited Companies (*Sociedades de Responsabilidad Limitada*).

• public limited companies (*Sociedades Anónimas*).

---

* In accordance with the OECD Model Convention

In accordance with Spanish company law, one of the main distinctions between the different types of companies is the degree of liability of the partners/shareholders. Thus, a distinction may be drawn between companies in which the liability of their members is limited to their contribution to the company (capital-based entities, called *Sociedades de base capitalista*) and those in which the members are personally liable, with all their current and future wealth, for the company's debts (partnerships, called *Sociedades de base personalista*).

Under this classification, public limited companies and private limited companies would belong to the first group (the shareholders' liability is limited to their contribution) and general and limited partnerships would belong to the second group (companies whose partners are personally liable for any partnership debts). However, in the case of limited partnerships with shares this assertion requires clarification.

Historically, the most common type of company used in Spain has been the public limited company. However, private limited companies have started to replace public limited companies as the main type of company.

General partnerships and limited partnerships are used mainly to set up firms of independent professionals, by large corporations that wish to avoid having to comply with certain advertising or auditing requirements or when setting up subsidiaries in certain countries where this form of business organisation is usual.

The Mercantile Registry

All companies must be registered with the relevant Mercantile Registry.

The Mercantile Registry is a public institution, dependent on the Ministry of Justice and is responsible, *inter alia*, for the registration of businesses and certain acts and contracts relating thereto, the legal recognition and publicising of official registers and accounting documents, and the centralisation and publication of information contained in the Register.

General partnership

This form of business organisation may be considered as being the closest to 'general partnerships' in countries influenced by legal institutions under Anglo-American law. The main characteristics of this type of partnership are as follows:

- No capital endowment is required for its formation. Any capital that exists is not divided up into units. As a result, there are no shares or unit participations.

- It may be administered by one or several partners. If no one is appointed to carry out the administrative duties, the business will be administered by all the partners.

- The name of the general partnership will comprise the names of all, several, or just one of its partners. In the last two cases, the name or names must be followed by the words *'y Compañía'*, and the abbreviation *'SC'* or *'SRC'*.

- Each partner has an unlimited joint and several liability for the partnership's debts.

- A partner's quota may not be transferred without the remaining partners' consent.

- General partnerships may be dissolved due to the death, incapacity or bankruptcy of any partner.

Limited partnership

In this form of business organisation, there are two types of partner:

- General partners (*Socios colectivos*) whose liability is unlimited;

- Limited partners (*Socios comanditarios*) whose liability is limited to the amount of their contributions to the company.

Limited partnerships may be ordinary or with shares.

Ordinary limited partnership (Comanditaria simple)

Ordinary limited partnerships will include the names of all, several or just one, of the general partners. In the last two cases, the name or names will be followed by the words *'y Compañía'* and by the words *'Sociedad en Comandita'* or the abbreviation *'S en C'* or *'S Com'*. If a limited partner includes his name, said limited partner will be subject to the same liability regime as the general partner. Limited partners:

- cannot administer the interests of the company, not even as representatives of the managing partners (all or some of the general partners).

- will only be able to examine the state and situation of the company's business affairs on the dates specified in the formation document or in subsequent documents.

Limited partnership with shares (Comanditaria por acciones)

Unlike general partnerships and ordinary limited partnerships, the capital of this limited partnership is divided into shares so that the limited partners are only liable for the amount of their contribution. In this form of organisation:

- At least one of the partners will be personally liable for the partnership's debts as general partner. The general partners manage the business in the same terms as an administrator of a public limited company.

- The name of the partnership will comprise the name of all, several, or just one of the general partners, or an objective name which must be followed by *'Sociedad en Comandita por Acciones'* or its abbreviation, *'S Com por A'*.

- Limited partnerships with shares are considered as a hybrid form of business organisation between a general partnership and public limited company. In fact, the Spanish Companies Act integrates and is applicable also to limited partnerships with shares on a subsidiary basis.

Private limited companies

Private limited companies (*Sociedad de Responsabilidad Limitada* or *SRL*) or simply named limited companies (*Sociedad Limitada* or *SL*), are currently the most commonly used business forms in Spain. Of newly incorporated companies 80 per cent are private limited companies.

The private limited company was relaunched with the enactment of Law 2/1995, of 23 March 1995, which provided these companies with a more extensive and detailed framework of independent regulations. Before said date, private limited companies were regulated by an antiquated and incomplete body of regulations dating from 1953, which proved insufficient for the actual business situation at the end of the century.

This form of business organisation is most commonly used both by small and medium size companies (minimum share capital is Ptas500,000 or €3005.06). It is also used by large companies (there is no maximum capital limit). The Articles of Association can describe the private limited company as a flexible structure that covers the necessary requirements.

The main characteristics of this type of company are:

- Shareholders' liability is limited to the capital they subscribe.

- Minimum share capital is Ptas500,000 (€3005.06). Capital must be paid up on the date of incorporation and may be in cash or in kind (capital goods, properties, etc) capable of being valued in monetary terms. Capital is divided into unit 'participations' (*participaciones*) which are not considered to be securities and may not be called shares (*acciones*). There may be different types of shares, although if they belong to the same class they must carry the same rights.

- Unlike in the case of public limited companies, the valuation of non-monetary contributions is not subject to a valuation report drawn up by an independent expert appointed by the Mercantile Registry.

- The incorporation must be recorded in a public deed and entered in the Mercantile Register.

- The formation deed must state, *inter alia*: the name and registered office of the company, its objects, the share capital figure, the date of commencement of business, the length of its financial year and year-end date. This information is contained in the Articles of Association, which are also included in the public deed and which lay down the rules for the internal functioning of the company and the regime governing the transfer of unit participations.

- A register of participation holders must be kept, setting out the unit participations held by each participation holder and any changes in ownership or encumbrances.

- A private limited company may be set up with only one founding participation holder. There is no maximum limit with respect to the number of participation holders.

- The Spanish Private Limited Companies Act does not allow any clauses in the Articles of Association that render practically free the voluntary transfer of unit participations *inter vivos*. Even when this is not specifically provided for in the Articles of Association, transfers of unit participations in private limited companies are subject to restrictions. However, unit participations may be freely transferable between participation holders.

- A general meeting (*Junta General de Socios*) must be held once a year, in the first six months of the year, to approve the annual accounts relating to the previous year and the management of the company's affairs.

- The company must have an administrative body that may be formed by:
  - a board of directors
  - a sole administrator
  - joint administrators, or
  - jointly and severally liable administrators.

Administrators/directors need not be participation holders or Spanish nationals. Companies may be administrators/directors provided they appoint an individual to represent them. Board members or administrators may be appointed for an indefinite period.

- The board of directors shall comprise a minimum of three members and a maximum of twelve and must, in any event, have a chairman and a secretary and where appropriate a vice-chairman and vice-secretary. The board may delegate all or some of its powers (except those that cannot be delegated by law) to an executive committee or to one or several managing directors.

- The administrators are answerable to the company, its participation holders and creditors for any damage caused by acts that are contrary to the law or the Articles of Association, or for any action that is taken without the due diligence expected of persons holding such posts. The powers of the administrators cannot be limited in any way *vis-à-vis* third parties. The company is liable to third parties acting in good faith.

- The participation holders or directors/administrators may receive financial assistance, advance payments, credits or loans and even guarantees in their favour, provided the general meeting considers this appropriate.

- The arrangement and guarantee of issues of debentures or other traded securities grouped for the purposes of their issue is prohibited.

Public limited company

In a public limited company (*Sociedad Anónima* or *SA*), the liability of the shareholders is limited to the amount of capital they subscribe. Until the nineties, it was the most commonly used form of business organisation in Spain, and it is the only form of company that may obtain a listing on Spanish stock exchange markets. The adaptation of the law to EU directives has resulted in a number of requirements and limitations, mainly aimed at protecting minority shareholding interests and third parties. Some of these limitations are those that govern reciprocal holdings and cross-shareholdings with other companies, prior publication of alterations to the Articles of Association and the public limited company's prohibition to grant financial assistance for the acquisition of own shares.

This form of business organisation is used mainly by companies with many shareholders of widely different kinds, and is the obligatory legal form for certain companies with specific objects (safety companies, finance companies, etc), and for being listed on the stock exchange. The basic requirements that must be complied with in the setting up of the company and the management of its affairs, are as follows:

- The incorporation of a public limited company must be recorded in a public deed executed before a notary and entered in the Mercantile Register.

- The formation deed, as in the case of private limited companies, must include the Articles of Association, and must state the business name and registered office, the type of activity to be carried out, the date of commencement of business, year-end date, share capital subscribed and paid up, etc.

- A public limited company may be set up with only one shareholder. There are no limits on the maximum number of shareholders.

- Minimum share capital is Ptas10 million (€60,101.21), and at least 25 per cent must be paid up at the time of incorporation. However, in certain sectors (safety, banking, insurance) a higher share capital figure is required as a guarantee measure, and/or a higher must be paid up at the time of incorporation. Share capital may be subscribed in cash or in kind, as equipment, properties etc, which may be valued in monetary terms.

- In the case of non-monetary contributions, the valuation attributed to such contributions must be verified by independent experts appointed by the Mercantile Registry.

- Share capital is comprised of shares that can be registered or bearer shares. Shares usually have the same par value, although they may have different par values if they belong to a different series. There may also be classes of shares so that shares of the same class carry the same rights.

- Share capital may be comprised of ordinary shares or preference shares. Non-voting shares may be issued up to a maximum of 50 per cent of nominal share capital with the right to an annual minimum dividend, fixed or variable, in accordance with the provisions of the Articles of Association.

- In principle, shares are transferable securities to the extent that although the transfer of shares can be restricted by the Articles of Association, no clauses can be agreed to that would make the shares untransferable. Thus, any limitations relating to the shareholders' possibility to sell their shares, which may only be established when the shares are registered shares, cannot prevent the sale thereof to third parties when certain conditions are not complied with.

- A general shareholders' meeting must be held at least once a year, in the first six months of the financial year, to approve the annual accounts and management of the company's affairs.

- The administrative body of a public limited company must be formed by
  - a board of directors
  - a sole administrator
  - two joint administrators, or
  - jointly and severally liable administrators.

  Administrators need not be shareholders or Spanish nationals. Companies can be directors/administrators provided they appoint an individual to represent them. Directors/administrators may be appointed for a period of up to five years and may be reappointed indefinitely.

- The points relating to the functioning of the board of directors and the liability regime of administrators in private limited companies are entirely applicable to public limited companies.

Single shareholder companies

Spanish legislation recognises the status of single shareholder companies for public limited companies and private limited companies, in which an individual or company owns all the shares either from the moment of incorporation or later.

In this respect, both the setting up of a single shareholder company and the declaration of the single shareholder status must be recorded in a public deed and entered in the Mercantile Register. This situation must be disclosed on all company documents, orders, invoices, etc.

In single shareholder companies, the sole shareholder has the powers pertaining to the general shareholders' meeting. Any decisions adopted by the single shareholder must figure in the relevant minutes which must be signed by the single shareholder or their representative.

Any contracts executed by the single shareholder must be in writing and entered in a company register which must be officially legalised by the Mercantile Registry. The company's annual report will expressly contain references to the main characteristics of each of these contracts.

If during the six month period following the date on which a company becomes a single shareholder company, such status is not registered with the Mercantile Registry, the single shareholder will have personal and unlimited liability, jointly and severally with the company, for any debts incurred during the period until the single shareholder status is entered in the Mercantile Register.

Accounting issues, financial information and advertising requirements

Spanish accounting practices and practices in respect of financial information have traditionally been very influenced by French accounting and tax criteria. Spanish mercantile law was reformed and adapted to EU directives on accounting matters. In December 1990, a new Spanish General Accounting Plan (*Plan General de Contabilidad*) was approved. The aim of the new regulations is to make accounting information more transparent and consistent and as a result facilitate comparative analysis between companies. Financial statements must provide a true and fair view of the company's financial situation and affairs using generally accepted accounting principles instead of tax criteria.

The main accounting requirements are set out in the following pages.

Accounting requirements
The rules for keeping accounting records are set out in the mercantile and tax legislation. The accounting records may be kept in data-processing form.

The official books of account are:

• Journal (*Libro Diario*).

• Book of Trial Balances and Annual Accounts (*Libro de Inventarios y Balances*), comprising the profit and loss account and the balance sheet.

• Minutes books for shareholders' meetings and board of directors' meetings.

• Shareholders' Register stating the shareholders who hold registered shares, or the Participations Register for private limited companies.

• Register of contracts concluded between the company and the single shareholder (only in the case of single shareholder companies).

All the mandatory books of account (for accounting and corporate purposes) must be legalised by the Mercantile Registry.

Financial statements
Companies are required to keep their accounting records and present their financial statements in accordance with the provisions of the General Accounting Plan. The Spanish General Accounting Plan divides the accounts into seven main groups, namely:

• **Group 1**   Basic financing – capital, reserves, long-term debts.

• **Group 2**   Fixed assets – buildings, plant and machinery, patents, etc.

• **Group 3**   Inventories – raw materials, finished goods, etc.

• **Group 4**   Creditors and debtors relating to trade operations, suppliers, trade debtors, etc.

• **Group 5**   Financial accounts – short-term loans, cash at bank and in hand, short-term investments.

• **Group 6**   Purchases and expenses.

• **Group 7**   Sales and income.

Given that certain sectors of activity have special requirements with respect to accounting matters (eg electricity companies, insurance companies) accounting plans have been drawn up and approved by the government for different sectors.

The majority of subsidiaries of foreign companies draw up their financial statements in accordance with parent company policies. However, under Spanish regulations, the financial statements must also conform to Spanish legislation. The financial statements must be drawn up in accordance with generally accepted accounting principles in Spain and filed with the Mercantile Registry.

Annual accounts

The annual accounts, which constitute one unit, comprise the balance sheet, profit and loss account and notes to the accounts. Where the company is required by law to draw up a directors' report and audit report, these must be filed with the Mercantile Registry each year. Failure to comply with this obligation may result in the imposition of penalties (suspension of entries at the Mercantile Registry) and fines (from Ptas200,000 to Ptas50 million) on the company. The contents of these documents are as follows:

● **Balance sheet.** Abridged balance sheets that have not been audited may be presented when two of the following limits are not exceeded:

Number of employees	50
Annual sales	Ptas790 million
Total assets	Ptas395 million

Companies that present an abridged balance sheet are not required to draw up a directors' report.

● **Profit and loss account.** An abridged profit and loss account may be presented when two of the following limits are not exceeded:

Number of employees	250
Total assets	Ptas1580 million
Annual sales	Ptas3160 million

● The notes to the accounts contain additional information (either figures or text) that clarify the contents of the financial statements.

The annual accounts, the directors' report, if appropriate, and the proposal for the appropriation of profit, and the consolidated annual accounts and the consolidated directors' report, if appropriate, must be drawn up by the company's administrative body within three months of the year-end.

The accounts must be approved by the general shareholders' meeting. Once the meeting has been convened, the documentation that will be put to the consideration of the meeting will be made available to the shareholders. A certificate of the resolution adopted by the general shareholders' meeting approving the accounts and the appropriation of profits, must be filed by the company with the Mercantile Registry, together with copies of these accounts, and, where appropriate, of the directors' report and audit report.

Filing the accounts of a branch

Foreign companies with branches in Spain are also required to file their annual accounts in Spain and, where appropriate, the consolidated accounts drawn up in accordance with the legislation of the country concerned.

If the accounts have already been filed in the Mercantile Registry of the foreign company, the classification by the Spanish Mercantile Registrar will be limited to verifying this point, which is called 'control of equivalence' (*control de equivalencia*). Where this is not possible, the parent company must draw up these accounts in relation to the activity of the branch and file them with the Spanish Mercantile Registry.

Auditing the annual accounts
All companies, except those authorised to present an abridged balance sheet (see above), are required to have their annual accounts audited by independent auditors. The auditors are appointed by the general shareholders' meeting for a minimum term of three years and a maximum of nine, and may be appointed annually once the initial term of engagement has ended. If the meeting does not appoint the auditors, any shareholder may request the Mercantile Registry to do so. Where a company is not obliged to have its annual accounts audited, a number of shareholders who hold an interest of at least 5 per cent may request that the Mercantile Registry appoint the auditors.

Foreign investments
Spain promotes foreign investments and, in recent years, there has been a steady flow of foreign capital into the country. As from Royal Decree dated 23 April 1999 (number 664), the restrictions and limitations affecting the movement of capital have been practically eliminated. This has led to the freedom of payments and trade between residents and non-residents and international bank transfers.

Definition of foreign investments
A foreign investment in Spain is an investment made by an individual, company or entity resident abroad, irrespective of their nationality or the origin of the funds invested or the procedure followed to make the investment.
Foreign investors are:

• Non-resident individuals (Spanish or foreign).

• Companies with registered offices located outside Spain.

• Foreign governments and public companies.

Types of investment
Foreign investments are classified as follows:

• Shareholdings in Spanish companies.

• Setting up and expansion of branches.

• Subscription and acquisition of negotiable securities representing loans issued by Spanish residents.

- Acquisition of real properties in Spain of a value above Ptas 500 million, or when, irrespective of the value, the foreign investment comes from a 'tax haven'.

The Spanish tax authorities consider that a certain group of countries, owing to their special tax circumstances (low or zero taxation) should be the object of special control as concerns investments which are made from or in said countries, in order to avoid any possible fraudulent behaviour.

The list of countries is subject to change by the Spanish administration on the basis of practice, or of changes in the economic situation or in international relations.

Regulations governing the investment
In general terms, foreign investments in Spain and foreign payments, collections or transfers are totally deregulated. Thus, a simple declaration for statistical purposes is required. There are specific cases where the investor is required to comply with certain prior administrative requirements and cases where the project is subject to prior official clearance. However, an attempt has been made to reduce the latter to a minimum. The reasons for maintaining prior clearance are the tax implications of the operation (the investment is made from a country classed as a 'tax haven').

Special investment regulations have to be considered on sectors with specific regulations (air transport, radio and television, gambling, national defence and private security), and sectors engaging in the manufacturing or sale of weapons, ammunitions, explosives and war materials.

4.3

Disputes and Arbitration

Juan Antonio Cuevas and Eduardo V Tejero, Landwell Abogados y Asesores Fiscales – A Correspondent Law Firm of PricewaterhouseCoopers

The Spanish judicial system is governed by an independent body known as the General Council of the Judiciary (*Consejo General del Poder Judicial*), which is characterised by its independence from the legislative and executive branches of government.

The judicial institutions that make up the Spanish judicial system are composed of judges who achieve their status through professional examinations that are open to law graduates. The judges apply the law individually in the courts of law or through collegiate tribunals. These judicial institutions are assigned competencies on the basis of the issues being judged, which may be grouped into four jurisdictional areas:

- Civil law.

- Criminal law.

- Cases involving action against the Administration (*contencioso-administrativo*).

- Employment law.

Civil law

The area of civil law covers litigation between private persons that is not expressly assigned to other areas of law. It therefore covers both civil issues (in the strict sense) and mercantile matters.

The most important proceedings in the area of mercantile law are the so-called declaratory actions (*juicios declarativos*), the procedural complexity of these being dependent on the amount of the claim involved. Through declaratory actions, the courts declare the relevancy of a given right, and the executory process (*juicios ejecutivos*) is implemented, where rights already deemed to be relevant are judicially enforced. These proceedings are carried out mainly in written form and comprise three stages: pleadings, evidence and conclusions. They are governed by the principle of the parties' right of rebuttal (*principio de contradicción*) and, with very few exceptions, require the involvement of a trial lawyer (*procurador*) and the technical supervision of a solicitor.

Together with the two procedures described above, also worthy of note are:

- Proceedings involving injunctions (*interdicto*) – aimed at securing an immediate solution which, due to its nature, cannot be delayed without prejudice to a party.

- Foreclosure proceedings (aimed at obtaining payment of a debt secured by mortgage).

- Marital proceedings.

- Bankruptcy cases.

Courts

The judicial institutions that are competent to hear suits in the first instance are courts with a single judge, which are authorised to approve the measures necessary to protect the parties' rights on a precautionary basis. They are known as Courts of the First Instance. Judgements delivered in the first instance, whether on a precautionary or final basis, may be appealed against in a higher court called the Provincial Court (*Audiencia Provincial*), which is made up of three judges. Appealing before this court does not preclude the possible provisional enforcement of the judgements already delivered in the court of first instance.

Criminal law

The area of criminal law covers proceedings against the perpetrators of offences specified in the Spanish penal code. The complexity of the procedures applied in this area of law vary depending on the sentence established for the offence concerned. They may be divided into:

- minor offence trials (*juicio de faltas* – sentence under six months' imprisonment);

- abbreviated proceedings (sentence under nine years' imprisonment);

- ordinary proceedings (sentence over nine years' imprisonment).

Criminal proceedings may be divided into two stages, consisting of the investigation of the offence (*instrucción*) and the trial itself, which is carried out orally and publicly as a single act.

Criminal proceedings may be instigated through the reporting of the facts by a private person or through a formal complaint whereby the person making the complaint acquires the status of plaintiff. In any event, criminal proceedings are characterised by the absolute independence between the judging institution and the accused, which is embodied in the separation between the state's act of judgement, performed through the courts of law, and the state's accusation which is handled by the Department of Public Prosecutions (*Ministerio Fiscal*). This independence of the judiciary is also expressed in the necessary separation between the investigating court and the court in which judgement is delivered.

Investigating magistrates are allowed to enforce precautionary measures of a penal character and also in relation to possible civil liability resulting from the offence concerned. In all cases, when final judgements are handed down the judges may include references to the consequences under civil law or in relation to property that derive from the offence committed. Juries have been provided for in Spanish legislation since 1995 but they are used only in a very limited number of cases, which include homicide and murder trials.

Courts

The investigation stage of criminal procedures is handled by the Magistrate Courts (*Juzgados de Instrucción*), whose judgements are delivered at courts with a single judge, called Criminal Courts (*Juzgados de lo Penal*), or by Provincial Courts comprising three judges. Whether the former or the latter is competent depends on whether the sentence to be applied exceeds three years' imprisonment. Judgements may be appealed against in the higher courts.

Employment law

Employment or labour law covers lawsuits between employers and employees, most of which relate to proceedings concerning dismissal, wage claims and collective bargaining. Labour proceedings commence with a writ of complaint, before which an out-of-court settlement may be sought from an independent government-controlled arbitration body.

Labour proceedings take place in single-judge courts in a single act which is predominantly oral in nature and based on the principle of the parties' right of rebuttal. A solicitor may or may not take part. Judgements can be appealed against before a second court comprising three judges.

Courts

Labour cases are heard before the Labour Courts (*Juzgados de lo Social*), whose rulings may be appealed against before a higher court with a regional scope called the High Court of Justice (*Tribunal Superior de Justicia*).

Action against the administration

This area of Spanish law (*jurisdicción contencioso administrativa*) is concerned with actions filed by private individuals against the public authorities, whether local, regional or central, and includes appeals against administrative rulings, the state's liability with respect to real property and all kinds of penalties. In such cases the state is defended by a body of functionaries known as the State Attorneys, composed of law graduates who have passed the relevant competitive examination.

For claims under Ptas500,000, a single oral process is applied. For higher claims, process is in writing and is divided into stages of pleadings, evidence and conclusions.

Courts may have one or more judges, depending on their competence. The main feature of this regime is that legal action against a public body requires a prior claim filed with an administrative court. These include the Central and Regional Tax and Treasury Courts (*Tribunales Económico Administrativos*), which are responsible for tax-related issues.

Proceedings require the technical supervision of a solicitor and may be instigated before the adoption of whatever precautionary measures are deemed necessary to avoid damages deriving from the appealed administrative action.

Courts

Courts consist of the Ordinary Administrative Courts (*Juzgados de lo Contencioso Administrativo ordinarios*) and the Central Administrative Court (*Juzgado Central de lo Contencioso Administrativo*), both with a single judge, as well as the High Court of Justice and the National Court (*Audiencia Nacional*) with various judges. Competence among these judicial bodies depends both on the amount of money involved and on the administrative body whose actions are the object of the claim.

Supreme court

The system of ordinary appeals ends with a collegiate court of the last instance called the Supreme Court, based in Madrid, and whose competence covers the entire state. Its function is to judge appeals for judicial review (*recursos de casación*) lodged against judgements delivered in an erroneous application of Spanish legislation. In such appeals for judicial review the court does not examine the events on which the relevant judgement was based, but limits itself solely to deciding whether Spanish legislation was appropriately applied in that judgement. An appeal for judicial review may be filed with the Supreme Court in all areas of law, providing the amounts involved exceed certain minimum limitations. A solicitor and trial lawyer are necessary.

Other courts

In addition to the institutions described above there are other, special courts which are not covered by judicial authority and which are competent to hear specific issues. These include the Constitutional Court, which is responsible for protecting the rights guaranteed by the Spanish Constitution, and arbitration institutions.

Constitutional court

The Constitutional Court is made up of various jurists of recognised prestige, who are not necessarily professional judges, and who are charged with the defence and protection of the basic rights guaranteed by the Spanish Constitution of 1978 through various appeal mechanisms that receive preferential treatment. This court also has the authority to interpret the Constitution and declare null and void any laws or regulations of any kind that infringe the Constitution.

Arbitration

Except in very few cases, Spanish legislation allows private persons to seek remedies through arbitration when the agreements or contracts in litigation include an arbitration clause or commitment.

The procedure governing the arbitration is determined by the parties themselves or, in the absence of agreement, by the arbitrators. In any event, the principles of hearing, the parties' right of rebuttal and equality of the parties apply. The parties may decide on the number of arbitrators, though there must always be an odd number. The parties may choose between arbitration in equity or at law. In the latter case the legislation to be applied in the arbitrators' award may be specified. In the absence of any such choice by the parties, arbitration in equity will apply.

Once the decision has been taken to submit a case to arbitration, no legal action may be taken in connection therewith. Likewise, the arbitrators' decision may not be appealed against, except where there are legally specified grounds for voiding the decision. In such case, appeals are filed before the ordinary courts, specifically the Provincial Court. Arbitrators' decisions have the same category as court judgements and therefore may be enforced directly before the courts, as can arbitration decisions issued in the course of international arbitration.

The fact that the arbitrators' decision must be issued within six months and enjoys the same status as a court judgement has been a decisive factor in the major increase in Spain in the use of arbitration in recent years, particularly with regard to mercantile matters.

4.4

Creating a Commercial Distribution Network

Miriam Ruiz de la Prada and Eduardo V Tejero, Landwell Abogados y Asesores – A Correspondent Law Firm of PricewaterhouseCoopers

When deciding on the strategies to adopt in order to promote their products, companies have the choice of creating an internal sales network or using external distribution channels. Prevailing legislation governing consumer protection and the retail trade must be taken into consideration when selling products directly to final customers. Retailing is understood to involve the sale of any kind of product to final users, whether through commercial premises or not.

Internal sales network

During the promotion and sale of products and/or services through the company's own internal network, sales staff may be employed under an ordinary employment contract or a special employment contract applicable to 'dependent sales representatives and travelling sales representatives'. This special employment relation is applicable when an individual represents one or more companies, receiving remuneration from them, in order to personally promote or arrange commercial transactions on behalf of the companies, without assuming any risk in this respect. The duration of these special employment contracts may be indefinite. If a specific duration is agreed it may not exceed three years.

These employees have the right to receive recognition from the company for the new clients secured by them in the course of their work and for the clients initially assigned to them. Among other implications, this means that the employees are entitled to a special indemnity in consideration of the increasing business with the clients secured by them, in addi-

tion to the indemnity to which they are entitled as a result of the termination of their employment contract. This applies when the contract is not
terminated due to breach of contract by the employee and provided that
the employee undertakes not to compete with the company or work for a
competitor after the contract has been terminated.

The internal distribution system enables the company to monitor its
employees' activities and the prices of its products more closely. On the
other hand, an internal sales network implies direct costs for the
employer, who must pay both sales staff salaries and related social security contributions.

External sales network

Products may be marketed and sold through independent companies or
individuals. A company may design its sales strategy based on independent third parties which may be classified based on the way in which they
operate, as outlined below:

- **Intermediaries:** Whether commercial agents (*agentes comerciales*)
  or commission agents (*comisionistas*), they usually act on behalf of
  the principal to promote and/or complete commercial transactions
  relating to the principal's products and/or services without assuming
  any risk in this respect.

- **Distributors:** Companies that promote the products and/or services
  of the principal while acting in their own name and right and assuming any risks that could derive from the sale of the products and/or
  services.

Intermediaries

A distinction may be made between agency agreements (*contratos de
agencia*), which are governed by special regulations, and commission
agreements (*contratos de comisión*).

Agency agreement
Spanish law defines the agency agreement as an agreement whereby an individual or a legal entity known as the agent undertakes to promote commercial acts or transactions on behalf of a third party on a continuous or regular
basis in exchange for remuneration, or to promote and complete such acts
or transactions on behalf of and representing a third party, as an independent intermediary, without assuming any risks relating to such transactions
unless otherwise stipulated. Unlike commercial distributors, a commercial
agent does not purchase the products from the manufacturer for resale, as
the products are sold directly by the principal to the final consumer.

In the course of the commercial agent's professional activity the agent is required to act in the best interest of the principal, as follows:

• The activity must be performed in accordance with the instructions received from the principal.

• Separate accounting records must be kept for each principal represented

• Any claims relating to defects or flaws in the quality or quantity of the products sold and services provided must be received on behalf of the principal.

Unless otherwise stipulated, the agent may engage in the agency activity on behalf of several principals. The following rules apply:

• The agent must obtain the consent of the principal employer in order to represent another company whose activity is related to products or services that are similar to or compete with those of that principal.

• An agent wishing to act through subagents must obtain authorisation from the principal.

• The agent's remuneration may consist of a fixed sum, a commission or a combination of the two. In practice, agents are usually paid by a commission based on the volume of sales promoted and, if applicable, completed by the agent.

The Spanish Agency Agreement Act grants a certain degree of protection to the agent, relating specifically to compensation that must be paid by the principal in the event that the agreement is terminated. Two types of special compensation are envisaged for the agent, one relating to customers and the other for damages:

• An agent that has secured new customers for the principal or considerably increased operations with existing customers will be entitled to customer-related compensation, provided that the activities performed are likely to continue bringing substantial benefits for the principal and the relevant no-competition agreements have been concluded. This compensation will not be payable, however, if the agency agreement is terminated due to the agent's failure to fulfil its legal or contractual obligations, or where it is terminated at the request of the agent, unless this is due to any breach of the contract by the principal.

• Additionally, in the event that the contract is terminated by the principal, the agent will be entitled to compensation for any damage caused by early termination.

Commission agreement
As indicated with respect to the agency agreement, a commission agent engages in business activities on behalf of the principal, although a com-

mission agent usually acts by concluding contracts in its own name. In practice, a commission agreement is conceived as an instrument to be used in one-off situations in order to effect a specific transaction, while the agency agreement usually regulates a more stable and lasting relationship whereby the principal effects transactions through an agent in a specific zone and on a regular basis.

As with the commercial agent, the commission agent must perform its activity in accordance with the instructions of the principal. If the commission agent acts in its own name it becomes directly liable as if it were the agent's own business *vis-à-vis* the parties with which contracts are concluded. The parties then may not bring action against the principal, nor the principal against the parties, any actions between the principal and the commission agent notwithstanding. While acting in its own name, the commission agent is not obliged to reveal to customers the identity of the principal. If the commission agent concludes contracts on behalf of the principal, however, the identity of the principal must be revealed, in which case the contract and related actions will have effect between the principal and the customers in question.

The principal's main obligation is to pay the agreed remuneration to the commission agent. The commission is generally a percentage of the value of the transaction.

Distributors

In certain cases, direct distribution by the manufacturer may imply high fixed costs which must be offset by large volumes of sales or high margins. Depending on various factors, some companies opt to use a distribution system based on distributors or franchise holders acting in their own name and at their own risk. Remuneration paid is the amount of the profit margin on sales made by them.

Under distribution agreements, the distributor purchases the products supplied by the manufacturer in order to resell them to consumers or to another distribution channel, in its own name, thus assuming any risk which could derive from the sale of the products. In such cases, and in accordance with competition law, the manufacturer is not always allowed to control the prices applied or the business activities performed by the distributors, although certain strategies may be adopted to control distribution.

Spanish legal doctrine usually refers to four main distribution systems:

- the extensive system whereby the number of distributors is not limited;

- the exclusive system in which the number of distributors is limited based on territorial criteria;

- the selective system where the number of distributors in limited based on criteria other than territorial considerations; and

- the franchise system.

It should be noted that in practice the agreements on which the distribution systems are based often contain clauses which could, in principle, be deemed to restrict competition. Consequently, when these agreements are drawn up it is advisable to determine whether they qualify for an existing Exemption by Category Regulation (*Reglamento de Exención por Categoría*) or, failing this, for any specific exemption or authorisation, in which case the Spanish competition authorities must be notified.

Exclusive distribution system
At present, under Community Law, the exclusive and selective distributional systems, and franchise agreements are basically governed by Regulation No. 2799/1999 of the European Commission. The Regulation comprises all kinds of vertical agreements, where the companies involved are on different levels in their production processes.

Other distribution systems

Spanish law provides for other systems for selling products, the most significant of which are distance selling and automatic selling. Both systems require prior official authorisation from the regional or central government, depending on the territorial scope of the activity, as well as entry in a Register.

Distance selling
Distance sales are sales made without the presence of the seller in the same physical location as the purchaser. The sale proposal is transmitted by the seller and accepted by the purchaser through any kind of distance communication media. The regulations governing sales of this kind are strongly influenced by the principles of consumer protection. Consequently, products may not be sent to consumers without their specific prior acceptance of the sale proposal, which must necessarily contain certain information, such as the identity of the supplier, price, method of payment, etc. The purchaser must be free to return the product within seven days of receipt. In the case of orders placed by telephone or electronically, in addition to the above-mentioned requirements the purchaser must receive written evidence stating the terms of the transaction effected.

Automatic selling
Automatic selling is a retail distribution system whereby the consumer may purchase the product or service in question by paying the price and activating some kind of mechanism. Spanish law requires that all vending machines must display a number of notices, such as the type of coins accepted, instructions for use, identity of the supplier or the address and telephone number for claims. When the machines are installed in premises occupied by a private company or activity the owners of this company are jointly and severally liable with the owner of the machine with respect to the purchaser for compliance with the obligations deriving from automatic selling.

4.5

Competition Law

Miriam Ruiz de la Prada and Eduardo V Tejero, Landwell Abogados y Asesores Fiscales – A Correspondent Law Firm of PricewaterhouseCoopers

Spanish competition legislation comprises mainly the following two laws, the Competition Act (*Ley de Defensa de la Competencia*) of 17 July 1989 and the Unfair Competition Act (*Ley de Competencia Desleal*) of 10 January 1991.

The Competition Act of 17 July 1989 is mainly drawn from European Union (EU) Treaty provisions concerning competition. This Act aims to protect the domestic market, assuring effective competition in it and protecting the Spanish market against any conduct that is contrary to the public interest. The main objectives of the Act can be analysed as follows:

- To avoid agreements, concerted practices or associations' decisions among companies that impede, restrict or distort competition in national territory.

- To avoid the abusive exploitation of dominant market positions.

- To oversee business combinations.

The Unfair Competition Act of 10 January 1991 seeks to safeguard competition in the interest of all market participants, and to this end prohibits unfair acts of competition. The Act includes a classification of 'disloyal acts', preceded by a general stipulation whereby any behaviour which is objectively contrary to the requirements of good faith is deemed to be unfair.

The Competition Act

Institutions

In Spain there are two administrative bodies, the Competition Defence Service (*Servicio de Defensa de la Competencia*) and the Competition

Defence Court (*Tribunal de Defensa de la Competencia*) that are responsible for monitoring compliance with Spanish competition legislation.

In general, the Competition Defence Service takes charge of instigating cases resulting from the application of the Competition Act, and oversees the enforcement and fulfilment of the rulings issued by the Competition Defence Court. This court is responsible for ruling on and, if appropriate, making proposals with respect to the cases instigated by the Service, in addition to its powers to impose penalties as provided in the Competition Act. The rulings of the Competition Defence Court are subject to the jurisdictional control of the courts.

Restrictive covenants

The Competition Act provides for a flexible system for controlling covenants*, whether horizontal (where the companies involved are on the same level in their production processes) or vertical (where the companies involved are on different levels in their production processes), which may, will, or are intended to have the effect of impeding, restricting or falsifying competition in the Spanish market. The Act gives a list, for illustrative purposes, of conducts that could be regarded as restrictive. These are very similar to those set out in the European Union Treaty. This means that other practices not expressly mentioned in the Act may also be classed as prohibited practices if they are deemed contrary to free competition.

For instance, the restrictive practices mentioned by the Act include fixing prices or other business conditions, limiting and controlling production, entering into agreements on sharing out markets and the subordination of the conclusion of contracts to the acceptance of supplementary services.

As a penalty, the Act provides that any conduct that is prohibited and is not covered by an individual or general exemption may be deemed null and void. In other words, the system adopted in Spain is very similar to that envisaged in EU legislation, in the sense that the prohibited practices may be permitted if the sectors concerned are exempted under legal regulations or if they qualify for authorisations, either individually or by applying an Exempt Category Regulation.

Conduct that, in principle, could be regarded as restrictive can be authorised by the Competition Defence Court if such conduct can contribute to improving the production or sale of goods and services, or encourage technological or economic progress. This is provided that, in addition, consumers benefit from its advantages, no restrictions are

---

* Covenants should be understood to include any collective decision or recommendation and any concerted or deliberately parallel practice.

placed on the companies involved except those that are essential, and that it does not cause the elimination of competition with respect to the products and services involved. Authorisation may also be obtained for practices, among others, which, provided that they are justifiable in view of the general economic situation and on the grounds of public interest, aim to balance supply and demand or produce relevant increase of the economic or social levels of depressed areas or sectors, or do not constitute a threat to free competition due to their limited relevance.

Abusive exploitation of a dominant position

Spanish law prohibits the abusive exploitation of a dominant position held by a business in all or part of the Spanish market. It should be noted that, as with EU law, a company's enjoyment of a strong position in a market is not banned in itself; what the law prohibits is the abusive exploitation of such a position. Examples of abusive practice include:

- imposing unfair prices or other business conditions;

- the unjustified refusal to meet product purchase orders;

- the application of unequal conditions for equivalent goods or services which places certain competitors at a disadvantage compared with others;

- the subordination of the conclusion of a contract to the acceptance of supplementary services which are not related to the object of the contract, predatory pricing, etc.

Considering that the spirit of Spanish law is to prevent any market operator with a dominant position from engaging in behaviour which, in the absence of holding a dominant position, would in principle be legitimate, it is important to analyse whether the company in question enjoys a dominant position before studying the events that could constitute abusive behaviour.

According to the doctrine of the Competition Defence Court, determining the existence of a dominant position requires a structural analysis of the market concerned, which in general means that it is necessary to first define the market concerned from both a geographical and a product viewpoint, and to determine:

- the market share of both the company concerned and its competitors;

- the company's behaviour and that of its subsidiaries;

- the degree to which the companies are dependent on the company in a dominant position;

- how long the market share has been held, and barriers to entry into the market concerned.

Penalties

Penalties for failure to comply with competition laws may consist of fines of up to Ptas150 million (€901,518.16), which may be increased by 10 per cent of the company's turnover for the financial year immediately preceding the year in which the penalty is imposed. When the offenders are legal entities, in addition to the penalties imposed on them, their legal representatives may be fined up to Ptas5 million (€30,050.61).

Apart from pecuniary penalties, the law provides for the nullification of any agreements, decisions or recommendations which are prohibited by the Competition Act and are not covered by an individual authorisation or by an Exempt Category Regulation.

Control over business combinations

Control over business combination operations is governed by the Competition Act and its enabling regulations.

Definition
Spanish law defines business combinations as those operations which entail a lasting change in the control structure of the entities involved, by means of:

- the merger of two or more previously independent companies;

- the take-over of all or part of a company or companies by any means or transaction;

- the creation of a common company and, in general, the obtention of joint control over a company when it engages on a permanent basis the functions of an economically independent entity and is not fundamentally designed to, or does not have the fundamental effect of, co-ordinating the competitive behaviour of companies that remain independent.

The Spanish legislator has chosen to establish a mandatory notification system, as is laid down in the EU regulations. Therefore, any business combination project or operation must be notified to the Competition Service. Business Combination include:

- as a result of the operation, a share acquired or increased equal to or higher than 25 per cent of the domestic market or of a defined geographical market therein, for a certain product or service; or,

- the overall volume of sales in Spain of the parties involved as a whole exceeds, in the last accounting period, Ptas40,000 million (€240,404,841.75), provided that the sales volume in Spain of at least two of the companies involved exceeds, individually, the sum of Ptas10,000 million (€66,101,210.44).

The above notification requirement does not affect combination operations which come under the scope of application of EEC Council Regulation 4064/89, amended by EEC Regulation 1310/97.

Procedure
The notification of the business combination operation must be submitted to the Competition Defence Service before performing the operation. The fact that the notification has been submitted will be made public.

Before submitting the notification, a request for a ruling may be submitted to the Competition Defence Service concerning whether a specific operation exceeds the minimum thresholds for notification.

Once the notification has been presented, the Ministry of Economy and Finance, at the proposal of the Competition Defence Service, passes on to the Competition Defence Court the files on any notified projects which, in its opinion, could hamper effective competition in the market. The Competition Defence Court, after hearing the interested parties, if appropriate, issues its decision within two months. It is understood that the administration does not oppose the operation if the notification is not passed on to the Court within one month of its being submitted to the Competition Defence Service. The Competition Defence Service will notify the interested parties of the date on which the proceedings are remitted to the Competition Defence Court.

In the event that a business combination project or operation which exceeds the minimum thresholds established is not reported, and the Service becomes aware of that project or operation, the Service, ex officio, may require the parties concerned to present the notification within twenty days as from the receipt of the requirement. If said period elapses without the notification having been presented, penalties may be imposed. Operations which are notified at the Service's requirement do not qualify for tacit authorisation.

Completion of the procedure
The decision issued by the Competition Defence Court is passed on to the Ministry of Economy and Finance and by this Ministry to the government, which within one month may decide:

● not to oppose the operation;

● to make approval subject to compliance with conditions that make a sufficient contribution to economic and social progress to compensate for the restrictive repercussions on competition;

● to disallow the operation, in which case the government is entitled to order that the transaction is stopped, if it has not commenced, or order appropriate measures to be implemented to establish effective competition, including demerger.

If the one month period elapses as from the date on which the Court's decision is received, or as from the date on which the period prescribed for the Court to issue its decision terminates, without the Cabinet having taken a decision, the operation is understood to be tacitly authorised.

When a business combination operation which does not entail the creation or strengthening of a dominant position gives rise to obstacles to competition that may be remedied easily. The Ministry of Economy and Finance, after first receiving a report from the Competition Defence Service, may request the parties to present compromise solutions or changes to the operation that do not qualify for tacit authorisation. The parties must reply within one month of receiving such a requirement, for the purpose, as appropriate, of reaching a conventional conclusion to the proceedings.

On the basis of the compromises achieved, the Ministry of Economics and Finance may:

- authorise the operation, if the compromises are deemed sufficient; or

- pass on the case to the Competition Defence Court.

Penalties
Failure to comply with the notification obligation will be penalised by the Director of the Competition Defence Service with a fine of up to Ptas5 million (€30,050.61). Notwithstanding, the Director of the Service will impose a fine of up to Ptas2 million (€12,020.24) per day's delay in making the notification when it has been required by the Service.

In the event of failure to comply with its instructions, the Cabinet may impose a fine of up to 10 per cent of turnover in Spain in the year in which the combination operation took place on each of the companies involved, without prejudice to the application of the execution measures envisaged in Spanish legislation

Unfair Competition Act

The Unfair Competition Act of 10 January 1991 aims to safeguard competition in the interest of all market players, and to safeguard the correct functioning of the competitive system, avoiding distortions caused by inappropriate practices.

Spanish law classifies the main cases of unfair competition that usually arise in practice. However, through a general provision, it prohibits all behaviour that is objectively contrary to the requirements of good faith. What the Act seeks with the inclusion of this general provision is to prevent protection against unfair competition becoming obsolete due to the continuous development of new business practices.

The acts of unfair competition expressly provided for in the Act may be classified on the basis of the following categories:

● The first category comprises all those acts or practices that consist of taking advantage of the efforts of other market players. This includes acts designed to mislead the service providers or clientele of a competitor; acts of exploitation of another's reputation, by giving the misleading impression that there is an association with these; acts of comparison, when comparative advertising is undertaken with the principal aim of benefiting from another's prestige; acts of imitation, when others' business practices or initiatives are imitated; acts of violation of secrets, when industrial secrets are stolen and exploited.

● A second category comprises those acts or practices that constitute direct attacks on other companies in the market. For instance, acts aimed at denigrating companies or products; acts aimed at encouraging another company's workers, suppliers or customers to commit breaches of contract; selling at a loss when this is part of a strategy designed to eliminate a competitor or group of competitors from the market; or discrediting the image of another business or its products.

● The third and last category comprises acts or practices that directly affect the scope of action of market players, impeding the smooth functioning of the market. For instance, acts of misleading offers, offering premiums that prevent or hamper the making of comparisons between prices of products or services; breaches of laws that place a competitor in a situation that is unjustly advantageous *vis-à-vis* its competitors.

Actions deriving from acts of unfair competition come under the jurisdiction of the ordinary civil courts, which will declare the act to be unfair and which may order the defendant to pay damages.

4.6

Industrial and Intellectual Property

Eduardo V Tejero and Miriam Ruiz de la Prada, Landwell Abogados y Asesores Fiscales – A Correspondent Law Firm of PricewaterhouseCoopers

Spanish legislation governing special forms of property involving intellectual activity draws a conceptual distinction between two main categories, according to the subject matter of the right to be protected. For this reason industrial property and intellectual property rights are regulated separately.

The purpose of industrial property law is to protect the inventions and distinctive signs of an enterprise or its products, whereas the purpose of intellectual property law is to protect original literary, artistic or scientific creations expressed in any form or medium.

Industrial property

The Spanish legislative provisions governing industrial property are essentially contained in the Patents Act 1986, which is modelled on the Munich Convention of 5 October 1973, and the Luxembourg Convention of 15 December 1975; and in the Trademarks Act 1988, which also embodies the principles underlying European trademark law. It should also be borne in mind that Spain has adhered to most current international treaties on industrial property. Both these treaties and European Community legislation must be specifically taken into account when considering industrial property rights in Spain.

Patents

Under Spanish law new inventions can be patented if they involve an inventive element and are capable of industrial application.

Patentable inventions
An invention must meet the following essential requirements in order to be patentable:

● **Novelty:** An invention is considered new when it does not form part of the state of the art; in other words, prior to the date of submission of the application, it was not accessible to the public through any means.

● **Inventive element:** It must not be obvious from the state of the art to an expert on the subject.

● **Industrial application:** The invention must be capable of industrial application; in other words, its subject matter may be manufactured or used in any kind of industry, including agriculture.

Even if they meet the patentability requirements, the following may not be patented:

● Inventions the exploitation or publication of which are contrary to public policy or to generally accepted principles of morality.

● Varieties of plants, breeds of animals and essentially biological procedures to obtain plants or animals, as well as methods for the treatment or diagnosis of the human or animal body.

● Discoveries, scientific theories and mathematical methods.

● Literary or artistic works or any other aesthetic creation, as well as scientific works.

● Plans, rules and methods for the performance of intellectual activities, for games or for financial and commercial activities, and computer programs.

● Forms of presenting information.

Holder of the patent
The patent, which may be freely transferred, belongs to the inventor or his assignees. If the invention was made by several persons together, the right to the patent is held jointly by all of them. If the invention was made by several persons independently, the right will be held by the person who first submits an application.

Inventions made by a worker while his employment contract is in force, and which are the result of research within the scope of his contract, belong to the employer. In such cases, the worker will be entitled to additional remuneration only where his personal contribution to the invention and the importance of such a contribution to the employer clearly falls outside the scope of his contract. The case of inventions made by a worker who was neither expressly nor tacitly engaged to carry out research in the field of the invention is different. If those inventions have been made with the assistance of the knowledge or resources acquired within the company that employs him, the latter may choose to claim ownership of the invention or reserve the right to use it, in both of which cases it must compensate the worker financially. All inventions of workers made in circumstances other than those mentioned above will belong to the worker. Any waiver in advance by a worker of the rights conferred on him in this respect by the Act is void.

Procedure for obtaining the patent
The process of registration of a patent in the Industrial Property Registry can be pursued by the applicant himself or can be handled by Industrial Property Agents (professionals duly authorised by the relevant authorities). Where the applicant is a foreigner not resident in the European Union he must act through such professionals.

In order to obtain a patent an application must be submitted containing certain information, most notably a full and clear description of the invention for which the patent is being requested, as well as the claims defining the subject matter for which protection is sought. The application will be followed by a preliminary analysis which, apart from considering whether it meets the formal requirements, must ascertain whether the application for the patent meets the patentability requirements. A report on the state of the art will also be required. Once the application has been examined, and if the result is favourable, a series of notices will be published in the *Official Industrial Property Gazette* for the purpose of safeguarding the rights of third parties to challenge the registration sought. Finally, the Registry will grant the patent applied for by publishing a notice to this effect in the *Gazette*.

Effects of the patent
Once the patent has been granted, the holder enjoys the exclusive right to use it for a twenty-year period, at the end of which it belongs to the public domain. The holder of the patent is required to use the invention patented, either personally or through a person authorised by him, either by producing the invention in Spain or in the territory of a member of the World Trade Organisation, so that such use is sufficient to meet demand in the domestic market. The use must occur within four years from the date of submission of the application for the patent, or three years from the date of publication of the grant of the patent in the *Official Industrial Property Gazette*.

The rights derived from the patent may be transferred by any means permitted by law. Patents may also be encumbered in certain ways. Spanish legislation regulates the grant of licences to use patents, which may be voluntary or obligatory. The former normally arises from a licence agreement, while the latter may be granted by the Industrial Property Registry in certain circumstances, such as the failure to use or inadequate use of the invention, interdependence of patents or the existence of public policy factors. The transfer, or any action relating to the patent, will only bind third parties from the registration of such transfer or action in the Spanish Patents and Trademarks Office.

The holder of the patent is entitled to file a number of legal actions against those injuring his rights. The most notable of the measures of redress that may be ordered by the courts are the suspension of acts that prejudice the patentee's rights; the seizure and vesting in the latter of ownership of items produced in violation of these rights and of the resources used exclusively for this purpose; orders for damages; and publication of the judgment at the defendant's expense. Together with these civil measures, Spanish law provides additional protection by considering the infringement of rights of use to constitute a criminal offence.

Additions to the patent
The holders of a patent may obtain additions to their patent in order to protect inventions that improve or develop the invention forming the subject matter of the main patent. Basically, the same requirements are demanded in the case of an application for an addition as those that apply to a patent application. The addition will have the same duration as the main patent upon which it depends. It may become an independent patent when its holder waives the main patent.

Utility models
The utility model protects inventions that confer upon an object a configuration, structure or constitution that benefits the use or manufacture of the object in question in a manner that can be appreciated in practical terms. The state of the art to be taken into account when examining the novelty and inventive element of utility models is the entire body of knowledge available in Spain prior to the date of submission of the application for protection as a model. The degree of inventive skill required is less than in the case of a patent. Reports on the state of the art or in-depth examinations of the patentability requirements are not needed for the granting of utility models. The model confers on its holder the same rights as a patent but only for a ten-year period. Additions are not admitted.

Distinctive business signs

Under Spanish legislation, trademark law refers generically to distinctive signs used by an enterprise to distinguish its activities, establishments, goods and/or services. Even though the Act that regulates this subject is called the Trademarks Act (perhaps this title was adopted as the trademark is the distinctive sign par excellence), it also regulates trade names and business house signs.

Trademarks
Under Spanish legislation, trademark means any sign or medium that distinguishes or serves to distinguish, within the marketplace, the goods or services of one person from identical or similar goods or services of another.

Selection of the trademark
The Trademarks Act lists, without restriction, the signs or media that may constitute a trademark. They are as follows:

- words;

- images, shapes, symbols and graphic representations;

- letters, numerals and combinations of both;

- three-dimensional forms, including wrappers, containers and the shape of goods or of their packaging;

- any combination of the above signs or media.

The Act also contains a series of signs or media that may not be registered as trademarks, establishing for this purpose certain absolute and other relative prohibitions.

- **Absolute prohibitions.** These include: generic signs or media; those that have become usual or customary in current language or practice; those that are contrary to public policy or accepted principles of morality; those that may deceive; colour, if it is not defined by a certainty shape; and imitations of official symbols, unless authorised, in which case they must form an accessory element of the main symbol.

- **Relative prohibitions.** These are prohibitions for the registration of which the prior authorisation of the person affected is required and, if necessary, the adoption of measures to avoid the risk of confusion. Among these are:
  - signs or media that, due to their phonetic, graphic or conceptual identity or similarity may lead to confusion with another trademark or trade name;
  - those that are identical to a business house sign applied for or registered relating to the same activities;
  - the forename, surnames, pseudonym or image that identifies a person other than the applicant for the trademark, or which the general public identifies with a person other than the applicant;
  - signs or media that imitate creations protected by intellectual or industrial property.

The representative in Spain of a third party who is the holder of a trademark in another country of the Paris Union may not register this trademark in his name without the latter's consent.

Registration of trademarks

The trademark right is granted by registration of the trademark in the Spanish Patents and Trademarks Office. In order to have the trademark registered an application must be submitted containing, *inter alia*, a description of the trademark; a receipt for payment of the relevant fee; a list of the goods or services to which the trademark applies, indicating the international nomenclature to which they belong; and, where foreign priority is claimed, a declaration to this effect, stating the date of priority and the country in which the right was acquired. If an Industrial Property Agent is involved, his name and address must be stated.

The application for registration may not cover more than a single class of goods or services from the international nomenclature. If the holder wishes to extend the goods or services protected by the trademark to some others included in the same class of the nomenclature, a new application must be submitted.

A trademark which, without having been the subject of an application, has been used in an official exhibition will enjoy the right of priority from the date of admission of the goods or services in the exhibition, provided that the application for registration is submitted within six months.

When the Spanish Patents and Trademarks Office has checked the correctness of the application, a notice will be published in the *Official Industrial Property Gazette* in which the following must be stated:

• name and address of the holder or holders;

• date of application and, where relevant, of priority;

• reproduction of the sign or medium;

• list of goods or services, indicating the international nomenclature.

Any interested party who considers that his interests are prejudiced may challenge the registration of the trademark within two months from the date of publication. When this period has expired, irrespective of whether or not the registration has been challenged, the Registry will, without being requested to do so, examine the application so as to verify that it meets the requirements established by law. In the event of any objection, the applicant may submit allegations and/or modify the trademark. The grant or refusal of the registration will be published in the *Official Industrial Property Gazette*.

The registration of the trademark is granted for ten years and may be renewed indefinitely for like periods, provided that it has been used. If, within ten years from the date of publication of the grant of the trademark, it has not been put to genuine and real use in Spain, or if such use has been suspended for an uninterrupted period of five years, the trademark will expire, unless there are good grounds for the failure to use it.

Rights conferred by the trademark

The registration of the trademark confers on the holder the exclusive right to use it in the course of trade. According to the provisions of the Trademarks Act, both the trademark and the application for registration of the trademark may be assigned by any means permitted by law. Furthermore, a trademark may be licensed for some or all of the goods or services for which it is registered and for the whole or part of Spanish territory. Licences may be exclusive or non-exclusive.

In order for an assignment or license of a trademark to be binding on third parties it must be documented in a deed and registered in the Spanish Patents and Trademarks Office. A trademark may be provided as security or be otherwise encumbered, but this must also be entered in the Spanish Patents and Trademarks Office if it is to be binding on third parties.

Trade name

The trade name is defined as the sign or name that serves to identify a natural or legal person in the performance of his/its business activity and to distinguish his/its activity from identical or similar activities. Among others, the following may constitute trade names: patronymics and the corporate name of legal persons, fanciful names, anagrams and names referring to the subject-matter of the business activity.

The registration of a trade name is optional and confers on the holder the exclusive right to use it in the course of trade. If the holder wishes to use the trade name as a trademark of goods or services, such trademark must be registered separately. The trade name may only be transferred with the business as a whole.

Business house sign

A business house or establishment sign is a sign or name that serves to make known a commercial establishment to the public and to distinguish it from others engaged in the same or similar activities.

Patronymics, corporate and fanciful names, names referring to the activity of the establishment and anagrams may, *inter alia*, constitute a business sign. A business house sign may not be registered if it is not sufficiently distinguishable from a trademark or trade name, or from another establishment sign registered for the same municipality.

Business signs are registered for the specific municipality or municipalities in which the main establishment and its branches, if any, are located. Not more than one establishment sign may be registered for any one retail establishment, and such sign may be used for the main establishment and the branches located in the municipality for which the sign has been registered.

Intellectual property

The Spanish legislative provisions that essentially regulate intellectual property are contained in the Royal Legislative Decree of 12 April 1996, approving the consolidated Intellectual Property Act, which reflects the main principles established by Directive 93/98/EC on the protection of copyright, and in the Act of 6 March 1998, which is incorporated into Spanish law Directive 96/9/EC on the legal protection of databases.

Subject matter

The concept of intellectual property under Spanish legislation comprises all original literary, artistic or scientific creations expressed in any form or medium, whether tangible or intangible, including, *inter alia*, the following works: books, pamphlets, lectures, musical compositions, audiovisual works, theatrical works, paintings, sculptures and computer programs.

In order for a work to constitute intellectual property, and as such to enjoy the legal protection established by the legislation on the subject, the following essential requirements must be met:

- **Creation.** The term creation refers to human intervention. In other words there must be a desire to create.

- **Originality.** The creation must be original, which means that the work created must differ in some respect from existing works. It is precisely the element of originality that confers on the author a property right to his creation.

- It must be a literary, artistic or scientific work.

- It must be expressed in any form or medium, whether tangible or intangible. It should be borne in mind that the legislation does not necessarily require a physical medium, although the latter is really the surest way of protecting the work.

In addition to the above-mentioned works, it should also be noted that intellectual property rights may also protect collections of works of others, of data or of other independent works, such as anthologies and databases, which due to the selection or arrangement of their contents constitute intellectual creations, without prejudice to any rights subsisting in those contents themselves. The protection conferred by the Act on the above-mentioned collections relates only to the structure as the form of expression of the selection and arrangement of their contents, but does not extend to such contents.

Authorship

The Act considers the natural person who creates a certain literary, artistic or scientific work to be the author. However, in certain cases expressly envisaged in the Act, legal persons may benefit from the protection conferred upon the author by the Act.

The Act establishes a presumption, in the absence of proof to the contrary, that the author is the person who appears as such on the work, in the form of his name, signature or other sign identifying him. Where a work (joint works) is the unitary result of the joint efforts of various authors, the intellectual property rights to that work will be held by all of them. The consent of all the co-authors will be required in order to circulate or alter the work. However, subject to what is agreed by the co-authors of the work, they may separately exploit their contributions where they are distinguishable and separable, unless they prejudice the joint exploitation of the work.

By way of exception to the general principle regarding authorship, in the case of collective works, unless agreed otherwise, the Act attributes the original ownership to the person who publishes and circulates the work under his name. A collective work means that it has been created at the initiative and under the co-ordination of a natural or legal person who publishes and circulates the work under his/its name. The work consists of a collection of contributions of different authors whose personal input is merged in a single independent creation, for which it was formed, so that no right to the work as a whole can be separately conferred on any of them.

Content

Intellectual property consists of a series of rights and powers that may be classified as follows.

- **Moral rights:** These are the strictly personal rights of the author that may not be waived or alienated. Among these are the following:

  - To decide whether the work is to be circulated and in what form.
  - To decide whether it is to be circulated under his name, a pseudonym or anonymously.
  - To demand that the integrity of the work is respected.
  - To withdraw the work from circulation, subject to payment of compensation to the holders of the rights of exploitation.

- **Rights of exploitation:** These are rights having a pecuniary value which confer the exclusive power to exploit the work and to prevent all others from doing so. In particular, the rights to reproduce, distribute, publicly transmit and transform the work constitute rights of exploitation. In general terms, these rights exist throughout the author's entire lifetime and for seventy years following his death or declaration of death; they may be transferred both *mortis causa* and *inter vivos*. In the case of computer programs, if the author is a legal person, the rights of exploitation are enjoyed for seventy years from the circulation of the program or from its creation, if it has not been circulated. *Inter vivos* assignments are limited to the right or rights assigned, to the forms of exploitation expressly stipulated and to the period and geographical area expressly established by the parties.

Where a work is created in the course of an employment relationship, the assignment to the employer of the rights of exploitation will be governed by the provisions of the contract, which must be entered into in writing. In the absence of a written agreement, the rights of exploitation will be presumed to have been assigned exclusively and to the extent necessary for the performance of the employer's habitual business activity at the time of the delivery of the work created, pursuant to such employment relationship.

Other rights, also having a pecuniary value, are also enjoyed, such as the right to a share and to remuneration per private copy, which constitute payments to the author for certain activities performed relating to the protected works.

Protection of intellectual property rights

The holder of intellectual property rights protected by the Act may institute both civil or, if necessary, criminal proceedings against anyone who violates them. The holder may seek a suspension of the offender's unlawful activity and the adoption of pre-emptive measures and demand, if necessary, compensation for damage to reputation and material loss caused.

Intellectual Property Registry

While registration of intellectual property rights is optional, the Act permits the registration of such rights in a public registry, it being presumed, in the absence of proof to the contrary, that the rights registered exist and belong to the holder in the manner established in the registry.

4.7

Duties and Responsibilities of Company Directors

Antonio J Padró and Eduardo V Tejero,
Landwell Abogados y Asesores Fiscales – A
Correspondent Law Firm of
PricewaterhouseCoopers

Introduction

In a business context, when reference is made to the management or senior managers of a company, this is broadly taken to mean the following persons:

- persons making up the company's administrative body;

- directors who fulfil duties that form part of the organisational nucleus of the company, with powers pertaining to the legal ownership of the company;

- the remaining senior personnel who hold positions of responsibility but who are not involved in the company's overall management.

Except in certain cases and in specific sectors (finance, tourism, etc), Spanish legislation does not contain a general body of regulations governing the rights and obligations of company directors (with the exception of employment law rules governing senior managers), and focuses only on regulating the duties and legal obligations of the members of corporate governing bodies, who, in a strictly legal sense, are considered to be responsible for managing the company's affairs.

It should therefore be noted that the rules governing directors' rights and liabilities do not apply to any persons that hold managerial posts or representative authority to act on the company's behalf, but who do not form part of the governing body.

Under Spanish legislation, the directors (*administradores*) are deemed to be those persons (natural or legal) who form part of a company's governing body. They represent the company in and out of court and their representative authority covers all actions included in its corporate objects.

A company's governing body will usually take one of the following forms (these are the only ones expressly contemplated for public limited companies (*sociedad anónima*) and private limited companies (*sociedad de responsabilidad limitada*):

- **Sole administrator:** a single individual who represents the company alone, with all the necessary powers.

- **Severally liable administrators:** each of whom is able to represent the company individually.

- **Jointly liable administrators:** in which case the power to represent the company is exercised jointly.

- **Board of directors:** which must act collectively. The board of directors may not have less than three members.

According to the legal regulations applicable to each type of company, the directors are obliged to perform a number of actions relating to the company's management, such as:

- convening general shareholders' meetings in accordance with the requirements of applicable legislation and the articles of association;

- certifying corporate minutes and resolutions;

- discharging their duties with the diligence of an orderly businessman and a loyal representative, and keeping confidential information secret;

- certain formal acts relating to shares (issue of shares, keeping the register of shareholders, etc);

- drawing up the annual accounts and directors' report.

Directors are subject to regulations governing conflicts of interest. According to these regulations the office of director may not be held by a person in certain *de facto* situations such as when working directly or indirectly in a similar or analogous activity. Similarly, directorships may not be held by persons in certain *de jure* situations (minors, legally disqualified persons, bankrupt or insolvent persons barred from doing business, etc). In addition, certain contracts between directors and the company may be subject to the prior approval of the general meeting.

Right to represent the company

The right of directors to represent the company depends on the legal form of the company.

General partnerships and ordinary limited partnerships

The common feature of both these types of organisation is that they are partnerships and therefore based on the mutual trust of the partners. In the absence of any specific agreement, the entity may be represented (ie the partnership's signature can be used) by all the partners (except industrial or limited partners). This means that resolutions must be adopted unanimously by partners attending meetings, a majority vote being insufficient. Each partner may oppose other partners' transactions before these become legally effective. No obligations should be incurred against such opposition, but if one were incurred it would not be annulled and would remain effective, without prejudice to the partner(s) responsible for the obligation answering to the remaining partners for any harm caused.

• Another possibility is to expressly appoint one or more directors, to carry out management functions without interference from the other partners.

• With respect to acts committed by partners who are not duly authorised to represent the partnership, only those committing the acts are answerable for them. They do not obligate the partnership, even if performed on its behalf using the partnership signature.

• Concerning the scope of representation of a partnership's directors, they may validly conclude contracts relating to anything forming part of the partnership's business operations.

Limited partnerships with shares, public limited companies (sociedades anónimas) and private limited companies (sociedades de responsabilidad limitada)

With respect to internal liability in these capital-based companies, the directors' powers of representation cover all actions included in the corporate objects described in the articles of association.

With respect to third parties, the entity is obligated by the actions of its directors even when these actions are not expressly allowed by the company's articles of association, as registered with the Mercantile Registry. This holds true only provided that the third parties have acted in good faith and without serious fault. This would therefore not be the case if the third party had known that the director was acting outside of his competence or if the third party might have been able to obtain information to that effect by exercising a minimum degree of diligence.

Incompatibility and conflict of interest

Directors are subject to a strict regime of disqualification and incompatibility, under which the following are disqualified from holding the office of director:

- Minors or persons disqualified under a final court judgement.

- Bankrupt and insolvent persons who have not been discharged.

- Persons barred from holding public office under a court judgement, for the duration of the sentence.

- Persons convicted of serious breach of employment-related laws or regulations.

- Persons unable to engage in business by reason of their occupation (judges, public prosecutors, notaries, etc).

- Public servants performing functions that are related to the activities of the company concerned.

- Directors of a competitor company or persons having opposing interests of any kind.

- The company's auditors.

Agreements between a company and its directors

In general, there are no specific regulations governing agreements and contracts between a company and its directors. However, the Limited Liability Companies Act (*Ley de Sociedades de Responsabilidad Limitada*) does clearly establish the need for the prior consent of the general meeting in two cases:

- Granting of advances, credits, loans, guarantees or financial assistance by the company to its directors.

- Establishment or alteration of any kind of relations involving the supply of services or work between the company and its directors.

In addition, the Spanish Companies Act (*Ley de Sociedades Anónimas*), which is applicable in this respect to private limited companies (*sociedades de responsabilidad limitada*), stipulates that the amount of advances and loans granted to members of the governing body must figure in the notes to the annual accounts. This also applies to any obligations assumed on the behalf of directors in the forms of guarantees given by the company.

Competition

Spanish commercial legislation restricts directors from undertaking activities that are deemed to compete with those of the company. In relation to public limited companies (*sociedades anónimas*), the Spanish Companies Act provides that directors may be legitimately dismissed due to conflicting interests. In such cases, they may be dismissed at the request of any shareholder and by resolution of the general meeting.

More clearly, the Limited Liability Companies Act expressly prohibits directors from engaging, on their own or for a third party's account, in activities that are identical, analogous or complementary to the company's objects, unless expressly authorised to do so by the company, by resolution of the general meeting. Any shareholder may petition the courts for the dismissal of a director who has violated this prohibition.

Directors' liability

A company develops along the paths that are chosen by its directors, who are therefore ultimately responsible for its success or failure. In addition to this overall responsibility that is inherent to their office, the directors must also answer for any harmful acts that their decisions may provoke. Under Spanish law, the directors are answerable to the company, the shareholders and the company's creditors for any damage caused by actions that are contrary to law or to the articles of association, or actions performed without the diligence required by their office.

As well as the above, various special laws classify as punishable certain instances of conduct by directors that are harmful to certain protected institutions or areas (the environment, the Treasury, commerce, etc).

Civil liability

An important aspect of any analysis of directors' liability is the degree of diligence that may be required of directors in the discharge of their duties. This provides the basis for determining the extent of a director's guilt or liability in the event of his having damaged the company's or a third party's interests while managing the company's affairs.

As previously mentioned, Spanish company law states that the directors shall perform their duties with the diligence of a prudent businessman and loyal representative. They must keep all confidential information secret, even after retirement from office.

The purpose of the above provisions is to establish guidelines or general norms of conduct so that the level of diligence in the fulfilment of the directors' duties can be assessed in each particular case. This is done without laying down an excessively strict set of rules that could make these provisions inapplicable.

- The specific criterion of 'the diligence of a prudent businessman' comes within the scope of professionalism, ie a director is to apply the same levels of attention, prudence, devotion and professional competence as may be expected of a prudent businessman. However, this does not mean that any specific qualifications are required to hold the office of director.

- The question of loyalty relates to the director's status as representative of the governing body (ie representative of interests other than his own), which is embodied in a duty of fidelity *vis-à-vis* the company.

- Concerning the duty of confidentiality, the law goes beyond establishing an obligation of prudence and care when dealing with confidential information, and provides for a higher degree of strictness and commitment. The law is not very specific concerning the scope and extent of this confidentiality requirement, which must therefore be construed flexibly, and the directors themselves must decide in each case which persons are covered by the obligation not to disclose confidential information and what the consequences of such disclosure would be.

Liabilities related to main duties of a director

The provisions of Spanish corporate legislation governing directors' liability are essentially based on the principle of relating such liability to professional performance. Spanish law states that directors shall be answerable to their company, to the shareholders and to the company's creditors for any harm they may cause through actions that are contrary to law or to the articles of association, or that are carried out without the due diligence expected of them in the performance of their duties.

The breaches of law or the articles are actions that can be classified objectively without difficulty. The due diligence is that commonly expected of a prudent businessman and of a representative who takes charge of another's affairs with all due loyalty. In this connection, it may be said that the directors are liable for both the actions and the omissions that may be attributed to them in the performance of their duties, assuming that some kind of harm is caused thereby. In other words, the directors are answerable for their conduct only when such conduct is harmful. In relation to the scope of liability, all the members of the administrative body are jointly and severally liable for the damage caused in the above cases.

The liability arises from both the execution and the adoption of the relevant resolution, and both the resolution itself and the act of executing it are deemed to be injurious. For a director to free himself from such liability, it is not sufficient that he did not take part in the adoption or execution of the resolution. He must be unaware of the act or resolution or, if aware of it, must take all proper steps to prevent the harm being done, or at least specifically express his opposition to it. The fact that the resolution has been adopted, authorised or ratified by the general meeting, ie by a superior body, will not free the director from his liability.

It is evident that any party wishing to bring an action for liability against the directors must prove that their actions or failure to act are contrary to the law, the articles of association or the duty to perform their functions with due diligence. Once the administrative body's liability has been established, however, all its members are jointly and severally liable unless they can prove that they took no part in and were unaware of, or took action against, the act or resolution concerned.

Criminal liability

Director and 'de facto' director
Under Spanish criminal legislation, criminal liability is wholly personal and applicable only to natural persons. In respect of companies, therefore, criminal liability is attributed to the members of the administrative body. Since the committing of a criminal offence requires actively fraudulent conduct, however, criminal liability cannot be attributed to all directors due simply to their holding such office.

In the case of a board of directors, it may be understood that the criminal liability will not affect the directors who opposed the resolution which caused the crime, or the directors who did not attend the meeting at which said resolution was adopted. The active conduct requirement makes it possible to argue that when there is a managing director or various managing directors, criminal liability will not necessarily also apply to the other board members (without executive powers), since the committing of a crime by omission does not appear to be feasible in these cases.

The intention of the Penal Code is to attribute liability to the person that exercises the ultimate decision-making powers in a company, even setting aside whether the person concerned is a director *de jure* (ie a director appointed by the general meeting who has accepted the office). As a result, criminal liability may also affect the so-called directors *de facto*. Decisions as to whether there are *de facto* directors and their identity must be made on a case-by-case basis depending on the specific circumstances. For illustrative purposes, we cite the following cases in which a *de facto* director may exist.

- Persons who formally hold the office of director, but whose appointment may be void due to defects of form or substance (for example, general meeting incorrectly convened, appointment expired, conflict of interests, etc).

- Persons who, though not formally directors, in fact control and govern the company, directing and giving orders to the formal directors. This is the case of some general managers who, while theoretically subordinate to the board of directors, are in fact the persons who run the company's affairs, while the directors restrict themselves to formally approving the general manager's performance. It would also be the case of a parent company when the action is taken against a company whose directors had been obliged to act in accordance with parent company instructions, although in this instance the possibility of liability being shared between both sets of directors should not be ruled out.

Criminal liability of the directors

The Spanish Penal Code contains highly important developments and envisages a wide range of offences in which company directors may be held criminally liable.

Within the field of crimes relating to economic and financial matters, the following groups of offences should be noted:

- Crimes against consumers.

- Crimes against the Treasury and social security authority.

- Crimes against workers' rights.

- Crimes against the environment.

- Crimes against the public authorities.

- Criminal insolvency.

The most typical crimes that can be committed by company directors are the so-called 'corporate offences', which were introduced for the first time in the Spanish legal system under the 1995 Penal Code. As a result, conduct that previously gave rise only to civil liability may now entail criminal liability, which evidently tightens the regulations governing directors' liability and the 'criminal' aspects of corporate life in general.

The most important offences (some are subject to prison sentences of up to four years) are the following (Penal Code Articles 290 to 297):

- Falsification of the annual accounts or other documents that must reflect the juridic or financial situation of the company. The falsification must be sufficiently serious to be capable of causing financial harm to the company, a shareholder or a third party. A longer sentence is applied if financial harm is actually caused.

- Utilisation, for one's own or a third party's benefit, of a majority position in the general meeting or in the governing body to impose an abusive resolution which is prejudicial to the other shareholders, without the resolution being of any benefit to the company.

- Utilisation, for one's own or a third party's benefit, of a resolution adopted by a fictitious majority obtained through means such as the abuse of blank signatures, illicit denial of voting rights or unlawful attribution of voting rights.

- Refusal to allow a shareholder to exercise his rights to receive information and to take part in the management or control of the company's affairs, or his right to the preferential subscription of new share issues.

- Blocking or impeding the functioning of the governing bodies responsible for inspecting and supervising the company's performance in certain heavily regulated sectors, such as the securities market, the insurance and banking sectors, etc.

- Fraudulent disposal, for one's own or a third party's benefit, of the company's assets, which causes pecuniary damage to the shareholders or owners of the assets administered by the company.

Insurance

Under Spanish civil legislation, civil liability is regarded as the legal obligation of each individual to remedy any damage caused, which entails the obligation to pay compensation for the harm caused to the injured party.

Under Spanish law, this obligation to remedy such damage caused covers not only actions and omissions of the individual concerned but extends to 'owners or directors of an establishment or company in respect of damage caused by their employees or when carrying out their duties'. However, this liability will cease when these persons prove that they acted with all necessary diligence to prevent the harm being done.

Under a third party liability insurance policy, the insurer undertakes to cover the risk (up to a certain limit) that arises in relation to the insured entity's obligation to indemnify a third party for any damage caused by an event covered by the insurance contract, in accordance with the relevant legislation.

As concerns the personal elements of the relationship covered by the insurance policy, it may be said that the insured party is insured against third parties, which are understood to be the actual company that arranges the policy, its shareholders, creditors, employees and in general, other injured parties.

In keeping with the principle of joint and several liability laid down for a company's governing body, the third party liability insurance policy will be arranged for all the members of the board of directors and not for each director on an individual basis. The benefits or scope of the policy coverage will normally be:

- payment of indemnities (up to certain limits);
- arrangement of bail or bond (in civil or penal cases);
- court costs and legal expenses.

However, certain cases such as those involving negligent actions or omissions performed by directors, fines or penalties, damage to the environment etc, are excluded from the liability cover and must be covered by a specific insurance policy.

4.8

Employment Law

Pilar Sierra and Eduardo V Tejero, Landwell Abogados y Asesores Fiscales – A Correspondent Law Firm of PricewaterhouseCoopers

In Spain there are many different types of labour regulations that are being changed periodically. It is important to bear in mind that Spanish employment regulations govern the *in dubio pro operario* principle whereby, in the event of dispute, the interpretation most favourable to the employee must be adopted. The main regulations are set out below.

Sources of labour law

The Labour Statute

The Labour Statute of 1980 has, since that date, undergone a number of changes aimed mainly at job creation. These changes have entailed the deregulation of the labour market by deregulating employment regulations and increasing the importance of employers and trade unions. These actors now have increased possibilities of regulating issues that relate to employer-employee relations under the applicable collective agreements that were previously regulated solely by the law.

The Labour Statute defines the respective rights of employees and employers, general terms of labour contracts, procedures for dismissal and collective bargaining rules.

Collective agreements

Collective agreements regulate the conditions contained in the Labour Statute in greater detail, and it is not uncommon for them to contain more favourable conditions than the Labour Statute. The agreements, which may be negotiated at industry, regional or company level, are concluded between an employer, a group of employers or employers' associations and one or several trade unions or, in the absence thereof, workers' representatives.

Specific regulations

There are specific regulations for different production sectors and certain groups of employed persons, such as commercial representatives and top management personnel. The employment and Social Security regulations for public servants are governed by special regulations determined by administrative law.

Labour authorities

Among others, the following bodies are responsible for all matters relating to employment:

- **INEM (National Institute for Employment):** A government agency responsible for helping the unemployed to find jobs or training courses and helping companies to fill vacation positions or implement outplacement plans.

- **The Labour Inspectorate:** A government department responsible for ensuring that employers comply with the provisions of labour laws and regulations and the various collective agreements (it handles the control of working conditions, employment, social security, occupational health and safety). Its inspectors have the right to visit a company's premises at any time and demand copies of all the documents that employers are legally required to keep. Breaches of certain labour laws may also, in certain cases, expose the employer to criminal proceedings.

- **The Mediation, Arbitration and Conciliation Unit:** An administrative body responsible for mediating in disputes between the company and employee. Conciliation is required to take place before any proceedings are instituted on grounds of dismissal before the labour court. The proceedings are very brief and usually take approximately 15 days as from the filing of the request.

Hiring of employees

A copy of the summary of the terms of the employment contracts, which must be concluded in writing (not including senior manager contracts that need only be notified) must be given to the workers' representatives. The workers' representatives will also be notified of any extensions and terminations.

- The INEM must be notified of any new employees hired. All contracts that must be concluded in writing must also be registered with the INEM.

- Disabled persons must account for at least 2 per cent of any workforce that has more than 50 permanent employees.

Employment contracts

In Spain, employment contracts may be concluded orally or in writing. Contracts must be concluded in writing when it is legally required. In any event, the following contracts are concluded in writing:

- training and apprenticeship contracts;
- those concluded for a specific work or service;
- contracts for workers that replace workers;
- part-time contracts;
- temporary contracts with a specific duration;
- contracts aimed at boosting employment;
- part-time contracts to attend to production requirements with a duration of more than four weeks.

Trial period

This will be taken to be the period (not mandatory) laid down in the collective agreement. If it is otherwise set, the trial period may not exceed six months for qualified specialists and two months for other employees (which may be extended to three months in companies with fewer than 25 employees).

Types of contract

Indefinite contracts

These contracts have no set term limit. A general principle of Spanish employment legislation states that contracts should be indefinite (either full-time or part-time), limiting temporary contracts to certain circumstances established by law.

Spanish legislation lays down a number of incentives for concluding indefinite contracts, consisting mainly of rebates and reductions in social security contributions. These incentives are applied to workers pertaining to certain groups for whom it is harder to conclude an indefinite contract, or the transformation of temporary contracts into indefinite contracts (full-time or part-time).

The groups to which the incentives and main benefits represented by these incentives are:

- unemployed persons under the age of 30;

- persons over the age 45 who have been unemployed for one year;

- women in professions or jobs in which they are under represented who have been unemployed for one year;

- unemployed disabled persons.

The aids and incentives will not apply in certain employer/employee relationships. These include the contracting of employees who, within the 24 months prior to the contract date, worked for the same company or group of companies under an indefinite contract, or workers who have terminated their indefinite employer/employee relationship within a period of three months prior to the contract date.

Contract to encourage long-term engagement of personnel
In 1997, a labour reform established this new type of indefinite contract in order to boost the stable engagement of workers who meet certain conditions and reduce employment. This type of contract may be concluded until 16 May 2001. A contract of this kind may not be used by companies that, in the preceding twelve months, have dismissed employees on objective grounds declared to be unjustified by the courts; or by companies that have made a group of employees redundant.

The severance indemnity for dismissals on objective grounds classified as unjustified by the labour courts amounts to 33 days' salary per year of service up to the limit of 24 monthly salaries. (Ordinary contracts: 45 days' salary per year.)

Temporary contracts

The most common temporary contracts are listed below.

Job-training contracts
The purpose of this type of contract is for the employee to acquire the technical and practical experience necessary to occupy a post. The duration of this contract is a minimum of 6 months and a maximum of two years. The working schedule must be full time. The requirements which must be complied with by the employees include the following:

- they must be between 16 and 21 years of age;

- they must not have held the same post in the company in the last 12 months.

Under the collective agreement, the maximum number of employees with this type of contract may be specified.

Work-experience contracts
The purpose of this type of contract is for the employee to gain practical experience suited to his studies. The duration of this contract is a minimum of six months and a maximum of two years. The requirements which must be complied with by the employees are as follows: they must be university graduates or have technical qualifications (provided that four years have not elapsed since the qualification was obtained).

Contract for a specific job or service
The object of this type of contract is to cover activities which do not form part of the company's normal activity. Although the performance is limited in time, the duration is not fixed. The duration will be equal to the duration of the work or service. The tasks which may be covered by these contracts are specified in the collective agreements.

Temporary contract due to specific production needs
The purpose of this contract is to meet market demand and deal with accumulated work or excess orders, even relating to the company's normal activity. The collective agreements can specify the activities covered by the contract and the number of contracts depending on the total number of employees. As a general rule, the duration will be a maximum of six months within a period of 12 months. However, the collective agreements can lay down a maximum period of 18 months with a maximum duration of three-quarters of this period.

Interim labour contract
This type of contract is used for hiring workers to replace other workers whose job is reserved for them by law, under the collective wage agreement or under an individual agreement, or for temporarily filling a job during the process of recruitment or promotion of the worker who is to hold the job permanently (in this case, the duration will not exceed three months).

Part-time contracts
The worker provides his services during a specific number of hours a day, a week, a month or a year, which is lower than the habitual number of hours in the specific activity. These contracts may be indefinite or temporary.

Senior management contracts
Senior management staff are employees who exercise, independently and with full responsibility, powers that are inherent to the legal ownership of the company and related to the company's general objectives. This employer-employee relationship is based on the mutual trust of the two parties, who act in good faith in the exercising of their rights and the ful-

filment of their obligations, governed by the agreements reached or by the provisions of Spanish civil or commercial law.

The general characteristics of the employer-employee relationship are as follows:

- Trial period of up to nine months.

- Temporary or indefinite contract.

- The contract may be terminated by either of the parties without any specific cause being given, provided that between three and six months' notice is given.

- In the event that the company wishes to terminate the employer-employee relationship, the senior manager is entitled to the indemnity agreed in the contract and, failing this, the senior manager is entitled to seven days' salary per year of service up to a maximum limit of 12 monthly salaries.

- If the termination of the employer-employee relationship is declared to be unjustified by the courts, the senior manager is entitled to an indemnity equal to 20 days' salary per year of service up to a maximum limit of 12 monthly salaries.

Wages and salaries

Wages and salaries consist of the total remuneration (cash and benefits in kind) received by the employee in return for working for the employer. Up to 30 per cent of the total remuneration may consist of benefits in kind. The minimum wage provision is determined by the government on an annual basis.

Hours of work

The hours of work are fixed by collective agreement or by individual employment contracts, however:

- the maximum number of working hours is an average of 40 hours a week calculated on an annual basis;

- the normal number of hours per day shall not exceed nine hours.

The collective agreements can establish a different distribution of working hours provided there are rest periods of at least 12 hours between working days and one-and-a-half days off on an uninterrupted basis each week.

Overtime is voluntary unless stipulated in an individual contract or collective agreement but, in general, overtime may not exceed 80 hours per year. Also, overtime compensated by time off in the 4 months after the overtime was worked will not be taken into account in the calculation of the 80 hour maximum.

Holidays

Employers are under a statutory obligation to give annual paid holidays to their employees. The holiday entitlement fixed by the collective agreement or individual contract may not be less than 30 days per working year. Employees are entitled to not more than 14 paid public holidays per working year.

Time off

There are statutory obligations for an employer to provide time off with pay to certain employees, based on special circumstances. Among such circumstances, mention may be made of the employee's marriage (15 days) and birth of children (two days).

Leave of absence

These are situations where the employment contract is suspended (work and remuneration are suspended) at the request of the worker.

In certain circumstances, a leave of absence must be granted by the company and the employee's position held open for them during that time. The reasons for granting compulsory leave of absence include:

- appointment or selection for a public office;
- carrying out union functions on a provincial or national level;
- temporary disability, up to a maximum of 18 months;
- military service.

An employee is also entitled to request a voluntary leave of absence. In this case, however, he is not entitled to have his position held open for him. Instead, the employee has a preferential right to return when a position in the company becomes vacant. To qualify for a voluntary leave of absence, the employee must have been with the company for at least one year. The minimum duration of a leave of absence is two years and the maximum five years.

Maternity provisions

A pregnant employee is entitled to maternity leave of up to 16 weeks. The father, where both parents work, may opt to take off up to the last four weeks of the benefit period.

With respect to adoption, the parental leave may be taken by either the mother or the father. The duration of the leave for the adoption of children under the age of six years is 16 weeks. The benefit is paid exclusively by social security.

Allowable time off work includes the time needed:

- to attend antenatal examinations and classes;

- to breast-feed a child under nine months (1 hour);

- to look after a child under six years of age.

In this last case, the time off entails a reduction in working hours and a proportional cut in remuneration of between one third and half the number of working hours.

Statute provides for a leave of absence not exceeding three years for the birth or adoption of a child as from the birth of the child. This right can only be exercised by the father or mother. During the first year of the parental leave of absence, the employee will be entitled to his/her position being held open for them. After the second year, the employee will be entitled to return to the company with a similar position.

Changes in work conditions

The management of a company may, for accredited economic, technological, organisational or production reasons, make changes in employment contracts in respect of working days, working hours, shifts, salary systems, work system, and output and work posts.

These changes in working conditions may be individual or collective. In the first case, it requires the employee to be notified by the employer and in the second case, it must be preceded by a consultation period with the employees' legal representatives.

- An employee who is affected negatively by substantial changes is entitled to terminate his employment contract and receive an indemnity amounting to 20 days salary for each year of service, up to a maximum of 9 monthly payments.

- A transfer is considered to be a change in an employee's place of work that necessitates a change in his permanent residence. In these cases, the employee concerned may accept the transfer or terminate the employment contract with the right to receive an indemnity totalling 20 days' salary for each year of service up to a maximum of 12 months salary.

- When the relocation is a temporary change in an employee's place of work that necessitates a change of residence, it must also be justified. If the relocation is for a period exceeding 3 months, the employee will be entitled to 4 days off for every three months and if the relocation exceeds 12 months in a period of 3 years, it will be considered to be a transfer.

Disciplinary and grievance procedures

The employer may impose penalties on any employee who breaches the statutory or the internal rules. Penalties cannot be imposed that entail a reduction in holidays or time off or docking of pay. Where the breach of discipline leads to dismissal, the employer must notify the employee in writing, detailing the events that led to the dismissal. Furthermore, employers may adopt appropriate disciplinary rules and procedures in order to provide safe working conditions.

Termination of employment

Termination at the employee's request

An employee can validly terminate an employment contract where there has been a substantial alteration to the conditions of employment to the detriment of the employee's professional training and/or dignity. Other reasons include a failure to pay the employee or a repeated delay in paying the employee, and any other serious failure on the part of the employer to discharge his contractual duties, except in cases of *force majeure*.

Statute states that the employee shall be entitled to the equivalent of 45 days pay for every year of service up to a maximum of 42 months pay.

Termination by employer for objective causes

The causes can be the following:

- Employee's ineptitude.

- Failure to adapt to technological changes in the job. They must be reasonable given the employee's skills and the employee must be given a period of two months to adapt to the changes.

- Cutting back on jobs. It must be proven that this is due to economic, technical, organisational or production reasons and that the termination contributes to overcoming any difficulties that prevent the success of the company's business performance, either due to its competitive position in the market or for demand, by organising resources more efficiently. It must affect less than 10 workers in companies employing less than 100 employees, 10 per cent in companies employing between 100 and 300 employees, 30 employees in a company employing more than 300 employees.

- Absence from work, even justified absences, when certain conditions are met that are basically related to the rate of absenteeism in the company.

The employer must allow 30 days between handing in the notice of termination of employment and actual termination, and should provide the employee with compensation equal to 20 days pay for each year of service up to a maximum of 12 months pay. During the notice period, the employee will be entitled to six hours off each week without loss of pay to look for other employment.

Where the dismissal is declared to be unfair, the employee will be entitled to an indemnity equivalent to 45 days pay for each year of service up to a maximum of 42 months pay. Failure to comply with the requirements specified, with the exception of the requirement relating to the notice period, will result in the termination being declared null and void.

Collective termination

Collective termination must be based on economic, technical, organisational or production reasons and the termination must contribute to overcoming an adverse financial situation or securing the future viability of the company and employment through a more efficient organisation of resources. It must affect at least:

- ten employees in companies engaging less than 100 (the dismissal will be considered as being for objective reasons if it affects the entire workforce and this is made up of less than five employees);

- ten per cent when the company employs between 100 and 300 employees;

- 30 employees in a company employing more than 300 employees.

The employer must obtain official authorisation from the competent labour authority and negotiate with the employees' legal representatives.

Employees who have their employment contracts terminated as a result of a collective termination are entitled to an indemnity amounting to 20 days pay for each year of service, up to a maximum of 12 months pay.

Termination on disciplinary grounds

The employer may terminate an employee's employment contract on disciplinary grounds where the employee is guilty of a serious and blameworthy breach of contract.

Consequences of termination of employment

If the employee does not agree with the dismissal, he may lodge an appeal before the labour courts, which will issue one of the following decisions:

- **Justified dismissal:** when the grounds for dismissal put forward by the company are legally acceptable and accredited. The employee is not entitled to any indemnity or salary during the litigation period.

- **Unjustified dismissal:** when the employer cannot substantiate the reasons for the termination. In this case the employer has the option to reinstate the employee, or pay the employee compensation in lieu of reinstatement. The amount of compensation equals 45 days salary for every year of service up to a maximum of 42 months pay, and an amount equal to the pay that the employee has forfeited between the date of termination and the date of judgement, or if earlier, the date that the employee commences alternate employment.

- **Null and void:** Termination will be considered null and void if the reason for dismissal is considered to reflect any type of discrimination prohibited by the Spanish Constitution or by law or if it occurs in violation of the employee's basic rights and liberties. Such a judgement will require the immediate reinstatement of the employee and payment of any outstanding wages accruing from the day termination came into effect.

Employee participation

Workers' right to participate in the company is discharged by shop stewards and works councils, without prejudice to other forms of participation. The shop stewards represent the workers in companies or plants with less than 50 and more than ten workers. Works councils are set up in each plant with a census of 50 or more workers; the number of components of works councils is based on the number of workers.

The rights of shop stewards and works councils include:

- receiving quarterly information on trends in the industry, company situation and programmes for the production and sales, and probable employment trends;

- receiving the annual accounts and any other documents supplied to shareholders; issuing reports prior to the implementation of decisions adopted by the employer (restructuring of work force and redundancies; total or partial relocation of facilities; introduction and review of organisational systems and control of work; bonus and incentive systems);

- ensuring that the company complies with the applicable regulations concerning social security and employment, and occupational health and safety conditions.

Shop stewards and the member of works councils, except where otherwise specified in collective agreements, have, among others, the following minimum guarantees:

- priority with respect to remaining in the company in the event of redundancy and in cases of geographical relocation for technical, organisational or production reasons;

- not to be dismissed or penalised during their term of office or in the following year, provided that the penalty is based on an act of the worker during the exercise of his representation.

Visas and work and resident permits

Nationals of non European Union (EU) countries

Under Spanish labour legislation, non-EU nationals intending to work in Spain must obtain a special work visa and a work and residence permit. The Spanish labour authorities grant different types of work permits depending on the type of work and duration of employment. Work permits are granted taking into account the employment situation of Spanish nationals for the same kind of work. However, there are certain preferential categories such as foreigners who have a Spanish spouse, workers necessary to set up foreign imported machinery, or top executives.

Nationals of EU member states

Nationals of EU member states are not subject to the requirement applicable to other foreigners to obtain a work permit as an employee or a self-employed person because the EU rules on the free movement of workers are fully in force. EU nationals must apply for an EU Resident Card.

Social security system

In Spain, social security benefits include health care, temporary and permanent disability benefit, retirement, widows' and orphans' pension, death benefit, family protection allowances, maternity and unemployment. The benefit types can be:

- **Contributory benefits:** benefits guaranteed by the social security system for all individuals who engage in paid employment and contribute to one of the system's schemes, and who therefore qualify for coverage; and

- **Non-contributory benefits:** periodic benefits guaranteed to individuals aged over 65 who lack financial means of their own, regardless of whether said individuals have contributed or not.

Social security contributions

The requirement to pay social security contributions commences when the employee starts working. Social security contributions must be paid by both employers and employees. Employers are required to ensure that both employers' and employees' contributions are paid to the social security and to present the relevant documentation. The contribution is calculated by multiplying the contribution base by the relevant percentage:

$$\text{Contribution} = \frac{\textit{Contribution base} \times \textit{rate}}{100}$$

All monthly salary payments received by the employee must be taken into account when determining the contribution base. Once the contribution base has been obtained by performing the above calculation, the maximum and minimum contribution bases and the percentages must be taken into account.

Annually, the government establishes maximum and minimum contribution bases for each professional category and also specifies the percentages by which contribution bases are to be multiplied.

- The general contribution rates are 30.8 per cent for the employer and 6.4 per cent for the employee.

- Employers must also pay premiums for accident at work and professional illness contingencies, governed by Royal Decree 2931 of 29 December 1979, on top of their share of social security contributions.

- With respect to employees on training contracts and employees on apprenticeship contracts, the social security contribution is lower.

The social security system – international regulations and treaties

Foreigners may take advantage of the public services offered to nationals in Spain. There are certain exceptions, however, such as the benefits offered by the Spanish social security, the enjoyment of which require the existence of an employer/employee relation unless expressly stated otherwise in a treaty signed by Spain.

Since 1986, EU social security regulations are applicable to Spain (Regulation 1.408/71 and Regulation 574/72). Two EU regulations ensure that the workers to whom they are applicable are not adversely affected by moving from one member state to another.

Part 5

Accounting Issues

5.1

Accounting Principles and Requirements

PricewaterhouseCoopers

Sources of generally accepted accounting principles

On admission to full membership of the European Community (EC) on 1 January 1986, Spain accepted the obligation to adapt existing legislation to comply with the EC Directives on company law. The process began with the promulgation of both the Audit Law (Eighth Directive) and Company Law Reform Act (First, Second, Third, Fourth, Sixth and Seventh Directives), which both took effect in 1990. The process was completed with the issuance of a revised General Chart of Accounts (including details of **generally accepted accounting principles (GAAP)** and the **form and content of accounts**), in December 1990 and rules for the preparation of **consolidated accounts** in December 1991.

Since then, the regulatory body (the Spanish Institute of Chartered Accountants, ICAC; see below) continues to make a number of statements to narrow the scope for interpretation.

In Spain, the Fourth Directive is applicable to *Sociedades Anónimas* (SA; Limited Liability Corporations) and to *Sociedades Limitadas* (SL; Private Limited Liability Corporations). With regard to other types of companies, such as insurance or finance companies, separate rules derived from EC Directives are prepared and supervised by the appropriate regulatory body.

Generally accepted accounting principles

Company law requires that a company's accounts comply with *the Plan General de Contabilidad* (PGC; General Chart of Accounts) and reflect a true and fair view of its financial position and results.

Statutory requirements for financial statement presentation and disclosure, general accounting principles and their methods of application are similar in Spain to those of other EU countries. The main sources of Spanish GAAP are as follows:

- **Código de Comercio (CCom; Commercial Code or fundamental text of mercantile law).** Parts of the Code were radically amended as part of the 1990 reform of company law.

- **Texto Refundido de la Ley de Sociedades Anónimas (LSA; Company Law).** The reformed LSA establishes certain accounting principles, the observance of which is obligatory for all companies.

- **Plan General de Contabilidad (PGC).** This is a statutory chart of accounts reissued in December 1990. The sections relating to format and content of accounts and accounting principles (*Normas de valoración*) are obligatory for all companies, irrespective of their legal, individual or corporate structure.

- **Normas para la Formulación de Cuentas Anuales Consolidadas.** These are the Rules, issued in December 1991, governing the preparation of consolidated accounts. Prior to that time, presentation of consolidated accounts by groups of companies was not obligatory and was in fact uncommon.

- **Instituto de Contabilidad y Auditoría de Cuentas (ICAC; Institute of Accounting and Auditing of Accounts).** (This government body under the Finance Ministry, was created by the 1988 Audit Law). The Royal Decree introducing the PGC establishes that this body may adopt and issue accounting rules as and when it deems necessary, compliance with which will be obligatory. The ICAC may propose amendments to the PGC, which are subject to review by the Finance Ministry (*Ministerio de Economía y Hacienda*). The PGC empowers the ICAC to issue statements that clarify or develop the PGC in the areas of accounting principles, rules for the preparation of annual accounts and the adaptation of those rules for specialised industries. The ICAC publishes a quarterly official bulletin (the BOICAC) in which its statements, resolutions, responses to queries and exposure drafts all appear.

- **Asociación Española de Contabilidad y Administración de Empresas (AECA).** This is a private body incorporating a number of professional accountants and representatives from the business and academic worlds. Membership is voluntary and observance of its pronouncements is not obligatory. Nevertheless, until the reform of company law, it was effectively the only body promoting the development of advanced accounting principles in Spain. All statements previously issued by AECA have been revised to reflect the changes brought about by the process of reform and restated. Generally, only a few AECA mentions are given in this chapter because they have no explicit legal recognition since official bodies in Spain do not follow the practice of giving recognition to private organisations.

In this respect, in reply to a query filed with the ICAC concerning its interpretation of **Principios Contables Facultativos**, the ICAC maintained the following:

- Currently in Spain, for the application of accounting legislation to be obligatory it must be laid down in appropriate legal regulations (Law, Regulations, ICAC Resolutions or rules issued by the competent public bodies). Common practice in this case does not qualify as a source of legislation.

- Obligatory accounting principles and standards are set out in Rule 22 of section five of the *Plan General de Contabilidad* (PGC) and Additional Provision Four of the Enabling Regulations of the Audit Law.

- In exceptional circumstances, the application of obligatory accounting principles is incompatible with the requirement to give a true and fair view of the company's financial situation, net worth and results of its operations, as is the ultimate objective of the accounts. In such cases, the most appropriate principles that make it possible to give such a true and fair view must be applied. Details of the reasons for the non-application and the effects on the Company's net worth, financial position and results are to be given in order to provide a correct understanding of the accounts.

- In such cases, it is possible to apply the criteria contained in the replies to a request for a ruling, filed with the ICAC, on this matter. These rulings are not binding, however, although they do reflect the ICAC's interpretation of the matters in respect of which the ruling was sought.

- At present, the accounting principles and policies contained in the documents or guides issued by both national and international Chartered Accountant Organisations are not obligatory for businesses since they would first need to be laid down in appropriate legal regulations.

Nevertheless, in relation to the above, it is common practice in the profession to use this literature due to the lack of official pronouncements in this respect in Spain.

Audit and public company requirements

Audits

Under the LSA, companies are required to appoint state-recognised auditors, who must comply with strict criteria of independence *vis-à-vis* the client. This requirement took effect for the financial years ending after 30 June 1990 and affects all corporations except those that satisfy at least two of the following conditions for two consecutive years:

- Total assets less than Ptas395 million.

- Turnover less than Ptas790 million.

- Work force less than 50 employees.

The original conditions have been modified in various laws since the promulgation of the Company Law Reform Act and Audit Law.

Auditors are appointed by the company (ie, the shareholders), in general meeting, for an initial period of no less than three and no more than nine years. On termination of the initial period of nomination, the auditor can be re-appointed for successive one-year periods. The auditors' fees, or the basis of their calculation, must be fixed for the entire period of the initial contract. Once appointed, auditors may not resign, or be removed without 'just cause'. What constitutes a 'just cause' is not, however, clearly defined.

Only persons whose names are inscribed in the *Registro Oficial de Auditores de Cuentas* (ROAC; Official Register of Auditors of Accounts), maintained by the ICAC, are eligible for appointment as statutory auditors. Inscription in the ROAC is open to all Spanish economics graduates who meet certain experience requirements, as well as to other similarly qualified EU nationals.

Auditing standards are established by the three professional bodies into which public accountants are grouped: the *Instituto de Auditores y Censores Jurados de Cuentas de Espana* (IACJCE; Spanish Institute of Auditors), the *Registro de Economistas Auditores* (REA; Register of Economics-Graduate Auditors) and the *Registro General de Auditores de Cuentas Titulares Mercantiles* (REGA; Register of Commerce Graduate Auditors). However, under the Audit Law, their standards do not become effective until approved by the ICAC and published in its official bulletin as *Normas Técnicas de Auditoría* (Audit Technical Rules). Although far less developed, the pronouncements of REA and IACJCE tend to adhere closely to International Standards on Auditing. The REA pronouncements, in particular, state that, in case of doubt, reference should be made to International Standards on Auditing or the standards of other leading national standard-setting bodies.

In addition to reporting on the accounts themselves, auditors are obligated to report on whether the Directors' Report (*Informe de Gestión*) is in agreement with the accounting information contained in the accounts. The auditor is also required by law to make specific mention of post balance sheet events 'that affect the operations of the business'. The auditor must also mention 'any infractions of law or of the company's by laws that come to light in the course of his or her work and that might affect the true and fair view the accounts must present'.

Public Companies (Empresas con Cotización Oficial)

There are no additional accounting rules or disclosure requirements for companies quoted on the Spanish Stock Exchange, though various rules regarding the filing of accounts apply. Audited annual accounts must be filed with the *Comisión Nacional del Mercado de Valores* (CNMV; the state body supervising the stock exchange) within two months of their approval by the shareholders, which, in turn, must be within six months of the year-end. Quarterly financial information must also be provided.

To issue shares to the public, a company is required to have a minimum of 100 shareholders and a minimum share capital of Ptas200 million. The annual accounts for the past three years must have been audited, and profit sufficient to permit payment of a dividend of at least 6 percent of share capital must have been made in the last two years or in at least three of the last five years.

Admission to quotation requires the prior consent of the CNMV. To retain quotation, a minimum capital of Ptas25 million is required and, although there is no minimum number of shareholders, at least 20 percent of the shares must be traded on the market. The company must have a contract with a broker who undertakes to provide a market in the shares.

Reference
LSA Articles 203–207; RLA Articles 5 and 17–23; RBI Article 32; SM1 RD 710/1986.

5.2

General Accounting

PricewaterhouseCoopers

Financial statements

Basic Accounting Concepts

Company law does not distinguish between fundamental or basic accounting concepts, underlying assumptions and accounting conventions. The *Plan General de Contabilidad* (PGC) enunciates a series of fundamental accounting principles (*principios contables*) and establishes specific accounting principles (*normas de valoración*), or valuation rules for each asset and liability. The *principios contables* are as follows:

- The prudence, going concern, accrual, matching and consistency principles.

- **Recording:** Transactions are recorded in the period in which the rights or obligations arise.

- **Historical cost:** All rights and assets are recorded at historical cost except where permitted otherwise by law (for an important exception, see the section on 'Property, Plant and Equipment' in the following chapter). Liabilities are recorded at the amount at which they are to be settled.

- **No offset:** Items of income and expense may not be offset against one another, nor may assets and liabilities. Each individual asset and liability must be valued separately.

- **Conflict of principles:** Where mandatory accounting principles conflict, priority is given to the principle that best reflects a true and fair view of the company.

- **Materiality:** Divergence from the above is acceptable where the effect is immaterial.

Without prejudice to the foregoing, the prudence principle always has precedence.

Format and Content of Financial Statements

Annual accounts comprise a balance sheet, a profit and loss account and the notes, or *memoria* (see below). They must he drawn up 'with clarity' and must present a true and fair view ('faithful image') of the net worth, financial position and results of operations of the company.

In the absence of any specialised industry requirements, the formats of the balance sheet and the profit and loss account must conform to the formats established in the *Texto Refundido de la Ley de Sociedades Anónimas* (LSA) and amplified in the PGC. The balance sheet and profit and loss account should be in the same format from one accounting period to the next, although, in exceptional cases, the format may be changed, but the fact must be indicated in the notes together with the reasons for doing so. Captions in the standard form of accounts may be subdivided or grouped, and the analysis presented in the *memoria* (notes), provided that the overall format is followed and that the main headings are disclosed.

Spanish legislation has created certain confusion in nomenclature because of the use of the word *memoria* to denote 'notes to the accounts and the Statement of Source and Application of Funds'. Previously, the word was used for 'annual report.' For clarity, *memoria* is generally translated as 'notes' in this chapter.

The law treats consolidated financial statements as separate from the individual statements of the parent company, to be approved and filed separately.

The statement of source and application of funds is described in the PGC as an obligatory element of the *memoria*. It is not clear why, under the legislation, this statement has not been given the status of a basic financial statement. The statement of source and application of funds has a tabular format, which does not use the direct method but rather adjusts net income for transactions of a non-cash nature. The statement, which must show comparative figures for the prior year, lists in separate columns all sources and applications of funds, lists the net source/application and then separately discloses all individual changes in working capital.

Legislation does not lay down the obligation to show comparative figures for the prior year for each note to the accounts, with the exception of the statement of source and application of funds which must contain comparative figures unless abridged accounts were prepared for the prior year.

It should be noted that, in accordance with the Technical Audit Rules issued by the ICAC, if the notes contain a complete set of comparative figures for the previous year and the current-year auditor was also the auditor in the previous year, the audit opinion should relate to the two years in question.

Small companies may present abridged accounts and are not obliged to present the Directors Report (*Informe de Gestión*). The rules distinguish between presentation of an abridged balance sheet and *memoria* on the one hand and an abridged profit and loss account on the other. A statement of source and application of funds is not required in consolidated financial statements, nor in the statements of companies entitled to file an abridged balance sheet. To qualify as a small company, companies must meet at least two of the following three criteria in both of the preceding two years:

	Abridged balance sheet and memoria	Abridged profit and loss account
Total assets at year-end must not exceed	Ptas395 million	Ptas1580 million
Turnover for the year must not exceed	Ptas790 million	Ptas3160 million
Average number of employees during the year must not exceed	50 persons	250 persons

Businesses incorporated other than as an SA and sole traders must, at a minimum, present abridged accounts.

Disclosure of Accounting Policies

The PGC lists practically all the account captions for which the accounting policies must be disclosed. In unusual circumstances, if a literal application of an authoritative pronouncement might render the financial statements misleading, it will be necessary to depart from the usual treatment. The practice followed and the reason for doing so and the effect on income and financial position of the departure should be disclosed in a note.

Consolidation (*consolidación de cuentas anuales*)

Principles of Consolidation

Under company law, the presentation of audited consolidated accounts became obligatory for financial years ended after 31 December 1990. The accounts of all group companies must be adjusted prior to consolidation to comply with the accounting principles followed by the parent.

The rules for preparation of consolidated accounts were published in December 1991.

Definition of Control

Consolidated financial statements must be prepared when the company holds investments in other companies if:

- It owns the majority of the voting rights.

- It has the power to appoint or remove the majority of the members of the board of directors.

- It controls, by virtue of agreements with other shareholders, the majority of the voting rights.

- It has appointed, by its sole vote, the majority of the members of the board of directors serving at the time the accounts are to be prepared and who have so served during the preceding two years.

The most significant exemption from the requirement to present consolidated accounts is when, at the end of the parent's financial year, the consolidated figures do not exceed the following limits:

	Until 31 December 1999	*Beginning 1 January 2000*
Total assets at year-end	Ptas2300 million	Ptas1580million
Turnover for the year	Ptas4800 million	Ptas3160 million
Average numbers of employees for the year	500 persons	250 persons

Alternatively, these limits are increased by 20 per cent and applied to the total of the corresponding figures of the individual annual accounts of each group company.

A further exemption arises when the reporting entity is at least 50 per cent owned by an entity domiciled in Spain or elsewhere in the EU, and minority shareholders holding 10 per cent of the shares have not requested, six months before the company's year end, that consolidated accounts be prepared. In such cases, the consolidated financial statements of the ultimate parent, translated into Spanish where appropriate, must be filed in the Spanish Mercantile Register.

Similarly, a parent company may account on the equity basis for a subsidiary that it would otherwise be obligated to consolidate on the line-by-line basis if the subsidiary:

- is immaterial;

- is subject to judicial intervention or receivership, effectively prohibiting preparation of consolidated accounts by the parent or affecting the parent's rights over the equity or the management of the subsidiary;

- cannot provide the information necessary for the preparation of consolidated accounts except at a disproportionate cost, or would delay the preparation of such accounts beyond the established time limits;

- has been acquired solely with the objective of resale in the near future;

- has activities very different from those of the parent, as a result of which its inclusion would not facilitate an understanding of the group's financial position or results of operations. This exemption is, however, available only if the subsidiary is a bank or insurance entity subject to specific regulation.

First Consolidation Surplus (diferencia de primera consolidación)

Where the purchase price exceeds the net book value of net assets acquired, after making the necessary adjustments to achieve consistency between the accounting principles of the acquired company and those of the acquiring company, such excess, called 'positive consolidation difference' may be allocated (net of deferred tax assets or liabilities, as appropriate) to the various assets up to their fair market value. The remaining excess is shown in the balance sheet as goodwill and amortised systematically in the year in which the goodwill contributes to the obtention of income for the group of companies. This is possible for a period of up to a maximum of twenty years (the amortisation period was changed from ten years to 20 and the change is applicable to the annual accounts drawn up after 31 December 1998, with no effect on the amortisation charged in previous years) and must be justified in the notes when the period exceeds five years.

When the consolidation difference is negative, it is allocated directly and, insofar as it is possible, to the assets and liabilities of the subsidiary, increasing the value of the liabilities or reducing the value of assets to their market value. The remaining difference is called Negative Goodwill and is classified as a separate balance sheet item (it may only be offset with the funds calculated in the same investee company) below minority interests, and absorbed in profit(/loss) in accordance with the nature thereof. In this respect, the following additional measures will be followed:

- In the case of first consolidation, the difference may be recognised as consolidated reserves if it relates to profits that have not been previously recognised by the parent company.

- The difference will only be recognised in cases where the acquisition cost is lower than the prior book value and for a maximum of the resulting amount.

- The book value recognised must be reverted to a specific period that avoids arbitrariness in the allocation thereof (it must relate to a system) and that takes into account the classification of said item at the date on which the portfolio was acquired.

Equity Method (método de puesta en equivalencia)

Associated companies must be accounted for under the equity method. An associated company is defined as one in which the reporting entity holds shares, with which it enjoys a lasting relationship and to whose development it contributes. A company is presumed to be associated when the reporting entity holds at least 20 per cent of the share capital (voting rights), or only 3 per cent if the company is quoted.

Proportional method (método de integración proporcional)

The proportional method of consolidation is also available under Spanish law for consolidation with other companies managed jointly by the participants (see section on *Joint Ventures* in this chapter). Such entities are referred to as 'multigroup' companies. Under this method, the financial statements of the multigroup company are first consolidated with those of any subsidiaries it may have, then adjusted for elimination of inter-company items and to bring them into line with the accounting principles of the parent. The resulting financial statements are then reduced, line by line, to reflect the reporting entity's proportional interest in the company and then added, line by line, to its statements.

Treatment of minority interests

In the consolidated balance sheet, that part of the net worth of subsidiaries attributable to outside shareholders must be shown separately (net of any unpaid calls on capital), immediately below shareholders' equity. The minority's share of income is shown in the profit and loss account as a deduction from after-tax income. If the subsidiary has a deficiency in assets, the entire deficiency must be ascribed to the parent company, unless the minority has agreed to make good its part.

Disclosure

The notes must contain for all subsidiary, associated and multigroup companies, whether consolidated or not:

- details of that company;
- the nature of ownership;
- 'reserves' held;
- consolidation treatment;
- the net worth and net income of associated companies;
- details of payables and receivables with unconsolidated group companies.

A separate analysis should be given by the company of movements in the carrying value of companies accounted for by the equity method. Disclosure should also be made of the accounting policy for amortisation of goodwill, and a schedule of movements in goodwill (with an analysis by originating investment) should also be shown.

In addition, the following should be separately disclosed:

- shares of any company in the group that are quoted;

- movements in minority interests (by company);

- the company's investment in its own shares (either directly or through any consolidated subsidiary or nominees).

Where there have been significant changes during a year in the composition of the group, the necessary information must be included in the notes to the accounts to enable suitable comparisons of the balance sheet, the profit and loss account and the statement of source and application of funds to be made.

Definition and types of mergers and spin-offs

Mergers

The merger of any company into a new public limited company, which could entail the extinction of each company, consists in the transfer *en bloc* of all the assets and liabilities to the new company which will acquire, by universal succession, all the rights and obligations of the mentioned companies.

If the merger derives from the absorption of one or more companies by an existing company, the latter will acquire all the assets and liabilities of the target companies that will be extinguished, and increase share capital by the amount required, unless the target company is wholly-owned by the acquiring company.

Depending on the financial nature of the operation, the following distinctions may be made:

- **Merger of interests**. Operations aimed at incorporating companies of the same size, where none of the companies involved in the merger (or the shareholders of such companies) can prevail over the other companies.

- **Merger by acquisition**. The economic substance consists of the acquisition of one or more companies by another company or companies. These mergers are characterised by the fact that the real net worth of the target company is lower than the net worth of the acquiring company.

- **Vertical mergers**. Mergers between related companies.

Spin-offs

In accordance with the Spanish Companies Act, a spin-off is considered as:

● The extinction of a company, where all its assets and liabilities are divided into two or more parts and each part is transferred *en bloc* to a newly-created company or to an existing company.

● The segregation of one or more parts of a company's assets and liabilities, without the company being dissolved, and the segregated portion is transferred *en bloc* to one or several newly-created companies or existing companies.

As in the case of mergers, a distinction may be drawn between the following types of spin-off operations:

● **Splitting of interests.** The object of these types of operation is to integrate assets and liabilities of similar amounts. Neither the transferee company nor the part of the assets and liabilities of the transferring company that correspond to the transferee company, prevail over each other. Splitting of interests is also considered to occur when the transferee company is a newly-created company.

● **Acquisition spin-offs.** The real value of the assets and liabilities acquired is considerably lower than the real value of the assets and liabilities of the transferee company or than the part of the assets and liabilities of the transferring company that corresponds to the transferee company.

● **Vertical spin-offs.** Spin-offs in which the transferee company and the transferring company are related before or after the spin-off. Vertical spin-offs are also considered to take place when the transferee company is incorporated into the group as a result of the spin-off and the transferring company leaves the group.

Accounting Treatment

The Spanish Institute of Chartered Accountants (ICAC) has drawn up draft Accounting Regulations applicable to mergers and spin-offs. The definitive regulations are pending publication, although they are being adapted by members of the accounting profession.

In accordance with the draft issued by said Institute, the applicable valuation rules are determined by applying the principle of the acquisition price:

● **Merger of interests.** The book values of the assets and liabilities of the company that results from the merger are stated at the book values recorded by each company before the merger.

- **Mergers by acquisition.** The assets and liabilities of the companies acquired are stated at the real values, after taxes, established in the merger process to fix the exchange relation without exceeding in any circumstances the acquisition cost.

- **Vertical mergers.** The assets and liabilities of related companies are valued in accordance with the criteria derived from the Regulations for the Drawing up of the Consolidated Annual Accounts.

- **Splitting of interests.** The assets and liabilities of the transferee company are stated at the book values recorded by each company before the split.

- **Acquisition spin-offs.** The rules applicable to this type of spin-off lay down the basis, according to which the assets and liabilities acquired are stated at the real values established for the purposes of the spin-off.

- **Vertical spin-offs.** The assets and liabilities of the transferee company, and of the part of the spin-off assets and liabilities, are valued in accordance with the Regulations for the Drawing up of the Consolidated Annual Accounts. This does not include the part that relates to minority shareholders or the proportional part of the assets and liabilities of the related company that corresponds to the interest in its capital not held by the transferring company or the transferee company. In this case, the book values recorded by each company before the merger remain unchanged.

Disclosure

The companies involved in merger or spin-off operations must inform the users of their annual accounts of their participation in such operations and of the most significant features of the operations, the current stage of the merger or spin-off processes and the foreseeable effects thereof.

Joint ventures

Accounting for Investments in Joint Ventures

In Spain there are three ways to set up a joint venture:

- a jointly controlled entity (*sociedad multigrupo*);

- a temporary Consortium (*unión temporal de empresas, UTE*);

- joint Venture Accounts (*cuentas en participación*).

For a jointly controlled entity, if the joint venture is incorporated, the participants should account for it in their individual annual accounts as an investment, at the lower of cost and market. In the consolidated accounts (if any) of the participants, the venture would generally be consolidated using the proportional method (see 'Consolidation') or, alternatively, the equity method.

For jointly controlled operations and jointly controlled assets, the accounting treatment in IAS 31 would be appropriate in Spain.

- **Temporary Consortium (*UTE*).** To the extent that the venture has no corporate identity, the participants incorporate into their individual (not consolidated) financial statements the appropriate percentages of the venture's assets, liabilities, income and expenses, as in the case of proportional method of consolidation.

- **Joint venture accounts (*cuentas en participación*).** Relate to a business managed by the parent entity (*partícipe gestor*), which records the contributions received from the participants in liability accounts and all income and expenses of the business. Accounts of expenses or income are used to transfer the corresponding profit or loss. The non-parent participant records the contribution made as an investment and the profit or loss attributed is recorded in income or expense accounts for the net amount.

Transactions between participants and the joint venture

The contribution of assets to a joint venture does not give rise to a gain on disposal in the contributor's financial statements. A loss would be recognisable on contribution to an incorporated joint venture where the deed of constitution attributed a lower value to the asset than its carrying value in the books of the contributor. In accounting for other transactions between the participants and the joint venture, the treatment would differ in the individual and consolidated accounts of the participant according to whether the venture was incorporated or unincorporated, with preference for deferral of recognition of profit and immediate recognition of any loss.

Disclosure

For incorporated joint ventures, the notes to the consolidated financial statements must include the following:

- Name and address of joint venture.

- Amount of investment and percentage interest held.

- Method of accounting used (if equity, a justification is required).

- Activities of the joint venture.

- Names of other participants.

If any joint ventures are excluded from consolidation, all of the above information is also required, together with the reason and justification for exclusion, and capital, reserves and results of the last available year.

Foreign currency translation (*conversión de divisas*)

Foreign Operations

The current rate method is used, except where the operations of the foreign subsidiary are such that they constitute 'a mere extension of the activities of one of the group's Spanish companies', in which case the temporal method is prescribed.

Under the current rate method, assets and liabilities are translated at the closing exchange rate; the profit and loss account is translated at the actual (or average) rate. The resulting difference in the balance sheet is taken to an 'exchange difference' reserve (*diferencias de conversión*).

Under the temporal method, non-monetary balance sheet items are translated at the historical rate, whereas the remaining items are translated at the closing rate. Translation differences, both positive and negative, are recorded in income in a special caption; alternatively, they may be treated in the same way as the parent company accounts for normal exchange differences.

Accounts of associated companies reported under the equity method are translated under the current rate method. Accounts of subsidiaries in highly inflationary countries should be translated under the temporal method or adjusted first in the foreign currency for changes in purchasing power.

The introduction of the euro will have no effect on the method used to account for a foreign investee domiciled in a European Monetary Union (EMU) Member State. The translation difference will, however, remain unchanged as from 1 January 1999 and while the shareholding is maintained. The necessary adjustments should be made in order to record assets at historical cost when the temporal method is used.

Domestic operations

The PGC stipulates the method of translation for all balance sheet items denominated in foreign currencies. Fixed assets, stock and variable return investments are translated at historical rates. All other balance sheet items are translated at the year-end rate. Transactions in foreign currencies are recorded in pesetas either at the rate prevailing at the time of the transaction or at an average rate for the period.

The rules are complex, but fundamentally the net unrealised exchange differences are, if positive, deferred and, if negative, charged to income.

If, however, losses have been expensed in prior years, a gain may be recorded up to the amount of the previously reported loss. Deferred gains are taken to income when realised or used to offset subsequent losses.

Subject to certain conditions, exchange differences on loans financing assets under construction may be capitalised. Nevertheless, this PGC rule is under review and it is probable that a new rule will be issued in line with IAS.

As a result of the introduction of the euro, exchange differences arising on transactions that have not yet fallen due at 31 December 1998, denominated in the currencies of EMU Member States, will be understood to have been realised and should therefore be taken to Profit and Loss at the year end 31 December 1998. As from 1 January 1999, foreign currency should be understood to relate to the currencies of non-EMU Member States.

Hedging transactions

In accordance with the draft accounting rule on Futures issued by ICAC, exchange differences relating to hedging operations covering the exchange exposure should be recorded by adjusting the valuation of the asset hedged.

Disclosure

The translation policy for foreign subsidiaries must be disclosed, together with the treatment of translation differences, which should be shown separately for each foreign entity. The basis of translation of balances denominated in foreign currencies must be disclosed, together with the policy for treatment of exchange differences. If assets and liabilities were originally recorded in a foreign currency, the basis of translation must similarly be disclosed.

As the standard profit and loss account format contains the captions for exchange profits and losses, the amounts recorded in income for the year must be disclosed, unless immaterial. Further, foreign currency lendings and borrowings (by currency), with details of hedging arrangements, must be disclosed.

As a result of the introduction of the euro, the following must be disclosed in the notes to the accounts:

- The quantification of exchange differences deriving from the introduction of the euro, the most significant transactions involved and the adjustments made. Maturity dates should be included together with the amounts of the most significant transactions.

- Should the Company record forward or future contracts involving the currencies of EMU Member States, the most significant transactions should be disclosed together with the accounting treatment afforded. Maturity dates should be specified as well as the amount of the exchange differences and the most significant transactions. A distinction should be drawn between items receivable and payable, respectively.

In the case of consolidated annual accounts:

• The amount of conversion differences relating to subsidiaries in EMU Member States, to which the year-end exchange rate is applied, should be disclosed.

• If the monetary–non-monetary method is applied to foreign companies whose accounts are denominated in the currencies of EMU Member States, information should be provided concerning the results of the conversion, indicating the method used to record the amount in question in Profit and loss. Specifically, information should be provided concerning the valuation differences with respect to historical cost arising in the foreign companies denominated in currencies of EMU Member States.

Changing prices/inflation accounting (*contabilidad para la inflación*)

General

Spain has no requirement to publish inflation-adjusted financial information. The only mention relates to the consolidation of investees in highly inflationary countries with respect to which the adjustments for inflation should be made in accordance with the rules laid down in this respect in the country in which the foreign company is located. If appropriate, in order to value an investment in a highly inflationary country in the individual accounts, the rules of the country in question should be used, or, alternatively IAS 29.

Disclosure

This situation, together with the principles and standards used to make the adjustments should, in any event, be disclosed in the notes to the consolidated accounts.

Accounting changes (*cambios en criterios valoración*)

Accounting treatment

The treatment in financial statements of a change in accounting policy is regulated in the *Plan General de Contabilidad* (PGC). In addition, a number of accounting rules emphasise the principle of consistency, indicating that where an accounting policy has been adopted, it must be followed consistently.

The cumulative effect at the beginning of the year of changes in accounting policies and methods should be accounted for as extraordinary items (see Chapter 5.4, 'Extraordinary or Unusual Items') in the year of change; changes in accounting estimates should be accounted for prospectively.

Disclosure

The notes must disclose the reason for the change and its effect on the financial statements. The CCom also requires an explanation in the notes if financial statements are not comparable with those of preceding years.

Prior period adjustments (*gastos e ingresos de otros ejercicios*)

Definition of adjusting items

In no case should previously reported results or reserves be adjusted, although reclassifications not affecting equity of a prior year's financial statements should be made to conform with the current year's presentation. The standard PGC profit and loss account format incorporates prior period items as an element of extraordinary items (see Chapter 5.4, 'Extraordinary or Unusual Items') entering into the determination of current year income. Nevertheless, certain industry-specific adaptations of the PGC allow, during the first year of adaptation (the PGC also allowed this during the year in which it came into force), certain adjustments resulting from the application of the new PYNCGA to be recorded against reserves.

Accounting treatment

The PGC includes captions under the general heading of extraordinary items (*resultados extraordinarios*) for reflecting income and expense of prior years. Only material items should be reported under this caption;

minor items should be classified as ordinary expense for the year. Prior year reported **retained earnings** are not adjusted (except as stated above).

Disclosure

Adequate explanation is to be given of prior year items, which are shown separately in the income statement.

Post-balance sheet events (*acontecimientos posteriores al cierre*)

Definition

Company law provides no definition of post balance sheet events, but classifies them in two categories:

• Events that do not affect the accounts, but knowledge of which is useful to the user.

• Events that affect the applicability of the going concern basis.

The Audit Technical Rules issued by the ICAC define post-balance sheet events as events or transactions that may arise after the balance sheet date but before the issuance of the report that have or may have a significant effect on the annual accounts. In certain cases these should therefore be included in the annual accounts and in other cases, should be disclosed in the notes to the accounts. A distinction is drawn between the following:

• Those events and transactions that provide additional evidence regarding conditions that already existed at the balance sheet date and that will lead to a change in the estimates made by the directors when initially drawing up the accounts.

• Those events and transactions that give rise to circumstances that did not exist at the year end and therefore do not entail the modification of the accounts but that, because of their importance, should be reported to the user of the annual accounts to avoid a misleading or incomplete interpretation.

Accounting treatment

Financial statements should be prepared based on conditions existing at the balance sheet date. Information regarding such conditions that comes to light during the preparation of the financial statements should be taken into account. Other material events should be disclosed.

Disclosure

Separate disclosure is required of information relating to any post balance sheet events that fall into either category (a) or (b) above.

Related party transactions (*transacciones con partes vinculadas*)

Definition

Definition of related parties is given in the CCom and the Introduction (Caption 19) of the *Plan General de Contabilidad* and specific disclosure in the annual accounts of certain types of transactions is required.

Accounting treatment

Transactions with related parties are accounted for using the same principles as for non-related party transactions. For purposes of tax assessment, the inspectorate may restate transactions with related parties on an arm's-length basis.

Disclosure

The only related parties for which disclosure is required are subsidiary, associated and multi-group companies, and remuneration of the directors of the reporting entity received by all companies included in the group.

For directors of the parent company, disclosure is required of the amount of salary, fees and any other form of remuneration from all consolidated companies, for whatever reason and classified by type of remuneration. This includes insurance premiums paid or the amount of any pension obligations (for present or former members), classified by type, and loans and advances (made by either the parent company or any consolidated company) together with related interest and any guarantee issued in their favour.

For subsidiaries, disclosure should be made of total transactions, classified by type (ie, sales, purchases and related year-end rebates, services received or given, interest received or charged, dividends or other profit distributions). For associated companies, disclosure is required of the amount of receivables/payables falling due in each of the following five years and the balance thereafter, appearing under each of the statutory balance sheet captions for receivables and payables.

Segmental information (*información por categoría de actividades*)

General

All companies are required to report segmental information by activity and geographical area. The criteria for an activity or a geographical area are subjective, based on the reporting entity's operations.

Segmental information may be omitted if its publication could prejudice the entity or if the entity may publish an abbreviated profit and loss account.

Disclosure

The notes must present a breakdown of turnover by activity and geographical area.

References

Financial statements: CCom Articles 34–38; PGC Parts 1.4 and 5; LSA Articles 173–201.

Consolidation: BOICAC 8, Issue 2; CCom Articles 25–49.

Mergers and spin-offs: Articles 233–259 of the Spanish Companies Act and the draft Accounting Regulations applicable to mergers and spin-offs issued by the Spanish Institute of Chartered Accountants (Official Gazette of the Spanish Institute of Chartered Accounts, 14).

Joint ventures: Consolidation Rules-Memoria 2, Order 127/93 Plan adapted to construction companies valuation rule 21 (BOICAC 12), Order 1228/94 Plan adapted to property companies valuation rule 21 (BOICAC 20), RD 437/98 Plan adapted to electricity companies valuation rule 22 (BOICAC 33) and PGC part 3.

Foreign currency translation: PGC Part 4, RD 2814/1998 Art. 5 and 6 Chapter 3, Draft Accounting Rule BOICAC 21.

Accounting changes: Consolidation rules Art. 57.

Changing prices/inflation accounting: CCom Articles 35 and 44; PGC Part 4 and 5.

Prior period adjustments: CCom Article 35; PGC Part 4.

Post-balance sheet events: PGC Part 4 and Audit Technical Rule on Reports and Audit Technical Rule of Post-balance sheet events issued by the ICAC.

Related party transactions: PGC Part 4; CCom Art. 48.

Segmental information: PGC Part 4; LSA Article 200.

5.3

Accounting Principles for Specific Items – Balance Sheet

PricewaterhouseCoopers

Property, plant and equipment (*inmovilizaciones materiales*)

Classification of Capital and Revenue Expenditure

The definition of assets to be recorded in specific *Plan General de Contabilidad* (PGC) accounts gives some guidance, as does the section on accounting principles (*normas de valoración*). In addition, the Spanish Institute of Chartered Accountants (ICAC) has issued a Resolution that lays down valuation rules for tangible fixed assets governing specific aspects of transactions involving tangible fixed assets such as donations, swaps and non-cash contributions

In addition, the ICAC has issued a Resolution in relation to production cost. The resolution states that financial expenses may be included, as an increase in the value of fixed assets in the course of construction, provided that such expenses have accrued before the fixed assets are ready to be brought into operation.

When such differences have resulted from debts in foreign currency (other than the euro maturing in more than one year), this resolution enables exchange differences to be included, as an increase in the value of fixed assets. This is also the same case where they are used specifically to finance the said fixed assets in which the potential gain or loss may be included as a decrease or increase in the cost of the relevant assets, provided that certain conditions are met. (See section on Inventories in this chapter.)

Basis of valuation

Company law explicitly states that the only basis for the carrying value of fixed assets is cost, with the single exception of legal actualisations (see below).

The last legal actualisation was issued by the RD-Law 7/1996. Consequently, assets acquired prior to 31 December 1996 are stated at cost plus any revaluations carried out in accordance with the provisions of RD-Law 7/1996 and the enabling regulations contained in RD 2607/1996.

Write-down of assets (other than normal depreciation) is unusual, although contemplated in the PGC. It must be reported separately in the profit and loss account and a provision set up until such time as the loss in value proves permanent, when it is written off against the asset.

On disposal of assets, the cost and accumulated depreciation accounts are adjusted and the profit or loss on sale is recorded in income as an extraordinary item (see Chapter 5.4, 'Extraordinary or Unusual Items').

Actualisation (actualización)

Actualisation, although now of decreasing significance, is a means of compensating businesses for the erosive effects of inflation. The government has, from time to time (most recently in 1981, 1983 and 1996), enacted legislation permitting optional revaluation of fixed assets by the application of specified coefficients based on the acquisition date of the assets and related annual depreciation. Revaluations were credited to an actualisation (revaluation) reserve that was part of shareholders' equity.

Application of the coefficients was legally subject to the overriding condition that the resulting carrying value should not exceed the 'real' value of the asset. In practice, however, most businesses applied the full coefficient without regard to that criterion, in order to maximise the benefit of future tax-deductible depreciation expense.

In accordance with Transitional Regulation 18 of Law 43/1995 on Corporate Income Tax, with effect as from the fiscal year commencing 1 January 1996 the Revaluation Reserve (Budget Law 1983) is freely available, provided that the necessary appropriation has been made to the legal reserve.

Concerning Revaluation Reserve Royal Decree-Law 7/1996, once the balance has been examined and agreed by the tax authorities, or after a three-year period has elapsed, it may be used to offset losses or to increase the Company's share capital. After ten years the balance may be transferred to freely available reserves, provided that capital gains have been amortised or the restated assets have been transferred or written off. The balance in the reserve may not be directly or indirectly distributed until the capital gain has been realised.

Thus, although with the passing of time, growth, inflation and the depreciation or sale of revalued assets, actualisation surpluses are of diminishing importance, there remain non-distributable reserves or parts of share capital that have their origin in a revaluation.

In addition, it should be noted that there is specific legislation governing the restatement of assets in certain autonomous regions (Basque Country, Navarre) that differs in certain aspects from the central government regulations.

Depreciation

Companies are required to allow for depreciation at rates calculated to write the cost of an asset down to its estimated net realisable value at the end of its economically useful life.

The depreciation method used is almost universally the straight-line method (subject to the variations explained below), although the reducing (declining) balance method is also acceptable.

Disclosure

A movements schedule must be presented for all tangible fixed asset accounts. Depreciation rates and, for each class of assets, details regarding assets acquired from group companies should be disclosed. An additional disclosure, which may be difficult for many businesses to comply with, is the requirement to indicate the net un-amortised portion of earlier revaluations or 'actualisations' and the revaluation-related amortisation charge for the year.

Other disclosure requirements include:

- the cost and accumulated depreciation of assets located abroad;

- the amount of any interest expense or exchange differences capitalised during the year;

- cost and accumulated depreciation of assets not used in operations;

- nature and amount of assets fully amortised, technically obsolete or not in use;

- assets subject to any mortgage, lien or reversion;

- firm purchase (and sale) commitments for fixed assets and expected sources of financing;

- and any other relevant information (such as rental of premises, insurance, lawsuits and embargoes).

Intangible assets (*inmovilizaciones inmateriales*)

Accounting treatment

The accounting treatment to be afforded to intangible fixed assets is that envisaged in the PGC, the ICAC Resolution on the valuation of intangible fixed assets and, insofar as it is applicable, the ICAC Resolution on the valuation rules of tangible fixed assets.

In general, intangible assets are recorded at cost, and, except where they conflict with specific rules, the same rules apply as for tangible fixed assets. Cost may include capitalisation of internal costs, if applicable. Treatments of specific types of intangible assets are as follows:

- **Patents and trademarks (*Propiedad industrial*).** This heading includes any amounts paid for the ownership or right to use patents or trademarks. All of those costs are capitalised under this heading once the patent/trademark is registered. The ICAC Resolution on the valuation of intangible assets states that they should be amortised over the period in which they are expected to contribute to income.

- **Research and development expenses (*investigación y desarrollo*).** As a general rule, they are treated as an expense for the year in which they are incurred, including those relating to projects commissioned to other research companies or institutions. However, these expenses may be capitalised if a series of conditions laid down in Section 2 of the ICAC's Resolution on intangible fixed asset valuation rules (see Chapter 5.4, 'Research and Development') are met.

- **Lease premiums (*Derechos de traspaso*).** Lease premiums are recorded at cost. They are to be amortised in the shortest time-period possible, which in no circumstances should exceed the period during which they contribute to income nor the period of the lease contract. In any event, the period over which they should be amortised should not exceed that laid down for goodwill (see 'Research and Development' in the following chapter).

- **Software.** Software is recorded at cost and amortised as a development expense (see Chapter 5.4, 'Research and Development') with a maximum of five years. Software maintenance may not be capitalised. The cost of producing software in house may be capitalised 'only in cases where it is expected to be used over various years'.

- **Preliminary, formation and capital increase expenses (*gastos de establecimiento, de constitución y de ampliación de capital*).** These are reported as start-up expenses, a deferred expense, rather than as intangible fixed assets. Preliminary expenses are defined as the cost of initial technical and economic viability studies, launching publicity, initial recruitment and training of personnel. Formation expenses are defined as the legal and fiscal costs of incorporation; costs of printing share certificates, prospectuses and similar items; and related publicity expense. Similar types of cost arising from increases in share capital are also included in this heading. Such expenses must be amortised systematically over a period not exceeding five years. While unamortised expenses of this kind remain in the balance sheet, distribution of profits is restricted (see 'Capital and reserves' in this chapter).

- **Goodwill (*Fondo de comercio*).** Goodwill can be included as an asset only when it has been acquired for valuable consideration. It must be amortised over its useful life, with a maximum of twenty years (the amortisation period has recently been changed from ten years and the change is applicable to the annual accounts prepared after 31 December 1998, with no effect on amortisation charged in previous years). Where the period of depreciation exceeds five years, justification for the excess period must be included in the notes to the accounts.

- **Loan formalisation expenses (*Gastos de formalización de deudas*).** Loan formalisation expenses are reported as a deferred expense, rather than as intangible assets. Expensing in the year incurred is encouraged, but they may be amortised over the life of the loan.

The PGC also includes as intangible fixed assets leasing rights (see 'Leases' in this chapter), research and development expenditures (see 'Research and Development' in the following chapter) and payments in advance on intangible assets.

Disclosure

A movements schedule is required for each category of intangible assets, and explanatory information must be given on material items.

Leases (*arrendamiento financiero*)

Classification

The PGC, on the treatment of leased assets, indicates merely that 'where it is evident from the economic terms of a leasing arrangement that it is an acquisition, it must be accounted for as such under intangible assets'.

The ICAC has provided guidance on the subject, to the effect that an asset acquired under a lease may be considered a finance lease and capitalised provided:

- the leasing contract includes an option to purchase.

- there is 'no reasonable doubt' that such an option will be exercised.

The following examples, amongst others, of 'no reasonable doubt' are given:

- When at the time of signing the contract, the option to purchase is less than the estimated value of the asset at the time of exercising the option.

- When the option price at the time of signing the contract is insignificant with respect to the total lease contract amount.

Accounting treatment in financial statements of lessees

Finance lease

Assets being acquired under finance leases should be recorded as intangible assets at the asset's cash value while total instalments payable plus the purchase option should be recorded under liabilities. The difference between both amounts, relating to financial costs, should be recorded under deferred expenses. The assets should be depreciated over their useful lives. When the purchase option is exercised, intangible assets and accumulated depreciation are adjusted accordingly and the relevant amount is included under the asset's value within Tangible fixed assets. Similarly, deferred expenses are taken to profit and loss using a financial method.

Before the reform, lease payments were almost universally expensed as paid. Transitional arrangements for finance leases in effect at the beginning of the first financial year commencing after 31 December, 1990 provided that companies could, at their option, either capitalise finance lease assets retroactively, with an adjustment to reserves, or continue to expense the lease payments as incurred.

Operating lease

Rental payments for operating leases should be expensed as incurred.

Sale and leaseback operations

If in substance a sale and leaseback transaction is a financing operation, the lessee should write off the net book value of the asset involved and simultaneously record an intangible asset for the same amount. At the same time, total instalments payable should be recorded under liabilities together with the amount of the purchase option. The difference between the debt and financing received should be recorded under deferred expenses.

Disclosure

The accounting policy used for assets acquired under finance leases must be disclosed. For all leases, disclosure must be made of the original cost, contract duration (including years expired), purchase option price and total leasing payments (shown separately for amounts paid in prior periods, paid during the year and outstanding).

Accounting treatment in financial statements of lessors

Leased assets, whether subject to finance or operating leases, are separately identified in the balance sheet under the property, plant and equipment caption and depreciated on either the straight-line or financial basis.

Finance lease
The total future leasing payments are recorded immediately in the customer account, with a credit to a deferred interest account and the balance to the future leasing instalments account. As each payment is made, an appropriate portion of the deferred interest account is released to income. At the same time, an amount equivalent to the balance of the payment is released from the future leasing instalments account. A financial method is used for depreciation of the asset, the monthly charge is equivalent to the amount released from the future leasing instalments account.

Operating lease
Rental receipts for operating lease should be recorded as income as incurred.

Disclosure

The accounting policy for assets sold under leasing arrangements must be disclosed. The assets subject to leasing are disclosed separately from operating assets and by appropriate category. Both the receivable and the future leasing instalments accounts must be analysed by the year in which they fall due.

Investments (*inmovilizaciones e inversiones financieras*)

Valuation

Treatment of long- and short-term investments is similar. Both are reported at the lower of cost or market value. Cost includes costs of acquisition and purchase of subscription rights. Where subscription rights attaching to shares are sold, the cost of such rights reduces the carrying value of the shares. Market value is determined as follows:

- **Shareholdings in the capital of Group and associated companies:** Proportional book value of the holding, adjusted to take into account any latent capital gains existing when the holding was acquired that still exist on the balance sheet date. If the latent capital gain is identified as goodwill in respect of the investee, for the purposes of recording the provision for amortisation, the amortisation thereof should be taken into account as if it had been recorded on the date of acquisition. Additional provisions should be made to reflect negative changes in the capital and reserve of the investee.

- **All other holdings:** Officially listed securities (when the shareholding is less than 3 per cent): the lower of the average listed price for the last quarter of the financial year and the price at the year-end.

- **Unlisted securities:** on the basis of the proportional book value of the holding as reflected in the latest available annual accounts.

In comparing cost with market value of fixed interest securities, accrued interest should be considered. Special accounting rules apply to treasury stock (own shares held), which are dealt with in the section on 'Capital and Reserves' later in this chapter.

Treatment of valuation reserve
The amount of any necessary provisions to reduce the carrying value of investments to market value must be shown in the profit and loss account separately for long- and short-term investments. Any provision established in this connection may not be carried forward when the conditions dictating its creation cease to exist.

Gains/losses

The difference between the net book value and the selling price of an investment is recognised in income when the investment is sold. Generally the practice would be to apply **average cost.** The profit or loss so determined is reported as an extraordinary item.

Disclosure

A schedule showing the movements of investments, by account category, should be provided. In addition, the notes are required to present detailed disclosures related to investments, such as any associated pledges or commitments, the currencies of issue, hedging arrangements, maturity dates and yields.

Accounts receivable (*deudores*)

Accounting treatment

Receivables are recorded at their face value. Interest included in the face value of trade receivables falling due after more than one year is recorded under Deferred income and taken to profit and loss on a yearly basis in accordance with a financial method. Any necessary provisions, such as for non-collection, are shown separately.

- **Recognition:** The recognition of **revenue,** and hence the related receivable, is as described in the section on 'Revenue Recognition' in the following chapter.

- **Discounts and rebates:** Cash discounts are regarded as a financial expense, irrespective of whether or not they are included in the invoice. Year-end rebates for achieving target levels of purchases are recorded in separate accounts from the related sale.

- **Allowances:** No specific method of calculating the provision for doubtful accounts is prescribed in the PGC. The generally accepted method consists of the individual identification of the relevant accounts.

For tax purposes, the provision for bad debts must be recorded on an individual account basis. Only in exceptional circumstances can provision be made on an overall basis using certain key figures (sales, debtor balances and other):

- **Individual system**: Provision may be made for the amount involved either in its entirety or in part provided that the risk of default is justified (bankruptcy, judicial complaint and doubtful debtors outstanding for more than one year).

- **Overall system**: Small companies may provide for bad debts by appropriating 1 per cent of the balance receivable at the year-end to the provision.

Factoring (*descuento de efectos y factoring without recourse*)

The discounting of receivables with banks is widespread. Most commercial transactions are for settlement in 90 days, and the most common means of settlement is by 'letra', an unaccepted bill of exchange drawn by the supplier and generally negotiated with the bank for immediate use of the funds. At maturity it is processed through the clearing system and presented to the customer. If it is not honoured, the bank has recourse to the supplier, whose account is debited. The PGC requires the recognition of the substance of the transaction; that is, the transaction should be accounted for as a bank loan secured against future cash flows, and accounts receivable should not be credited until the customer makes payment. In almost all cases, the up-front interest charge on discounting is not apportioned between accounting periods, although this treatment does not strictly conform with the matching principle.

Factoring without recourse is treated as a sale of the relevant account receivable when risk is fully transferred to the financial institution involved.

Disclosure

Standard captions in the PGC require separate disclosure of trade receivables (third parties); accounts receivable from group and associated companies; sundry debtors; employees; state entities; and advances received from customers.

Provisions for doubtful accounts and other allowances must be separately disclosed, as must the charge for the year, split between increases in the provision and write-offs.

Inventories (*existencias*)

General accounting treatment

Under the PGC, inventory is categorised as follows:

- Goods purchased for resale without processing.

- Finished goods manufactured by the company and ready for sale.

- Work in progress, whatever its stage of manufactured, where destined for incorporation into finished products.

- Raw materials for incorporation into the production process.

- Other supplies, such as fuel, lubricants, packing materials and spares that do not fall into any of the foregoing categories, plus saleable scrap and by-products.

- Provisions (such as for obsolescence).

- Advances to suppliers for purchase of inventory items.

Valuation

Inventory is valued at the lower of cost or market value. The cost of purchased raw materials includes direct expenses incurred to the point at which the goods enter the warehouse (such as transportation, customs duties and insurance), but excludes interest, storage and other internal expenses.

Production cost consists of the acquisition price of raw materials and other consumables needed in the production process as well as costs directly attributable to the product and the part of indirect costs that may be reasonably attributed. Costs should be attributed to the product until the product is completed.

Financial expenses may be included as an increase in the value of inventories in the course of construction with long production cycles, not taking interruptions into account and provided that such financial expenses have accrued before the inventories are ready for final consumption or utilisation by other companies.

Exchange differences involving currencies other than the euro should not be regarded as adjustments to the production cost of fixed assets or inventories. The company may, nevertheless, opt to include the potential gain or loss as a decrease or an increase in the cost of the relevant assets, when the exchange differences result from debts in foreign currencies, (other than the euro maturing in more than one year). This is also the case where they are used, specifically, to finance fixed assets or inventories in the course of construction involving long production cycles, provided that all the following conditions are met:

- The amount payable that generated the differences has been unequivocally used to construct a fixed asset or manufacture inventories that have been specifically identified.

- The period over which the fixed asset is constructed or the inventories are manufactured exceeds twelve months.

- The variation in the exchange rate takes place before the fixed assets are ready for operation or the inventories are ready for final consumption or utilisation by other companies.

- The amount resulting from their inclusion in cost in no circumstances exceeds the market or replacement value of the fixed assets or inventories.

For inventories whose acquisition cost or production cost may not be identified on an individual basis, the weighted average price or weighted average cost method is generally used. Only if the company considers that the FIFO, LIFO or other similar methods are more suitable for management purposes and that they give a more accurate true and fair view of the company's state of affairs can these other methods be used. Standard cost is not acceptable unless the differences that would have resulted as compared with the application of other methods, as accepted in this Resolution, are not significant.

Once a valuation method has been adopted, it must be applied consistently to all inventories with similar characteristics and of a similar nature.

Market value of goods purchased from third parties is their replacement value or net realisable value, if less. Market value of manufactured items is their net realisable value. For work in progress, market value is defined as the net realisable value of the related finished product less costs to be incurred in its completion.

Long-term contracts

The method of valuation of long-term contracts is not prescribed by legislation, although the ICAC has developed specialised industry Accounting Charts that regulate this area.

There are two methods for recording income:

• **Percentage of completion method:** under which income is recognised as the contract is performed and it is therefore possible to apportion income and expenses over the term of the contract. In order to apply this method, two conditions must be fulfilled:

  – the company must have a cost system which allows it to reasonably and reliably estimate contract budgets, income, costs and level of completion at any given date; and
  – there must be no unusual or extraordinary risks that could jeopardise the successful performance of the contract or collection of the amount involved.

• **Completed contract method:** under which income is realised when the goods or services envisaged under the contract have been substantially provided. Inventories under construction are valued at the costs incurred that may be attributed to the contract.

This method is also used when it is not possible to apply the percentage-of-completion method because the necessary resources to make reasonable estimates are not available. It should be borne in mind that this method is incompatible with the accrual principle and its application must therefore be approved by the authorities.

Disclosure

The basis of valuation of inventory and the method of determining provisions for obsolescence should be disclosed. In the balance sheet, there should be separate presentation of the different types of inventory listed above, followed by any related provisions for obsolescence. The profit and loss account must also show separately the purchases made during the year, together with the changes in inventory and provisions for obsolescence. It should be noted that the PGC profit and loss account format does not disclose (or permit calculation of) a cost of goods sold figure. Other disclosures include details of significant purchase and sales agreements, and details (with values) of any charges or liens on inventory or goods on consignment.

Current liabilities (*pasivo circulante*)

Accounting treatment

Current liabilities, as defined by the PGC, include short-term loans and debts arising from the purchase of services or goods. The criterion for long-term/short-term distinction is 12 months. The PGC provides specific captions for the presentation of liabilities whose maturity exceeds 12 months. Liabilities must be reflected at their face value. Accrued liabilities are reflected in a separate caption.

- Income received in advance (deferred income) is recognised as income when it accrues; until that time, it is shown as a long- or short-term liability.

- Loans are shown at the amount drawn down; any undrawn balance is disclosed in a note.

- Generally, proposed dividends are not provided for in the accounts, but there is an obligation to disclose them in the notes.

Creation of general and specific provisions

Provision 'for risks and responsibilities', disclosed between shareholders' equity and long-term debt in the balance sheet. Under the PGC its use is restricted to specific, certain and probable risks; in addition to information on the risks covered, a movements schedule must be provided. General provisions are therefore no longer permitted.

Disclosure

The format of the standard PGC balance sheet provides for separate disclosure, where material, of the short-term portion of debentures (split between convertible, nonconvertible, other debt and accrued interest), borrowings (loans and accrued interest), related party liabilities, commercial creditors (customer advances, trade creditors and debts represented by bills of exchange), nontrade creditors (state entities, debts represented by bills of exchange, accrued payroll, short-term deposits and others), provisions for guarantees and sales returns, accrued expenses and short-term deferred income.

In addition, details of significant purchase commitments, circumstances that might give rise to lawsuits and details of guaranteed liabilities should be disclosed.

Long-term debt (*acreedores a largo plazo*)

Accounting treatment

Long-term debt is reported at the amount at which it is to be repaid, including premium, if any. The discount on issuance plus the repayment premium, if any, are reported as a deferred charge and are written off on a suitable basis. Companies are encouraged to write off expenses of issuance in the year incurred, although 'exceptionally' they may be written off over the life of the issue. Any portion of loan principal repayable within 12 months of the balance sheet date is classified as a current liability.

Debt restructuring/paying off (*restructuración y amortización anticipada de deuda*)

No specific rules or guidelines are mentioned in the PGC for Debt Restructuring/Paying off. However, the *Asociación Española de Contabilidad y Administración de Empresas* (AECA) has issued document no. 18: 'Financial liabilities', which develops the accounting treatment of the issues that may arise in the event of paying-off or modification of financial liabilities. These include a change of creditor, maturity of convertible loan stock, maturity of debentures that may be exchanged for shares, conversion of other financial liabilities into capital and transformation of loans into grants. In addition, ICAC has issued a Rule in Draft about the accounting treatment of 'Suspension of payments'.

Disclosure

The standard balance sheet format requires separate disclosure of 14 different categories of debt, distinguishing among various types of debentures, loans, bills of exchange and other debt arrangements. The amount of principal repayable should be analysed for each of the following five years and the total amount thereafter for each debt category. The total should be broken down by group, or by associated and other companies.

In addition, disclosure is required of the amount of unpaid accrued interest; details of mortgages securing debt; details of each issue of debentures or bonds (such as interest rate, repayment date, security given and conversion particulars); and details of unused lines of credit.

Contingent liabilities (*pasivos contingentes*)

General Accounting Treatment

Accounting law gives little guidance on the treatment of loss **contingencies** and is silent on gain contingencies. Most quoted companies appear to have been broadly following US principles.

Disclosure

The amounts of any guarantees given with respect to third parties must be disclosed, analysed by type of guarantee and broken down by group, associated and other companies. For each, the amount, if any, provided in the accounts must be disclosed.

Generally, for each contingency, there must be disclosure of its nature, the basis on which it is evaluated, factors on which it depends and its potential impact on net worth or an explanation of why it cannot be quantified, indicating maximum and minimum risks.

Capital and reserves (*fondos propios*)

General

Capital and Reserves constitute the shareholders' contribution to the financing of operations. In Spain, the minimum capital for an SA is Ptas10 million. The PGC contemplates shareholders' equity being divided into share capital, share premium, legal reserve, reserves for the purchase of its own (or parent company) shares, reserves from retained earnings, and profit or loss for the year less dividends paid on account during the year.

Share capital (capital social)

Businesses incorporated under the *Texto Refundido de la Ley de Sociedades Anónimas* (LSA) may issue shares in either registered or bearer form; shares issued in the latter form must be fully paid. Shares must have a par value, expressed in pesetas. A company's share capital may consist of different classes of shares, each with differing voting, dividend and capital repayment rights. Unpaid capital is shown as an asset, representing the company's rights against the shareholders. Uncalled amounts are shown above (ie, as less liquid than) fixed assets, while called but unpaid amounts are shown as the first item in current assets.

No company may subscribe to its own shares or to those of its parent on issuance, but may acquire them on the market subsequently, provided that:

- they are fully paid;
- the holding does not exceed 10 per cent;
- the acquisition is authorised by the parent company in a general meeting.

Share premium (reserva prima de emisión)

The share premium account is credited with the proceeds in excess of par value of new share issues. The law imposes no restriction on its use, merely indicating that it may be used to increase capital.

Legal reserve (reserva legal)

Company law requires that 10 per cent of the net profit in each year be appropriated to this reserve until such time as the balance equals 20 per cent of the share capital. This reserve is not available for distribution (except to the extent that it exceeds 20 per cent of share capital) but may be used to offset losses where no other reserves are available. It may also be used to increase capital, but only if, after the increase, the balance of the reserve is not less than 10 per cent of the new capital.

Reserves (for purchase of own, or related company, shares)

A company may not subscribe on issuance for either its own shares or shares issued by its parent company. A company may, however, acquire its own shares or those of its parent company provided the following conditions are met:

- Acquisition is approved by a shareholders' meeting that sets the maximum and minimum price, maximum number of shares that can be acquired and the duration of the authorisation, which cannot exceed 18 months.

- The nominal value of the shares acquired, including those already held by the company and its subsidiaries, may not exceed 10 per cent of share capital (5 per cent if shares are quoted).

- The shares acquired have been fully paid up.

- A reserve must be created without reducing capital or undistributable reserves equal to the carrying value of the company's own shares or of the shares of the parent company. Such a reserve must be maintained until the shares are sold.

Crossholdings of shares also give rise to the obligation to set up a reserve. Thus, if a company ('A') acquires, directly or indirectly, more than 10 per cent of the shares in another ('B'), it must immediately notify the other company of the fact. Where crossholdings in excess of 10 per cent arise involuntarily, the company that is first notified of the fact (say, B) must reduce its holding in the company issuing the notification (in this case A) below 10 per cent. Until it has disposed of the excess, B must set up a 'reserve for crossholdings' equal to the net cost of that part of its holding in A that exceeds 10 per cent. The reserve may be released when the excess is disposed of.

The transfers to and from the reserves listed above are recorded in one of the distributable reserves.

Dividends paid on account (dividendo a cuenta)

Dividends paid on account during the year are shown separately on the face of the balance sheet as a deduction under capital and reserves. Proposed but not approved dividends are not recognised as a liability but disclosed by note. Where a dividend has been paid on account, the notes must include an 'accounting forecast' covering the 12 months from payment *'estado contable previsional'*.

Disclosure

Details of authorised and issued share capital, including rights associated with founders' shares and convertible debentures, with a schedule of movements during the period should be provided. If capital is increased, details of the shares issued should be given. The amount of any authorised and un-issued capital and restrictions on distribution of reserves should also be disclosed. The notes should disclose details of own shares held, directly or indirectly, indicating their ultimate use and amount of reserve. Holdings in excess of 10 per cent of a reporting entity's capital should be disclosed.

Restrictions on the payment of dividends

The distribution of freely available reserves as well as the distribution of profits for the year is subject to the following restrictions:

- The distribution would reduce the remaining reserves to an amount less than the sum of the un-amortised balance of preliminary and formation expenses plus research and development expenses and goodwill (see earlier in this Chapter, 'Intangible Assets' and Chapter 5.4, 'Research and Development').

- The balance of the Revaluation Reserve Royal Decree – Law 7/1996 of 7 June 1996 (see beginning of this Chapter, 'Property, Plant and Equipment') may not be directly distributed until the capital gain has been realised and, if appropriate, the purchase option exercised. If the balance of the Revaluation reserve Royal Decree – Law 7/1996 is being used to increase share capital and/or appropriated to freely available reserves, the balance of that account may not be indirectly distributed in the event of a capital reduction involving the reimbursement of contributions or distribution of reserves when the amount of capital or reserves resulting from said reduction or distribution is lower than the undistributed part of the revaluation reserve included in share capital and/or freely available reserves.

References

Property, plant and equipment: PGC Part 5; LSA Article 195; RD-Law 7/1996 and ICAC Resolutions (BOICAC 6 and 42).

Intangible assets: PGC Parts 4 and 5; LSA Articles 194 and 195 and ICAC Resolution (BOICAC 8).

Leases: PGC Parts 4 and 5; AECA Document 2 and ICAC Resolution (BOICAC 8).

Investments: PGC Parts 4 and 5.

Accounts receivable: PGC Parts 3, 4 and 5.

Inventories: PGC Parts 4 and 5 AECA Document 8, and ICDC Resolution (BIOCAC 42).

Current liabilities: PGC Parts 4 and 5.

Long-term debt: LSA Article 197; PGC Parts 4 and 5. 21. Draft Technical Rule 'Suspension of Payments'

Contingent liabilities: PGC Part 4 and AECA Document 11.

Capital and reserves: LSA Articles 49–54, 75–84, 157 and 214; BOICAC 2 and PGC Part 4.

5.4

Accounting Principles for Specific Items – Income Statement

PricewaterhouseCoopers

Revenue recognition (*reconocimiento de ingresos*)

General principles

Income is recorded when a service has been provided, the transfer of ownership in an asset has been effected or the right to the income arises. Normally, in the case of sale of goods, the time of recognition of income is on delivery of the goods. In the case of income from services, income is recognised when the services are completed. Income is recorded at its gross amount, and deductions for discounts or other rebates are shown separately. Interest income must be shown separately.

Long-term contracts

Revenue recognition for long-term contracts is described in the section on 'Inventories' in the previous chapter.

Instalment sales (*ventas a plazo*)

Receivables on instalment sales are recorded at face value. If a credit sale extends over more than 12 months, the interest element is credited to a deferred income account and written back to income on a financial basis.

Rights of return (*ventas con derecho de devolución*)

Sales where a right of return exists are generally recorded as firm sales, and appropriate provision is made for probable returns. No specific requirements exist, however, in this area.

Disclosure

The principal income captions in the profit and loss account distinguish between income arising from the sale of goods or the provision of services, deductions for rebates and returns, investment income (various categories), profit on translation or conversion, extraordinary income, work on own assets and increases in inventory of finished and in-process stock. The effect on income of any change in valuation criteria or method of presentation of income should also be shown.

Government grants and assistance (*subvenciones recibidas*)

Accounting treatment

Non-reimbursable capital grants (ie, grants whose conditions have been fulfilled or where there is no reasonable doubt as to their being fulfilled) are generally deferred in a special balance sheet caption and written off to income at the same rate as the related assets. It is also theoretically possible to credit the entire grant against the cost of the related asset.

In addition to capital grants in cash, there are also operating grants and total or partial relief from state or local taxes. All such grants are accounted for as operating income in the profit and loss account.

Disclosure

The amount, description and conditions attaching to subsidies and grants received, the un-amortised balance, amount amortised during the period and accounting policy used must be disclosed. If the grant assists the purchase of property, plant and equipment, details of the grant must be provided under that caption.

Research and development (*investigación y desarrollo*)

Definitions of research and development expenses

Research and development expenses are defined as expenses incurred for the purpose of improving technological and scientific know-how, perfection of new applications, improvement of the business or similar activity. As long as un-amortised cost of this type remains in the balance sheet, distribution of profits is restricted as set out in the section on 'Capital and Reserves' in the previous chapter.

Accounting treatment

Research and development expenditures may be capitalised only when:

- The projects are specifically identified and costs clearly defined so that they may be amortised.

- There is good reason to believe that the projects will be successful and the product profitable.

Amortisation should be over as short a period as possible, within a maximum of five years from the end of the development project in the case of development costs and, in the case of research costs as from the year in which they are capitalised. If any doubt as to the commercial viability of the project arises, costs must be expensed immediately. When the process or product becomes protected by patent or otherwise, the related deferred costs should be transferred to the caption patents and trademarks (propiedad industrial); see the section on 'Intangible Assets' in the previous chapter.

Disclosure

A schedule of movements of the research and development account should he provided, and the criteria followed for the deferral and amortisation disclosed.

Capitalised interest costs (*intereses capitalizados*)

Accounting treatment

In the case of fixed assets and inventories, as stated by the Spanish Institute of Chartered Accountants (ICAC) and *Plan General de Contabilidad* (PGC), purchase cost may include interest accrued prior to the date of the asset becoming ready to be put into use or for final consumption or utilisation by other companies (inventories). The amount of interest capitalised relates to interest charged by the supplier and interest and commissions on loans for financing the acquisition. In addition, if there are sources of borrowing that have not been obtained specifically for the acquisition or construction of fixed assets and inventories, accrued interest expense may be capitalised for these debts in accordance with certain rules.

Disclosure

The interest capitalisation policy and the amount capitalised during the year should be disclosed.

Implicit interest in not-trade debtor accounts (*intereses implícitos en deudas no comerciales*)

Accounting treatment

Debt is stated at the amount at which it is to be repaid, and any excess over the actual proceeds of the loan is reported as deferred interest and written off to expense on a financial basis. While there is no specific requirement to write down loans or other long-term debt to net present value where agreements are entered into at lower-than-market rates of interest, this might be required on occasion in order to present a true and fair view.

Disclosure

The method of recognising imputed interest must be disclosed. In addition, disclosure of the net amount outstanding and interest rate imputed would appear to be required under the caption 'any other significant information'.

Extraordinary or unusual items (*resultados extraordinarios*)

Definition

Terminology used for extraordinary items in Spain may be confusing, as two levels of extraordinary items are reported. Under the PGC, virtually all items of income and expense not relating to operating and financing activities are identified separately as extraordinary (*resultados extraordinarios*), on both the income and expense sides of the profit and loss account. '*Resultados extraordinarios*' include the following captions:

- Extraordinary results-positive:
  - Profit on sale of fixed assets;
  - Profit on dealings in own shares;
  - Grants on fixed assets transferred to income;
  - Extraordinary income;
  - Prior year items-profits.

- Extraordinary results-negative:
  - Asset write-downs;
  - Loss on sale of fixed assets;
  - Loss on dealings in own shares;
  - Extraordinary expenses;
  - Prior year items-losses.

As may be seen, within the above there are further specific captions for extraordinary income and expenses. These should record 'those profits or losses of material amount which a user or reader of the financial statement would consider nonrecurring when estimating likely future results of operations'. Generally, an income or expense is considered an extraordinary item if it originates from events or transactions that are outside the normal activities of the business and there is a reasonable expectation that they will not recur with frequency.

The PGC gives various examples of transactions to be recorded as extraordinary items, such as losses arising from flood, fire or other accidents; costs of an unsuccessful take-over bid; fines; fiscal and legal penalties; and recovery of receivables previously considered irrecoverable. The list is not all-inclusive.

Disclosure

Apart from disclosure in specific captions of the income statement as described above, an explanation of the nature of any type of extraordinary income or expense should be given.

Income taxes (*impuesto sobre sociedades*)

Accounting treatment

The PGC requires that income tax be accounted for as an expense and the liability disclosed on the balance sheet. Deferred taxes are recognised under the liability method, and deferred tax assets are carried forward only to the extent that their recovery is reasonably assured. The full provision method, therefore, is likely to be used.

Timing differences giving rise to tax credits may only be treated as such when their future realisation is reasonably assured. Otherwise, they should be treated as permanent differences.

However, timing differences giving rise to tax liabilities should at all times be regarded as such. There is no limit on the period over which they may reverse.

Reasonable doubts are assumed to exist regarding the future realisation of tax credits resulting from timing differences in the following circumstances, *inter alia*:

- When they are expected to reverse in over ten years as from the year end.

- In the case of companies habitually reporting losses.

- In the case of credits relating to tax loss carry-forwards, such losses must have arisen due to atypical circumstances, the causes of which do not persist, and there must not be reasonable doubts regarding the existence of future tax profits against which to offset the losses in question.

Tax losses may, subject to approval, be offset against profits for the succeeding ten tax years.

Disclosure

Disclosure should include a reconciliation of the reported pre-tax income and taxable income, details of tax loss carry-forwards and tax incentives/credits, and any other material information relating to the tax position. This could include, for example, which years are open to inspection by the tax authorities – a major factor in assessing the financial position of a Spanish company. A schedule analysing movement in the deferred tax provision should be shown.

Post-retirement benefits (*pensiones y obligaciones similares*)

Accounting treatment

The PGC provides an account entitled 'Provision for pensions and other liabilities', under which should be reported sums set aside to cover legal or contractual pension obligations.

As a transitional arrangement, companies that at their year-end immediately preceding 1 January 1990 had incurred pension obligations are required to quantify the related actuarial liability at that date and to amortise it as follows:

* Portion relating to active employees – over 15 years.

* Portion relating to retired employees – over seven years.

In both cases, the method of amortisation must be 'systematic' (ie in most cases, straight line).

An order of the ICAC of 30 June, 1991, specifically relating to electrical utilities only, set out to extend the above transitional periods to 20 and ten years respectively. It introduced the principle that the annual amortisation should be charged to reserves to the extent possible and, only where those are insufficient, to profit for the year.

The requirement to account for post-retirement benefits mentions only pensions. It may be assumed that other benefits should be similarly accounted for.

In accordance with Law 30/1995 of 8 November 1995, on Private Insurance, pension commitments assumed by companies, including benefits to retired employees, must be arranged in the form of insurance contracts or a pension plan or both, as from the time on which the related cost accrues. Such commitments may not be covered through the setting up of internal funds or similar instruments in the company, which entail the Company's continued ownership of the funds in question.

The Order of the Ministry of Finance, dated 29 December 1999 and published on 1 January 2000, sets out the Transitional Regime to be applied for accounting purposes to the externalisation of the pension commitments governed by Royal Decree 1588/1999. This Order lays down the accounting treatment to be applied by entities with pension commitments to be externalised, and addresses the differences that may arise between the amounts to be externalised and the amounts covered by the provisions for pensions in the balance sheets.

Disclosure

In addition to the accounting policy, 'a general description of the method of calculation' of the liability must be disclosed. A schedule of movements on the pension provision should also be given.

Discontinued operations (*actividades abandonadas*)

Accounting law does not specify any treatment for discontinued operations. Similarly, no pronouncement has been issued by the AECA.

The IASC has published IAS 35, 'Discontinuing Operations'. The Standard contains requirements and guidance for the identification and disclosure of information in relation to significant operations of an enterprise which have been discontinued during the reporting period.

Earnings per share (*beneficio por acción*)

There is no requirement in Spain to present earnings per share data and it is not a common disclosure. The IASC has issued IAS 33 in this respect.

References
Revenue recognition: PGC Parts 4 and 5 and AECA Document 13.
Government grants and assistance: PGC Part 4.
Research and development: PGC Parts 4 and 5 and ICAC Resolution.
Capitalised interest costs: PGC Parts 4 and 5; ICAC Resolution (BOIC C 42) and AECA Document 8.
Implicit interest in not-trade debtor accounts: PGC Parts 4 and 5.
Extraordinary or unusual items: PGC Account Definitions of Part 4.
Income taxes: PGC Parts 4 and 5; AECA Document 9 and ICAC Resolution NV 16[a].
Post-retirement benefits: PGC Part 5, Royal Decree 1588/1999.

5.5

Compliance with International Accounting Standards

PricewaterhouseCoopers

Do Spanish standards or prevalent practice substantially comply with international accounting standards?

Topic	Substantially Complies with IAS?	Comments
Basic accounting concepts and conventions	Yes	Although there are certain differences in the basic accounting concepts and contents of financial statements for example in the cash
Contents of financial statements	Yes	flow statement.
Consolidation	Yes	With the exception of the negative difference on consolidation. In Spain, this item is analysed and if it proves to be a provision for liabilities and charges, it is accounted for as such, or it is recorded as a decrease in the value of the assets acquired. Otherwise, it is left as a liability, which may be taken to income only in the event of a downturn in the company's results or when the asset generating the difference is disposed of. For IAS purposes, the non-allocated portion may be considered as deferred income to be taken to income in a systematic manner.
Joint Ventures	Yes	In Spain, a parent company's individual accounts reflect the investment in a subsidiary only at the acquisition price. Provision is made for the difference with respect to the attributable portion of net worth adjusted by the amount of underlying capital gains existing when the acquisition is made and which subsist in the subsequent valuation. In consolidation accounts the

		proportional method of integration or equity method is used.
Foreign currency translation	Yes*	Unrealised gains on exchange resulting from domestic operations are deferred in Spain, while under IAS in general the exchange gains/losses are integrated into profit and loss for the year. The Spanish accounting rule for futures is in draft.
Inflation accounting	Yes	
Accounting changes	No	In Spain the cumulative effect at the beginning of the year of changes in accounting policy should be accounted for as extraordinary items in the profit and loss account.
Prior period adjustments	No	In Spain, the change is deemed to take place at the beginning of the year and the accumulated effect of variations in assets and liabilities calculated at that date are included under extraordinary items in the profit and loss account. Reserves are not adjusted unless the annual accounts are redrafted. IAS 8 only treats fundamental errors
Post balance sheet events	Yes	
Related party transactions	No	The definition of related party and the extent of disclosure are more limited than in IAS 24
Segmental information	No	Industry and geographical analysis is required for sales only
Property, plant and equipment	Yes*	In Spain revaluations are only permitted if they are allowed by law. Last Spanish revaluation is not in line with IAS rules.
Intangible Assets	Yes*	Except that in Spain formation and start-up expenses may be capitalised. This is not allowed under IAS. Concerning development expenses, these must be written off over a maximum of five years while under IAS the maximum period is that of utilisation. In Spain research expenses may be capitalised, which is not possible under IAS.
Leases	No	The Spanish rule is less extensive than the International. The definition of leases in Spain is based more in legal than economic considerations.
Investments	No	Investments in Spain are valued at lower of cost or market value. In Spain revaluations are only permitted if they are allowed by law and fair value (IAS 39 and 40) is only permitted exceptionally.

Accounts receivable	Yes	
Inventories and work in progress	Yes	
Current liabilities	Yes	Except that there is no requirement for disclosure of contingent gains
Long-term debt	Yes	
Contingent liabilities	Yes	Under Spanish legislation, provisions can sometimes be recorded for probable losses even when there is no commitment with a third party.
Capital and reserves	Yes*	Although the Spanish treatment for own shares is not allowed in IAS.
Revenue recognition	Yes	
Government grants and assistance	Yes	
Research and development	Yes	Except that research expenses are not capitalised following IAS.
Capitalisation of interest costs	Yes	
Imputed Interest	Yes	
Extraordinary or Unusual Items	No	The range of items that may be classified as extraordinary is wider than is permitted by IAS 8.
Income Tax	No	Deferred taxes are recognised under the liability method (timing differences), and deferred tax assets are carried forward only to the extent that their recovery is reasonably assured. The recording of deferred tax assets is somewhat more restrictive in Spain, and only tax credits deriving from tax-loss carry-forwards are allowed.
Post-retirement benefits	Yes*	Spanish rule is less developed. So there is no definition of an actuarial valuation method and there is no treatment for actuarial gains and losses. Ttransitional arrangements for un-amortised past service costs at the time the standard came into force are different from IAS 19.

Comparison in this table is made to International Accounting Standards in force at 1 September 2000.
*Yes, but with certain differences, as explained in *Comments*.

International accounting standards not developed in Spanish rules

- Earnings per share
- Financial Instruments: Recognition and Measurement, Disclosure and Presentation
- Interim Financial Reporting
- Impairment of assets
- Discountinuing operations

Part 6

Taxation

6.1

Corporate Income Tax For Residents

PricewaterhouseCoopers

Introduction

The current corporate income tax regulations are contained in Law 43/1995 of 27 December 1995 (Corporate Income Tax Act – CITA), in respect of which the enabling regulations are set out in Royal Decree 537/1997, of 14 April 1997.

The aim of the changes introduced by said law is to determine taxable income for corporate income tax purposes on the basis of book profit(/loss), corrected by the exceptions defined by the law, in order to obtain greater legal security for the taxpayer. The law also aims to bring together the various special regimes, currently dispersed among different bodies of regulations, into a single law. This reform is considered to be an adaptation of the Spanish economy to the recent international flows of capital.

Entities subject to corporate income tax are those that are deemed to be resident in accordance with the CITA, ie entities that meet one of the following requirements:

- they have been set up in accordance with Spanish legislation;

- their registered office is located in Spain;

- their place of effective management is located in Spain.

Calculating the tax base

The tax base consists of the amount of income obtained during the year, irrespective of its source or origin, determined in accordance with mercantile legislation, reduced by the offsetting of prior year tax-loss carry-forwards and adjusted by applying the specific rules contained in the CITA.

As a rule, the deductibility of expenses is contingent upon the following requirements being met:

• documentary evidence;

• recording for accounting purposes;

• matching with income.

Corrections to the value: depreciation/amortisation

Amounts that are considered depreciation/amortisation of tangible or intangible fixed assets, and that correspond to an effective decline in value of the asset concerned can be deducted.

In this respect, a decline in value will be deemed to be effective when:

• It is calculated by applying the straight-line depreciation rates laid down in the officially approved depreciation/amortisation tables.

• It is calculated by depreciating or amortising the value by a constant percentage rate.

• It is calculated by applying the sum of the digits method, determined on the basis of the depreciation/amortisation periods established in the officially approved depreciation/amortisation tables.

• It is the result of a special depreciation/amortisation plan drawn up and put into effect by the taxpayer and accepted by the Tax Administration.

• The amount of the decline in value can be documented and proven.

Deduction for investments to settle up enterprises abroad

The tax base may be reduced in the effective investments done in the fiscal year, to acquire an interest in non-resident entities that give a majority of the voting rights thereof, provided:

• The subsidiary carries out business activities abroad, excluding real estate, financial or assurance activities or services rendered to Spanish related companies.

• The said activities had not been carried out under another ownership previously.

• The subsidiary is not resident in a country member of the EU or in a tax haven.

The limit for the deductions is Ptas5000 million and never exceeding 25 per cent of the tax base of the fiscal year. It will be reduced in the provision for the decline of value, of such an investment, if it has been deductible.

The amounts deducted will be added to the tax base in the following fiscal years that conclude within the four subsequent years, in equal amounts.

This deduction is not compatible with the tax credit for export activities described below.

Provisions for risks and expenses

As a general rule, under the CITA, appropriations made to provisions for risks and expenses are not deductible when there is uncertainty as to whether the relevant risks and expenses were real.

As specific rules, among others, the CITA lays down that appropriations to provisions for third party liabilities are deductible when they may be justified, even if the amount thereof has not been specifically determined. Also deductible are provisions to cover guarantees for repairs and reviews, within the limits laid down by legislation.

Bad debts provision

Appropriations to cover the risk of possible bad debts are considered deductible when one year has elapsed since payment fell due, or when the debtor has been declared to be bankrupt by a court. The regulation specifically excludes the deductibility of these appropriations for bad debts in certain cases. These cases include appropriations based on global estimates of risk, those that concern related entities, such as subsidiaries for example, and debts for which payment has been guaranteed by third parties.

Provision for decline in value of the investment portfolio

Appropriations made to a provision for the decline in value of investments in undertakings listed on a secondary market can be deductible. They are deductible up to the limit of the difference between the theoretical book value at the beginning and at the end of the year, bearing in mind any contributions or repayments, and provided the investee company is not resident in a country classed as an official tax haven. Appropriations to the provision for the decline in the value of fixed interest securities will be deductible up to the limit of the global decline in value of the portfolio during the year.

Non-deductible expenses

The tax regulations are separate from the accounting criteria in relation to the deductibility of certain expenses, through a specific list thereof. This includes any kind of profit distribution, the corporate income tax expense recorded, criminal and administrative fines and penalties and fixed penalty charges for the late filing of returns, gaming losses, donations and gifts and expenses arising from operations with persons or entities resident in territories officially classed as tax havens, unless an effective transaction is proved.

Application of the normal market value

As a general rule, assets are valued at their acquisition or production cost. This notwithstanding, the CITA lays down that the normal market value will be applied to assets when they are acquired by virtue of:

- donations;

- contributions to entities and values received in consideration;

- transfer to shareholders as a result of the winding up of the company, withdrawal of the members, capital decreases with the return of contributions, distributions of share premiums and profit distributions;

- transfers as a result of mergers, absorption or spin-offs;

- acquisitions through swaps, exchange or conversion.

In order to include as taxable income the positive income obtained from the transfer of fixed assets such as property, the CITA provides for an adjustment method to account for inflationary effects on capital gain.

Operations between related persons or entities

The CITA provides for the possibility of the Tax Administration valuing operations between related persons or entities at their normal market value, without taking into account its accounting valuation. The aim is to avoid, through the use of prices that are not normal market prices, the transfer of income from one entity to another, resulting in a lower taxation of the related parties or a deferral of such taxation.

In order to apply the valuation of certain operations at their normal market prices, the parties concerned must be related. To this effect, the following are considered to be related persons or entities:

- a company and its shareholders when these hold an interest of 5 per cent or more (1 per cent in the case of companies listed on a stock exchange);

- a company and its directors or administrators;

- a company and the spouses, ascendants or descendants of the shareholders, directors or administrators;

- two companies that form part of the same group in accordance with the provisions of the Code of Commerce;

- a company and the shareholders, directors or administrators of another company or their spouses, ascendants or descendants, when both companies form part of the same group of companies;

- two companies when one of them indirectly holds at least 25 per cent of the share capital of the other;

- two companies in which the same shareholders, their spouses, ascendants or descendants hold, directly or indirectly, at least 25 per cent of the share capital;

- a company resident in Spain and its permanent establishments abroad or vice versa;

- two companies when one of them exercises decision-making power over the other.

The mechanisms laid down by CITA for making said valuation are a reflection of the methods established by the OECD in order to determine the normal market value, opting for a bilateral adjustment.

These methods are basically the following:

- comparable price method;

- resale price method;

- cost-plus method: this method, together with the above, is applied secondarily to the market price method;

- profit distribution method, considering its possible application in the event of not being able to apply the above methods.

The deductibility of contributions to research and development activities and management support services between related companies is contingent upon the compliance of certain additional requirements, in accordance with the OECD recommendations.

In any event, and prior to the commencement of the activities, the taxpayer can submit a proposal for the valuation of operations between related entities, to the Tax Administration. The proposal will be based on the normal market value.

International tax transparency

Under this regime, the CITA aims to avoid the use of special purpose companies set up between the source of the income and the ultimate owner of the income and that are domiciled in territories with a low taxation rate. This is achieved by deferring the taxation of income until it can be taxed at the headquarters of the last beneficial owner, when the income is distributed.

Thus, all income obtained by companies located in countries with low taxation, which according to the criteria of CITA is not deemed to be income obtained from the carrying out of economic activities, will be considered income obtained directly by the shareholders and taxed accordingly.

Income will be designated taxable income when the following requirements are met:

• the income in question is not business income;

• the income obtained by the non-resident entity is taxed, through the provisions of a tax similar in nature to Spain's corporate income tax, but the tax is less than 75 per cent of what the tax would have been under Spanish tax laws;

• the interest in the non-resident entity must be equal to or greater than 50 per cent of capital, equity, results or voting stock.

The income attributable to the entity resident in Spain, will, in general, be the income obtained by the non-resident entity from any of the following sources, provided it is not considered, for corporate income tax purposes, as income obtained when carrying out business activities:

• real property investment income, both from rural and urban property, which is not related to the business activity;

• interest in the equity of any type of entity and assignment to third parties of own resources (investment from capital);

• Income obtained from credit, financial or insurance activities, or supplies of services carried out directly or indirectly with related entities resident in Spain, provided they entail a tax deductible expense for the resident entity;

• transfer of goods and rights that generate real property income or securities investment income.

Thin capitalisation

When the average net direct or indirect interest-bearing borrowings by a company (excluding financial institutions) from a non-resident related individual or company are greater than three times said company's average fiscal capital, the interest paid in respect of the surplus will be treated as dividends. Fiscal capital is deemed to be the company's net worth not including profit or loss for the year.

When a treaty for the avoidance of double taxation exists with the country of residence of the related entity and provided there is reciprocity, taxpayers may submit a proposal for the application of a coefficient other than that mentioned. The proposal will be based on the borrowing that the taxpayer would have been able to obtain under normal market conditions.

Offsetting tax loss carry-forwards

Tax loss carry-forwards and tax losses generated in tax periods ending prior to 1 January 1999, may be offset against taxable income relating to the years ending in the immediately successive ten years. Before this date, the offsetting period had been seven years.

In the case of newly created entities, the computation of the offsetting period will commence in the first period in which taxable income is obtained.

Tax liability

Tax rate

The standard tax rate is 35 per cent. However, there is a reduced rate of 30 per cent for small-size entities applicable to taxable income up to Ptas15 million.

There are special rates for collective investment funds (1 or 7 per cent), certain tax protected co-operative societies (20 per cent), certain non-profit making foundations and entities (25 or 10 per cent) and entities engaging in mineral oil research and exploitation (40 per cent), among others.

Deductions for the avoidance of double taxation

Through this mechanism, the CITA aims to palliate the phenomenon of double taxation which results from the inclusion in the taxpayer's taxable income of income which has already been taxed, either in another company (internal double taxation) or in another country (international double taxation). In the case of international double taxation, the aim is to avoid juridical double taxation, i.e. when the same taxpayer has paid tax on the same income in two different countries, and economic double taxation, when two taxpayers have paid tax on the same income in two different countries.

In the case of the deduction for the avoidance of internal double taxation, the deduction is 50 or 100 per cent if the interest is greater than 5 per cent of share capital and this interest has been held uninterruptedly during the year prior to the date on which said profits are distributed.

As concerns the deduction for the avoidance of international double taxation, although the method laid down by the CITA is the allocation of income, in practice this works out to being equivalent to the exemption method, as foreign tax paid may be deducted by 100 per cent if certain requirements are met. As from 1 January 2000, the exemption method is directly applicable.

The International Deduction for Double Taxation (DDT) may include the following scenarios:

• Deduction in order to avoid double taxation arising on income, obtained by the taxpayer, which is taxed in Spain and abroad. The method is based on the attribution of the income to the taxpayer's tax base and the subsequent deduction of the lower of the following amounts:

    – The amount actually paid abroad under an identical or similar tax to corporate income tax, payable on income received.
    – The amount of the tax payable in Spain that would have been payable if the income had been obtained in Spain.

    In order to apply this deduction, companies must be taxable in Spain as a resident, which means that foreign companies operating in Spain through a Permanent Establishment (PE) are excluded, and Spanish entities operating abroad through a PE are included.

• The amounts not deducted may be deducted over the following 10 years.

• Deduction that is intended to avoid international double taxation arising when income obtained by a certain permanent establishment (PE) is subject to the same tax in Spain and abroad. If, in a previous period, the entity's tax base was decreased by losses deriving from the PE, the deduction shall be reduced by the amount resulting from the application of the tax-loss carry-forwards at the rate applicable to the company applying for the deduction.

    The requirements to apply for this deduction are as follows:

    – The PE must be subject to a tax similar to CIT and not be located in an area deemed to be a tax haven.
    – The income must arise from the carrying-on of business activities by the PE abroad, in accordance with the limits set by the corporate income tax act in terms of the definition of business activities.

• Deduction in order to avoid the double taxation arising when a parent company residing in Spain receives dividends or shares in the profits of its foreign subsidiaries, to the extent that the profit giving rise to the dividends has already been taxed in the country in which the subsidiary resides. The amount of the deduction shall be the amount of the tax actually paid by the non-resident company on profits on which the dividends are based. This deduction is compatible, up to the limit of the tax that would be payable in Spain on this income, with the International DDT regarding tax payable in the event that the parent company has paid a foreign tax on the dividend distributed.

    The following requirements must be met in order to apply this deduction:

- Shareholding of at least 5 per cent in the non-resident subsidiary (direct or indirect).
- Maintenance of this shareholding uninterruptedly for the year prior to the day on which the dividend falls due for payment.
- The deductible foreign tax may have been paid both by the subsidiary of the company applying the deduction or by subsidiaries of that subsidiary, provided that the requirements referred to above are met.
- The amounts not deducted due to the above-mentioned limit being exceeded are not deemed to be a deductible expense for tax purposes. The provision for the decline in value of the portfolio as a result of the payment of the dividend is not deductible either, unless the profits were taxed in Spain when the shareholding was previously transferred.

- Tax credit for dividends and capital gains arising abroad, designed to avoid double taxation. This, for instance, applies when a company resident in Spain receives dividends from its subsidiaries established abroad or transfers its shares in these subsidiaries, since both the dividend and the capital gain have already been taxed abroad as part of the income obtained by the subsidiaries. In the case of the dividends, this method provides an alternative to the method described above, and is more advantageous due to being based on the exemption method, directly applicable as from 1 January 2000.

Until 31 December 2000, the deduction is calculated by applying the tax rate that is applicable to the company that requests the deduction to the gross amount of the dividends or capital gains (previously included in the resident's taxable income).

The following requirements must be met in order to apply this deduction:

- Minimum interest of 5 per cent in the subsidiary, held for one year prior to the day on which the dividend falls due for payment.
- The investee company must be subject to and not exempt from a tax similar to Spanish corporate income tax and may not be resident in a tax haven.
- The dividends must derive from income obtained from business activities carried out by the non-resident company.
- The decline in value of the shareholding in the subsidiary as a result of the payment of the dividend is not a deductible expense unless the profits have been taxed in Spain due to an earlier transfer of the shareholding.

Tax credit for scientific research and technology innovation activities

Research and Development (R&D) activities allow for the deduction of 30 per cent of expenses incurred for this item during the year, after reducing such expenses by 65 per cent of any grants received to promote such activities. Any expense incurred in the year, in excess of the average expense in the two preceding years, qualifies for a deduction of 50 per cent.

This tax credit may be applied to activities carried out in Spain and abroad provided that the core activity is carried out in Spain and the amount invested abroad does not exceed 25 per cent of the total investment.

An additional deduction of 10 per cent is applicable on personnel expenses correspondent to scientists involved in R&D projects, and expenses related to R&D projects entered into with universities or Innovation and Technology Centres.

There are some other activities known as 'technology innovation activities' which qualify for a 10 or 15 per cent deduction of the expenses incurred, such as obtaining new products or production processes, or substantial technological betterments thereof.

Tax credit for export activities

A deduction of 25 per cent of the amount invested in the creation of branches or permanent establishments abroad, or in the acquisition of shareholdings in foreign companies, or in the setting up of subsidiaries directly related to export activities is applicable, provided the interest is greater than 25 per cent.

Advertising expenses relating to the launching of products, to the opening and research of markets and to attending fairs abroad or international fairs held in Spain, also qualify for this type of deduction.

Tax credit for investments in items of cultural interest, cinema productions and book publishing

Investments in items of cultural interest, cinema productions and book publishing qualify for a deduction of 10, 20, and 5 per cent respectively. Any part of the investment financed with grants is not included in the calculation of the amount qualifying for a deduction. The CITA defines a party known as the financial co-producer in cinema productions, who may deduct 5 per cent of the investment financed, subject to a limit of 5 per cent of the income derived from such investments in that period.

Tax credit for investments in environmental protection

Investments in tangible fixed assets including industrial or commercial vehicles of road transport to protect the environment and reduce air or pollution or to reduce and recover industrial waste qualify for a tax credit of 10 per cent of the investments made. In order for this tax credit to be applied, the investments must be made under an agreement with the competent environmental authorities, which must issue a validation certificate. Any part of the investment financed with grants is not included in the calculation of the amount qualifying for a deduction.

Tax credit for professional training expenses

Expenses incurred in professional training qualify for a deduction of 5 per cent of such expenses, after 65 per cent of the grants received for these activities has been subtracted. Any expenses in excess of the average expenses incurred for this item in the previous two years will qualify for a deduction of 10 per cent.

Tax credit for the creation of jobs for disabled employees

The deduction is Ptas800,000 for each disabled employee taken on each year, if employed with an indefinite full-time contract.

The amounts not deducted of the described tax credits may be used over the following five years, and 10 years in the case of scientific research and technology innovation activities.

Special regimes

Tax transparency

Companies are considered transparent when they meet any of the following requirements for at least 90 days in the year:

- More than half their assets consist of securities and holding entities when more than 50 per cent of the capital of these companies belongs to the same family group or ten or less shareholders.

- More than 75 per cent of their income derives from professional activities when the professional *individual* who generates such income is entitled to a profit participation, together with his relations, of at least 50 per cent of said profit.

- Companies in which more than 50 per cent of the income is earned through artistic or sporting performances by individuals when they, together with their relations, are entitled to a profit participation of at least 25 per cent of said income.

In the event that the entire body of shareholders is made up of non-transparent companies, the regime will not be applicable. Nor would it apply to the part of the taxable base that corresponds to non-resident shareholders.

The transparency regime entails the allocation of the company's taxable income to its respective shareholders, in proportion to their holding, as well as the tax credits and allowances to which the company is entitled, partial payments, withholdings and payments on account and tax paid or allocated to the transparent company.

Tax loss carry-forwards will not be allocated to the shareholders and may be offset by the transparent company in the immediately successive 10 years.

Regime for groups of companies

Under the CITA, a company and its investee companies may be taxed under the tax consolidation regime as a single taxpayer *vis-à-vis* the Administration, provided certain holding requirements are met. This notwithstanding, there is a formal obligation to file returns without tax payment for each and every entity that makes up the group.

The group is made up of a parent company resident in Spain and of its subsidiaries, which will not, under any circumstance, be transparent companies or subsidiaries of another parent company. The parent company will have a direct or indirect interest of at least 90 per cent, which must be held uninterruptedly during the year prior to the first day of the tax year in which the regime for groups of companies is to be applied and during the year in question. The taxable income of the group is determined by adding together the taxable income of all the companies that form the group, less the relevant reductions or plus the relevant additions.

The application of this regime allows the group's tax loss carry-forwards to be offset against the taxable income of the group. Tax loss carry-forwards generated in a company prior to its inclusion in the group may be offset against the taxable income of the group, up to the limit of the taxable income of the company that generated the tax losses.

The decision to apply this regime must be notified to the Administration in the year prior to its application. The regime may be applied during three years and may be extended for periods of the same duration.

Regime for mergers, spin-offs, contributions and exchanges of securities

The special tax regime contained in the CITA is the result of the development of Directive 90/434/EEC in this matter, after it was initially introduced to Spanish regulations by the now abolished Law 29/1991, on the Adaptation of Certain Tax Items to EU Directives and Regulations.

Operations that qualify for this special regime are mergers, full or partial splits, including those of holdings that provide control of a third company, non-cash contributions of branches of activity and exchanges of securities representing the share capital.

The characteristics of this regime include:

- In general, any income that arises in Spanish territory as a result of applying the normal market value must be excluded from the taxable income. However, the tax payer may opt to be taxed, on such income, totally or partially.

- The right to offset tax loss carry-forwards when the transaction is carried out is transferred to the acquiring entity, albeit with certain limitations, as are the tax benefits and obligations relating to the transferred assets and rights.

- The goodwill included in the acquisition price of the holding must be deductible in mergers where the acquiring entity holds at least 5 per cent of the capital of the transferor, provided certain requirements are met.

- The retroactive effect of the merger for mercantile and tax purposes is identical.

Foreign securities holding companies (ETVE)

The CITA lays down a specific regime for holding companies resident in Spain whose corporate purpose is to hold securities in non-resident entities and manage securities abroad. This regime applies as long as the entities whose securities are being held are subject to and not exempt from a tax that is identical or analogous to corporate income tax and are not resident in territories classed as official tax havens. In order to benefit from this regime, the taxpayer must file an application and prove that it complies with the requirements laid down by the Administration.

Under this regime, the income obtained by the foreign securities holding company derived from the distribution of profits to its investee companies and the transfer of its interest to a third party are exempt. If that third party is resident in Spain, it can only benefit from the regime if the entity is not related to the foreign securities holding company.

The contribution to the foreign securities holding company of shareholdings in entities that are not resident in Spanish territory is treated under the special regime mentioned in the section immediately above.

Tax incentives for small-sized companies

The CITA offers a number of incentives for companies that are classed as being of a reduced size, their net turnover in the immediately preceding year being less than Ptas499 million (€3 million).
In general terms, the main incentives are as follows:

* Freedom of depreciation for investments in new fixed assets which in turn generate job creation.

* Freedom of depreciation for low value investments.

* Accelerated depreciation for tax purposes of investments in new fixed assets not associated with job creation and of investments in intangible assets.

* Deductibility of appropriations to the bad debt provision based on a global estimate of the risk of 1 per cent.

* As of 1 January 1999, reinvested capital gains are no longer exempt though accelerated depreciation in certain cases involving the sale of tangible assets is allowed.

* Tax credit of 10 per cent in the fiscal year investments and expenses in the development of communication and information technologies, in particular, access and presence in internet, e-business, etc. Any part of the expense or investment financed with grants does not qualify for a deduction.

Tax payments on account

Partial payments

Taxpayers are required to make a partial payment by 20 April, 20 October and 20 December on account of the definitive tax assessment for the year and, relating to the tax period in progress, on 31 March, 30 September and 30 November, respectively.

The CITA lays down two different methods for the calculation of tax payments depending on whether or not turnover in the preceding tax period exceeded Ptas 1,000 million. The first method entails an estimate arrived at by calculating 18 per cent of the tax payable on the last corporate income tax return to have been filed, and deducting any previous partial payments made and any withholdings paid to date.

The second method is compulsory for companies with turnover greater than Ptas 1,000 million in the preceding tax period. It consists of applying a 25 per cent rate to taxable income from the first day of the tax period to the last day that the payment on account relates to.

Transparent companies do not have to make partial payments with respect to the part of the taxable base to be apportioned to their resident shareholders.

Withholdings

The Corporate Income Tax provides for the application of withholdings on account of securities investment income obtained by taxpayers, income from the transfer or redemption of shares and holdings in collective investment institutions. The applicable withholding rates are 15 and 18 per cent, respectively.

The amounts withheld may be deducted in the final tax assessment and, where appropriate, a refund may be claimed for the excess amount with respect to the net tax payable. Likewise, companies are required to make withholdings on account for personal income tax or corporate income tax in respect of salaries and income from professional activities paid, and on any securities investment income or real property investment income that they are required to pay. The tax is paid on a quarterly or monthly basis, depending on whether the turnover of the company making the withholding exceeds Ptas1,000 million.

Special tax regime for the Basque country

The three historic provinces that make up the Autonomous Region of the Basque Country (Alava, Guipúzcoa and Vizcaya) have concluded an Economic Agreement (*Concierto Económico*), governed by Law 12/1981, dated 13 May with the central government, whereby the provinces are granted the right to regulate their tax regimes.

Coinciding with the recent reform of the Spanish Corporate Income Tax Act, the provincial authorities of Vizcaya have altered their regulations to incorporate certain items that make the area more attractive to taxpayers from the viewpoint of corporate income tax.

Tax rates

Tax rate provisions include:

- The general rate has been reduced to 32.5 per cent.

- A reduced rate of 30 per cent applies to small companies, provided more than 80 per cent of their share capital is owned by individuals.

- A rate of 25 per cent applies to companies that are officially listed on the Bilbao stock exchange for the first time and to brokerages.

- To calculate the tax base, the following must be taken into account:

- Tax loss carry-forwards may be offset over a period of 15 years.

- Goodwill, brands, transfer rights, etc, may be written off over a period of five to 10 years.

- Financial goodwill may be deducted through a provision over five to 10 years.

- Shorter depreciation periods for fixed assets.

Tax credits

A 10 per cent tax credit may be applied to investments in new tangible fixed assets, subject to certain requirements relating to the amount of the investment. Investments in software also qualify for tax credits. In the province of Vizcaya only, the tax credit is of 15 or 20 per cent if the number of employees with indefinite employment contracts is increased by 5 per cent over a three-year period.

Subject to certain requirements being met, appropriations of profit to a Special Reserve for Productive Investments (SRPI) entitle the taxpayer to a credit of 10 per cent of the amount appropriated. In the province of Vizcaya, this credit is of 15 per cent if the number of employees with indefinite employment contracts is maintained; the tax credit can reach 20 per cent if this number is increased by 5 per cent over a three-year period.

Applicable only in Vizcaya (although until 1999, this tax regime was also applicable in Alava, and Guipúzcoa).

Co-ordination, management, and finance centres have been introduced to enable the formation of international entities. Subject to certain requirements, the applicable tax regime will be as follows:

- Tax base equal to 25 per cent of expenses incurred (excluding financial expenses). The standard corporate income tax rate and tax credits apply, and the tax payable is equal to 8.125 per cent of expenses (excluding financial expenses).

- Tax base in line with general principles (transfer pricing regulations).

The tax benefits for investing in securities, subject to certain requirements being met, are:

- Tax credit of 5 per cent of the investment.

- Investments in companies with shares listed on a stock market and capital increases in any company qualify for a tax credit of 6.5 per cent

- This last credit increases to 8.5 per cent for companies listed on the Bilbao stock exchange.

Promotion of other activities include:

- R&D expenses, 30 per cent; 50 per cent if the expenses exceed the average expenses for the previous two years. (Certain expenses related with R&D activities, additional 10 per cent.)

- Environmental conservation and improvement or energy saving expenses, 15 per cent.

- Investment to promote exports by the Spanish company (foreign advertising, forming companies and branches abroad), 25 per cent.

- Staff training, 10 per cent; 15 per cent if the investment exceeds the previous year's investment.

Employment creation incentives:

- Ptas600,000 for each post created and for each year in which the average workforce is increased, provided that indefinite employment contracts are concluded and the increase is maintained for two years.

- Ptas1,100,000 for each position created and for each year in which the average workforce is increased provided that indefinite employment contracts are concluded and persons who have special difficulties in finding employment are engaged.

Incentives to reduce working hours – companies that agree to a reduction in working hours and a 10 per cent increase in the workforce to be maintained over three years receive:

- Free depreciation of existing and new tangible fixed assets.

- 35 per cent tax credit instead of 15 per cent, for investments in new fixed assets.

- Ptas750,000 for each position created and for each year in which the average workforce is increased, provided that indefinite employment contracts are concluded and the increase is maintained for two years.

Dividends paid by Basque companies out of income not included in the taxable income, in accordance with the criteria laid down for the avoidance of international double taxation of dividends, are not subject to withholding tax in Spain when the recipient is an individual or entity not resident in Spanish territory. The above provisions shall not apply when the recipient of the dividend is a resident of a country or territory officially classed as a tax haven.

Special tax regime for Navarre

Reinvestment exemption

- Exclusion from the tax assessment base of income obtained from the transfer of assets used in the company's activities.

- Exemption relates to the transfer of both tangible and intangible fixed assets.

- The reinvestment may be made in tangible or intangible fixed assets.

- Reinvestment is understood to be investments made between the year prior to the transfer and the subsequent three years.

Special investment reserve

The main features are as follows:

- Minimum balance of Ptas25 million.

- Appropriations may be made to this reserve against profits of the fiscal year in question.

- Reduction in the tax assessment base of 45 per cent of the amounts appropriated to the reserve against book profits for the year; this reduction may not exceed 40 per cent of the tax base for that year.

- The amount included in the reserve must be invested, within the two years following the end of the year of which the profits were used to create the reserve, and must be invested in certain specified goods.

- Items subject to excise duty on Specific Means of Transport are excluded.

Incentives for new companies

- Applicable to companies that do not file consolidated tax returns and are not subject to the tax transparency regime or the specific regimes governing Spanish or European economic interest groupings or temporary consortia.

- 50 per cent reduction in gross tax payable for the consecutive tax periods closed within the seven years following the commencement of the company's activity, with a maximum limit of four periods as from the first period in which a positive net tax base is made within said seven-year term.

- The company must start business with a minimum capital of Ptas20 million.

- During the first two years of activity, the company must make investments of a minimum of Ptas100 million.

Deductions for investments in new tangible fixed assets

- The Navarre Regional Government authorises the application of a special regime for new companies that allows a deduction from net tax payable of up to 15 per cent of the investments made during the year, without any limitation on that net tax payable.

- In addition, companies may apply a deduction from net tax payable of 10 per cent of the investments made in new tangible fixed assets, excluding land. This deduction is applicable subject to a ceiling of 35 per cent of net tax payable.

Deduction for vocational training expenses

A deduction may be applied to net tax payable consisting of 15 per cent of the expenses relating to staff training initiatives, excluding expenses regarded as earned income. The deduction consists of 15 per cent of the expenses incurred during the year.

Deduction for environmental conservation and improvement activities

Deduction of 15 per cent of investments in new tangible fixed assets directly used in the reduction and containment of pollution caused by the company's activity.

Research and development deduction

Applicable to goods and expenses relating to R&D programmes, a 30 per cent deduction for investments made in this area. Free depreciation may also be applied to the assets concerned.

Tax benefits for job creation

The following benefits, which may not be enjoyed simultaneously, are available:

- Ptas700,000 deduction for each person-year increase in average staff with an indefinite employment contract.

- Ptas250,000 deduction for each person-year increase in average staff with an indefinite employment contract, without an increase in the total average workforce being necessary.

- Ptas250,000 deduction for each person-year increase in average staff with an indefinite employment contract, when the total workforce is reduced.

- Ptas900,000 and Ptas300,000 deductions, respectively, in each of the cases mentioned above when the increase derives from the hiring of disabled workers.

The above deductions for job creation are compatible with any direct financial assistance also granted to the taxpayer for job creation purposes.

6.2

Corporate Taxation for Non-Residents

PricewaterhouseCoopers

Introduction

The determining factor of the tax regime for non-resident entities is whether or not these have a permanent establishment in Spain. In any event, non-resident entities are only subject to tax on the income that is obtained in Spain. This income comprises both earned income and capital gains obtained by non-resident taxpayers.

The contents of this chapter shall be considered without prejudice to the Treaties and Conventions ratified by the Kingdom of Spain, which prevail over internal legislation.

Until 1999, the tax treatment of income obtained by non-residents was set out in the Personal Income Tax Act or Corporate Income Tax Act, and was contingent upon whether the non-resident taxpayer was an individual or a company. As of 1 January 1999, the taxation of income obtained in Spain by non-resident individuals and companies has been governed by the new Law 41/1998, of 9 December 1998, on Non-Residents' Income Tax.

Income obtained in Spain

The following income is deemed to have been obtained in Spain:

- Income from business activities or operations carried out through a permanent establishment in Spain.

- Income from business activities or operations carried out without a permanent establishment in Spain:
  - where such activities or operations are carried out in Spain.
  - where services are provided and used in Spain, such as studies, projects, technical assistance, management support.

– where such income derives directly or indirectly from the activities of artists or athletes in Spain, even when received by a person other than the artist or athlete.

• Earned income derived directly or indirectly from work performed in Spain.

• Dividends and other income derived from shares held in companies resident in Spain.

• Interest, royalties and other securities investment income paid by residents or permanent establishments in Spain or relating to capital invested in Spain.

• Income derived directly or indirectly from real property located in Spain or from rights relating to such property.

• Income allocated to individual taxpayers that own municipal property located in Spain, which is not used to carry out business activities.

• Capital gains derived from:
– securities issued by persons or entities residing in Spain.
– other moveable property located in Spain.
– rights that must be observed or are exercised in Spain.
– real property located in Spain or rights relating to such property.

• Income received from individuals engaged in business activities and entities resident in Spain, and from permanent establishments located in Spain, with the following exceptions:
– Income received in respect of business activities or operations carried out abroad, particularly that which relates to international purchases and sales of goods (including agents' commissions and related expenses).
– Income received in relation to services provided in Spain, particularly in relation to studies, projects, technical assistance or management support, where such services are used entirely outside Spain and relate directly to business activities carried out abroad by the paying party, unless assets located in Spain are involved.
– Income received by non-resident individuals or entities from permanent establishments located abroad where the services are directly related to the permanent establishment's activity abroad.
– Earned income relating to work performed entirely abroad subject to personal income tax in the country in question.
– Income from real property located abroad.

Income exempt from tax

The following income is exempt from tax:

- Income classified as exempt in the Personal Income Tax Act, when obtained by individuals.

- Interest and other income obtained by lending capital to third parties, as well as capital gains derived from moveable property obtained without a permanent establishment by residents of another EU member state, provided it is not obtained through countries or territories officially classed as tax havens.

(These exemptions do not apply to capital gains from the transfer of shares, holdings or other rights pertaining to a company whose assets consist mainly of real property located in Spain or if, during the 12 months prior to the transfer, the taxpayer has at any time held a direct or indirect interest of 25 per cent or more in the company in question.)

- Income obtained from Spanish government securities without a permanent establishment, provided it is not obtained through countries or territories officially classed as tax havens.

- Income derived from securities issued in Spain by non-resident individuals or entities without a permanent establishment, unless the holder is a permanent establishment located in Spain.

- Income derived from accounts held by non-residents, with certain exceptions.

- Profits distributed by subsidiaries resident in Spain to their parent companies resident in an EU member state, provided that the following requirements are met:
  - Both companies must be subject to and not exempt from one of the taxes levied on company profits in EU member states referred to in Directive 90/435/EEC of 23 July 1990 on the regulations governing parent companies and subsidiaries of different member states.
  - The profit must not be distributed as a result of the winding-up of the subsidiary.
  - The legal structure of both companies must be included in the Appendix to the above-mentioned Directive.
  - An entity is deemed to be parent company if it holds directly at least 25 per cent of the Spanish subsidiary, uninterruptedly, during the year prior to the date in which the profit is due, or otherwise, is kept the necessary lapse of time to complete a year.

This exemption does not apply if the majority of the parent company's voting rights are held, directly or indirectly, by individuals or legal entities that are not residents of an EU member state. Further, for the exemption to apply, the parent company must engage in a business activity directly related to its subsidiary's activity and must be involved in administering and managing the subsidiary. Or, the parent company must be able to show that the subsidiary has been established for valid business reasons and not for the purpose of taking undue advantage of the exemption.

Additionally, this exemption is not applicable if the parent company is a resident, for tax purposes, of a territory officially classed as a tax haven.

- Income obtained from transfers of securities effected on official Spanish secondary securities markets by non-resident individuals or legal entities without a permanent establishment in Spain, which are residents of a state with which Spain has concluded a double taxation treaty containing an information exchange clause.

- Dividends received from holding companies (ETVE) by non-residents not resident in territories officially classed as a tax haven.

- Income allocated to non-resident individuals in respect of timeshare rights that entitle the holder to use a building for no more than two weeks per year.

Income obtained through a permanent establishment located in Spanish territory

A company is understood to operate through a permanent establishment when it has installations or a place of business of any type, on a continuous or habitual basis, from which it carries out all or part of its activity. This is also true of a company that operates in Spain through an agent authorised to conclude contracts in the name and on behalf of the non-resident company that habitually exercises such powers.

The following are considered to constitute a permanent establishment: a branch; an office; a factory a workshop; a warehouse; shops and other establishments; a mine; an oil or gas well; a quarry; an agricultural undertaking; a building site, construction or installation project if it lasts more than 12 months.

Calculating taxable income

The Corporate Income Tax Act lays down three ways in which a permanent establishment can obtain income. The tax treatment is different in each case.

General case
In general, taxable income is determined in accordance with the general regime for residents, with the following special characteristics:

- Payments made by the permanent establishment to its local office or any of its permanent establishments in respect of royalties, interest, commission in exchange for technical assistance or for the use of other rights and services, are not deductible.

- The reasonable part of general management and administration expenses that relates to the permanent establishment is deductible provided the following requirements are met:
  1. Reflection in the accounting statements.
  2. Consistency through an informative report filed with the return, of the amounts, criteria and distribution methods.
  3. Consistent and rational criteria of the allocation methods adopted.

Under no circumstances will the amounts relating to the cost of capital belonging to the entity, relating directly or indirectly to the permanent establishment, be deductible.

The permanent establishment can offset its tax losses in accordance with the general corporate income tax rules. Operations carried out by the permanent establishment with the central office of the non-resident entity or with other permanent establishments of the entity, located in Spanish territory or abroad, or with other related companies, are valued in accordance with the valuation rules laid down in the section relating to resident entities.

Operations carried out in Spain by a permanent establishment that do not close a complete business cycle and that lead to income in Spain
This heading refers to cases in which the closing of a business cycle requires the intervention of the local office or another of its permanent establishments, with no consideration except the coverage of the expenses of the permanent establishment. It also refers to cases where all or part of the services or products is not provided to third parties other than to the non-resident entity itself.

- **General rule:** Income and expenses are valued at market prices and the tax liability is determined in accordance with the rules of the general regime.

- **Rules of secondary application:** The taxable income is calculated by applying 15 per cent to the total gross expenses incurred when carrying out the activity of the permanent establishment, without any reductions or offsetting. The ancillary income such as royalties, interest, capital gains and losses derived from the assets used in the permanent establishment is added to the above gross amount. Gross tax payable is calculated by applying to the tax base the standard tax rate. Any deductions or allowances under the general regime will not be applicable.

Permanent establishment with sporadic activity in Spanish territory
This refers to construction, installation or assembly works with a duration of more than twelve months, seasonal business activities or activities relating to the prospecting for natural resources.

- **General rule:** The tax is levied in accordance with the rules laid down for income obtained in Spain from business activities without the involvement of a permanent establishment, the following rules being applicable in this respect:

– The rules relating to accrual and filing of returns in respect of income obtained without the involvement of a permanent establishment.

– Taxpayers are exempt from the general accounting and registration obligations. However, all supporting documentation relating to income obtained and corporate income tax payments made must be kept at the disposal of the Tax Administration, and where appropriate, the documentation relating to withholdings and payments on account made and the relevant returns filed.

● **Optional method:** The non-resident can opt to apply the general regime laid down for the above-mentioned permanent establishments. In any event, the application of the system indicated in the general rule will be compulsory if the permanent establishment does not have separate accounting records for the income obtained in Spanish territory. The option must be declared at the same time as the registration in the Index of Entities is requested.

Tax liability

In general, 35 per cent tax is levied on taxable income determined in accordance with the above.

In addition, when the income obtained in Spain is transferred abroad, a complementary tax of 25 per cent will be levied on the amount transferred and on any payments in respect of royalties, interest, commissions and technical assistance services, use or assignment of goods and rights. The complementary tax is not applicable, provided there is a reciprocal agreement, to income obtained in Spanish territory through permanent establishments, by entities that have their registered office for tax purposes in another EU member state.

The following may be applied to gross tax payable:

● Rebates and deductions established in the general regime for resident entities, with the exception of deductions for international double taxation.

● The amount of withholdings on the permanent establishment, payments on account and partial payments which have been made.

Tax period

The tax period coincides with the business year declared by the permanent establishment and cannot exceed twelve months. The tax period is considered to end when the permanent establishment ceases its activity, when the permanent establishment is transferred or when the local office transfers its residence. Tax accrues on the last day of the tax period.

Accounting obligations, registration and formal obligations

Permanent establishments are required to keep separate books of account and comply with registration, accounting and formal obligations like resident entities, except when the permanent establishment engages in sporadic activities that avail themselves of the tax rules for non-resident entities operating without a permanent establishment.

The obligation to assess the tax is, therefore, similar to that which applies to resident entities both in terms of manner and time periods.

Payments on account

Permanent establishments come under the general regime in respect of payments on account on the income received, and make withholdings and payments on account on the same conditions as resident entities.

Tax representative

A tax representative only needs to be appointed in cases where there is an exceptional deduction of certain general expenses relating to purchases, consumption and salaries paid, when calculating taxable income. The appointment of a tax representative may also be required by the Tax Administration depending on the amount and nature of the income obtained in Spanish territory.

Joint and several liability

Since 1 January 1999, the weight of this liability has been shifted towards the withholding entity. The party with joint and several liability for paying the tax continues to be the depository or administrator of the goods or rights of non-residents without a permanent establishment, or the payer of the income. The new regulation however, which contains an exemption from such liability in cases where withholdings and payments on account must be made, limits the joint and several liability. In practice, liability is limited to the depository or administrator who are jointly and severally liable for the payment of tax relating to income derived from the goods and rights they manage, and to individuals who pay income aside from carrying out a business activity.

The party with joint and several liability can file the non resident's personal income tax returns and pay the relevant amount.

The Administration may claim the payment of the tax directly from payers of income accrued without a permanent establishment and, in the case of depositories and administrators, after the liability has been transferred.

The withholding entity

Withholdings and payments on account must be made in respect of income subject to non-residents' income tax paid by the following persons or entities:

- entities resident in Spain;

- resident individuals in respect of income paid when carrying out their business activity;

- non-resident entities with a permanent establishment in Spanish territory.

The withholding entity must not, in any event, withhold an amount on account of the final tax payable by the taxpayer, but an amount equal to that tax. This amount is calculated in accordance with the rules laid down in the Non-Residents' Income Tax Act (except in the case of donations, certain expenses paid, and the special tax paid by the taxpayer) and the tax rates governed by the relevant treaties for the avoidance of double taxation.

No withholdings must be made in respect of:

- income paid to non-residents without a permanent establishment that attest to the payment of the tax or the applicability of the exemption;

- profits distributed by a foreign securities holding company (ETVE) to a non-resident shareholder;

- income declared exempt under the Non-Residents' Income Tax Act;

- income declared exempt by virtue of the provisions of the relevant double taxation treaty;

- capital gains, with the exception of:
  - prizes obtained in games, competitions, raffles or random combinations;
  - transfers of real property located in Spanish territory by non-residents acting without a permanent establishment;
  - income derived from transfers or redemption of shares or participation in the capital or net worth of collective investment institutions.

Income obtained without the involvement of a permanent establishment

Calculating taxable income

In general, income obtained without the involvement of a permanent establishment is valued at the gross amount thereof, in accordance with the provisions of the Personal Income Tax Act. The exception to this is that the multiplying percentages will not be applied to certain investment income or the reductions envisaged therein for irregular income.

When calculating taxable income in cases of supplies of services, technical assistance, installation or assembly works and, in general, any other business activity, one can deduct the gross amount of staff costs, supplies of material incorporated into the works or supplies. In any event, as in the case of personal income tax, the rates for the restatement of the acquisition value can only be applied to real property. In the case of income derived from reinsurance activities, the taxable income will consist of the amounts of the premiums, assigned for reinsurance, to the non-resident reinsurer.

In the case of capital gains obtained from transfers for valuable consideration or for no consideration, the taxable income is the difference between the transfer value and the acquisition value of the assets acquisitions, and the capital gain coincides with the market value thereof. These entities cannot offset losses against future profits or capital gains.

Tax payable

The following rates will be applied to any taxable income determined in accordance with the regulations set out above:

- General rate: 25 per cent

- Reinsurance operations: 1.5 per cent

- Sea or air navigation companies/entities resident abroad whose ships or aircraft touch Spanish territory: 4 per cent.

- Capital gains: 35 per cent.

- In the case of pensions and passive income, there is a progressive scale that starts at 8 per cent for the band under Ptas1.6 million and reaches 40 per cent for amounts over Ptas2.5 million.

- The draft of the Budget Bill for 2001 establishes an 18 per cent rate for dividends, interest and other income obtained by lending capital to third parties, and the capital gain obtained as a consequence of the transfer of shares in collective investment institutional or reimbursements thereof.

When a non-resident without a permanent establishment transfers real property located in Spain, the acquirer is required to withhold and pay 5 per cent of the price agreed to in respect of the relevant payment on account. This withholding is not made when the owner of the property is an individual who, at 31 December 1996, had owned the property for more than ten years without making any improvements to the property during said time. Likewise, contributions of property in the formation or increase of capital of companies resident in Spain are not subject to the 5 per cent payment on account.

Assets transferred are subject to the payment of the lower of the withholding and payment on account or the relevant tax.

Deductions

Tax payable can only be reduced by the deductions allowed for donations and withholdings and payments on account made in respect of the income of the non-resident entity.

Formal obligations

Non-resident entities without a permanent establishment are only required to comply with accounting, registration or formal obligations in the following cases:

- Non-residents who obtain income from carrying out business activities, in which when calculating taxable income, staff costs and the supply costs of materials may be deducted, are required to:
  - keep a register of income and expenses; and
  - keep the invoices issued, numbered chronologically, the invoices received, and any other types of supporting documentation.

- Non-residents obliged to make withholdings or payments on account must:
  - file tax returns;
  - file an annual statement of withholdings and payments on account;
  - issue the relevant certificate to the taxpayer attesting to the withholdings and payments on account made.

Accrual

There is no single date for accrual, ie tax accrues for each operation when the relevant income, in turn, accrues. For this reason, there is no set time period for filing the tax return relating to this income.

Therefore, income obtained without the involvement of a permanent establishment is taxed separately on each total or partial accrual of income subject to tax. For these purposes, such income is understood to accrue:

- in the case of yields, when they become payable or on the date of collection, if earlier;

- in the case of capital gains, when the alteration in equity takes place;

- in the case of allocated income relating to urban property, on 31 December each year;

- in the case of assumed income, when it becomes due, or in the absence thereof, on 31 December each year.

Withholdings

Likewise, non-residents operating in Spain without the involvement of a permanent establishment are required to make withholdings and payments on account on the salaries they pay and on other types of income subject to withholding, which constitute a deductible expense from income received.

International treaties for the avoidance of double taxation on income and capital

The Double Tax Treaties concluded between Spain and third countries that are based on the model OECD Double Taxation Treaty, aim to reduce the taxation in Spain of income obtained by entities without a permanent establishment in Spain.

International treaties prevail over internal tax legislation by direct application of the Spanish Constitution.

Once officially published, the validly concluded international treaties form part of the internal regulations and any modification, elimination or suspension thereof is only possible in the manner laid down therein or in accordance with general international law rules.

In general, the business profits and capital gains not derived from real property, and obtained by entities without a permanent establishment in Spain that are resident in a country with which Spain has concluded a Double Taxation Treaty, are not subject to tax in Spain. However, capital gains derived from the sale of shares in a company can be subject to tax in Spain under specific clauses of certain treaties. Other types of income, such as royalties, interest or dividends, are in general subject to tax in Spain (withholdings at source) at reduced tax rates.

For illustrative purposes, below is a chart setting out the tax rates applicable to dividends, interest and royalties in accordance with the Double Taxation Treaties concluded with Spain.

Table 6.2.1 Double taxation treaties

Country	Dividends (%)	Interest (%)	Royalties (%)
Germany	15/10	10/0	5
Argentina	15/10	12/5	15/10/5/3
Australia	15	10	10
Austria	15/10	5	5
Belgium	15/0	10/0	5
Bolivia	15/10	15/0	15/0
Brazil	15	15/10	15/10
Bulgaria	15/5	0	0
Canada	15	15	10
China	10	10	10
Denmark	15/10	10	6
Ecuador	15	10/5/0	10/5
Slovakia	15/5	0	5/0
United States of America	15/10	10/0	10/8/5
Philippines	15/10	15/10/0	20/15/10
Finland	15/10	10	5
France	15/0	10/0	5
Hungary	15/5	0	0
India	15	15/0	20/10
Ireland	15/0	0	10/8/5
Italy	15	12/0	8/4
Japan	15/10	10	10
South Korea	15/10	10/0	10
Luxembourg	15/10	10/0	10
Morocco	15	10	10/5
Mexico	15/5	15/10	10/0
Norway	15/10	10	5
The Netherlands	15/10/5	10	6
Poland	15/5	0	10/0
Portugal	15/10	15	5
United Kingdom	15/10	12	10
Czech Republic	15	0	5/0
Romania	15/10	10	10
Russia (URSS)	15/10/5	5/0	5
Sweden	15/10	15/0	10
Switzerland	15/10	10/0	5
Thailand	15	15/10/0	15/8/5
Tunisia	15/5	10/5	10

Special tax on property owned by non-residents

Non-resident entities that own property in Spain, by any title, or the right to the use and enjoyment of such property, are subject to a special tax that accrues on 31 December each year and is declared and paid in the following January.

Taxable income for this tax consists of the rateable value of the property, or in the absence thereof, of the value determined for wealth tax purposes. The applicable tax rate is 3 per cent.

The following qualify for exemption:

- non-profit making entities;
- state and public foreign institutions;
- international organisations;
- companies whose shares are listed on a secondary stock market.

Also exempt are entities covered by an international double taxation treaty with a clause on exchange of information, and any direct or indirect non-corporate owners of such entities who are resident in Spain or in a country with which Spain has concluded a Treaty in those terms.

This special tax may be deducted from any non-residents' income tax that the owner of the property may be subject to.

6.3

Personal Income Tax

Pricewaterhousecoopers

On 1 January 1999, Law 40/1998, of 9 December 1998, on Personal Income Tax, came into effect. This law is applicable to income obtained after said date and to income pending allocation that was obtained under the old Law 18/1991 of 6 June 1991, on Personal Income Tax.

Similarly, Law 41/1998 of 9 December 1998 on Non-Residents' Income Tax (NRIT), in force since 1 January 1999, regulates the taxation of income obtained in Spain by non-resident individuals and companies, independently of the new Personal Income Tax Act.

The main criterion for determining which law is applicable is the residence of the taxpayer. The law provides that persons have a habitual abode in Spain when any of the following requirements are met:

- they remain for more than 183 days of the calendar year in Spain; or

- their main place of business or professional activities or centre of economic interest is located in Spain.

In this respect, the new Personal Income Tax Act maintains the assumption that, unless otherwise proven, the habitual abode, in accordance with the above criteria, is in Spain if the taxpayer's spouse (not legally separated) and dependent children reside in Spain.

In addition, the new Personal Income Tax Act introduces an anti-abuse rule. This now means that Spanish nationals who have become residents for tax purposes in any country or territory officially classed as a tax haven, continue to be liable for personal income tax during the year in which the change of residence takes place and in the following four tax years.

Taxation of residents

Taxable base

Taxpayers who are considered to be residents of Spain in accordance with the above criteria are taxed on their world-wide income in accordance with the rates laid down by the central government and the Autonomous Regions. In this respect, it should be stressed that personal income tax is a central government tax, albeit partially transferred to the Autonomous Regions. This is as a result of the regime for the financing of Autonomous Regions, derived from Law 14/1996 on the Transfer of Taxes from the Central Government to the Autonomous Regions, a regime applied by nearly all the Autonomous Regions. Thus, the Autonomous Regions have legislative powers in relation to this tax, although limited to the rates laid down in the official tax tables applicable to the general tax base (together with the general rates) and the relevant reductions in tax payable.

One of the most significant changes is that the application of the tax now centres on so-called 'available income'. This being the income available to taxpayers after covering their needs and those of any dependent persons. In order to define available income, the so-called minimum 'personal' or 'family' income is declared exempt. This amount varies depending on the circumstances of the taxpayer.

Worthy of note in the chart of personal income tax exemptions are indemnities for physical and psychic damages in legally recognised amounts or by an amount imposed by the courts, academic grants, relevant literary, artistic or scientific awards, certain lottery and gambling prizes and unemployment benefits, subject to certain limits.

Under the new law, there is a new exemption for earned income received for work carried out abroad – up to a limit of Ptas10 million – provided such income is subject to a foreign tax similar or analogous to personal income tax. This requirement is understood to be met when the taxpayer pays at least 50 per cent of the tax that would be applicable in Spain by applying the average effective rate of personal income tax to said income.

The tax base for personal income tax purposes is made up of a general part and a special part. The general tax base is made up of earned income, real property and securities investment income, income from business activities, capital gains and losses and allocations of income established by the Personal Income Tax Act. Net income consists of the difference between income subject to tax and deductible expenses.

The main deductible expenses are:

- **For earned income:** the amount of fees paid to professional associations if membership of these is obligatory, and expenses relating to legal assistance in the event of a legal dispute with the employer, up to a maximum of Ptas50,000.

- **For real property investment income:** the financing expenses invested in the acquisition or improvement of assets or rights derived from such income, and the depreciation of said assets.

- **For securities investment income:** expenses relating to the administration or deposit of traded securities.

Capital gains and losses consist of the difference between transfer and acquisition values. The relevant reductions applicable to each source of income are applied to the above amounts. The main reductions are:

- In respect of income generated over a period of more than two years or obtained in an irregular manner in time, a 30 per cent reduction is generally applied.

- In respect of earned income, an additional reduction is applied to net income that ranges between Ptas375,000 and Ptas500,000, depending on the amount involved.

Tax liability

The general tax base is obtained by adding up all the above components. The single central government and Autonomous Region tax scale is applied to the individual or joint tax return after reducing the tax base by the amount corresponding to the legally established personal or family exempt minimum. Under no circumstances can the result of the above result in a negative tax base.

The scales in pesetas applicable to the general tax base are as follows in Table 6.3.1:

Table 6.3.1 Scales applicable to general tax base (Ptas)

Taxable income up to	Gross tax payable	Rest of taxable income up to	Applicable rate (%)
0	0	612,000	15.00
612,000	91,800	1,530,000	20.17
2,142,000	400,401	2,040,000	23.57
4,182,000	881,229	2,550,000	31.48
6,732,000	1,683,969	4,488,000	38.07
11,220,000	3,392,551	And over	39.60

The personal income tax scale of the Autonomous Region or the complementary scale is applied to the general tax base when the relevant Autonomous Region has not made use of its legislative powers relating to this tax and has not approved its own tax scale. In these cases the following scale in pesetas applies:

Table 6.3.2   Scales applicable to special tax base (Ptas)

Taxable income up to	Gross tax payable	Rest of taxable income up to	Applicable rate (%)
0	0	612,000	3.00
612,000	18,360	1,530,000	3.83
2,142,000	76,959	2,040,000	4.73
4,182,000	173,451	2,555,000	5.72
6,732,000	319,311	4,488,000	6.93
11,220,000	630,329	And over	8.40

The special tax base includes net capital gains generated over a period of more than one year. In the case of capital gains derived from the transfer of assets not used in business activities that were acquired before 31 December 1994, a transitional regime is applicable whereby the reducing consolidated coefficients at 31 December 1996, in force under the abolished regulations, may be applied thereto. In any event, 18 per cent tax will be applied to the special tax base (15.3 per cent relating to the central government and 2.7 per cent to the Autonomous Regions).

After obtaining these amounts, a number of reducing factors are applied. These include deductions for investment in habitual dwelling, for business investments envisaged in the Corporate Income Tax Act for those taxpayers who carry out business activities, for donations, for income obtained in Ceuta or Melilla, and for investments and expenses relating to items of cultural interest. Once these deductions have been applied, the net tax payable is obtained.

In turn, net tax payable will be reduced by the following: deduction for double taxation (internal and international); withholdings; payments on account and partial payments on account of the tax. In this way, the amount payable by or refundable to the Spanish resident is obtained.

Withholdings and payments on account

The law establishes a system for making withholdings and payments on account in respect of certain types of income that are considered as payments on account of the definitive tax. The following types of income are subject to withholding or payment on account:

- Earned income (including benefits in kind). The withholding rate applied is the rate that results from the new method of calculation, which is similar to that of the definitive tax assessment and which takes into account the personal and family situation of the taxpayer.

- Securities investment income. The withholding rate is 18 per cent.

- Income for professional activities, 18 per cent and income from agricultural and farming activities, between 1 and 2 per cent.

- Capital gains obtained from the transfer or redemption of shares and holdings representing the capital or net worth of collective investment institutions, which will be subject to a 18 per cent rate.

- Income from the leasing and sub-letting of urban property, which will be subject to a withholding rate of 15 per cent.

- Income from copyright, industrial property rights and supplies of technical assistance services, and from the leasing and sub-letting of movable property, businesses or mines, which is subject to 18 per cent withholding.

- Income from the assignment of the right to the use of image rights is subject to 20 per cent withholding.

In general terms, withholdings and payments on account must be made by the following persons or entities:

- Companies and other entities, including entities using the tax flow-through system.

- Taxpayers who carry out business activities when they pay out others' incomes for the carrying out of their activities.

- Individuals, companies and other entities not resident in Spain and that operate in Spain with a permanent establishment.

- Individuals, companies and other entities that are non-resident in Spain and that operate in Spain without a permanent establishment. This is only in respect of salaries they pay and other income subject to withholding or payment on account, which constitute a deductible expense for the obtaining of certain income specified in Law 41/98 on NRIT.

The above persons and entities obliged to make withholdings or payments on account must, by 20 April, 20 July, 20 October and 20 January, file a statement of amounts withheld and payments on account relating to the immediately preceding calendar quarter and pay the relevant amounts into the Treasury.

However, when the party making the withholding is considered to be a large-size company, the above statement must be filed by the 20th day of each month in relation to amounts withheld and payments on account relating to the immediately preceding month.

Taxation on non-residents

Taxpayers deemed non-residents in accordance with the requirements set out above are taxed in Spain on their gross income in cash or in kind obtained in Spain as laid down in Law 41/1998 on Non-Residents' Income Tax (IRNR). This Act is interpreted as laid down in the personal and corporate income tax regulations, depending on the case.

It should be noted that the provisions of the IRNR Act must respect both the provisions of the double taxation treaties concluded by Spain governing income and assets and the provisions of EU legislation. The key factor when defining taxation of non-residents is whether or not the income that is taxable in accordance with rules governing non-residents is obtained through a permanent establishment located in Spain.

Income obtained through a permanent establishment

Please refer to Chapter 6.2, on corporate taxation for non-residents.

Note that, among the special rules relating to non-resident individuals, there are no additional taxes levied on income obtained by the permanent establishment and transferred to its non-resident individual owner.

Income obtained without a permanent establishment

As indicated above, please see the chapter on corporate taxation for non-residents. Set out below are the most significant special rules affecting non-resident individuals:

- In the case of transfers of real property located in Spain by non-resident individuals without a permanent establishment, the purchaser is not required to withhold and make an interim payment of 5 per cent of the agreed price on account of the non-residents' tax. This is true provided that the building has been owned by the non-resident for more than ten years at 31 December 1996, and that no improvements have been carried out during that period.

- Gains derived from the transfer of assets not used in business activities that were acquired prior to 31 December 1994, and obtained by non-resident individuals, qualify for the transitional regime already described, whereby the reducing rates that were in effect at 31 December 1996 may be applied to the gains.

- As regards the tax treatment of pensions and passive income received by non-resident individuals, a fixed rate of 8 per cent is applied where the income does not exceed Ptas1.6 million. There is a progressive scale of 8 to 40 per cent for amounts exceeding Ptas2.5 million.

- Note that there is an optional tax regime the application of which may be requested by individuals resident in other EU member states. This is provided that their earned income or income from business activities obtained in Spain represents at least 75 per cent of their total income and that the individuals have paid IRNR during the period. These taxpayers may benefit from the provisions of the Personal Income Tax Act applicable to residents in order to obtain, since 1 January 1999, a refund of excess tax paid.

6.4

Miscellaneous Taxes

PricewaterhouseCoopers

Wealth tax

Wealth tax is a direct and personal tax levied on the net worth of individuals at 31 December each year. Spanish residents are subject to wealth tax on their world-wide net worth, irrespective of the place in which their assets and rights are located or may be exercised. Non-residents are subject to wealth tax on any assets and rights that are located or may be exercised in Spain.

Any charges and encumbrances may be deducted from the net worth figure, as well as personal debts and obligations for which the taxpayer is liable. With respect to non-resident taxpayers, these charges and debts are limited to the assets and rights owned or which may be exercised in Spain.

Assets that form part of the national or regional heritage, certain works of art and antiques, personal effects, vested rights in pension plans, assets and rights used in business activities, and shares in 'family' businesses that are not transparent for tax purposes, the habitual home up to Ptas25 million, among others, are exempt from wealth tax. The valuation methods applicable to each asset and right that forms part of net worth are established in the law on wealth tax. There is an exempt minimum figure of Ptas18 million that does not apply to non-resident taxpayers.

The rates laid down in the official tax tables to be applied to the wealth tax assessment base are illustrated in Table 6.4.1 as follows:

Table 6.4.1   Rates applicable to wealth tax assessment base (Ptas)

Taxable base, up to	Gross tax payable	Remainder of base, up to	Tax rate
0	0	27,808,000	0.20
27,808,000	55,616	27,807,000	0.30
55,615,000	139,037	55,614,000	0.50
111,229,000	417,107	111,229,000	0.90
222,458,000	1,418,168	222,458,000	1.30
444,916,000	4,310,122	444,916,000	1.70
889,832,000	11,873,694	889,832,000	2.10
1,779,664,000	30,560,166	Higher	2.50

Certain powers to regulate wealth tax have been transferred to the regional governments, which are allowed to establish their own official tax tables and exempt minimum figure.

Inheritance and gift tax

Inheritance and gift tax is a direct tax levied on certain capital increases *inter vivos* or *mortis causa* that are obtained gratuitously by individuals. The tax is levied on individuals that are resident in Spain for tax purposes, on capital gains obtained gratuitously, irrespective of where the assets or rights acquired are located or may be exercised. The tax is levied on non-resident individuals who obtain such capital gains from assets or rights that are located or may be exercised in Spain. This applies to heirs, legatees and transferees.

Inheritance and gift tax is levied on the following:

• acquisition assets or rights through inheritance, bequest or any other type of transfer of estate;

• acquisition of assets or rights in the form of gifts or other gratuitous transfers *inter vivos*;

• receipt of sums of money by beneficiaries of life insurance contracts where the policyholder is not the beneficiary.

In general, the taxable base is the actual value of the assets and rights acquired. The value declared by the taxpayer may be verified by the tax authorities.

The taxable base is reduced by 95 per cent in the case of transfers to family members, whether *inter vivos* or *mortis causa*, from sole proprietor businesses, professional businesses and shares in 'family' businesses exempt from wealth tax. The following legal requirements must be met in order to reduce the taxable base:

- The transferee may not sell the assets or shares acquired for at least ten years or perform acts or effect corporate operations that result in a substantial decline in the value of such assets or shares.

- The sole proprietor businesses, professional businesses and shares in 'family' businesses must remain exempt, for the purposes of the transferee's wealth tax, for the following ten years (not required in the case of transfers *mortis causa*).

- In the case of transfers *inter vivos*, the transferor must have reached the age of 65 or be in a situation of permanent and absolute or major disability. Similarly, the transferor must discontinue his management responsibilities, if applicable, and receive no remuneration in this respect as from the date of transfer.

The amount of tax payable will vary, based, among other circumstances, on the nature of the transfer (*inter vivos* or *mortis causa*), the relationship between the transferee and transferor and certain personal circumstances of the former, such as age, physical or mental condition and net worth before the transfer. The tax rate may vary between 0 and 80 per cent depending on these circumstances.

The regional governments have the power to regulate certain aspects of the tax, including the tax rate and the cases in which the taxable base may be reduced.

The tax rates applicable in 1999 are set out in Table 6.4.2 below:

Table 6.4.2   Tax rates for 1999 (Ptas)

Taxable base, up to	Gross tax payable	Remainder of taxable base, up to	Tax rate (%)
0	0	1,330,000	7.65
1,330,000	101,745	1,329,000	8.50
2,659,000	214,710	1,329,000	9.35
3,988,000	338,972	1,329,000	10.20
5,317,000	474,530	1,329,000	11.05
6,646,000	621,384	1,329,000	11.90
7,975,000	779,535	1,329,000	12.75
9,304,000	948,983	1,329,000	13.60
10,633,000	1,129,727	1,329,000	14.45
11,962,000	1,321,767	1,329,000	15.30
13,921,000	1,525,104	6,635,000	16.15
19,926,000	2,596,657	6,635,000	18.70
26,561,000	3,837,402	13,270,000	21.25
39,831,000	6,657,277	26,520,000	25.50
66,351,000	13,419,877	66,351,000	29.75
132,702,000	33,159,299	higher	34.00

There are currently three double taxation treaties on gifts and inheritance concluded by Spain (with Greece, France and Sweden) that contain special rules governing this issue.

Value Added Tax (VAT)

VAT is an indirect tax levied on the consumption of goods and services produced or marketed by businesses or professionals for a fee in the course of their business or professional activity. The following operations constitute taxable events for VAT purposes:

- Supplies of goods or services.

- Intra-Community acquisitions of goods.

- Imports of goods.

Intra-Community acquisitions of goods are taxed at destination on a provisional basis, a procedure that will be replaced in the future by taxation at source, more suitable for trade in the single European market.

Certain operations are exempt from VAT, including specific banking, financial and insurance services, health and education services, etc.

The VAT assessment base is the total amount paid in relation to the relevant transactions by the recipient or by third parties. The tax rates vary depending on the nature of the good or service:

- The standard rate of 16 per cent is applied to most goods and services.

- The reduced rate of 7 per cent is applied to certain food products, medical services, pharmaceutical products, housing construction, passenger transport services, hotel and catering services, etc.

- The low rate of 4 per cent is applicable to certain staple foods, medicines, printed publications, etc.

VAT is applied throughout Spain, the only exceptions being in the Canary Islands, Ceuta and Melilla.

Transfer tax and stamp duty

Transfer tax and stamp duty is an indirect tax levied on certain taxable events grouped into the three categories described below.

Capital transfers for consideration (transmisiones patrimoniales onerosas, TPO)

Levied on transfers of assets and rights *inter vivos* and the establishment of certain real property rights, loans, guarantee deposits, leases and administrative concessions. The scope is limited to transfers between individuals. The taxable base is the actual value of the asset transferred or right established or assigned. The value declared may be verified by the tax authorities.

The tax rate applicable to these operations is 6 per cent for real property, 4 per cent for moveable property and 1 per cent for the establishment of certain guarantees and the execution of certain contracts, albeit different rates are in force in several Autonomous Regions.

Transfers of rural land and second transfers of buildings are exempt from VAT and subject to 6 per cent transfer tax. If the transfers are effected by companies, businesses or professionals in the course of their business or professional activity, however, and the transferee is a business or professional able to deduct all input VAT, the seller may charge VAT, waiving the exemption and thus avoiding the higher cost of transfer tax.

Finally, transfers of shares in companies more than 50 per cent of whose assets consist of real property located in Spain are subject to 6 per cent transfer tax if, as a result of the transfer, the transferee holds more than 50 per cent of the share capital.

Corporate operations (operaciones societarias, OS)

Levied on the most relevant corporate financing operations, among others, including company formation, capital increases, winding-up, capital reduction, transfer to Spain of a company's place of effective management or registered office in certain circumstances, etc. The tax rate applied to these corporate operations is 1 per cent.

Transactions evidenced by legal documentation (actos jurídicos documentados, AJD)

Levied on notarial, mercantile and administrative transactions. The tax rate applied to the more common operations is 0.5 per cent. In the case of notarial documents (documentos notariales, DN), this rate is applied to the value declared in the documents.

Several taxable events may arise from a single act that may be subject to different taxes or both VAT and transfer tax. In order to avoid this situation, incompatibilities have been established as shown in Table 6.4.3:

Table 6.4.3   Established tax compatabilities/incompatabilities

TPO	Incompatible with	OS and AJD (DN)
TPO	Incompatible with	IVA
OS	Incompatible with	TPO and AJD (DN)
OS	Compatible with	VAT
AJD, Mercantile documents (DM)	Compatible with	TPO and OS
AJD	Compatible with	VAT
AJD, Notarial documents (DN)	Incompatible with	ISD*, TPO and OS

* Inheritance and Gift Tax

Excise duties

Excise duties are indirect taxes applicable to specific types of consumption and levied, on a one-off basis, on the production, import and, if applicable, introduction into Spain of certain goods, as well as the registration of certain means of transport. Excise duties are levied on the consumption of alcohol and alcoholic drinks such as beer, wine, fermented beverages and intermediate products. The consumption of fossil fuels and tobacco is also subject to excise tax.

In general, these taxes are not applicable in the Canary Islands or Ceuta and Melilla, although alcohol and beer are taxed in the Canary Islands and tobacco in Ceuta and Melilla.

The excise duty on certain means of transport is levied on a one-off basis on the registration in Spain of certain means of transport (cars, ships and aircraft). The tax rates vary depending on the means of transport, as shown in Table 6.4.4.

Table 6.4.4   Transport tax rates

Class of vehicle	Mainland Spain Balearic Islands (%)	Canary Islands	Ceuta and Melilla (%)
I*	7	6	0
II**	12	11	0

* Private vehicles with petrol engines smaller than 1600 c.c. or diesel engines smaller than 2000 c.c.
** Other means of transport.

On 1 January 1998, an excise duty on electricity was introduced which is levied on a one-off basis on the production, import and, if applicable, intra-Community acquisition of electricity. The taxable base is obtained by multiplying the total amount of the taxable base for VAT purposes by the coefficient 1.05113. The tax rate is 4.864 per cent.

Customs duties on imports

Customs duties are levied on imports of goods. An import is understood to involve the entry into Spain of merchandise from non-European Union (EU) countries or from territories not covered by the scope of EU customs authorities that are held by EU member states (eg Ceuta and Melilla).

The tariff payable on goods imported into the EU is determined based on the following factors:

* correct customs classification according to the EU tariff list;

* origin of the merchandise, which in turn determines whether or not duty benefits may be applied;

* the value for customs purposes, to ensure that the base for calculating the tariff is declared correctly.

Since 1987 the EU's harmonised classification tariff (TARIC) and exemptions system have been in force in Spain.

Tax on insurance premiums

Introduced on 1 January 1997, tax on insurance premiums is levied on insurance and capitalisation operations deemed to be effected in Spain, or arranged by insurance companies operating in Spain, including non-resident companies operating under a free supply of services regime. Such operations are also subject to, but exempt from, VAT.

The tax is levied on all kinds of insurance operations and capitalisation operations based on actuarial techniques that would include, in principle, the following operations:

* life insurance;

* direct non-life insurance;

* reinsurance of the above operations;

* capitalisation operations based on actuarial techniques that consist of obtaining certain commitments as regards duration and amount, in exchange for pre-established lump-sum or regular payments.

The following operations, among others, are exempt:

* mandatory welfare cover and group insurance policies through which systems alternative to pension funds or plans are arranged;

* capitalisation operations based on actuarial techniques;

* life insurance operations;

- reinsurance operations;

- operations relating to the international transport of merchandise or passengers.

These operations are subject to this tax when effected in Spain, as defined below:

- where the risk or commitment is located in Spain;

- where there are no specific rules determining the location and the contracting party, acting in the course of its business or professional activities, a business or professional resident in Spain for tax purposes or operating through a permanent establishment in Spain.

The taxpayers, ie the insurance companies, must pass on to persons contracting the relevant insurance the entire amount of tax payable on the operations in question. The provisions of the VAT Act must be taken into account in this respect. The taxable base is the net insurance premium, or payment made by the policyholder or by a third party. The tax accrues on payment of premiums at a rate of 6 per cent.

6.5

Local and Regional Taxes

Pricewaterhouse Coopers

Local taxes

Although central government laws determine the basic aspects of local taxes, the municipalities have certain powers to regulate these taxes that may give rise to differences in the practical application of a tax in each municipality. There are two types of local tax:

- mandatory taxes that must be levied by local councils; and

- optional taxes that require a specific agreement by each town council.

Mandatory taxes

Property tax
Property tax is a direct tax on real property, the management of which is shared by the central government and town councils.
    The taxable events are as follows:

- ownership of rural or municipal real property;

- ownership of the usufruct right or surface right to such real property;

- ownership of an administrative concession in respect of public property.

The taxable base is the rateable value of the real property, which may not exceed the market value. The taxable base is reduced in the event that the rateable value has recently been reviewed. Tax payable is calculated by applying to the taxable base a tax rate that varies between 0.4 per cent and 1.3 per cent for municipal property and 0.3 per cent and 1.22 per cent for rural property.

Tax on business and professional activities
This tax accrues on an annual basis and is levied on the mere performance of business activities within the municipality. The regularity of operations and existence of a profit is irrelevant for the purposes of this tax. Tax

payable is calculated based on several factors (type of activity, number of employees, status of the activity, etc) and local councils have a considerable margin for reducing the final tax burden.

Motor vehicle tax
Tax on motor vehicles accrues on an annual basis and is levied on the ownership of motor vehicles suitable for use on public thoroughfares. Tax payable is calculated based on the vehicle's specifications (power, number of seats, etc) and the population of the municipality in question.

Optional taxes

Tax on buildings, installations and works of construction
This tax is levied on all works of construction or installation carried out within the municipality for which a building permit or planning permission must be obtained. The taxable base is the actual cost of the building, installation or work of construction and the tax payable is calculated by applying a tax rate of between 2 per cent and 4 per cent depending on the official population of the municipality.

Municipal land value increment tax

This tax is levied on capital gains obtained in respect of municipal land due to the transfer of ownership or the establishment or assignment of any right of usufruct to such land. The taxable base is the actual increase in the value of the land over a maximum period of 20 years. This increase is determined by applying to the value of the land at the date of accrual a rate that varies depending on the official population of the municipality and the period over which the value has increased. The tax payable is calculated by applying a rate of between 16 per cent and 30 per cent to the taxable base, again depending on the official population of the municipality.

Special regional regimes

Canary Islands

Introduction
In addition to a special European Union (EU) statute, the Canary Islands has a special regime called the Economic and Fiscal System of the Canary Islands (*Regimen Economico Fiscal de Canarias*), which is basically governed by Laws 20/1991 and 19/1994. Its special characteristics are as follows:

- Value Added Tax (VAT) is not applicable. Instead, the General Canary Islands Indirect Tax is applied (*Impuesto General Indirecto Canario*).

The structure of this tax is very similar to VAT, with the following differences:

- The tax rates are significantly lower: 'zero', 2, 4.5 and 13 per cent, the standard rate being 4.5 per cent. It is not associated with VAT. Therefore, the introduction of tangible property in the Canary Islands, irrespective of its origin, is taxed as an import.

- Supplies of deliveries of goods carried out within the scope of retail trade activities are exempt.

- Imports of tangible property in the Canary Islands are subject to the Special Canary Islands' Import Tax (*Arbitrio sobre la Producción e Importación en Canarias*), a temporary tax that is still expected to be in force in the year 2000 and which is currently levied at 0.05 per cent and 2.3 per cent.

- Spanish excise duties established, in general, are not applicable in the Canary Islands except for those relating to alcohol, beer and certain means of transport. The applicable rates are lower than those laid down in Spain and the Balearic Islands.

In addition, the following specific incentives are laid down for operations and/or investments carried out in the Canary Islands:

Canary Islands investment reserve

Profits obtained in the Canary Islands may be transferred to this special reserve up to the limit of 90 per cent of retained earnings. This gives rise to a reduction in taxable income for corporate income tax purposes in the amount provided for, or with respect to individual businessmen, a reduction in personal income tax payable.

In order to benefit from the above reduction, the appropriations to the Canary Islands Reserve must subsequently be invested, in a period of three years, in the assets specified below. These must be held by the taxpayer during a period of five years or during the estimated useful life of the asset, if this is lower.

- Fixed assets located and used in the Canary Islands that are necessary for the activities of the taxpayer. The assets may be new or used, provided certain requirements are met.

- The subscription of government stock up to the limit of 50 per cent of the amount transferred from profits each year.

- The subscription of interest in the capital of companies that carry out an activity in the Canary Islands, which subsequently invest in the fixed assets specified above.

Rebate for production activities in the Canary Islands
A 50 per cent rebate in corporate income tax payable is available in respect of profits obtained as a result of activities carried out in the Canary Islands relating to the production of tangible property, in respect of agricultural, farming, industrial and fishing activities. This rebate is also applicable to the personal income tax of individual businessmen and women subject to the direct evaluation method.

Tax regime of the special register for ships and shipping companies
Ships and shipping companies that meet the requirements established in Law 27/1992 may register with the Special Register for ships and shipping companies and may thereby enjoy:

• Exemption from transfer tax in respect of all acts and contracts relating to the ships registered in said Register.

• Personal income tax exemption is granted for 50 per cent payroll received by the crew of such ships.

• A 90 per cent reduction in tax payable relating to taxable income generated from the exploitation of the ships registered in the Special Register.

Tax credits – Fixed assets investments
In relation to all tax credits referred to under the Corporation Tax general regime, when the investments are located and used in the Canaries, or activities are carried out therein, the credits are between 25 and 80 per cent points higher while application limits are also increased. Besides which, there remains a 25 per cent tax credit, in the Canaries, for investments in fixed assets, and even used fixed assets, when certain requirements are met.

Deduction for investments
In relation to investments in the Canary Islands, in addition to the current general regime, the deduction regime contained in the previous corporate income tax legislation (Law 61/1978), remains in force. As a result, the deduction for investments in new fixed assets, and even used fixed assets when certain requirements are met, remains in force. As concerns all types of deduction, the credit generated is increased and the period over which it may be applied to corporate income tax payable is extended.

Incentives for new activities or improvements in existing activities
Exemption from transfer tax and stamp duty is available on the setting up of companies domiciled in the Canary Islands and on capital increases of existing companies. This exemption also applies to acquisitions of capital goods by said companies during a period of three years as from the date on which the formation deed is executed or the capital increase carried out.

Exemption from the Canary Islands Indirect Tax is available on supplies and imports of capital goods to the above companies during a period of three years as from the date on which the formation deed is executed or the capital increase carried out.

Special Canary Islands' zone (zona especial de Canarias – ZEC)

The ZEC was approved in January 2000 by the European Union (EU) and the Spanish main regulation was passed in 23 June 2000, while further development regulations will be passed throughout the year 2000.

The main regulations being as follows:

• New companies may apply for authorisation from ZEC authorities to be registered as ZEC entities until 31 December 2006, so that they will be allowed to enjoy the special ZEC tax regime until 31 December 2008. The EU could, under revision, extend the ZEC tax regime in the future.

• The ZEC territory includes all the Canaries except for those ZEC entities that intend to carry out industrial or commercial activities involving tangible goods which must be located in specific controlled areas.

• Application for registration as a ZEC entity requires submitting a complete report regarding intended activities and requires the compromise to:

 – make an investment in fixed assets located in the ZEC territory for a minimum of €100,000 within the first two years of activity.
 – create at least five new jobs in the Canaries.

• ZEC entities are subject to special accounting requirements so as to keep proper separate detailed registers for the operations qualifying for the special tax regime. They are also allowed to operate outside the Canaries through branches conditioned to keeping separate accounting books.

• ZEC allowed activities include a wide range of industrial and commercial activities, as well as a wide range of service activities (see Appendix 1). Nevertheless, credit and insurance entities, as well as Co-ordinated Centres and Intra-group Services' activities are excluded.

• ZEC entities do enjoy reduced Spanish Corporate Tax rates for the taxable base arising from the allowed ZEC activities. Such rates range from 1 per cent to 5 per cent, depending on the year of the ZEC entity registration, type of activity and job creation. The referred tax rates are limited up to certain taxable base amounts, which are also dependent on the type of activities to be carried out and job creation. The rest of their taxable base will be subject to general Corporate Tax rate (35 per cent), where other REF incentives would also be available.

- ZEC entities will enjoy relevant exemptions regarding IGIC, Transfer Tax and Stamp Duty, as well as relevant reductions and simplified rules for local taxes.

- Exemption from the Spanish Non-Residents Income Tax is granted regarding the following income when paid by ZEC entities to non-residents, except when the referred returns shall be obtained through territories considered as tax havens under Spanish regulations:

  - Interest, dividends or other returns obtained by the assignment of own capital to third parties.
  - Capital gains derived from moveable property obtained without an intermediary permanent establishment. However, this exemption shall not be applicable to capital gains arising from the transfer of shares, interests or other rights in a ZEC entity. This is especially the case when the assets of the ZEC entity mainly consist of, directly or indirectly, real property located in Spain. Or, when, at some time in the 12 months preceding the transfer, the non-resident has held, directly or indirectly, at least 25 per cent of the capital of the ZEC entity.

- Dividends paid by ZEC entities to its shareholders – wherever they are resident, except for tax havens under Spanish regulations – will enjoy the tax benefits stated in the EU's Parent-Subsidiary Directive and therefore no Spanish taxation.

- No double taxation deductions on dividends received are granted to Spanish shareholders of ZEC entities (companies or individuals).

6.6

Taxation: Infringements and Penalties

Pricewaterhousecoopers

The most common tax cycle begins either with the tax payer's self-assessment or with a tax return that contains complete information so that the tax authorities may assess the relevant tax owed. The latter is currently not common practice. The information contained in the tax returns may be verified and rectified by the competent body of the tax authorities, the controlling bodies and the Tax Inspectorate during the four years following submission.

The current legislation establishes the obligation of tax payers to furnish tax-related information to the Tax Administration regarding their economic, professional or financial activities with third parties. The information can either be provided in general by using the relevant forms to this effect or as a result of receiving an official notification from the authorities.

Regarding the obligation to pay taxes, the different consequences arising from the tax legislation in force enables us to establish the following paying schemes and results:

- voluntary payment within the voluntary payment period;

- voluntary payment, without official notification from the authorities, made after the voluntary payment period has elapsed. The General Tax Law establishes tax liabilities, without official notification from the tax authorities. The fixed charges are 5, 10, or 15 per cent of the tax due, depending on whether tax is paid within three, six or twelve months after the last day of the voluntary payment period. A fixed charge of 20 per cent plus the relevant late-payment interest is applicable if the tax is paid more than twelve months following the last day of the voluntary payment period;

- payment after receiving official notification entails a 20 per cent collection charge and late-payment interest.

The General Tax Law and the regulations governing the different taxes, spell out several acts (or omissions) that constitute a breach of tax regulations. Different penalties are imposed, the nature and amount of which are contingent upon whether or not the breach is considered as serious or minor. In addition, the presence of fraudulent intent and the amount of unpaid tax may determine the committing of a tax offence. Additionally, penalties may be monetary or non-monetary penalties, the latter being ancillary to the former.

The most common serious infringement is the failure to pay taxes. Such omissions are penalised with fines of between 50 and 150 per cent of the unpaid amount. Additional charges may be imposed due to the existence of aggravating circumstances. On the other hand, if the taxpayer agrees with the proposed fine, the fine is reduced by 30 per cent. Fines for minor infringements are generally between Ptas1000 and Ptas150,000. (Or Ptas200,000 per item, in cases of failure to provide information, subject to certain limits.)

Non-monetary penalties may consist of forfeiting the right to apply tax benefits, receive subsidies or any other public grants, conclude contracts with the state or other public agencies, in general, for a period of up to two or five years, depending on whether the breach is minor or serious.

Although the law, in the case of legal entities, generally establishes the legal representatives or directors as having a secondary liability for the tax liability, there are certain cases in which, because of their consent or participation in the committing of the infringement, such liability becomes joint and several.

As in the case of assessments, claims may be filed either with the body raising the assessment (voluntarily in this case) or with the relevant administrative courts, against any penalties imposed (one or two appeals depending on the amount of the penalty). An appeal may be filed with the relevant Court of Justice against the final judgement issued.

Whenever there is a fraudulent non-payment of tax exceeding Ptas15 million (per tax and year) a tax offence is committed. Additionally, the offence of fraudulently receiving subsidies is established when subsidies of more than Ptas10 million are obtained from the authorities. Finally, there are several accounting actions that may be typified as an accounting offence, such as having two different accounting records, failure to comply with the accounting obligations, falsifying or omitting accounting entries, or recording non-existent operations.

Tax offences are punishable by imprisonment of between six months and six years, and fines of up to six times the amount defrauded. In the case of legal entities, penalties are imposed on the legal directors or representatives.

Profiles of the Autonomous Regions

SEPI

Andalusia

Population:	7,258,168
Population density (inh/sqkm):	83
Area (sqkm):	87,595
GDP (US$ million):	75,645
GDP structure (%):	
Agriculture:	10.89
Industry:	14.49
Construction:	8.67
Services:	65.96
GDP per capita (US$):	10,422
Imports (US$ million):	7,990.31
Exports (US$ million):	8,866.91
Active population:	2,774,609
Activity rate (%):	48.23
Unemployment rate (%):	23.57
Tourism (visitors/year):	8,981,298

Major companies

Delphi Automotive System España (automotive); Carbonell (food industry); Cruzcampo Grup (food industry); Abengoa Grup (construction); Siderúrgica Sevillana (iron and steel); Alcatel Citesa (telecommunications); Siemens Matsushita Components (electronics and electrical equipment); Tioxide Europe (chemicals and pharmaceuticals); Fujitsu (electronic and computer devices); Visteon (automotive).

Infrastructure supporting the economy

Airports: Sevilla, Jerez, Málaga, Córdoba, Granada, Almería
Ports: Huelva, Sevilla, Málaga, Bahía de Cádiz, Bahía de
              Algeciras, Almería–Motril
Motorways: A-4 Sevilla–Cádiz; N-IV Madrid–Sevilla.

Capital grants

Maximum levels of non-refundable capital grants to productive investments: Up to 60 per cent of the eligible investment amount.

Aragon

Population:	1,181,814
Population density (inh/km²):	25
Area (km²):	47,720
GDP (US$ million):	18,707
GDP structure (%):	
Agriculture:	5.68
Industry:	28.72
Construction:	6.86
Services:	58.74
GDP per capita (US$/inh.):	15,829
Imports (US$ million):	4,730.18
Exports (US$ million):	5,539.09
Active population:	522,953
Activity rate (%):	51.88
Unemployment rate (%):	8.42
Tourism (visitors/year):	1,385,473

Major companies

General Motors (automotive); Adidas España (textiles and footwear);
Schindler (mechanical industry); Saica (paper and press); Valeo Térmico
(automotive); Lecitriler (automotive); Siemens Elasa (electronics and
electrical equipment)

Infrastructure supporting the economy

Airports: Zaragoza
Motorways: A-68 Bilbao–Logroño–Zaragoza; N-II Madrid–Zaragoza;
              A-2 Zaragoza–Barcelona

Capital grants

Maximum levels of non-refundable capital grants to productive investments: Between 20 and 60 per cent of the eligible investment amount.

Asturias

Population:	1,080,103
Population density (inh/km^2):	102
Area (km^2):	10,604
GDP (US$ million):	13,654
GDP structure (%):	
Agriculture:	3.90
Industry:	27.63
Construction:	8.09
Services:	60.38
GDP per capita (US$/inh):	12,641
Imports (US$ million):	1,654.75
Exports (US$ million):	1,479.23
Active population:	412,338
Activity rate (%):	44.91
Unemployment rate (%):	17.22
Tourism (visitors/year):	814,500

Major companies

Alsa (transportation); Suzuki Motor (motorcycles); Naval Gijón (naval construction); Thyssen Industrie (metallic and mineral products); Hunosa (coal mines); Du Pont (chemical); Fluor Daniel (engineering); Celulosas de Asturias (paper and press); Danone (food industry); Saint Gobain (glass industry); Limpac Plastics (plastics and rubbers); Tenneco (automotive)

Infrastructure supporting the economy

Airports:	Avilés
Ports:	Gijón, Avilés
Motorways:	A-66 León–Campomanes; highway network between Oviedo, Gijón and Avilés

Capital grants

Maximum levels of non-refundable capital grants to productive investments: Up to 50 per cent of the eligible investment amount.

Balearic Islands

Population:	801,023
Population density (inh/km^2):	160
Area (km^2):	4,992
GDP (US$ million):	17,120
GDP structure (%):	
Agriculture:	1.46
Industry:	7.43
Construction:	5.25
Services:	85.86
GDP per capita (US$/inh):	21,373
Imports (US$ million):	1,043.69
Exports (US$ million):	526.79
Active population:	366,667
Activity rate (%):	56.49
Unemployment rate (%):	9.53
Tourism (visitors/year):	5,648,155

Major companies

Ibernostar Grup (hotels and tourism); Sol Meliá (hotels and tourism); Barceló Grup (hotels and tourism); Riu Hotels Grup (hotels and tourism); Air Europa (air transportation – tourism); Gesa Grup (electricity, water and gas); Coflusa (textiles and footwear); Casa Buades (iron and steel)

Infrastructure supporting the economy

Airports:	Palma de Mallorca, Menorca, Ibiza
Ports:	Baleares-Mallorca

Canary Islands

Population:	1,639,795
Population density (inh/km^2):	218
Area (km^2):	7,492
GDP (US$ million):	24,167
GDP structure (%):	
Agriculture:	3.80
Industry:	8.51
Construction:	9.07
Services:	78.62
GDP per capita (US$/inh):	14,738

Imports (US$ million):	3,079.22
Exports (US$ million):	669.30
Active population:	710,079
Activity rate (%):	54.19
Unemployment rate (%):	16.74
Tourism (visitors/year):	3,047,361

Major companies

Unelco (electricity, water and gas); Freiremar (Sea-food industry); Binter Canarias (Air transportation – tourism); Flick Canarias (automotive); Disa Red de servicios Petrolíferos (petrochemical)

Infrastructure supporting the economy

Airports:	Tenerife (Northern & Southern), Lanzarote, Las Palmas, Fuenteventura, La Palma, Hierro
Ports:	Sta Cruz de Tenerife, Las Palmas

Cantabria

Population:	526,557
Population density (inh/km^2):	99
Area (km^2):	5,321
GDP (US$ million):	7,072
GDP structure (%):	
Agriculture:	4.23
Industry:	24.03
Construction:	7.36
Services:	64.39
GDP per capita (US$/inh):	13,431
Imports (US$ million):	1,538.88
Exports (US$ million):	1,201.07
Active population:	211,668
Activity rate (%):	47.15
Unemployment rate (%):	17.00
Tourism (visitors/year):	706,569

Major companies

Eléctrica de Viesgo (electricity, water and gas); Teka industrial (metallic and mineral products); Alcatel Cable Ibérica (electronics and electrical equipment); Plásticos Españoles (plastics and rubber); Transportes Gerposa (transportation); Edcha España (automotive); Derivados del Fluor (chemicals and pharmaceuticals); Solvay (chemicals and pharmaceuticals)

Infrastructure supporting the economy

Airports: Santander
Ports: Santander
Motorways: A-8 Santander–Irún (French border); A-67
              Santander–Gijón–Oviedo; N-611 Palencia

Capital grants

Maximum levels of non-refundable capital grants to productive investments: Up to 40 per cent of the eligible investment amount.

Castilla – La Mancha

Population:	1,719,756
Population density (inh/km^2):	21
Area (km^2):	79,461
GDP (US$ million):	19,848
GDP structure (%):	
Agriculture:	12.29
Industry:	23.62
Construction:	11.70
Services:	52.39
GDP per capita (US$/inh):	11,541
Imports (US$ million):	2,469.18
Exports (US$ million):	1,880.71
Active population:	666,620
Activity rate (%):	46.74
Unemployment rate (%):	13.94
Tourism (visitors/year):	1,311,008

Major companies

Basf Coating (chemicals and pharmaceuticals); Magneti Marelli Ibérica (automotive); Liebherr Ibérica (mechanical industry); Thomson TV España (electronics and electrical equipment); Schmalbach Lubeca Pet Cont. Ibérica (chemicals and pharmaceuticals)

Infrastructure supporting the economy

Motorways: N-II Madrid–Guadalajara; N-III Madrid–Albacete; N-IV
              Madrid–Sevilla; N-V Madrid–Badajoz; N-401 Toledo

Capital grants

Maximum levels of non-refundable capital grants to productive investments: Between 40 and 60 per cent of the eligible investment amount.

Castilla – Leon

Population:	2,478,391
Population density (inh/km^2):	26
Area (km^2):	94,224
GDP (US$ million):	33,047
GDP structure (%):	
Agriculture:	8.86
Industry:	24.57
Construction:	8.73
Services:	57.84
GDP per capita (US$/inh):	13,334
Imports (US$ million):	7,347.00
Exports (US$ million):	7,376.66
Active population:	1,054,616
Activity rate (%):	49.61
Unemployment rate (%):	15.29
Tourism (visitors/year):	2,621,988

Major companies

Nissan Vehículos Industriales (automotive); Antolín Irausa Grup (automotive); Siro (food industry); Rhone Poulenc Animal Nutrition España (chemicals and pharmaceuticals); Fasa Renault Grup (automotive); Michelin (plastics and rubbers)

Infrastructure supporting the economy

Airports:	León, Valladolid, Zamora
Motorways:	N-I Madrid–Burgos; N-VI Madrid–La Coruña; A-I Burgos –Armiñon; N-620 Salamanca–Valladolid–Burgos

Capital grants

Maximum levels of non-refundable capital grants to productive investments: Between 40 and 60 per cent of the eligible investment amount.

Catalonia

Population:	6,154,987
Population density (inh/km^2):	191
Area (km^2):	32,113
GDP (US$ million):	110,162
GDP structure (%):	
Agriculture:	1.62
Industry:	29.03
Construction:	6.72
Services:	62.64
GDP per capita (US$/inh):	17,898
Imports (US$ million):	38,469.02
Exports (US$ million):	29,214.76
Active population:	2,762,856
Activity rate (%):	53.69
Unemployment rate (%):	12.25
Tourism (visitors/year):	7,525,014

Major companies

Seat (automotive); Volkswagen Audi España (automotive); FCC (construction); Gas Natural (electricity, water and gas); Nissan Motor Ibérica (automotive); Bayer Hispania (chemicals and pharmaceuticals); Basf Grup (chemicals and pharmaceuticals); Nestlé (food industry); Sony (electronics and electrical equipment); Henkel Ibérica (chemicals and pharmaceuticals)

Infrastructure supporting the economy

Airports:	Barcelona, Sabadell, Girona, Reus
Ports:	Barcelona, Tarragona
Motorways:	A-2 Zaragoza–Barcelona; A-19 Montgat–Malgrat; A-18 San Cugat–Terrasa–Manresa; A-16 Tunels de Garraf; A-7 Mediterranean coast

Valencia

Population:	4,033,902
Population density (inh/km^2):	173
Area (km^2):	23,255
GDP (US$ million):	57,969
GDP structure (%):	
Agriculture:	4.35

Industry:	25.52
Construction:	7.64
Services:	62.50
GDP per capita (US$/inh):	14,370
Imports (US$ million):	10,094.40
Exports (US$ million):	14,138.93
Active population:	1,702,903
Activity rate (%):	51.98
Unemployment rate (%):	16.27
Tourism (visitors/year):	3,336,224

Major companies

Famosa (toys); Reebok Leisure (textiles and footwear); Francisco Ros Casares Group (iron and steel); MB España (toys); Porcelanosa Group (construction); Johnson Controls España Group (automotive); Plastic Omnium (plastics and rubbers); Ford (automotive); Ube Industries (chemicals and pharmaceuticals)

Infrastructure supporting the economy

Airports:	Valencia, Alicante
Ports:	Valencia, Alicante, Castellón
Motorways:	A-7 Mediterranean Coast; N-III Madrid–Valencia

Capital grants

Maximum levels of non-refundable capital grants to productive investments: Between 30 and 50 per cent of the eligible investment amount.

Extremadura

Population:	1,069,098
Population density (inh/km^2):	26
Area (km^2):	41,634
GDP (US$ million):	11,323
GDP structure (%):	
Agriculture:	16.87
Industry:	16.91
Construction:	10.19
Services:	56.04
GDP per capita (US$/inh):	10,591
Imports (US$ million):	293.23
Exports (US$ million):	611.52

Active population:	428,176
Activity rate (%):	48.65
Unemployment rate (%):	18.88
Tourism (visitors/year):	812,550

Major companies

Acorex (agriculture and livestock); AG Siderúrgica Balboa (iron and steel); Alfonso Gallardo (metallic and mineral products); Deutz Diter (automotive); Chistian Lay (trade); Mercoguadiana (agriculture and livestock); Industrias y promociones alimenticias (food industry)

Infrastructure supporting the economy

Airports:	Badajoz
Motorways:	N-V Madrid–Badajoz

Capital grants

Maximum levels of non-refundable capital grants to productive investments: Up to 60 per cent of the eligible investment amount.

Galicia

Population:	2,722,637
Population density (inh/km²):	92
Area (km²):	29,575
GDP (US$ million):	33,443
GDP structure (%):	
Agriculture:	9.23
Industry:	20.70
Construction:	9.15
Services:	60.92
GDP per capita (US$/inh):	12,283
Imports (US$ million):	6,821.89
Exports (US$ million):	5,892.89
Active population:	1,185,412
Activity rate (%):	52.07
Unemployment rate (%):	13.80
Tourism (visitors/year):	1,839,754

Major companies

Inditex Group (textiles and footwear); Financiera maderera (wood and furniture); Calvo Group (fish canning factory); La Lactaria Española (milk factory); Astilleros y Talleres del Noroeste (naval construction); Coren Group (food industry); Adolfo Domínguez (textiles and footwear); Citröen Hispania (automotive); Pescanova Group (food industry)

Infrastructure supporting the economy

Airports:	A Coruña, Santiago, Vigo
Ports:	Ferrol–San Ciprián, A Coruña, Marín–Pontevedra, Vigo, Vilagarcía
Motorways:	N-VI & A-6 Madrid–A Coruña; A-9 A Coruña–Vigo

Capital grants

Maximum levels of non-refundable capital grants to productive investments: Up to 60 per cent of the eligible investment amount.

Community of Madrid

Population:	5,100,500
Population density (inh/km^2)	634
Area (km^2):	8,028
GDP (US$ million):	94,876
GDP structure (%):	
Agriculture:	0.45
Industry:	15.71
Construction:	6.61
Services:	77.23
GDP per capita (US$/inh):	18,601
Imports (US$ million):	32,039.00
Exports (US$ million):	11,459.85
Active population:	2,279,843
Activity rate (%):	53.53
Unemployment rate (%):	11.09
Tourism (visitors/year):	5,045,036

Major companies

Repsol Group (petrochemical); Telefónica Group (telecommunications); El Corte Inglés (stores); Endesa Group (electricity, water and gas); Cepsa (petrochemical); Aceralia Group (iron and steel); IBM España (computers); Saint Gobain (glass industry)

Infrastructure supporting the economy

Airports: Madrid; Barajas, Madrid; Cuatro Vientos
Motorways: N-I Madrid–Burgos; N-II Madrid–Barcelona; N-III Madrid–
              Valencia; N-IV Madrid–Sevilla; N-V Madrid–Badajoz;
              N-VI Madrid–A Coruña; A-6 Villalba–Adanero; N-401
              Madrid–Toledo

Murcia

Population:	1,119,082
Population density (inh/km²):	99
Area (km²):	11,314
GDP (US$ million):	12,820
GDP structure (%):	
Agriculture:	8.14
Industry:	20.77
Construction:	9.41
Services:	61.68
GDP per capita (US$/inh):	11,456
Imports (US$ million):	2,020.93
Exports (US$ million):	2,775.12
Active population:	461,996
Activity rate (%):	51.68
Unemployment rate (%):	15.34
Tourism (visitors/year):	614,353

Major companies

El Pozo (food industry); Hero España (food industry); Misiva envases (bottles, cans); García Carrión (food industry); GE Plastics de España (plastics and rubbers)

Infrastructure supporting the economy

Airports: Murcia–San Javier
Ports: Cartagena
Motorways: A-7 Mediterranean coast; N-340 Murcia–Almería

Capital grants

Maximum levels of non-refundable capital grants to productive investments: Up to 50 per cent of the eligible investment amount.

Navarra

Population:	530,394
Population density (inh/km^2):	51
Area (km^2):	10,391
GDP (US$ million):	9,068
GDP structure (%):	
Agriculture:	4.47
Industry:	36.41
Construction:	6.52
Services:	52.60
GDP per capita (US$/inh):	17,097
Imports (US$ million):	3,174.73
Exports (US$ million):	4,390.59
Active population:	230,266
Activity rate (%):	50.64
Unemployment rate (%):	9.19
Tourism (visitors/year):	359,359

Major companies

Volkswagen Navarra (automotive); BSH Electrodom España (electronics
and electrical equipment); Aceralia Transformados (iron and steel); Vis-
cofán (plastics and rubbers); Delphi Unicables (automotive); Cementos
Portland (cement factory); SKF Española (automotive); Nissan Forklift
España (electronics and electrical equipment); Sanyo España (electronics
and electrical equipment)

Infrastructure supporting the economy

Airports:	Pamplona
Motorways:	A-15 Zaragoza–Pamplona–San Sebastián; N-I Pamplona–Vitoria; N-121 Soria–Pamplona–Hendaya (French border)

Capital grants

Maximum levels of non-refundable capital grants to productive investments: Up to 15 per cent of the eligible investment amount.

Basque Country

Population:	2,095,900
Population density (inh/km^2):	290
Area (km^2):	7,234
GDP (US$ million):	35,043
GDP structure (%):	
Agriculture:	1.95
Industry:	35.45
Construction:	6.15
Services:	56.45
GDP per capita (US$/inh):	2,436,080
Imports (US$ million):	7,431.52
Exports (US$ million):	10,555.40
Active population:	909,920
Activity rate (%):	51.04
Unemployment rate (%):	16.13
Tourism (visitors/year):	1,313,295

Major companies

Gamesa (aeronautics); Tubos Reunidos (iron and steel); Sidenor (iron and steel); Petróleos del Norte (petrochemicals); Bridgestone Firestone Hispania (plastics and rubbers); GKN Transmisiones España (automotive); Pepsi Cola España (food industry)

Infrastructure supporting the economy

Airports:	Bilbao, Vitoria, San Sebastián
Ports:	Bilbao, Pasajes
Motorways:	A-8 Bilbao–San Sebastián–Behobia (French border); A-68 Bilbao–Logroño–Zaragoza

Capital grants

Maximum levels of non-refundable capital grants to productive investments: Up to 25 per cent of the eligible investment amount.

La Rioja

Population:	263,512
Population density (inh/km^2):	52
Area (km^2):	5,045
GDP (US$ million):	4,337
GDP structure (%):	
Agriculture:	8.33
Industry:	30.50
Construction:	7.46
Services:	53.71
GDP per capita (US$/inh):	16,458
Imports (US$ million):	528.66
Exports (US$ million):	837.46
Active population:	121,763
Activity rate (%):	54.61
Unemployment rate (%):	8.61
Tourism (visitors/year):	300,238

Major companies

Delphi Componentes (automotive); BTR Sealing Systems Ibérica (plastics and rubbers); Bodegas Dinastia Vivanco (wine); Tobepal (paper and press); Barpimo (chemicals and pharmaceuticals); Ramodín (metallic and mineral products)

Infrastructure supporting the economy

Motorways: A-68 Bilbao–Logroño–Zaragoza

Ceuta and Melilla

Population:	132,467
Population density (inh/km^2):	4,132
Area (km^2):	32
GDP (US$ million):	1,422
GDP structure (%):	
Agriculture:	0.83
Industry:	7.61
Construction:	5.22
Services:	86.35
GDP per capita (US$/inh):	10,735
Imports (US$ million):	421.46

Exports (US$ million):   10.71
Active population: 55,073
Activity rate (%):   53.79
Unemployment rate (%):   17.38
Tourism (visitors/year):   119,599

Infrastructure supporting the economy

Airports: Melilla
Ports: Ceuta, Melilla

Sources

Population: INE
Population density (/km^2):
Area (km^2):   INE
GDP (US$ million):   BBV 98
GDP per capita (US$/inh):
Imports (US$ million):   ICEX 98
Exports (US$ million):   ICEX 98
Active population: BBV 98
Activity rate (%):   BBV 98
Unemployment rate (%):   BBV 98
Tourism (visitors/year):   INE 98

Major companies: Actualidad Económica 1999
Infrastructure supporting the economy: DGT; AENA; Puertos españoles

Appendix 2

Chambers of Commerce for Business, Industry and Shipping

What is the role of the Chambers of Commerce for business, industry and shipping in Spain?

For business, industry and shipping in Spain, the Chambers of Commerce should:

- deal with matters of general interest;

- defend those general interests and to act as a consulting body for the Administration;

- promote economic activity; and

- represent companies and take an active role in matters dedicated to the general development of company activity.

There are 85 chambers of commerce in Spain which, along with their regional offices, make up a network of 150 bodies. These chambers of commerce are regulated by a law of March 1993 and all bodies, while independent of each other, are represented at the national level by the Higher Council of Spanish Chambers of Commerce.

The Spanish Chambers of Commerce are similar to public law firms (advisers to the Administration) and are managed by businessmen in councils that are renewed every four years. The Spanish Chambers of Commerce, like the majority of European ones, differ from those in Britain as they each depend upon their regional chapters, to which they must pay an annual fee.

The pooling of resources contributed by companies to the chambers of commerce enable these bodies to fund activities in the general interest that, due to their scope, few companies could fund individually. The main objective of these corporations is to defend the general interests of all their member companies, whatever sector or trade they happen to be in, and to promote and improve their business and economic turnover.

The official Chamber of Commerce, Industry and Shipping in Barcelona is a 100-year-old institution, founded in 1886, but previously known as the Shipping Consulate or the Royal Council for Private Commerce, originating in the Middle East. The Chamber in Barcelona is a useful instrument for the benefit of the 320,000 businesses it represents and for the economic activity within its area of interest.

The role of the Chamber of Commerce in Barcelona consists of two different, but complementary, parts: to promote and improve economic and business activity in Catalonia through projects that will indirectly also benefit its member firms and to offer services of an individual nature to these firms.

The chambers of commerce also act as a consultative and advisory body for the government. Within its area of initiative, actions that are worth noting are:

- proposals for economic policy;

- proposals for reform and change of current regulations – in financial and business contexts – in order to bring regulations in line with economic reality;

- the writing of reports and opinions relating to regulations and projects developed by governmental bodies (land, localisation of industry and commerce);

- contesting and opposing regulations that prejudice the interests of the productive economy.

What is noticeable is that the Chamber of Commerce in Barcelona partakes in the financing and management of companies alongside the promotion of the business and economic fabric of Catalonia, including:

- The Barcelona Fair.

- The Consortium for Tourism in Barcelona.

- The Foundation for the Promotion of Barcelona.

- The Barcelona Foundation – Centre for Design.

- Airport Management and Promotion.

The 85 Spanish Chambers of Commerce must by law devote a large part of their annual grant to improving the international nature of companies. Over the year 2000, they will have given Ptas7000 million towards making businesses more international, of which Ptas800 million will go to Barcelona-based companies.

In 1992, the Barcelona Chamber of Commerce launched an initiative that aimed to modernise the institution in order to help businesses become more competitive. The Chamber has fought to become a pioneer in digital and electronic business, by being the first Spanish Chamber of

Commerce to set up a system that allows companies to carry out business transactions more securely.

Further information can be found at the following websites:
http//www.cambrescat.es
http//www.cscamaras.es

Appendix 3

Spanish Chambers of Commerce and Industry

General Councils for the Chambers of Commerce

Consejo Regional de Camaras de Comercio e Industria de Castilla y Leon
Plaza San Juan Bautista de la Salle 2
Entreplanta
47006 Valladolid
Spain
Tel: +34 983 37 48 59/12
Fax: +34 983 37 49 69
E-mail: crcastillaylcon@camerdata.es *or* cocicyl@cocicyl.es
Website: www.cocicyl.es
President: Manuel Vidal Gutiérrez
Director: Valentín Fernández-Soto Vélez

Consejo de Camaras Oficiales de Comercio, Industria y Navegacion de la Comunida Valenciana
Plaza de Alfonso el Magnánimo 12–1°–2ª
46003 Valencia
Spain
Tel: +34 96 353 40 72
Fax: +34 96 353 40 73
E-mail: consejocamarascv@camerdata.es
President: Arturo Virosque Ruiz
Director General: José Luis Colvée Millet

Consejo de Camaras Oficiales de Comercio, Industria y Navegacion de Cataluña
Avenida Diagonal 452–454
08006 Barcelona
Spain
Tel: +34 93 416 94 57
Fax: +34 93 416 93 01
President: Antoni Negre Villavecchia
Secretary Director General: Narcís Bosch Andreu

Spanish Commercial Bureau in the European Union
Boulevard du Regent 52
1000 Brussels
Belgium
Tel: +32 2 509 86 11
Fax: +32 2 511 19 40
Business Adviser: Rafael Coloma

Consejo Superior de Camaras de Comercio (EU Delegation)
Boulevard Genéral Wahis 15
1030 Brussels
Belgium
Tel: +32 2 705 67 50
Fax: +32 2 705 66 40
Director: Emiliano Alonso Pelegrín

Instituto Español de Comercio Exterior (Spanish External Trade Institute – ICEX)
Paseo de la Castellana 14–16
28046 Madrid
Spain
Tel: +34 913 496 100
Fax: +34 914 316 128
Website: www.icex.es

Regional Chambers of Commerce

Alava*

(Vitoria) Cámara de Comercio e Industria
C/ Eduardo Dato 38
01005 Alava
Spain
Tel: +34 945 14 1800
Fax: +34 945 14 31 56
E-mail: Cocia-jet.es
Website: www.camaradealava.com
President: Josu de Lapatza Urbiola
Secretary General: Lorenzo Bergareche Capa

Albacete

Cámara de Comercio e Industria
C/ Tesifonte Gallego 22
02002 Albacete
Spain
Tel: +34 967 59 00 93; (President) +34 967 59 01 53; (Secretary General) +34 967 59 01 52
Fax: +34 967 23 53 45
E-mail: comext.alba@camerdata.es
Website: www.camerdata.es/albacete
President: Marcos Montero Ruiz
Acting Secretary General: Esteban Villanueva Soriano

Alicante

Cámara de Comercio, Industria y Navegación
C/ San Fernando 4
03002 Alicante
Spain
Tel: +34 965 20 11 33; +34 965 20 12 34/5
Fax: +34 965 20 14 57
E-mail: cexterior@camara-alc.es
Website: www.camara-alc.es
President: Luis Esteban Marcos
Secretary General: Tomás Morató Norte

Almeria*

Cámara de Comercio, Industria y Navegación
C/ Conde Ofalia 22 – Entlo.
04001 Almeria
Spain
Tel: +34 950 23 44 33
Fax: +34 950 23 48 50
E-mail: camaralm@larural.es
President: Francisco Martínez-Cosentino Justo
Secretary General: José María Cosano Pérez

Avila*

Cámara de Comercio e Industria
C/ Eduardo Marquina 6
05001 Avila
Spain
Tel: +34 920 21 11 73
Fax: +34 920 25 51 59
Website: www.camerdata.es/avila
E-mail: ca0500@camerdata.es/avila
President: José Angel Dominguez González
Secretary General: Francisco Isaac Pérez de Pablo

Aviles

Cámara de Comercio, Industria y Navegación
Plaza de Camposagrado 1
33400 Asturias
Spain
Tel: +34 985 54 41 11; +34 985 54 43 33
Fax: +34 985 54 15 28
E-mail: ccinaviles@camerdata.es
Website: www.camerdata.es/aviles
President: Antonio Sabino y García-González
Secretary General: Carlos Rodríguez de la Torre Rodríguez

Airport office:
Tel: +34 985 51 05 51
Fax: +34 985 51 05 51
E-mail: cocinas@ctv.es

Badajoz

Cámara de Comercio e Industria
Avenida Europa 4
06004 Badajoz
Spain
Tel: +34 924 23 46 00
Fax: +34 924 24 38 53
E-mail: ccibadajoz@camerdata.es
Website: www.camerdata.es/badajoz
President: Juan José Hernández Ramírez
Secretary General: Angel María Sánchez Pocostales

Barcelona

Cámara de Comercio, Industria y Navegación
President: Antoni Negre Villavecchia
Managing Director: Carles Castells i Oliveres
Secretary General: Luis Solá Vilardell

Corporate headquarters:
Casa Lonja del Mar
Pº de Isabel II 1
08003 Barcelona
Spain
Tel: +34 93 319 24 12/16/54

Offices and services:
Avenida Diagonal 452–454
08006 Barcelona
Spain
Tel: +34 93 416 93 00; (airport office) +34 93 478 67 99
Fax: +34 93 416 93 01
E-mail: msancerni@mail.cambrabcn.es
Website: www.cambrabcn.es

Bilbao*

Cámara de Comercio, Industria y Navegación
C/ Alameda Recalde 50
48008 Bilbao
Spain
Tel: +34 94 470 65 00; (President/ Secretary) +34 94 470 65 10
Fax: +34 94 443 61 71; (President) + 34 94 443 32 95
E-mail: infor@camaracombilbao.es
President: Ignacio Mª Echeberría Monteberría
Managing Director: Juan Luis Laskurain Argarate
Acting Secretary General: Juan Carlos Landeta Basterrechea

Burgos*

Cámara de Comercio e Industria
C/ San Carlos 1–1º
09003 Burgos
Spain
Tel: +34 947 20 18 44; + 34 947 20 89 60; +34 947 26 30 70
Fax: +34 947 26 36 26
E-mail: cexterior.cocibu@camerdata.es
President: Antonio Miguel Méndez Pozo
Secretary General: José Luis Miguel de la Villa

Caceres

Cámara de Comercio e Industria
Plaza del Doctor Durán 2
10003 Caceres
Spain
Tel: +34 927 62 71 08
Fax: +34 927 62 71 09
E-mail: ccicaceres@camerdata.es
Website: www.camerdata.es/caceres
President: José Manuel González Calzada
Secretary General: Teófilo Amores Mendoza

Cadiz*

Cámara de Comercio, Industria y Navegación
C/ Antonio López 4
11004 Cadiz
Spain
Tel: +34 956 22 30 50/54; +34 956 21 14 58
Fax: +34 956 25 07 10
E-mail: sgcadiz@camerdata.es
President: Angel Juan Pascual
Secretary General: Adolfo González-Santiago Cabadas

Cantabria*

Cámara de Comercio, Industria y Navegación
Plaza de Velarde 5
39001 Santander
Spain
Tel: +34 942 31 80 00
Fax: +34 942 31 43 10
E-mail: ccincantabria@camaracant.es
Website: www.camaracant.es
President: Modesto Piñeiro García-Lago
Secretary General: Agustín Gutiérrez-Cortines y Lanuza

Castellon

Cámara de Comercio, Industria y Navegación
Avenida Hermanos Bou 79
12003 Castellon de la Plana
Spain
Tel: +34 964 35 65 00
Fax: +34 964 35 65 10
E-mail: mjarenos@camaracs.es
Website: www.camaracs.es
President: Salvador Martí Huguet
Acting Secretary General: Vicente Casañ

Ceuta

Cámara de Comercio, Industria y Navegación
C/ Muelle Cañonero Dato s/n
51001 Ceuta
Spain
Tel: +34 956 50 95 90
Fax: +34 956 50 95 89
E-mail: cocinceuta@camerdata.es
President: Luis Moreno Naranjo
Acting Secretary General: María del Rosario Espinosa Suárez

Ciudad Real

Cámara de Comercio e Industria
C/ Lanza 2
13004 Ciudad Real
Spain
Tel: +34 926 22 12 20; +34 926 22 11 49; +34 926 22 25 31; +34 926
22 21 10
Fax: +34 926 25 38 13
Website: www.camerdata.es/ccicreal
President: Juan Antonio León Triviño
Secretary General: José Cano Martínez

*Cordoba**

Cámara de Comercio e Industria
C/ Pérez de Castro
14003 Cordoba
Spain
Tel: +34 957 29 61 99; +34 957 29 63 99; +34 957 29 65 99
Fax: +34 957 20 21 06
E-mail: comext@alcavia.net
President: José Adame Fernández
Secretary General: José Enrique Fdez. de Castillejo y Cerezo

Corunna

Cámara de Comercio, Industria y Navegación
C/ Alameda 30–32–1º
15003 Corunna
Spain
Tel: (general information) +34 981 21 60 72; (headquarters) +34 981 21 60 73; (foreign trade)+34 981 21 60 74; (Presidency and Secretary General) +34 981 21 60 75
Fax: +34 981 22 52 08
E-mail: ccincoruna@camerdata.es
Website: www.camerdata.es/coruna/
President: José Antonio Quiroga y Piñeyro
Secretary General: Gonzalo Ortíz Amor

Cuenca*

Cámara de Comercio e Industria
C/ Calderón de la Barca 30
16001 Cuenca
Spain
Tel: +34 969 22 23 51; (President) +34 969 22 22 30
Fax: +34 969 22 89 23
E-mail: cicuenca@camerdata.es
Website: www.camerdata.es/cuenca
President: Eduardo Fernández Palomo
Acting Secretary General: Carlos Martínez García

Gijon*

Cámara de Comercio, Industria y Navegación
C/ Dr Fleming s/n
33203 Gijon
Spain
Tel: +34 985 18 01 80
Fax: +34 985 18 01 06
E-mail: ccingijon@camerdata.es
Website: www.camerdata.es/gijon
President: Guillermo Quirós Pintado
Secretary General: Pedro García-Rendueles Aguado

Girona

Cámara de Comercio, Industria y Navegación
C/ Gran Vía Jaume I 46
17001 Girona
Spain
Tel: +34 972 41 85 00; (President) +34 972 41 85 31
Fax: +34 972 41 85 01
E-mail: npuigvert@cambrescat.es
Website: www.cambra.gi
President: Antonio Hostench i Figueras
Managing Director: Joaquín Abadal Montal
Secretary General: Santiago Coquar Oriol

*Granada**

Cámara de Comercio, Industria y Navegación
C/ Paz 18
18002 Granada
Spain
Tel: +34 958 53 61 52
Fax: +34 958 53 62 92; (President and Secretary) +34 958 53 62 80; (Director) +34 958 53 62 79
E-mail: cexccigranada@camerdata.es
Website: www.camerdata.es/granada/
President: Antonio Robles Lizancos
Director: Jaime Parra Parra
Secretary General: Fernando Mir Gómez

Guadalajara

Cámara de Comercio e Industria
C/ Mayor 28
19001 Guadalajara
Spain
Tel: +34 949 24 70 32
Fax: +34 949 24 72 45
E-mail: cciguadalajara@camerdata.es
President: Ramón Silgo Martínez
Secretary General: Luis Fernando González Gálvez

Guipuzcoa*

Cámara de Comercio, Industria y Navegación
C/ Ramón María Lili 6
20002 San Sebastián
Spain
Tel: +34 943 27 21 00
Fax: +34 943 29 31 05
E-mail: jzabaleta@camaraguipuzkoa.com
Website: www.camaragipuzkoa.com
President: Fermín Mendizabal Oyarzabal
Managing Director: Félix Iraola Escrihuela

Huelva

Cámara de Comercio, Industria y Navegación
C/ Sor Angela de la Cruz 1
21003 Huelva
Spain
Tel: +34 959 24 59 00/43; +34 959 26 19 49
Fax: +34 959 24 56 99
President: Antonio Ponce Fernández
Acting Secretary General: Arsenio Martínez Barea

Huesca*

Cámara de Comercio e Industria
C/ Santo Angel de la Guarda 7
22005 Huesca
Spain
Tel: +34 974 24 46 31/99
Fax: +34 974 22 96 44
E-mail: ccihuesca@camerdata.es
President: Antonio Ruspira Morraja
Acting Secretary: Aurelio Biarge López

Jaen

Cámara de Comercio e Industria
C/ Hurtado 29
23001 Jaen
Spain
Tel: +34 953 24 17 29; +34 953 24 79 50; +34 953 24 01 32
Fax: +34 953 24 07 38
E-mail: ccijaen@camerdata.es
Website: www.camerdata.es/jaen
President: Francisco Espinosa García-Olalla
Director: Manuel Luis Fernández Ruiz
Secretary General: Juan Francisco Montiel Bueno

La Rioja

Cámara de Comercio e Industria
C/ Portales 12
26001 Logroño
Spain
Tel: +34 941 24 85 00
Fax: +34 941 23 99 65
E-mail: sfernandez@camararioja.com
President: Miguel Angel Martínez Berriobeña
Director General: Rafael Citoler Tormo
Secretary General: Luis Maraver Alonso

Las Palmas

Cámara de Comercio, Industria y Navegación
C/ León y Castillo 24
35003 Las Palmas
Spain
Tel: +34 928 37 10 00
Fax: +34 928 36 23 50
E-mail: mariscal@camaralp.es
Website: www.camaralp.es
President: Angel Ferrera Martínez
Director General: Luis Padrón López
Secretary General: José Juan Melián Pérez

Leon*

Cámara de Comercio e Industria
C/ Fajeros 1
24002 Leon
Spain
Tel: +34 987 22 44 00/04
Fax: +34 987 22 24 51
E-mail: cextleon@camerdata.es
Website: www.camerdata.es/leon/
President: Angel Panero Florez
Secretary General: Antonio Miguel Díaz Carro

Lugo*

Cámara de Comercio, Industria y Navegación
C/ Avenida de Ramón Ferreiro 18
27002 Lugo
Spain
Tel: +34 982 28 43 00; (President) +34 982 28 48 77
Fax: 34 982 24 43 01; (President) +34 982 28 48 81
E-mail: comexlugo@camerdata.es
Website: www.camerdata.es/lugo
President: Alfredo H. Mosteirín Castañer
Director General: Alberto Fernández Piñeiro
Secretary General: Vicente Silva Meilán

Lleida

Cámara de Comercio e Industria
C/ Anselmo Clavé 2
25007 Lleida
Spain
Tel: +34 973 23 61 61
Fax: +34 973 24 74 67
E-mail: jpanades@cambrescat.es
President: Joan Simó i Burgués
Secretary General: Salvador Roig Bonet

Madrid*

Cámara de Comercio e Industria
President: Juan Luis Mato Rodríguez
Managing Director: Roberto Molero Gómez-Elegido
Secretary General: Alberto Durán Ruiz de Huidobro

Corporative headquarters:
C/ Huertas 13
28012 Madrid
Spain
Tel: +34 91 538 35 00
Fax: +34 91 538 36 77
E-mail: dcel@camaramadriDes
Website: www.camaramadriDes

Offices and services:
Plaza Independencia 1
28001 Madrid
Spain
Tel: +34 91 538 35 00
Fax: +34 91 538 37 18

(airport branch):
Tel: +34 91 305 88 07/08

Malaga*

Cámara de Comercio, Industria y Navegación
C/ Cortina del Muelle 23
Palacio de Villalcazar
29015 Malaga
Spain
Tel: +34 952 21 16 73; +34 952 21 37 85/86
Fax: +34 952 22 98 94
E-mail: ccinmalaga@camerdata.es
President: José Joaquín Erroz-Lecumberri
Secretary General: Agustín Palacios Luque

Majorca, Ibiza and Formentera*

Cámara de Comercio, Industria y Navegación
C/ Estudio General 7
07001 Palma de Mallorca
Majorca
Balearic Islands
Tel: +34 971 72 78 51; +34 971 71 01 88
Fax: +34 971 72 63 02
E-mail: cextmallorca@camerdata.es
President: Miguel Lladó Oliver
Secretary General: Antonio Grimalt Llofriu

Ibiza and Formentera:
C/ Historiador J Clapés 4
07800 Ibiza
Balearic Islands
Tel: +34 971 30 14 92
Fax: +34 971 30 71 10

Melilla*

Cámara de Comercio, Industria y Navegación
C/ Miguel de Cervantes 7
52001 Melilla
Spain
Tel: +34 952 68 48 40; +34 952 68 55 21
Fax: +34 952 68 31 19
E-mail: ccinmelilla@camerdata.es
President: Margarita López Almendariz
Secretary General: Jesús Fernández de Castro y Pedraja

Minorca*

Cámara de Comercio, Industria y Navegación
C/ Miguel Verí 3-A
07703
Mahón
Minorca
Balearic Islands
Tel: +34 971 36 31 94
Fax: +34 971 36 84 16
E-mail: camaracomercio@menorca.infotelecom.es
President: Hipólito Mercadal Pascual
Secretary General: Pedro Monjó Cerdá

Murcia*

Cámara de Comercio, Industria y Navegación
Plaza de San Bartolomé 1
30004 Murcia
Spain
Tel: (switchboard) +34 968 22 94 00; (President) +34 968 22 94 06;
+34 968 22 94 04; (Secretary) +34 968 22 94 05; (Vice Secretary) +34
968 22 94 04
Fax: +34 968 22 94 24; +34 968 22 94 25
E-mail: fmartinez@cocin-murcia.es
Website: www.cocin-murcia.es
President: Pedro García-Balibrea Martínez
Acting Secretary General: Enrique Torres Tortosa

Navarra

Cámara de Comercio e Industria
C/ Yanguas y Miranda 27
31003 Pamplona
Spain
Tel: +34 948 29 02 01; (President) +34 948 29 01 20; (Secretary) +34
948 29 06 56
Fax: +34 948 24 28 94; +34 948 23 19 75
E-mail: marian@camerdata.es
Website: www.camerdata.es/navarra/
President: Fco Javier Taberna Jiménez
Director General: Marta Vera Janín
Secretary General: Ignacio Galañena Sainz

Ourense

Cámara de Comercio e Industria
Avenida de la Habana 30 bis
32003 Ourense
Spain
Tel: +34 988 23 21 14; +34 988 23 31 16
Fax: +34 988 23 30 88
E-mail: adocampo@camerdata.es
Website: www.camerdata.es/ourense
President: Jorge Bermello Fernández
Acting Secretary General: Elisa Rodríguez Dacosta

Oviedo*

Cámara de Comercio, Industria y Navegación
C/ Quintana 32
33009 Oviedo
Spain
Tel: +34 985 20 75 75
Fax: +34 985 20 72 00
E-mail: ccioviedo@camerdata.es
Website: www.camerdata.es/oviedo
President: Jesús Serafín Pérez Díaz
Secretary General: Jesús Torres García

Palencia

Cámara de Comercio e Industria
Plaza Pío XII 7
34002 Palencia
Spain
Tel: +34 979 72 95 98; +34 979 71 00 35; +34 979 72 75 94
Fax: +34 979 73 09 70
Website: www.cocipa.es
President: Vicente Villagrá Blanco
Secretary General: Juan Carlos Garrán García

Pontevedra*

Cámara de Comercio, Industria y Navegación
C/ Jardines Vicenti 4–2°
36001 Pontevedra
Spain
Tel: +34 986 85 14 88; +34 986 86 63 03
Fax: +34 986 86 26 43
E-mail: tribadulla@camerdata.es
President: Manuel Durán Couto
Secretary General: María del Rosario Lorenzo Pontevedra

Salamanca*

Cámara de Comercio e Industria
Plaza de Sexmeros 2
37001 Salamanca
Spain
Tel: +34 923 21 17 97
Fax: +34 923 28 01 46
E-mail: rosam@mmteam.interbook.net
President: Fernando Prado Juan
Secretary General: Gabriel Hortal Castaño

Santa Cruz de Tenerife*

Cámara de Comercio, Industria y Navegación
Plaza de la Candelaria 6
38003 Santa Cruz de Tenerife
Tenerife
Canary Islands
Tel: +34 922 24 53 84/85; (Secretary) +34 922 24 11 76
Fax: +34 922 24 24 28
E-mail: ccintenerife@camerdata.es
Website: www.camerdata.es/tenerife/
President: Ignacio González Martín
Director General: Ramón Gil-Roldán Sansón
Secretary General: Rafael Espejo Castro

Segovia*

Cámara de Comercio e Industria
C/ Fernán García 1–1§
40001 Segovia
Spain
Tel: +34 921 43 23 00/11
Fax: +34 921 43 05 63
E-mail: raznar@camerdata.es
President: Jesús Postigo Quintana
Director General: Carlos Figuero Espadas
Acting Secretary General: Rafael Aznar Mendiola

Seville*

Cámara de Comercio, Industria y Navegación
Plaza de la Contratación 8
41004 Seville
Spain
Tel: +34 954 21 10 05; +34 954 21 10 04/6
Fax: +34 954 22 56 19
E-mail: nturrion@camerdata.es
Website: www.camerdata.es/sevilla
President: Ramón Contreras Ramos
Secretary General: Francisca García García

Soria*

Cámara de Comercio e Industria
C/ Venerable Carabantes 1C–1°
42003 Soria
Spain
Tel: +34 975 21 39 44/45
Fax: +34 975 22 86 19
E-mail: ccisoria@maptel.es
President: Julio Santamaría Calvo
Secretary General: Luis Martínez Escolar

Tarragona*

Cámara de Comercio, Industria y Navegación
Avenida Pau Casals 17
43003 Tarragona
Spain
Tel: +34 977 21 96 76; (President) +34 977 21 96 77; (Secretary) +34
977 21 89 77
Fax: +34 977 24 09 00
E-mail: rbarros@cambrescat.es
Website: www.cambrescat.es
President: Jaume Carrera Güerri
Secretary General: José Ramón Gispert Magarolas

Teruel*

Cámara de Comercio e Industria
President: Florencio Muñoz Rodríguez
Secretary General: Santiago Ligros Mancho

C/ Amantes 17
44001 Teruel
Spain
Tel: +34 978 61 81 91
Fax: +34 978 61 81 92

Plaza Dean 2
44600 Alcañiz
Spain
Tel: +34 978 83 46 00
Fax: +34 978 83 16 56
E-mail: cserrano@camarateruel.com
Website: www.camarateruel.com

Toledo*

Cámara de Comercio e Industria
Plaza de San Vicente 3
45001 Toledo
Spain
Tel: +34 925 28 01 11
Fax: +34 925 28 00 04
Tel Euroventanilla: +34 925 28 01 12
Fax Euroventanilla: +34 925 28 00 07
E-mail: cctolcex@ctv.es
President: Pedro Jesús Santolaya Heredero
Director General: Joaquín Echevarría Cuesta

Valencia

Cámara de Comercio, Industria y Navegación
C/ Poeta Querol 15
46002 Valencia
Spain
Tel: +34 96 351 13 01; (President) +34 96 352 98 07; (Secretary) +34 96 351 60 17
Fax: +34 96 351 63 49; +34 96 351 35 58
E-mail: vriera@camerav.es
Website: www.camerdata.es/valencia/
President: Arturo Virosque Ruiz
Secretary General: Antonio Rico Gil

Valladolid

Cámara de Comercio e Industria
Avenida Ramón Pradera s/n
47009 Valladolid
Spain
Tel: +34 983 37 04 00
Fax: +34 983 37 06 60
E-mail: exterior@cociva.es
Website: www.cociva.es
President: Vicente Garrido Capa
Director General: Arturo Rodríguez-Monsalve
Secretary General: Federico Sanz Rubiales

Zamora*

Cámara de Comercio e Industria
C/ Pelayo 6
49014 Zamora
Spain
Tel: +34 980 53 00 50; +34 980 53 31 82
Fax: +34 980 51 85 94
E-mail: ccizamora-ext@retemail.es
President: Manuel Vidal Gutiérrez
Secretary General: Francisco J Díaz Rincón

Zaragoza

Cámara de Comercio e Industria
C/ Isabel Católica nº 2 (antigua Feria de Muestras)
50009 Zaragoza
Spain
Tel: +34 976 30 61 61; (Presidency and Secretary) +34 976 30 61 64
Fax: +34 976 35 79 45; (President) +34 976 35 98 52
E-mail: exterior@camarazaragoza.com
Website: www.camarazaragoza.com
President: Javier Rico Gambarte
Secretary General: Luis Fernández Ordoñez

Foreign Chambers of Commerce and Commercial Offices in Spain

Argentina

Argentine Chamber of Commerce
Caracas 10–2º izda
28010 Madrid
Spain
Tel: +34 91 308 59 36; +34 91 319 09 36
Fax: +34 91 308 59 54
E-mail: uei0595903110@eurociber.es
President: Silvio Starosta
Executive Secretary: Jorge Alberto Laspiur Nölting

Austria

Austria Commercial Office
Orense 11–6º B
Edificio Centro
28020 Madrid
Spain
Tel: +34 91 556 43 58; +34 91 556 43 62
Fax: +34 91 556 99 91
E-mail: ahstmad@mail.ddnet.es
Website: www.embajada-de-austria.es/oficina-comercial
Business Adviser: Walter M Resl
Commercial Attaché: Hedwig Brandl

Belgium and Luxembourg

Belgium & Luxembourg Chamber of Commerce
Claudio Coello 99–1° dcha
28006 Madrid
Spain
Tel: +34 91 435 48 99
Fax: +34 91 578 05 27
E-mail: ccble@retemail.es
President: Luis Fernando López-Chicheri
Director: Angeles Osorio Iturmendi

Brazil

Brazil Chamber of Commerce
Jacometrezo 4–3ª – 3
28013 Madrid
Spain
Tel: +34 91 522 48 44
Fax: +34 91 522 48 44
President: Felipe Carballo
Secretary General: Lea del Para Netto

Canada

Canadian Economic & Commercial Service
Núñez de Balboa 35 (Edificio Goya)
28080 Madrid
Spain
Tel: +34 91 423 32 50
Fax: +34 91 423 32 52
E-mail: mdrid@dfait-maeci.gc.ca
Website: www.canada-es.org or www.canada.gc.ca
Business Adviser: Louis Poisson

Chile

Chile Chamber of Commerce
Diputación 256–4º – 1ª
08007 Barcelona
Spain
Tel: +34 93 481 32 90
Fax: +34 93 317 32 06
E-mail: camchile-esp@teclata.es
President: Angel de la Rubia Pérez
Director General: Jaime Balic

Denmark

Danish–Spanish Commercial Association
Claudio Coello 91 – 4º
28006 Madrid
Spain
Tel: +34 91 575 37 86
Fax: +34 91 431 91 68
President: Tomás A Barrera
Secretary: Birte Brenner

European Commission

European Commission (Representation in Spain)
Castellana 46
28046 Madrid
Spain
Tel: +34 91 423 80 30/3
Fax: +34 91 576 03 87
Director: Miguel Moltó Calvo

France

France–Spain Chamber of Commerce and Industry
Ruíz de Alarcón 7
28014 Madrid
Spain
Tel: +34 91 522 67 42
Fax: +34 91 523 36 42
E-mail: chambre@teleline.es
President: M Etienne Obert de Thieusies
Director: Bertrand Barthélemy

French Chamber of Commerce and Industry
Passeig de Gracia 2 – 3°
08007 Barcelona
Spain
Tel: +34 93 270 24 50
Fax: +34 93 270 24 51
E-mail: ccfbcn@ccfbcn.es
President: Michel Arpa
Director General: Philippe Saman

French Commercial and Economic Service
Marques de la Ensenada 10
28004 Madrid
Spain
Tel: +34 91 700 78 50
Fax: +34 91 700 78 51
E-mail: frescomcesatel.es
Website: www.dree.org/
Advisory Minister for Economic Affairs: M Bruno Le Gal
Business Adviser: Mme Arlette Chadebec

Germany

German Chamber of Commerce
Avenida Pío XII 26–28
28016 Madrid
Spain
Tel: +34 91 353 09 10
Fax: +34 91 359 12 13
E-mail: ahk_spanien@compuserve.com
President: Manuel García Garido
Secretary General: Peter Moser

Greece

Greek Commercial Office
Avenida Dr Arce 24
28002 Madrid
Spain
Tel: +34 91 564 45 92
Fax: +34 91 563 02 83
Adviser for Economic and Commercial Affairs: Georgios E Dudumis

Indonesia

Indonesia Commercial Office
Agastia 65
28043 Madrid
Spain
Tel: +34 91 413 02 94; +34 91 413 05 94
Fax: +34 91 519 49 50
E-mail: atperdag@lander.es
Commercial Attaché: Adriano Adlir

Ireland

Ireland Commercial Office
Paseo de la Castellana 46–3º
28046 Madrid
Spain
Tel: +34 91 436 40 86
Fax: +34 91 435 66 03
Website: www.irish-trade.ie
Director: J Fintan Keogh

Israel

Israel Commercial Office
Velázquez 150–7ª
28002 Madrid
Spain
Tel: +34 91 411 13 57
Fax: +34 91 564 00 02
E-mail: comercial@embajada-israel.es
Advisory Economics Minister: Rachel Roei

Italy

Italy Commercial Office
Lagasca 98
28006 Madrid
Spain
Tel: +34 91 423 33 00
Fax: +34 91 577 67 69
E-mail: ambcommsp@cempresarial.com
Business Adviser: Marco Rocca

Italian Chamber of Commerce
Cristobal Bordiú 54
28003 Madrid
Spain
Tel: +34 91 534 25 09; +34 91 534 49 84
Fax: +34 91 534 50 89
E-mail: ccis@adv.es or italcamera@adv.es
President: Luigi Michetti

Japan

Japan Commercial Office
Serrano 109
28006 Madrid
Spain
Tel: +34 91 590 76 00; +34 91 590 76 21
Fax: +34 91 590 13 21
E-mail: Kenichi.hosoda@mota.go.Jp
Commercial Attaché: Kenichi Hosoda

Japan External Trade Organisation (JETRO)
Plaza de Colón 2
Torre de Colón Torre 1
28046 Madrid
Spain
Tel: +34 91 391 21 00
Fax: +34 91 310 36 59
Director General: Kunimichi Hashida

Korea

Korea Chamber of Commerce
Pº de la Castellana 95 – 10º
Torre Europa
28046 Madrid
Spain
Tel: +34 91 556 62 41
Fax: +34 91 556 68 68
E-mail: madridktc@maDservicom.es
Website: www.kotra_spain.com
Director General: Hyung-Soo Kim

Mexico

Mexican Chamber of Commerce, Trade and Tourism
Iriarte 3
28028 Madrid
Spain
Tel: +34 91 726 00 99
Fax: +34 91 361 06 30
E-mail: jgutierrezar@hexo.es
President: Lic. Víctor Manuel Torrones López
Executive Vice-President: José Gutiérrez Navas

Netherlands

Dutch Commercial Department
Avenida Comandante Franco 32
28016 Madrid
Spain
Tel: +34 91 359 09 14
Fax: +34 91 359 21 50
E-mail: nlgovmad@ctv.es
Website: www.Embajadapaisesbajos.es
Adviser for Economic and Commercial Affairs: Aart Jacobi

New Zealand

New Zealand Trade Development Board
Plaza de la Lealtad 2–3°
28014 Madrid
Spain
Tel: +34 91 531 09 97; +34 91 531 51 82
Fax: +34 91 523 01 71
E-mail: elena.ortuno@tradenz.govt.nz
Website: www.tradenz.govt.nz
Commercial Director: Elena Ortuño

Norway

Norway–Spain Chamber of Commerce
Fray Luis de León 11
28012 Madrid
Spain
Tel: +34 91 528 90 65
Fax: +34 91 467 15 59
President: Jan Skybak
Director: Oyvind Fossan

Portugal

Portugal–Spain Chamber of Commerce
President: Antonio Garrigues y Díaz-Cañabate
Zurbano 67–5° B
28010 Madrid
Spain
Tel: +34 91 442 23 00
Fax: +34 91 442 22 90

Taiwan

Taiwan Trade Center SA
Paseo de la Castellana 56–1§ dcha.
28046 Madrid
Spain
Tel: +34 91 563 94 44
Fax: +34 91 563 93 24
E-mail: ttc@maDservicom.es
Website: www.cetra.org.tw.
Director: Arturo Wang

United Kingdom

United Kingdom Commercial Department
Fernando el Santo 16
28010 Madrid
Spain
Tel: +34 91 700 82 00
Fax: +34 91 700 83 11
E-mail: commercial@embrit.es
Business Adviser: Michael Connor

United States of America

American Chamber of Commerce
Tuset 8 Entlo 3ª
08006 Barcelona
Spain
Tel: +34 93 415 99 63
Fax: +34 93 415 11 98
E-mail: 101643.715
President: James A Baker
Executive Director: José A Manrique

USA Commercial Service
Serrano 75
28006 Madrid
Spain
Tel: +34 91 564 89 76
Fax: +34 91 563 08 59
Website: www.embusa.es
Business Adviser: Rafael Fermoselle
Commercial Attaché: Stephen Morrison

Venezuela

Venezuela Chamber of Commerce
Condado de Treviño 2
Portal 2
28033 Madrid
Spain
Tel: +34 91 302 70 31
Fax: +34 91 766 15 69
E-mail: venezuela@cideiber.com
Website: www.cideiber.com/infopaises/
President: Ignacio Fierro Viña
Executive Vice-President: José Lorenzo García Martín

(*) New President

Appendix 4

Useful Addresses

The following institutions provide location consulting services for foreign companies with overseas investment projects, as well as for companies already operating in Spain and planning new investments or expansion projects. While the Investment Promotion Bureau (SEPI) acts with a national scope as a 'one-stop shop' to foreign investors, other entities provide a regional scope.

Investment Promotion Bureau (SEPI)
Velázquez 134
28006 Madrid
Spain
Tel: +34 913 961084
Fax: +34 913 961226
E-mail: jberbel@sepi.es
Website: www.sepi.es
Contact: Juan José Berbel; Jordi Giro

Instituto Gallego de Promoción Económica (IGAPE)
C/Fray Rosendo Salvado 16 – Bajo
15701 Santiago de Compostela
Spain
Tel: +34 981 541127
Fax: +34 981 541114/590467
E-mail: promocion@igape.es
Website: www.igape.es

Instituto de Fomento Regional (IFR)
Parque Tecnológico de Asturias
33420 Llanera
Spain
Tel: +34 98 5980020
Fax: +34 98 5264455
E-mail: promocion@ifrasturias.com
Website: www.ifrasturias.com

Sociedad Para el Desarrollo Regional de Cantabria (SODERCAN SA)
Avenida de los Infantes 32
39005 Santander
Spain
Tel: +34 942 290003
Fax: +34 942 273240
E-mail: informacion@sodercan.cantabria.org
Website: www.sodercan.cantabria.org

Sociedad de Promoción y Reconversión Industrial (SPRI) Basque Country
Gran Vía 35 3º
48009 Bilbao
Spain
Tel: +34 94 479 7000
Fax: +34 94 479 7023
E-mail: info@spri.es
Website: www.spri.es

Sociedad de Desarrollo de Navarra (SODENA)
Avenida Carlos III nº 36–1º–Dcha
31003 Pamplona
Spain
Tel: +34 948 421942
Fax: +34 948 421943
E-mail: info@sodena.com
Website: www.sodena.com

Agencia de Desarrollo Económico de la Rioja (ADER)
C/Muro Francisco de la Mata 13–14
26071 Logroño
Spain
Tel: +34 941 291500
Fax: +34 941 291544
E-mail: ader@ader.es
Website: www.ader.es

Agencia de Desarrollo Económico (ADE)
C/Duque de Victoria 23
47001 Valladolid
Spain
Tel: +34 983 361235/411857
Fax: +34 983 361244
E-mail: Carlos.Martin@dire.ade.cict.jcyl.es
Website: www.jcyl.es/jcyl/cict/ade

Instituto Aragonés de Fomento (IAF)
C/Teniente Coronel Valenzuela 3
50004 Zaragoza
Spain
Tel: +34 976 702100
Fax: +34 976 702103
E-mail: jmartinez@iaf.es
Website: www.iaf.es

Catalonia Office of Foreign Investment (CIDEM)
C/Provença 339 – 5ª Planta
08037 Barcelona
Spain
Tel: +34 93 4767284
Fax: +34 93 4767303
E-mail: mfarres@cidem.gencat.es
Website: www.catalonia.com

Instituto Madrileño de Desarrollo (IMADE)
C/ Gran Vía 42
28013 Madrid
Spain
Tel: +34 1 5802777/5801560
Fax: +34 1 5801972
E-mail: imade.inversiones@comadrid.es

Sociedad de Fomento Industrial de Extremadura (SOFIEX)
C/Moreno de Vargas nº 2
06800 Merida
Spain
Tel: +34 924 319159
Fax: +34 924 319212
E-mail: Fomento@bme.es
Website: www.bme.es/fomento

Consejeria de Industria y Trabajo (Castilla-la-Mancha)
Rio Estenilla s/n Polígono Industrial Santa María Benquerencia
45071 Toledo
Spain
Tel: +34 925 267802
Fax: +34 925 267845
E-mail: pcaballero@jccm.es
Website: www.jccm.es

The Valencian Institute of Export (IVEX)
Plaza de América 2
46004 Valencia
Spain
Tel: +34 96 3952001
Fax: +34 96 3954274
E-mail: fax@ivex.es
Website: www.ivex.es

Instituto Balear de Desarrollo Industrial (IDI)
C/General Ricard Ortega 4
07006 Palma de Mallorca
Majorca
Balearic Islands
Tel: +34 971 774031
Fax: +34 971 465601
E-mail: info@idi.es
Website: www.idi.es

Instituto de Fomento de la Región de Murcia (INFO)
Avenida de la Fama 3
30003 Murcia
Spain
Tel: +34 968 366180/362800
Fax: +34 968 362835
E-mail: inv.murcia@info.carm.es
Website: www.murcia-inversiones.com

Instituto de Fomento de Andalucia (IFA)
C/Torneo 26
41002 Seville
Spain
Tel: +34 95 5030 712/721/700
Fax: +34 95 5030 775/780
E-mail: pexterior@ifa.es
Website: www.ifa.es links.htmlinks.htm

Sociedad Canaria de Fomento Económico, SA (SOFESA)
E-mail: promoción@sofesa.csz.rcanaria.es
Website: www.csz.rcanaria.es/

Tenerife office:
Imeldo Serís 57 6ª Planta
38003 Santa Cruz de Tenerife
Tenerife
Canary Islands
Tel: +34 922 248 245
Fax: +34 922 248 630

Gran Canaria office:
Nicolás Estévanes 30 2ª Planta
35008 Las Palmas
Gran Canaria
Canary Islands
Tel: +34 928 221 554
Fax: +34 928 221 453

A public and private network of institutions is devoted to providing assistance to different economic activities carried out by companies in Spain, from trademarks and patents register to R&D, technology transfer, innovation programmes assistance, international trade fairs and congresses organisation, or training and employment support. In parallel with these institutions, private initiatives are focused mainly in extremely active venture capital firms as well as a vast network of financial institutions and professional services devoted to business development. These are predominantly in growing sectors such as telecommunications and IT, advanced technologies, environment or international shared-services.

Oficina Española de Patentes y Marcas (Spanish Office of Patents and Trademarks)
C/Panamá 1
28071 Madrid
Spain
Tel: +34 913 495331/495335
Fax: +34 913 495379; +34 914 572586
E-mail: secretaria@oepm.es *or* difusion@oepm.es
Website: www.oepm.es

Centre for the Development of Industrial Technology (CDTI)
Paseo de la Castellana 141
28046 Madrid
Spain
Tel: +34 915 815500
Fax: +34 915 815594/84/76
E-mail: Info@cdtl.es
Website: www.cdti.es

Feria de Madrid (Madrid International Fair)
Tel: +34 917 225180
Fax: +34 917 225801
E-mail: infoifema@ifema.es
Website: www.ifema.es

Feria de Valencia (Valencia International Fair)
Avenida De las Ferias s/n
46035 Valencia
Spain
Tel: +34 963 861100
Fax: +34 963 636111/644064
Website: www.feriavalencia.com

Feria de Barcelona (Barcelona International Fair)
Avenida Reina Mª Cristina s/n
08004 Barcelona
Spain
Tel: +34 932 332222
Fax: +34 932 332198
Website: www.firabcn.es

Feria de Bilbao (Bilbao International Fair)
D Alberto Insula
Ayala 128–6°
28006 Madrid
Spain
Tel: +34 91 576 8401
Fax: +34 91 576 7162
Website: www.feriaint-bilbao.es

Feria de Gijon (Gijon International Fair)
Parque Isabel La Católica s/n
33202 Gijón
Spain
Tel: +34 985 180 100/105/112
Fax: +34 985 337 711
E-mail: fid@adv.es
Website: www.fidma.com

Feria de Zaragoza (Zaragoza International Fair)
Carretera Nacional II Km 311
50012 Zaragoza
Spain
Tel: +34 976 764700
Fax: +34 976 330649
Website: www.feriazaragoza.com

Ministerio de Ciencia y Tecnología (Science and Technology Ministry)
Paseo de la Castellana 160
28071 Madrid
Spain
Tel: +34 913 494 976/4961/4999/4974
Fax: +34 914 578 066
Website: www.mcyt.es

Ministerio de Economia (Economy Ministry)
Alcalá, 9
28071 Madrid
Spain
Tel: +34 915 958 000
Fax: +34 915 958 841
Website: www.mineco.es

Ministerio de Hacienda (Treasure Ministry)
Alcalá, 9
28071 Madrid
Spain
Tel: +34 915 958 000
Fax: +34 915 958 837
Website: www.minhac.es

INEM (National Employment Institute)
C/Espartinas 10
28001 Madrid
Spain
Tel: +34 91 520 6000
Website: www.inem.es
Contact: Ildefonso Hernández Sanz, Director

Spanish Employers Confederation
C/Diego de León 50
28006 Madrid
Spain
Tel: +34 915 663400
Fax: +34 915 628023
E-mail: ceoe@ceoe.es
Website: www.ceoe.es

Fundacion Para La Formacion Continua (On-Going Training Foundation)
C/Arturo Soria 126–128
28048 Madrid
Spain
Tel: +34 913 837845/009400/880771
Fax: +34 917 599698
Website: www.forcem.es

Appendix 5

Sources of Economic and Business Information

Banco de España (Bank of Spain)
Alcalá 50
28014 Madrid
Spain
Tel: +34 91 338 5000
Fax: +34 91 338 5320
Website: www.bde.es
Main publications: annual report, quarterly inflation report, monthly statistical report and quarterly economic report.

BBVA (Bilbao Vizcaya–Argentaria Bank)
Plaza San Nicolás 4
48005 Bilbao
Spain
Tel: +34 94 487 5555; +34 91 374 7000 (studies service)
Website: www.bbv.es
Main publications: weekly and quarterly reports, *Latinwatch*, *UEM–11* (with historical series), economic situation reports, workshops, regional distribution income reports, economic surveys, etc.

Consejo Superior de Camaras (Superior Chambers Council)
Velázquez 157 1°
28002 Madrid
Spain
Tel: +34 91 590 6900
Fax: +34 91 590 6908
E-mail: csc@cscamaras.es
Website: www.cscamaras.es

Eurostat Data Shop (EUROSTAT/INE)
Paseo de la Castellana 183 of:009
28046 Madrid
Spain
Tel: +34 91 583 9167
Fax: +34 91 579 7120
E-mail: datashop.eurostat@ine.es
Website: www.eurostat.eu.int/comm/eurostat
Main publications with an EU scope: *Statistics in Focus, Panorama of the European Union, Methods and Nomenclatures,* detailed tables, other EU-15 compared official statistics.

Foundation of the Spanish Savings Bank Confederation for Social and Economic Research (FUNCAS)
Juan Hurtado de Mendoza 19
28036 Madrid
Spain
Tel: +34 91 350 4400
Fax: +34 91 350 8040
Website: www.funcas.ceca.es
Main publications: *Papeles de Economia Española, Cuadernos de Información Económica,* workshops, economic studies of Spanish regions, *Financial System Perspective,* etc.

International Labour Office (branch office in Spain)
Alberto Aguilera 15 1° piso
28015 Madrid
Spain
Tel: +34 91 548 2066/4575
Fax: +34 91 547 4422
E-mail: MADRID@ilomad.mtas.es
Website: www.ilo.org
Main publications: *Yearbook of Labor Statistics, Encyclopaedia of Occupational Health and Safety, Labor in the World,* etc.

National Employment Institute (INEM)
Condesa de Venadito 9
28027 Madrid
Spain
Tel: +34 91 5859888
Fax: +34 91 377 5881
Website: www.inem.es
Main publications: monthly summary of basic data, working population and other labour-related issues.

Spanish External Trade Institute (ICEX)
Pº de la Castellana 14–16
28071 Madrid
Spain
Tel: +34 91 349 6100
Fax: +34 91 431 6128
Website: www.icex.es
Main publications: business guides, country profiles, foreign trade handbook.

Spanish National Statistics Institute (INE)
Pº de la Castellana 183
28071 Madrid
Spain
Tel: +34 91 583 9100
E-mail: info@ine.es
Website: www.ine.es
Main publications: *Population Census, Working Population Survey, Hospital Indicators Survey, Household Budget Continuous Survey, Quarterly National Accounts, Consumer Price Indices, Labour Cost Survey, Industrial Production Index*, etc.

Newspapers and specialised Spanish economic reviews

Main economic daily newspapers: *Expansión, Cinco Días, Gaceta de los Negocios*
Main socio-economic yearbooks: *El País* and *El Mundo* yearbooks

General economic reviews: *Actualidad Económica, Información Comercial Española, BICE (Boletín de Información Comercial Española), Economistas, Dinero, Inversión, Economía Industrial, Expansión, Actualidad Financiera*, etc.

Sectoral information sources

ANFAC (National Association of Vehicles and Trucks Manufacturers)
C/Fray Berbardino Sahagún 24 – Planta Baja
Tel: +34 91 343 1343
Fax: +34 91 345 0377/359 4488
Website: www.anfac.com

ANIEL (National Electronic Industries Association)
C/Príncipe de Vergara 74–4° planta
28006 Madrid
Spain
Tel: +34 91 590 2300
Fax: +34 91 411 4000
E-mail: aniel@aniel.es
Website: www.fti.es/aniel

FEIQUE (Spanish Chemical Industries Federation)
C/Hermosilla 31–1° Ext Dcha
28001 Madrid
Spain
Tel: +34 91 431 7964
Fax: +34 91 576 3381
E-mail: feique@interbook.net
Website: www.feique.org

SEDISI (Information Technology source)
C/Príncipe de Vergara n° 43–8°
28001 Madrid
Spain
Tel: +34 91 577 4466
Fax: +34 91 576 5554
Website: www.sedisi.es

SERNAUTO (Automotive Components Manufacturers Association)
C/Castelló 120
28006 Madrid
Spain
Tel: +34 91 562 1041/1595/3431
Fax: +34 91 561 8437
E-mail: sernauto@sernauto.es
Website: www.sernauto.es

Appendix 6

Retail Contacts

Grocery chains

Head Office: Carrefour
(incorporating the former Pryca and Continente management functions)
Campezo 16
Poligono Las Mercedes
28022 Madrid
Spain
Tel: +34 91 301 8900
Fax: +34 91 301 8911
Website: www.carrefour.com

El Corte Ingles
Hermosilla 129
28009 Madrid
Spain
Tel: +34 91 309 0988; +34 91 401 4700; +34 91 402 8112
Fax: +34 91 309 3433
Website: www.elcorteingles.es

London buying office:

Ibérica Trading Co
41–42 Eastcastle Street
London W1N 7PE
United Kingdom
Tel: +44 20 7580 6434
Fax: +44 20 7323 1564

Alcampo Sa
Santiago de Compostela Sur s/n
28029 Madrid
Spain
Tel: +34 91 730 6666
Fax: +34 91 738 1084
Website: www.alcampo.es

Eroski Soc Coop
Barrio San Agustín de Etxebarria s/n
48230 Elorrio
Vizcaya
Spain
Tel: +34 94 621 1211
Fax: +34 94 621 1222
Website: www.grupoeroski.mcc.es

Mercadona SA
C/Valencia 5
46016 Tabernes Blanques
Valencia
Spain
Tel: +34 96 388 3333
Fax: +34 96 388 3302
E-mail: mercadona@vlc.servicom.es

Autoservicios Caprabo SA
C/Ciencias 135
08908 L'hospitalet de Llobregat
Barcelona
Spain
Tel: +34 93 261 6000
Fax: +34 93 261 6020
Website: www.caprabo.es

Makro
Campezo 7
28022 Madrid
Spain
Tel: +34 91 321 9500
Fax: +34 91 321 9675

Superdiplo
Carretera Nacional 340 Km 3 6
11130 Chiclana de la Frontera
Cádiz
Spain
Tel: +34 956 470600
Fax: +34 956 470622

Gallega de Distribuidores de Alimentacion SA (GADISA)
Polígono de Piadela
Apartado 99
15300 Betanzos
La Coruña
Spain
Tel: +34 981 779600
Fax: +34 981 779608

LIDL – Autoservicio Descuento
Avenida Alcalde Barnils s/n
Edificio Gestetner 3ª planta
08190 Sant Cugat
Barcelona
Spain
Tel: +34 93 544 1270
Fax: +34 93 544 1999

Tengelmann España SA – Superplus Descuento
Paseo de la Castellana 40
28046 Madrid
Spain
Tel: +34 91 436 3100
Fax: +34 91 575 5433

Grupo Unigro SA
Forja 93
Polígono industrial de Argales
47008 Valladolid
Spain
Tel: +34 983 413500
Fax: +34 983 413501

Grupo Ahorramas
Carretera de Arganda a Velilla de San Antonio Km 5
28891 Velilla de San Antonio
Madrid
Spain
Tel: +34 91 660 2100
Fax: +34 91 660 8174

Clothing chains

El Corte Ingles
(see above)

Industrias de Diseño Textil SA (INDITEX)
Polígono Industriel Sabon
Parcela 79
15142 Arteixo
La Coruña
Spain
Tel: +34 981 185400
Fax: +34 981 185488
Website: www.inditex.com

Cortefiel SA
Avenida del Llano Castellano 51
28034 Madrid
Spain
Tel: +34 91 387 3400
Fax: +34 91 387 3931
Website: www.grupocortefiel.com

Punto-Fa (Mango) SL
Mercader 9–11
Poligono Industriel
Riera de Caldes
08184 Palau de Plegamus
Barcelona
Spain
Tel: +34 93 864 4444
Fax: +34 93 864 9170 (Purchasing Department)
Website: www.mango.es

Adolfo Dominguez E Hijos SA
Polígono Industrial San Ciprián de Viñas
Calle 4
32901 Orense
Spain
Tel: +34 988 383 705
Fax: +34 988 246 761; +34 988 226 927
Website: www.adolfo_dominguez.com

Other useful contacts

Food From Britain (SPAIN) SL
Castelló 95 2B
28006 Madrid
Spain
Tel: +34 91 578 3962
Fax: +34 91 577 1379

Asociación Española de Marketing Directo (AEMD)
Avda. Diagonal 437
08036 Barcelona
Spain
Tel: +34 93 343 414/5272
Fax: +34 93 343 201/2988

Asociación Española de Comercio Electronica
Website: www.aece.org

Asociación Español de Centros Comerciales
Rafael Calvo 30–1°C
28010 Madrid
Spain
Tel: +34 91 308 4844
Fax: +34 91 310 5535

Appendix 7

Contributor Contact Details

Mikel Navarro Arancegui
ESTE – University of Deusto
Mundaiz 50
E-20012 San Sebastian
Spain
Tel: +34 94 332 6292
Fax: +34 94 327 3932
E-mail: mnavarro@ud-ss.deusto. es

Bové Montero & Cia
Mariano Cubi 7-9
Atico 2a
08006 Barcelona
Spain
Tel: +34 93 218 0708
Fax: +34 93 237 5925
E-mail: bcn@bovemontero.com
Web-site: www. Bovemontero.com
Contact: Brigitte Pollinger
Email: polling@bovemontero.com

Cranfield School of Management
Cranfield
Bedford, MK43 0AL
England, UK
Tel: +44 01234 751122
Fax: +44 01234 75 1806
Contact: Elena Liquete Collis
E-mail: m.e.liquete-collis@cranfield.ac.uk
Professor Chris Brewster BA (Econ), PhD MIPD
E-mail: c.j.brewster@cranfield.ac.uk

Elsie Fairbanks
Fairbanks Consultancy
9 The Woodlands
Hebden Bridge
West Yorkshire
HX7 6JP
England, UK
Tel: +44 01422 844649
Fax: +44 01422 843257
E-mail: fairbank@surfaid.org

Hay Consulting SA
Paseo de Gracia 8–10, 4°2^B
08007 Barcelona
Tel: +34 93 270 3960
Fax: +34 93 412 5807
E-mail: hay@hayconsulting.com
Contact: Mr H U Hay

Carmen Hernansanz
BBVA Research Department
Paseo Recoletos 10
Planta Baja Ala Norte
28001 Madrid, Spain
Tel: +34 91 374 6122
Fax: +34 91 374 6362
E-mail: carmen.hernan@grupobbva.com

Investment Promotion Bureau (IPB), SEPI
Velázquez, 134
28006 Madrid, Spain
Tel: +34 91 396 1084/1177
Fax: +34 91 396 1226
E-mail: jberbel@sepi.es
Web-site: www.sepi.es
Contact: Marga Lainez, Josefa Mateos, Juan José Berbel

Jones Lang la Salle
Paseo de la Castellana, 33
Planta 14
28046 Madrid
Spain
Tel: +34 91 577 0956
Fax: +34 91 789 1200

PricewaterhouseCoopers
Paseo de la Castellana 43
28046 Madrid
Spain
Tel: +34 915 684 400
Fax: +34 913 083 566
Contact: José Luis Gonzalez Ferreras
E-mail: jose.l.gonzalez@es.pwcglobal.com

Joaquim Vergés
Department of Business Economics, Universitat Autònoma de Barcelona
Department d'Economia de l'Empresa
Universitat Autònoma de Barcelona, Campus, edifici B
08193, Bellaterra (Barcelona), Spain
Tel: +34 93 581 1210
Fax: +34 93 581 2555
E-mail: joaquim.verges@uab.es
Web-site: www.selene.uab.es/jverges

Index

References in italic indicate figures or tables.

Index of Advertisers